Joint Workshop of the 5th Financial Technology and Natural Language Processing (FinNLP) and 2nd Multimodal AI for Financial Forecasting (Muffin) in conjunction with IJCAI 2023 (FinNLP-Muffin 2023)

Macao, China
20 August 2023

ISBN: 978-1-7138-9051-5

Printed from e-media with permission by:

Curran Associates, Inc.
57 Morehouse Lane
Red Hook, NY 12571

Some format issues inherent in the e-media version may also appear in this print version.

Printed with permission by Curran Associates, Inc. (2025)

For permission requests, please contact the Association for Computational Linguistics at the address below.

Association for Computational Linguistics
209 N. Eighth Street
Stroudsburg, Pennsylvania 18360

Phone: 1-570-476-8006
Fax: 1-570-476-0860

acl@aclweb.org

Additional copies of this publication are available from:

Curran Associates, Inc.
57 Morehouse Lane
Red Hook, NY 12571 USA
Phone: 845-758-0400
Fax: 845-758-2633
Email: curran@proceedings.com
Web: www.proceedings.com

FinNLP-Muffin 2023

Joint Workshop of the 5th Financial Technology and Natural Language Processing (FinNLP) and 2nd Multimodal AI For Financial Forecasting (Muffin) in conjunction with IJCAI 2023

Proceedings of the Workshop

August 20, 2023

Macao

Preface

Welcome to FinNLP, a forum dedicated to fostering international collaboration and knowledge-sharing in the application of Natural Language Processing (NLP) within the dynamic domain of FinTech. As we gather in this workshop, our aim is to explore the intersection of FinTech and NLP, identifying challenging problems, shaping future research directions, and expanding the horizons of this interdisciplinary field. The 5th FinNLP is a joint workshop with the 2nd workshop on Multimodal AI For Financial Forecasting (Muffin).

In the current year, FinNLP-Muffin continues to be enriched by the participants, who bring forth novel ideas and share their latest findings on pertinent issues. Once again, we are thrilled to collaborate with 3DS Outscale (formerly Fortia) in organizing the shared tasks in FinNLP, with a focus on Multi-Lingual ESG Issue Identification (ML-ESG).

This workshop would not have been possible without the contributions of numerous individuals, and we extend our heartfelt gratitude to each of them. Dr. Juyeon Kang, who led a dedicated team in successfully orchestrating the shared task. Additionally, we are indebted to all the program committee members who invested substantial time and expertise in providing insightful comments on the submissions and guiding the selection process for FinNLP-Muffin-2023.

Last but not least, we extend our sincere thanks to the project JPNP20006, commissioned by the New Energy and Industrial Technology Development Organization (NEDO), for their invaluable financial support. Their partnership has been instrumental in enabling us to realize the goals of FinNLP-Muffin and advance research in this domain.

We hope that FinNLP-Muffin will continue to serve as a catalyst for groundbreaking research and meaningful connections, propelling the realms of FinTech and NLP towards new heights of innovation and excellence.

Chung-Chi Chen, Puneet Mathur, Ramit Sawhney, Hiroya Takamura
FinNLP-Muffin 2023 Organizers
August 2023

Organizations

General Chairs, FinNLP
Chung-Chi Chen, AIST, Japan
Hiroya Takamura, AIST, Japan

General Chairs, Muffin
Puneet Mathur, University of Maryland College Park, USA
Ramit Sawhney, Mohamed bin Zayed University of Artificial Intelligence, Abu Dhabi

Organizing Committee
Dinesh Manocha, University of Maryland College Park, USA
Preslav Nakov, Mohamed bin Zayed University of Artificial Intelligence, Abu Dhabi
Hen-Hsen Huang, Institute of Information Science, Academia Sinica, Taiwan
Hsin-Hsi Chen, Department of Computer Science and Information Engineering, National Taiwan University, Taiwan
Hiroki Sakaji, School of Engineering, The University of Tokyo, Japan
Kiyoshi Izumi, School of Engineering, The University of Tokyo, Japan

Advisory Committee
Franck Dernoncourt, Adobe Research, USA
Fu-Ming Guo, Fidelity Investments, USA
Lucie Flek, University of Marburg, Germany
Sanghamitra Dutta, University of Maryland College Park, USA
Sudheer Chava, Georgia Institute of Technology, USA

Shared Task Organizers
Chung-Chi Chen, AIST, Japan
Yu-Min Tseng, Department of Computer Science and Information Engineering, National Taiwan University, Taiwan
Juyeon Kang, 3DS Outscale (ex Fortia)
Anaïs Lhuissier, 3DS Outscale (ex Fortia)
Min-Yuh Day, Graduate Institute of Information Management, National Taipei University
Teng-Tsai Tu, Graduate Institute of International Business, National Taipei University
Hsin-Hsi Chen, Department of Computer Science and Information Engineering, National Taiwan University, Taiwan

Program Committee

Table of Contents

Model-Agnostic Meta-Learning for Natural Language Understanding Tasks in Finance

Bixing Yan[*†], **Shaoling Chen**[*], **Yuxuan He**[*], **Zhihan Li**[*]
Center for Data Science, New Your University, New York, NY 10012
{by783, sc6995, yh2857, zl2516}@nyu.edu

Abstract

Natural language understanding(NLU) is challenging for finance due to the lack of annotated data and the specialized language in that domain. As a result, researchers have proposed to use pre-trained language model and multi-task learning to learn robust representations. However, aggressive fine-tuning often causes over-fitting and multi-task learning may favor tasks with significantly larger amounts data, etc. To address these problems, in this paper, we investigate model-agnostic meta-learning algorithm(MAML) in low-resource financial NLU tasks. Our contribution includes: 1. we explore the performance of MAML method with multiple types of tasks: GLUE datasets, SNLI, Sci-Tail and Financial PhraseBank; 2. we study the performance of MAML method with multiple single-type tasks: a real scenario stock price prediction problem with twitter text data. Our models achieve the state-of-the-art performance according to the experimental results, which demonstrate that our method can adapt fast and well to low-resource situations.

1 Introduction

It has been a trading practice tradition to utilize textual data to improve modeling of the financial market dynamics(Xing et al., 2018). Nowadays financial operators have access to a growing volume of information, provided by financial reports, news articles, press releases, etc. The enrichment of text sources has also lead to diverse types of unstructured and structured data, for example, social media websites like Twitter, Facebook, etc. are generating rich text content, which can be used as a supplement to support prediction. As a result, there have been increasing attempts to try to utilize deep learning methods on solving financial tasks, including financial opinion mining and question answering (Maia et al., 2018), financial sentiment analysis(Araci, 2019), financial named entity recognition(Wang et al., 2014) and other natural language understanding(NLU) tasks.

However, traditional deep neural network based methods faces several drawbacks. First, they often require vast amount of annotated data which requires high manual labeling cost. Second, language model that trained on Wikitext or other general dataset may be ineffective in solving financial tasks (Araci, 2019) because text data in financial field often exhibits a different pattern compare to text data collected in other domain. Thus, aiming at solving this issue, researchers and investors in financial NLU field has shifted their attention to use transfer learning technique, i.e. to learn a general representation of financial text and adapt it to other new tasks.

Researchers have presented several approaches for transfer learning in Finance NLU field. One of the approach is FinBERT(Araci, 2019), which exploits the powerful pre-trained language model, BERT(Devlin et al., 2019) fine-tunes it using texts in financial field then uses it for new tasks. Further, another approach is to apply multi-task learning to representation learning, where (Liu et al., 2019) proved that BERT model could be improved with multi-task learning strategy as the MT-DNN model. It has achieved descent results on GLUE datasets. However, (Dou et al., 2019) pointed out that multi-task learning may prefer tasks with significantly larger datasets than others and further suggested meta-learning algorithms for multiple types of low resource language understanding tasks. Meta-learning algorithms try to learn a meta-policy for updating model parameters or a good initialization that can be useful for fine-tuning on various tasks with minimal training data, which makes them promising alternatives to multi-task learning. Meta-learning has been proved useful in few-shot learning(Finn et al., 2017),single-type multi-

[*]The authors contributed equally and are presented in alphabetical order.

[†]Bixing Yan is the corresponding author.

Proceedings of the Joint Workshop of the 5th Financial Technology and Natural Language Processing (FinNLP) and 2nd Multimodal AI For Financial Forecasting (Muffin), Macao, August 20, 2023.

tasks learning. Indeed, (Gu et al., 2018) extends meta-learning algorithm for low-resource neural machine translation, framing low-resource translation as a meta-learning problem and adapting to low-resource languages based on multilingual high-resource language tasks.

Inspired by these work, in this paper, we investigate the applications of meta-learning algorithms, specifically the Model-Agnostic Meta-Learning(MAML) algorithm(Finn et al., 2017), to try to solve the fundamental representation learning issue in financial text data.

The main contribution of this paper is two-fold:

- We study the performance of MAML method with multiple types of tasks. We combine the MAML algorithm with MT-DNN model, train the model using four high-resource datasets, evaluate it on other low-resource datasets, and then adapt the model to Financial PhraseBank, a financial sentiment analysis dataset, where we achieve the state-of-the-art. Our experiments also justify the superior property in fast adaptation and over-fitting avoidance of the MAML model.

- We study the performance of MAML method with multiple tasks in single type. We develop a few-shot learning method for the task of stock price movement prediction with news texts, and propose a competitive MAML-BERT model for stock price prediction.

The rest of the paper is structured as follows: Section 2 briefly describes the relevant literature in multi-task learning, meta-learning and financial natural language understanding tasks. Then, Section 3 introduces the methods we use: BERT model and MAML algorithm. In Section 4, we present multiple experiments being conducted, including datasets, implementations and their results. We conclude with Section 5 and discuss the future work in Section 6.

2 Related Work

In this section, we introduce the relevant literature in multi-task learning, meta-learning and two financial natural language understanding tasks including financial sentiment analysis and stock price prediction.

2.1 Multi-Task Learning

Multi-task learning (MTL) is a sub-field of machine learning, which exploits commonalities and differences across tasks and solves multiple learning tasks at the same time. Biologically, we often apply the knowledge we have acquired in related tasks to learning new tasks. For example, a baby first learns to recognize faces and can then recognize other objects by applying this knowledge. Similarly, multi-task learning can result in improved learning efficiency and prediction accuracy for the task-specific models, compared to training the models separately (Baxter, 2000).

Multi-task learning penalizes all complexity uniformly, and as a result, regularization induced by requiring an algorithm to perform well on a related task can be superior to regularization that prevents over-fitting. One situation where MTL may help is if the tasks share significant commonalities and are generally slightly under sampled[(Hajiramezanali et al., 2018)].

In the context of Deep Learning, it's the most commonly approach for multi-task learning to use hard parameter sharing, generally applied by sharing the hidden layers between all tasks, while keeping task-specific output layers. MT-DNN model is a one of the typical hard parameter sharing application in NLU tasks(Liu et al., 2019).

2.2 Meta Learning

Meta-learning, or learn-to-learn, has recently attracted much attention in the machine learning community (Lake et al., 2015). Basically the goal of meta-learning is to train a learner that is able to fast adapt to new task with limited training data.

There are three common approaches to meta-learning: metric-based, model-based, and optimization-based.

Metric-based Metric-based meta-learning is similar to nearest neighbors algorithm and kernel density estimation. The model predicts a probability y over a set of known labels by a weighted sum of labels of support set samples. The weight is generated by a kernel function k_θ, which measures the similarity between two data samples.

$$P_\theta(y|x, S) = \sum_{(xi,yi)\in S} k_\theta(x, x_i)y_i$$

To train a successful metric-based meta-learning model requires researchers to specify a good kernel that could learn the distance function over objects well. However, kernel functions are highly depends on specific problem, the inputs and the representation space of tasks.

Most of the frequently-used metric-based models learn embedding vectors of input data explicitly and use them to design proper kernel functions, see Convolutional Siamese Neural Network(Koch et al.), Relation Network (Sung et al., 2018), etc.

Model-based Model-based meta-learning model requires a model designed for fast learning. By modifying the internal model architecture or adding an additional meta-learner model on top of original model, it could achieve the fast learning goal, i.e. to update its parameters rapidly within a few training steps.

The representative works in this category include Memory-Augmented Neural Network(Santoro et al., 2016), Meta Network(Munkhdalai and Yu, 2017), etc.

Optimization-based Optimization-based meta-learning algorithms aim to achieve the fast adaptation goal by adjusting the optimization algorithms. As we all know, deep learning models learn through back-propagation of gradients. Yet, since the gradient-based optimization does not work well on small number of training samples and won't converge within a small number of optimization steps, a model is designed to modify the gradient based optimization algorithm.

The most popular optimization-based meta-learning algorithm is model-agnostic meta-learning(MAML), which is also what we mainly aim to investigate in this paper. (Finn et al., 2017) achieved state-of-the-art performance by directly optimizing the gradient towards a good parameter initialization for easy fine-tuning on low resource scenarios without introducing any additional architectures or parameters.

Figure 1 visually illustrates the differences between classical multi-task learning and meta multi-task learning. The classical multi-task learning tends to get to a point where the current gradients from different tasks are balanced, which may still result in over-fitting and tend to favor tasks with significantly larger amounts of data than others, while meta-learning aims to minimize the future loss of different task respectively.

2.3 Financial NLU Applications

2.3.1 Financial Sentiment Analysis

General sentiment analysis aims to extract people's opinions or tendency from language. Yet there is a key specialty in financial sentiment analysis that the purpose of financial sentiment analysis is usually targeted towards the market. Indeed, it usually aims to analyze the text data to facilitate understanding of how the markets will react with the information presented in the text.

Most popular methods in solving sentiment analysis tasks include RNN, LSTM network models. Extending upon these models, (Maia et al., 2018) adds a text simplification layer and then applies it to LSTM network. Despite the success in general sentiment analysis, there is still a huge gap to utilize the neural networks to their fullest potential in solving tasks in finance domain due to the lack of high quality annotated datasets in the domain.

(Araci, 2019) has tackled this issue with FinBERT model. As we have discussed before, it essentially is to initialize the model with pre-trained values and fine-tuning the model with respect to the classification task. In FinBERT, the author used Reuters data to pre-training the BERT model and achieved promising results on Financial PhraseBank.

We address this problem from a different perspective. We utilize the meta learning model by training it with multiple NLU tasks to facilitate learning of a more robust and generalized representation. Then fitting the model to Financial PhraseBank dataset so that the model can quickly adapted on learning the sentimental relations in the text. We have compared our results against their reported accuracy.

2.3.2 Stock Price Prediction

Stock price prediction has long attracted researchers and investors. In financial natural language processing field, the two primary content resources for stock market prediction are public news and social media data (mainly from twitter). Classical research relies primarily on feature engineering but their results tends to be highly volatile. With the prevalence of deep learning(Le and Mikolov), event driven approaches were studied and models with LSTM, RNN become dominant. More recently, (Hu et al., 2019) proposed a novel method to feed news sequence directly from text with hierarchical attention mechanisms for stock trend

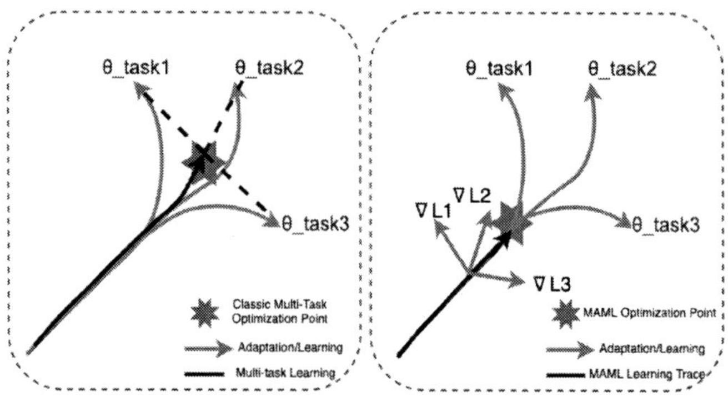

Figure 1: The illustrative comparisons between representations learned by (a) classical multi-task learning and (b) meta multi-task learning.

prediction. Further, language model such as BERT has also inspired researchers with development of new models.

However, stock price prediction is widely considered difficult due to three factors: high market stochasticity, chaotic market information and temporally-dependent prediction. Stock prices are not influenced solely by news information or tweeter information. Other factors influencing the stock price are not directly observable or measurable. Thus the traditional prediction are mainly resulting in a random-walk pattern(Malkiel, 1996).

In order to tackle the temporally-dependent prediction issue, researchers choose to frame the data to fit for a time series problem. In other word, they have to incorporate the temporal dependency between stock prices movements in to the model. For example, when a company experienced some good news on day d_1, its stock price will be slowly affected and thus will have an upward trend pattern in the following days until d_n. Similarly, when a company suffered from some scandal, its stock price will needs time to absorb the affect of the scandal in the following n days.

Yet the time series model explained above did not address the chaotic market information issue. Different stock may correlated in different level with text data. Some stock may suffer from inefficient data issue. Transfer learning provides a viable way to alleviate this issue by using meta-learning. Previously, Zhaojiang has used MAML in tackling a similar issue: use text data from Chinese Weibo to predict sales for different company(Lin et al., 2019). This strategy used non-parametric model to leverage historical information of other brands, and used them as prior knowledge and thereby allows the model for fast adaptability.

In this paper, we are going to adopt the methodology of MAML to test the effectiveness of MAML on stock price prediction task.

3 Method

In this section, we present the main methods used: pre-trained Language Model of BERT and Model-Agnostic Meta-Learning algorithm, and how we combine them.

3.1 Pre-trained Language Model: BERT

We use Bidirectional Encoder Representations from Transformers (BERT)(Devlin et al., 2019) as our pre-trained model, which will be shared across all the tasks.

BERT is first trained on unlabelled text, including Brown Corpus and English Wikipedia which has more than 2.5 billions of words. Fine-tuned on downstream nature language processing jobs, BERT has obtained state-of-art results on 11 different tasks, such as text classification, named entity recognition, sentiment analysis and question answering. Unlike ELMo which predicts the next word of an ordered sequence of tokens, BERT is trained on the entire sentence by randomly masking 15% of the set of words. Therefore, instead of learning the context based on the previous or next word, it can learn the representation of words through all words in the sentence simultaneously. With transformer and bi-directional structure implemented, BERT helps with disambiguation of polysemous words and homonyms by focusing attention on a specific token.

BERT has two versions: BERT-Base, with 12 encoder layers, hidden size of 768, 12 multi-head attention heads and 110M parameters in total, and BERT-Large, with 24 encoder layers, hidden size of 1024, 16 multi-head attention heads and 340M parameters. Considering about the computation resources, we only use BERT-Base in our experiments.

3.2 Algorithm: Model-Agnostic Meta-Learning

The basic idea of MAML(Finn et al., 2017) and its variants is to use a set of source tasks to find the initialization of parameters, and by using that parameters, it would require only a small number of training examples to learn a target task.

Given a set of tasks $\{\mathcal{T}_1, ..., \mathcal{T}_k\}$ drawn from a distribution of $p(\mathcal{T})$, which consist of a training set $train(\mathcal{T})$ and a testing set $test(\mathcal{T})$, consider a model represented by a parameterized function f_θ with parameters θ.

When adapting to new tasks $\mathcal{T}_i$, we can update the model's parameter θ to θ'_i using one or more gradient update(We use one gradient update here to simplify the case, but usually real applications use multiple gradient updates):

$$\theta'_i = \theta - \alpha \nabla_\theta \mathcal{L}_{\mathcal{T}_i}(f(\theta))$$

This is the inner loop update, where $\mathcal{L}_{\mathcal{T}_i}$ is the loss function for $\mathcal{T}_i$.

To achieve a good generalization across various tasks, we aim to optimize the meta-objective, which is as follows:

$$\min_\theta \sum_{\mathcal{T}_i \sim p(\mathcal{T})} \mathcal{L}_{\mathcal{T}_i}(f(\theta'))$$
$$= \sum_{\mathcal{T}_i \sim p(\mathcal{T})} \mathcal{L}_{\mathcal{T}_i}(f(\theta - \alpha \nabla_\theta \mathcal{L}_{\mathcal{T}_i}(f(\theta))))$$

We perform the meta-optimization over the model parameters θ, with the objective computed using the updated model parameters θ. As a result, a few gradient steps on a new task will produce maximum influence on that task.

So for the outer loop, model parameters θ are updated as follows:

$$\theta \leftarrow \theta - \beta \nabla_\theta \sum_{\mathcal{T}_i \sim p(\mathcal{T})} \mathcal{L}_{\mathcal{T}_i}(f(\theta))$$

where β is the meta step size. The full algorithm is outlined in Algorithm 1, adapted from (Finn et al., 2017).

3.3 Proposed Framework

The architecture of the MAML model is similar to MT-DNN(Liu et al., 2019). A word sequence (either a sentence or a pair of sentences packed together) is firstly input to BERT, which is the shared semantic representation trained by our meta multi-task objectives. On the top are the task-specific layers, where for each task, task-specific representations are generated by task-specific layers. And after that, there are some necessary operations for classification, relevance ranking, etc.

Generally, there are three steps in our method: the pre-training step as in BERT, the meta-learning step and fine-tuning step. In meta multi-task learning step, we use stochastic gradient descent (SGD) for inner loop update and Adamax optimizer for outer loop adaptation. In each epoch, a batch of tasks is selected, and the model is updated according to the sum of all multi-task objectives over the tasks.

4 Experiments

In this section, we discuss two specific instantiations of MAML for multi-task learning settings. One is multi-types of NLU tasks and another is multiple NLU tasks in single type, which differ in the loss function's form and in how data is generated by the tasks and presented to the model, but the same basic adaptation mechanism are applied in both cases.

4.1 Multi-Types NLU Tasks

In this part, we study the performance of MAML model with multiple types of tasks.

4.1.1 Datasets

We briefly describes the GLUE, SNLI, and SciTail datasets, as summarized in Table 1.

GLUE The General Language Understanding Evaluation (GLUE) benchmark (Wang et al., 2018) is a tool for evaluating and analyzing the performance of natural language understanding models across nine NLU tasks: Single-Sentence Tasks, Similarity and Paraphrase Tasks and Inference Tasks.

Four high-resource datasets(MNLI, QQP, SST, QNLI) are used as training datasets, and four other

Algorithm 1: Model-Agnostic Meta-Learning(MAML)

Require: $p(\mathcal{T})$:distribution over tasks
Require: α,β: step size hyperparameters
randomly initialize θ;
while *not done* **do**
  Sample batch of tasks $\mathcal{T}_i \sim p(\mathcal{T})$;
  forall $\mathcal{T}_i$ **do**
    Evaluate $\nabla_\theta \mathcal{L}_{\mathcal{T}_i}(f(\theta))$ with respect to K examples;
    Compute adapted parameters with gradient descent: $\theta_i' = \theta - \alpha \nabla_\theta \mathcal{L}_{\mathcal{T}_i}(f(\theta))$;
  end
  Update $\theta \leftarrow \theta - \beta \nabla_\theta \sum_{\mathcal{T}_i \sim p(\mathcal{T})} \mathcal{L}_{\mathcal{T}_i}(f(\theta))$;
end

low-resource datasets(CoLA, MRPC, STS-B, RTE) are used as testing datasets, according to (Dou et al., 2019). In our experiments we do not train or test models on the WNLI dataset because of previous work (Devlin et al., 2019).

SNLI The Stanford Natural Language Inference dataset (Bowman et al., 2015) is a naturalistic corpus of 570k sentence pairs labeled for entailment, contradiction, and independence.

We use this dataset to examine the algorithm's fast adaptation ability in this study.

Sci-Tail This is a Textual Entailment Dataset from Science Question Answering (Khot et al.). Hypotheses from science questions are created while the corresponding answer candidates and premises from relevant web sentences are retrieved from a large corpus. These linguistically challenging sentences, combined with the high lexical similarity of premise and hypothesis for both entailed and non-entailed pairs, makes the new entailment task particularly difficult.

We use this dataset examine the algorithm's fast adaptation ability in this study.

Financial PhraseBank(FPB) The sentiment analysis dataset (Malo et al., 2013) consists of 4845 english sentences selected randomly from financial news found on LexisNexis database, which is annotated by 16 people with finance and business background. The annotators were asked to give labels according to how they think the information in the sentence might affect the mentioned company stock price.

This dataset is our first step to generalize our model to financial domain in this study.

4.1.2 Implementation Details

Our implementation of MAML is based on PyTorch implementation of MT-DNN (Liu et al., 2019). We use Adamax with a learning rate of 5e-5 as our outer optimizer, batch size of 32 and the maximum number of epochs of 5. We also set the update step to 3 and α, the inner learning rate of SGD to 5e-5. The dropout rate of all task specific layers is 0.1, except 0.3 for MNLI and 0.05 for CoLA. A linear learning rate decay schedule with warm-up over 0.1 is used. The gradient norm is clipped within 1 to avoid exploding gradient problem. The pre-trained BERT-Base is used to initialize the model. Tasks are sampled according to the size of their datasets.

An Amazon p3.8.xlarge EC2 instance with 4 GPUs, and 90 GiB of host memory is used to train the models.

Experiment details are presented in Figure 2. We compare our MAML model against various state-of-the-art baselines.

For GLUE, SciTail and SNLI datasets, We use the public code of BERT-Base (Devlin et al., 2019) model and MT-DNN model(Liu et al., 2019) to obtain their results. For Financial PhraseBank dataset, we target the results in FinBert model(Araci, 2019).

4.1.3 Results

The experiment results on GLUE, SNLI, SciTail and Financial PhraseBank datasets are the following.

GLUE Main Results We first train the MAML model using four of the GLUE datasets and their fine-tuned results are presented in Table 2. Then we test the model with four GLUE datasets. The results for the testing datasets are presented in Table 3.

Corpus	Task	Train	Dev	Test	Label	Metrics
CoLA	Acceptability	8.5k	1k	1k	2	Matthews Corr
SST-2	Sentiment	67k	872	1.8k	2	Accuracy
MNLI	NLI	393k	20k	20k	3	Accuracy(match/mismatch)
RTE	NLI	2.5k	276	3k	2	Accuracy
WNLI	NLI	634	71	146	2	Accuracy
QQP	Paraphrase	364k	40k	391k	2	Accuracy/F1
MRPC	Paraphrase	3.7k	408	1.7k	2	Accuracy/F1
STS-B	Similarity	7k	1.5k	1.4k	1	Pearson/Spearman Corr
QNLI	QA/NLI	108k	5.7k	5.7k	2	Accuracy
SNLI	NLI	549k	9.8k	9.8k	2	Accuracy
SciTail	NLI	23.5k	1.3k	2.1k	2	Accuracy
FPB	Sentiment	2.9k	1.0k	1.0k	3	Accuracy

Table 1: Benchmarks: GLUE, SNLI, SciTail, FPB

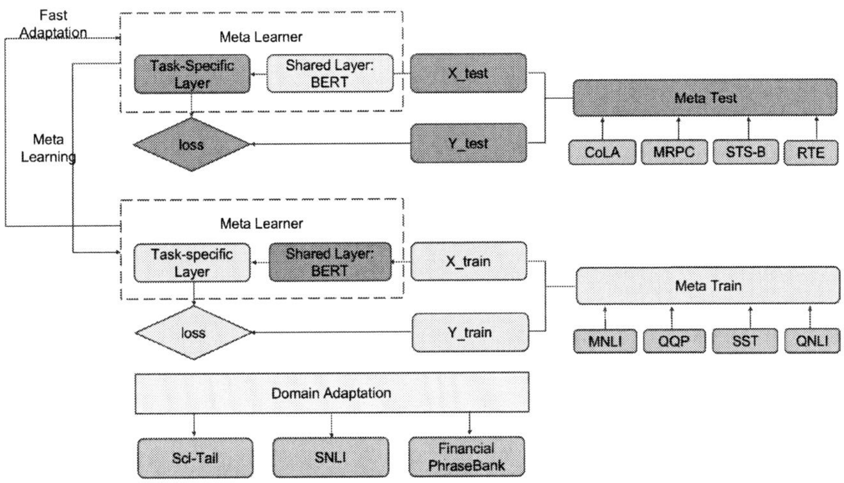

Figure 2: Multi-types NLU Tasks Learning

Basically, the MAML model achieves better or equal performance in almost all tasks, which indicates the effectiveness and reliability of our model.

Model	MNLI	QQP	SST	QNLI
BERT	84.6/83.4	71.2	93.5	90.5
MT-DNN	84.3/84.5	86.9	92.9	90.8
MAML	84.0/84.4	87.1	92.7	90.5

Table 2: Training Results on GLUE Datasets. MAML and MT-DNN uses BERT-Base to initialize their shared layers. We fine-tuned three models for each of the four GLUE task using task-specific data.

Fast Adaptation on SNLI and SciTail We transfer our model to two new tasks. We randomly sample 0.1%, 1%, 10% and 100% of their training data and thus obtain four sets of training data for SciTail including 23, 235, 2.3k, 23.5k training samples, and four sets for SNLI including 549, 5.5k, 54.9k and 549.3k training samples respectively.

We observe that MAML model outperforms the BERT and MT-DNN baselines with fewer training examples used, with more details provided in Table 4. For example, with only 0.1% of the SciTail training data, MAML achieves an accuracy of 77.531% while BERT's is 51.2% and MT-DNN's

Model	CoLA	MRPC	STS-B	RTE
BERT	52.1	84.8/88.9	66.4	87.1/85.8
MT-DNN	55.9	87.2/90.5	74.4	89.6/89.6
MAML	56.9	87.3/90.7	78.3	89.3/89.3

Table 3: Testing Results on GLUE Datasets. MAML and MT-DNN uses BERT-Base to initialize their shared layers. We fine-tuned three models for each of the four GLUE task using task-specific data.

is 66.411%.

Similar results are also verified in SNLI dataset.

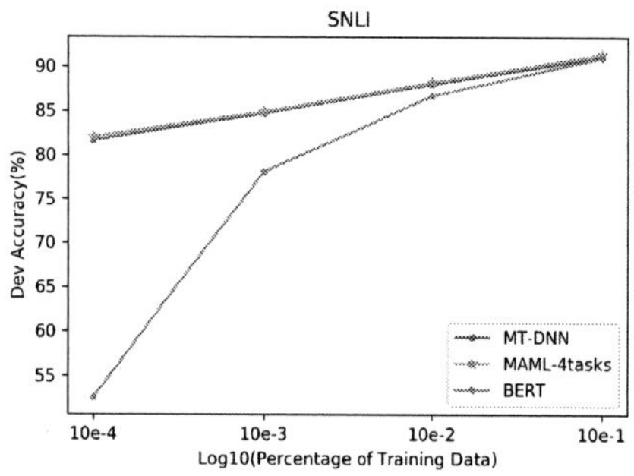

Figure 3: Results on SNLI Dataset. The X-axis indicates the amount of domain-specific labeled samples used for adaptation.

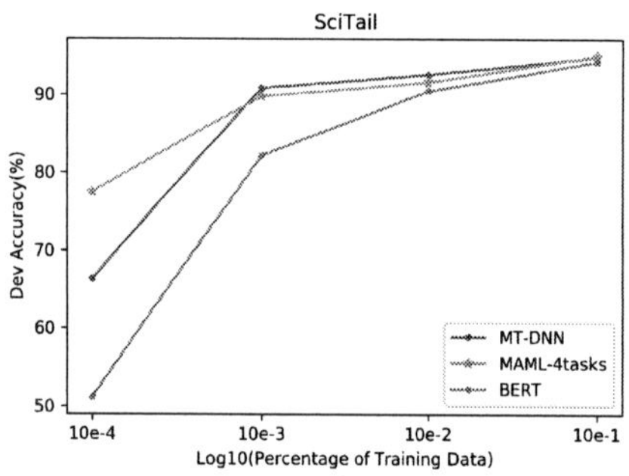

Figure 4: Results on Scitail Dataset. The X-axis indicates the amount of domain-specific labeled samples used for adaptation.

Domain Adaptation on Financial Dataset Based on above experiments, we further extend our model to Financial PhraseBank dataset. From Table 5, we could see that the MAML model achieves an accuracy as good as FinBert, without any financial specific further pre-training. Moreover, with only 1% or 10% training data, it reaches a fairly good performance.

4.2 Single-Type NLU Tasks - Stock Price Prediction

The experiments above show the effectiveness of MAML in handling multiple tasks together. In this part, we aim to apply MAML to solve single-type financial NLU task, stock price prediction.

4.2.1 Dataset

We obtain the dataset from (Xu and Cohen, 2018). There are two main components in our dataset, a Twitter dataset and a historical price dataset. The historical prices for the 88 selected stocks to build the historical price dataset from Yahoo Finance. the text data includes two-year price movements from 01/01/2014 to 01/01/2016 of 88 stocks separated into 9 industries: Basic Materials, Consumer Goods, Healthcare, Services, Utilities, Conglomerates, Financial, Industrial Goods and Technology. The table blow shows that there is an imbalance issue lies within stocks and industries which we have to deal with in training/evaluation phase.

4.2.2 Implementation-Single Stock Price Prediction Task

Inspired by (Xu and Cohen, 2018), we assume that predicting the stock movement between trading day d and d+1 can be benefit from historical prices of previous days and previous price movements on its former trading days. Under this premise, we adopt the data processing techniques from (Xu and Cohen, 2018). First, we find all T eligible trading days referred in a sample stock and group them by $t \in [1, T]$. Thus each sample should contain twitter text and stock price data with in the range of t days. Let us use $S = [s_1, s_2, ..., s_t], P = [p_0, p_2, ...p_t]$ to represent the twitter text collected in each sample which collected by aligning to each trading day. Then we transform the text data and stock price in to the features we desired. We calculate stock price movement $Y = [p_1 - p0, p_2 - p_1, ..., p_t - p_{t-1}]$. Note here we further transform the Y into three classes: moving up, moving down, no movement.

SNLI(Dev Accuracy %)				
#Training Data	0.1%	1%	10%	100%
BERT	52.5	78.1	86.7	91.0
MT-DNN	81.6	84.7	88.0	91.08
MAML	82.0	84.9	88.2	91.4
Sci-Tail(Dev Accuracy %)				
#Training Data	0.1%	1%	10%	100%
BERT	51.2	82.2	90.5	94.3
MT-DNN	66.411	90.874	92.638	94.862
MAML	77.531	89.801	91.648	95.015

Table 4: Domain Adaptation Results on SNLI and Sci-Tail using the shared embeddings generated by MAML, MT-DNN and BERT, respectively.

FPB(Dev Accuracy %)			
#Training Data	1%	10%	100%
Fin-Bert	-	-	86.00
MAML	61.26	77.38	86.47

Table 5: Domain Adaptation Results on Financial PhraseBank.

Number of Twitter Text Per Industry	
#Industry	#Num Twitter Text
Material	4405
Consumer Goods	22491
Healthcare	7984
Services	19025
Utilities	6095
Cong	268
Finance	9291
Industrial Goods	5764
Tech	31015

Table 6: Number of Twitter Text Per Industry During 01/01/2014 - 01/01/2016.

The architecture of the model is shown below. We first use BERT to process the twitter data and concat it with the previous days stock price. Then we feed it into a RNN model with T layers which represent T days in the lag. Finally, we integrate the final result with a softmax function in order to output the confidence distribution over up and down.

4.2.3 Implementation- MAML-BERT Model

We then transform the model to multitask structure by adding multiple tasks together and applying MAML method to it. The scenario is, suppose we are given a new stock with limited twitter text data, with MAML model pre-trained on multiple stock-text data, the model should be able to capture the intrinsic parameters for this new stock quicker and thus reach good accuracy faster.

To test our hypothesis scenario, we design experiments by selecting 8 stocks to train the meta learner for 10 epoch and test the model with a new stock dataset. We conduct 4 experiments and finally evaluate its accuracy against a direct prediction model listed in 4.2.2. The setting structure is shown in Figure 6.

4.3 Results

As described in previous sections, stock prediction is a challenging task and a minor improvement could lead to large potential profits. An the accuracy of 56% is generally reported as a satisfying result for binary stock movement prediction(Nguyen and Shirai, 2015). We evaluate the model in the following four settings and the results are illustrated in the graph below. The selection of the stocks is according the the amount of twitter text data we obtain.

As shown in the table and graph below, we have reached promising evaluation accuracy on all different models. The highest result is generated by Mixed Model. It is trained on 8 stocks with the maximum number of twitter text data from all industry and evaluated on AAPL stock which is not included in the industry for all training stock. The

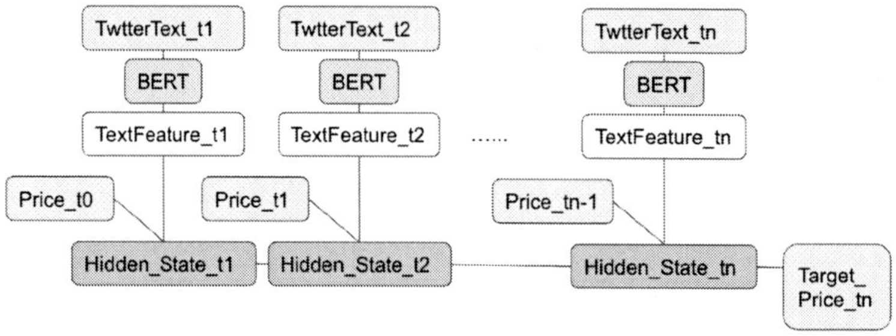

Figure 5: The architecture of Single Stock Prediction Task. We use the main target tn for prediction and the lag size of n for illustration

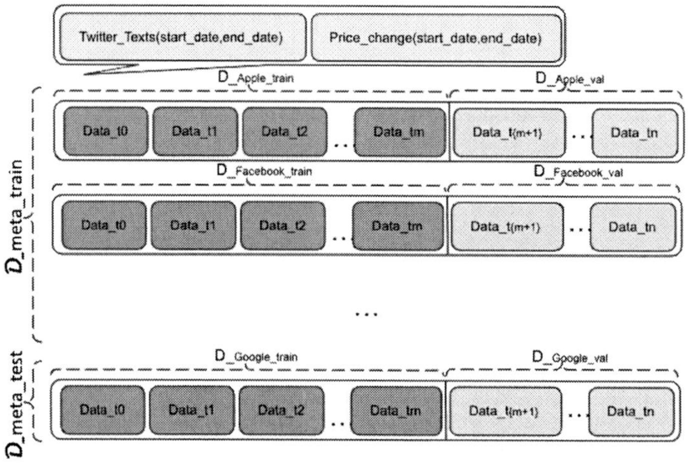

Figure 6: MAML-Model task structure

Model Industry	Train Stocks	Eval Stock	(Train Acc %)	(Eval Acc%)
Consumer	PG,BUD,KO,PM,TM,PEP,..	AAPL	59.21	57.14
Services	AMZN,BABA,WMT,CMSCA,..	MCD	58.82	56.91
Tech	GOOG, MSFT,FB,T,CHL,ORCL,..	CSCO	58.42	56.15
Mixed	CELG,PCLN,JPM,GE,FB..	AAPL	60.27	57.94

Table 7: Training and Evaluation Results on Different Groups of Stock Data.

final dev accuracy we have reached is of 57.94% for MAML-mixed model.

We have also evaluate the adaptation rate of our model(MAML-Mixed) against a baseline model that was not pre-trained on other stocks. The graph below shows that the MAML model converged in a faster rate compared to the baseline model.

5 Conclusions

In this paper, we investigate model-agnostic meta-learning algorithm for general NLU tasks, and also evaluate its performance on two financial applications - financial sentiment analysis and stock price prediction. Experiments show our MAML model is able to learn general representations, which can be adapted to new tasks with limited samples effec-

Stock Price Prediction (Dev Accuracy %)	
RAND	50.89
ARIMA	51.39
BERT-Baseline	54.07
BERT-MAML-Mixed	57.94
Stocknet (Xu and Cohen, 2018)	57.64

Table 8: Domain Adaptation Results on Stock Price Prediction Tasks.

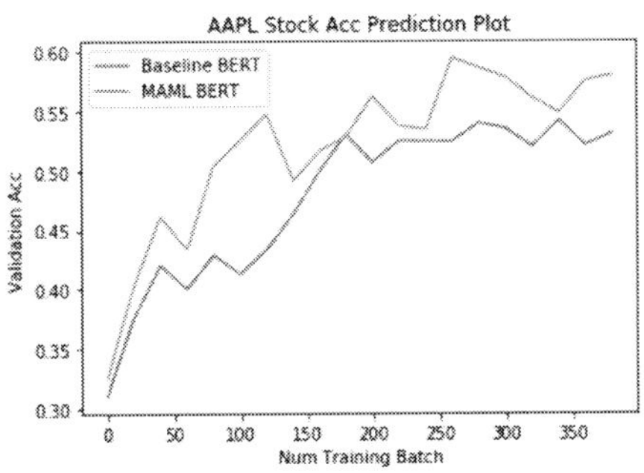

Figure 7: Results on Stock Price Prediction Task from BERT Model and BERT-MAML model

tively, and is also robust to the task specific scales without over-fitting. Our study suggests promising applications of meta-learning algorithms in low-resource financial natural language understanding tasks.

Acknowledgements

The authors are grateful to the project advisers from Center for Data Science and Dr. Zulkuf Genc, Dmitri Jarnikov and Dogu Araci from Prosus AI team for their constructive comments and advisement. The computational resources are provided by Prosus AI team.

References

Dogu Araci. 2019. FinBERT: Financial Sentiment Analysis with Pre-trained Language Models. *arXiv:1908.10063 [cs]*. ArXiv: 1908.10063.

J. Baxter. 2000. A Model of Inductive Bias Learning. *Journal of Artificial Intelligence Research*, 12:149–198. ArXiv: 1106.0245.

Samuel R. Bowman, Gabor Angeli, Christopher Potts, and Christopher D. Manning. 2015. A large annotated corpus for learning natural language inference. In *Proceedings of the 2015 Conference on Empirical Methods in Natural Language Processing*, pages 632–642, Lisbon, Portugal. Association for Computational Linguistics.

Jacob Devlin, Ming-Wei Chang, Kenton Lee, and Kristina Toutanova. 2019. BERT: Pre-training of Deep Bidirectional Transformers for Language Understanding. *arXiv:1810.04805 [cs]*. ArXiv: 1810.04805.

Zi-Yi Dou, Keyi Yu, and Antonios Anastasopoulos. 2019. Investigating Meta-Learning Algorithms for Low-Resource Natural Language Understanding Tasks. *arXiv:1908.10423 [cs]*. ArXiv: 1908.10423.

Chelsea Finn, Pieter Abbeel, and Sergey Levine. 2017. Model-Agnostic Meta-Learning for Fast Adaptation of Deep Networks. *arXiv:1703.03400 [cs]*. ArXiv: 1703.03400.

Jiatao Gu, Yong Wang, Yun Chen, Kyunghyun Cho, and Victor O. K. Li. 2018. Meta-Learning for Low-Resource Neural Machine Translation. *arXiv:1808.08437 [cs]*. ArXiv: 1808.08437.

Ehsan Hajiramezanali, Siamak Zamani Dadaneh, Alireza Karbalayghareh, Mingyuan Zhou, and Xiaoning Qian. 2018. Bayesian multi-domain learning for cancer subtype discovery from next-generation sequencing count data. In S. Bengio, H. Wallach, H. Larochelle, K. Grauman, N. Cesa-Bianchi, and R. Garnett, editors, *Advances in Neural Information Processing Systems 31*, pages 9115–9124. Curran Associates, Inc.

Ziniu Hu, Weiqing Liu, Jiang Bian, Xuanzhe Liu, and Tie-Yan Liu. 2019. Listening to Chaotic Whispers: A Deep Learning Framework for News-oriented Stock Trend Prediction. *arXiv:1712.02136 [cs, q-fin]*. ArXiv: 1712.02136.

Tushar Khot, Ashish Sabharwal, and Peter Clark. SciTail: A Textual Entailment Dataset from Science Question Answering. page 9.

Gregory Koch, Richard Zemel, and Ruslan Salakhutdinov. Siamese Neural Networks for One-shot Image Recognition. page 8.

B. M. Lake, R. Salakhutdinov, and J. B. Tenenbaum. 2015. Human-level concept learning through probabilistic program induction. *Science*, 350(6266):1332–1338.

Quoc Le and Tomas Mikolov. Distributed Representations of Sentences and Documents. page 9.

Zhaojiang Lin, Andrea Madotto, Genta Indra Winata, Zihan Liu, Yan Xu, Cong Gao, and Pascale Fung. 2019. Learning to Learn Sales Prediction with Social Media Sentiment. In *Proceedings of the First Workshop on Financial Technology and Natural Language Processing*, pages 47–53, Macao, China.

Xiaodong Liu, Pengcheng He, Weizhu Chen, and Jianfeng Gao. 2019. Multi-Task Deep Neural Networks for Natural Language Understanding. *arXiv:1901.11504 [cs]*. ArXiv: 1901.11504.

M. Maia, A. Freitas, and S. Handschuh. 2018. Finsslx: A sentiment analysis model for the financial domain using text simplification. In *2018 IEEE 12th International Conference on Semantic Computing (ICSC)*, pages 318–319.

Macedo Maia, Siegfried Handschuh, André Freitas, Brian Davis, Ross McDermott, and Alexandra Balahur Manel Zarrouk. 2018. FiQA - 2018.

Burton Gordon Malkiel. 1996. A random walk down Wall Street: including a life-cycle guide to personal investing. *Choice Reviews Online*, 33(08):33–4629–33–4629.

Pekka Malo, Ankur Sinha, Pyry Takala, Pekka Korhonen, and Jyrki Wallenius. 2013. Good Debt or Bad Debt: Detecting Semantic Orientations in Economic Texts. *arXiv:1307.5336 [cs, q-fin]*. ArXiv: 1307.5336.

Tsendsuren Munkhdalai and Hong Yu. 2017. Meta networks. *Proceedings of machine learning research*, 70:2554–2563.

Thien Hai Nguyen and Kiyoaki Shirai. 2015. Topic Modeling based Sentiment Analysis on Social Media for Stock Market Prediction. In *Proceedings of the 53rd Annual Meeting of the Association for Computational Linguistics and the 7th International Joint Conference on Natural Language Processing (Volume 1: Long Papers)*, pages 1354–1364, Beijing, China. Association for Computational Linguistics.

Adam Santoro, Sergey Bartunov, Matthew Botvinick, Daan Wierstra, and Timothy Lillicrap. 2016. Meta-learning with memory-augmented neural networks. In *Proceedings of The 33rd International Conference on Machine Learning*, volume 48 of *Proceedings of Machine Learning Research*, pages 1842–1850, New York, New York, USA. PMLR.

Flood Sung, Yongxin Yang, Li Zhang, Tao Xiang, Philip H.S. Torr, and Timothy M. Hospedales. 2018. Learning to Compare: Relation Network for Few-Shot Learning. In *2018 IEEE/CVF Conference on Computer Vision and Pattern Recognition*, pages 1199–1208, Salt Lake City, UT. IEEE.

Alex Wang, Amanpreet Singh, Julian Michael, Felix Hill, Omer Levy, and Samuel Bowman. 2018. GLUE: A Multi-Task Benchmark and Analysis Platform for Natural Language Understanding. In *Proceedings of the 2018 EMNLP Workshop BlackboxNLP: Analyzing and Interpreting Neural Networks for NLP*, pages 353–355, Brussels, Belgium. Association for Computational Linguistics.

S. Wang, R. Xu, B. Liu, L. Gui, and Y. Zhou. 2014. Financial named entity recognition based on conditional random fields and information entropy. In *2014 International Conference on Machine Learning and Cybernetics*, volume 2, pages 838–843.

Frank Z. Xing, Erik Cambria, and Roy E. Welsch. 2018. Natural language based financial forecasting: a survey. *Artificial Intelligence Review*, 50(1):49–73.

Yumo Xu and Shay B. Cohen. 2018. Stock Movement Prediction from Tweets and Historical Prices. In *Proceedings of the 56th Annual Meeting of the Association for Computational Linguistics (Volume 1: Long Papers)*, pages 1970–1979, Melbourne, Australia. Association for Computational Linguistics.

ChatGPT as Data Augmentation for Compositional Generalization: A Case Study in Open Intent Detection

Yihao Fang[2,3], **Xianzhi Li**[1,2], **Stephen W. Thomas**[3] **and Xiaodan Zhu**[1,2]

[1]Department of Electrical and Computer Engineering, Queen's University
[2]Ingenuity Labs Research Institute, Queen's University
[3]Smith School of Business, Queen's University
{yihao.fang, 21xl17, stephen.thomas, xiaodan.zhu}@queensu.ca

Abstract

Open intent detection, a crucial aspect of natural language understanding, involves the identification of previously unseen intents in user-generated text. Despite the progress made in this field, challenges persist in handling new combinations of language components, which is essential for compositional generalization. In this paper, we present a case study exploring the use of ChatGPT as a data augmentation technique to enhance compositional generalization in open intent detection tasks. We begin by discussing the limitations of existing benchmarks in evaluating this problem, highlighting the need for constructing datasets for addressing compositional generalization in open intent detection tasks. By incorporating synthetic data generated by ChatGPT into the training process, we demonstrate that our approach can effectively improve model performance. Rigorous evaluation of multiple benchmarks reveals that our method outperforms existing techniques and significantly enhances open intent detection capabilities. Our findings underscore the potential of large language models like ChatGPT for data augmentation in natural language understanding tasks.

1 Introduction

Open intent detection, a key component of natural language understanding, aims to identify previously unseen intents in user-generated text. This task is of paramount importance for a wide range of applications, such as conversational AI systems, where the ability to recognize new intents can substantially improve the user experience. Although the field has made significant strides in recent years, a major challenge remains in addressing compositional generalization, which refers to the capability of models to handle unseen combinations of language components. This capability is essential for the successful deployment of AI systems in real-world scenarios, where users may express intent in unforeseen ways.

In this paper, we present a case study that investigates the potential of ChatGPT, a state-of-the-art large language model, as a data augmentation technique for enhancing compositional generalization in open intent detection tasks. Our study begins by identifying the shortcomings of existing benchmarks in evaluating this problem, which underscores the need for the development of datasets tailored to assess compositional generalization in open intent detection tasks.

To address this issue, we leverage ChatGPT to generate synthetic data that is then incorporated into the training process. By doing so, we aim to improve the model's ability to recognize new combinations of language components, thereby enhancing its open intent detection capabilities. Through rigorous evaluation of multiple benchmarks, we demonstrate that our proposed method outperforms existing techniques and leads to significant performance improvements.

Our findings highlight the potential of large language models, such as ChatGPT, for data augmentation in natural language understanding tasks. This case study offers valuable insights into the development of more effective dialogue systems capable of handling a wider range of user intents and fostering better human-computer interactions.

Our primary contributions to the literature include:

- Dataset Construction for Compositional Generalization: We construct compositionally diverse subsets derived from existing open intent detection benchmark datasets.
- ChatGPT Data Augmentation: We propose using ChatGPT to generate paraphrases of training dataset instances, thereby enhancing model generalization and performance on unseen compositions.
- We evaluate three different strategies for incorporating ChatGPT-generated paraphrases into

Proceedings of the Joint Workshop of the 5th Financial Technology and Natural Language Processing (FinNLP) and 2nd Multimodal AI For Financial Forecasting (Muffin), Macao, August 20, 2023.

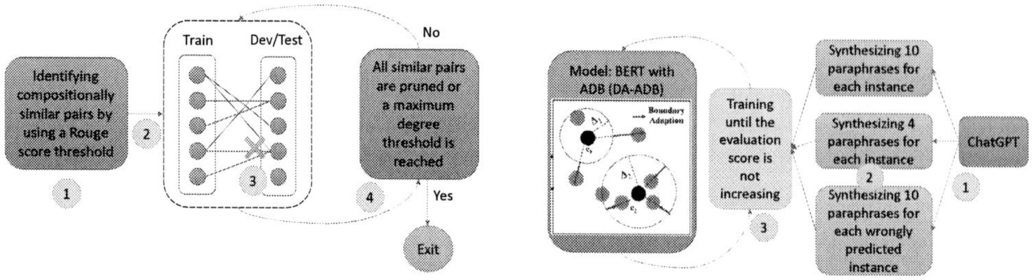

(a) Dataset construction

(b) ChatGPT data augmentation

Figure 1: a-1) Compositionally-similar utterance instances are identified by a Rouge score threshold. a-2) An undirect graph is created by connecting compositionally-similar instances with edges. a-3) Node (instance) degrees are counted in the undirected graph and highest-degree nodes and their edges are first pruned. a-4) This process iterates until all similar pairs are pruned or a maximum degree threshold is reached. b-1) Paraphrases are generated by ChatGPT for utterances in the training dataset. b-2) Paraphrases are incorporated into the BERT training process through three different strategies. b-3) The training process iterates until the evaluation score (accuracy) is not increasing.

the training process of BERT (Devlin et al., 2019) with ADB (Zhang et al., 2021b) (DA-ADB Zhang et al., 2023).

The rest of the paper is organized as follows: Section 2 provides a background on open intent classification and reviews related work. Section 3 describes our proposed method in detail. Section 4 presents the experimental setup, results, and analysis. Finally, Section 5 concludes the paper and suggests directions for future research.

2 Related Work

Open intent classification is an important problem in natural language understanding and dialogue systems, aiming to identify known intents and detect unseen open intents using only the prior knowledge of known intents. Several recent studies have explored various techniques for addressing this challenging task.

One line of research involves aligning representation learning with scoring functions. For instance, the unified neighbourhood learning framework (UniNL) was proposed to detect OOD intents by designing a KNCL objective for representation learning and introducing a KNN-based scoring function for OOD detection (Mou et al., 2022b). Another study proposed a unified K-nearest neighbour contrastive learning framework for OOD intent discovery, which focuses on inter-class discriminative features and alleviates the in-domain overfitting problem (Mou et al., 2022a).

Another direction focuses on learning discriminative representations and decision boundaries for open intent detection. The Deep Open Intent Classification with Adaptive Decision Boundary (**ADB**) method learns an adaptive spherical decision boundary for each known class, balancing both the empirical risk and the open space risk without requiring open intent samples or modifying the model architecture (Zhang et al., 2021b). Similarly, the **DA-ADB** framework successively learns distance-aware intent representations and adaptive decision boundaries for open intent detection by leveraging distance information and designing a loss function to balance empirical and open space risks (Zhang et al., 2023).

In summary, various methods have been proposed to address the challenges associated with detecting unseen intents. However, none of them have explored compositional generalization in open intent detection tasks. We highlight the need for constructing datasets and leverage ChatGPT to generate synthetic data to address this problem. Our proposed method in detail is given in the following section.

3 Methodology

3.1 Dataset Construction for Compositional Generalization

The construction of the dataset starts with identifying compositionally-similar utterance instances by utilizing a Rouge score threshold (Figure 1a). The Rouge score is a widely-used metric for evaluating the similarity between a pair of text sequences by comparing the number of overlapping n-grams (Lin, 2004). By setting a threshold value, instances with Rouge scores above this threshold are deemed to be compositionally similar, allowing for the effective detection of instances with a high degree of overlap in content or structure.

Once the compositionally-similar utterance instances are identified, an undirected graph is created by connecting these instances with edges. In this graph, each node represents an instance, and an edge is drawn between two nodes if their corresponding instances are compositionally similar according to the Rouge score threshold. This representation allows for a better understanding of the relationships between the instances, making it easier to discern patterns and outliers in the data. Furthermore, the graph-based approach facilitates the efficient pruning of highly similar instances in subsequent steps.

To refine the dataset and ensure maximum diversity, the highest-degree nodes and their connecting edges are first pruned. In this context, the degree of a node refers to the number of edges connected to it. By pruning the highest-degree nodes, the instances with the most similarities to other instances are removed from the dataset. This process iterates until all similar pairs have been pruned or a maximum degree threshold is reached. The result is a dataset with a high degree of diversity and helps to access the compositional generalizability of the model trained on this dataset.

The aforementioned approach is utilized on three open intent detection benchmark datasets: **Banking** (Casanueva et al., 2020), **OOS** (Larson et al., 2019) and **StackOverflow** (Xu et al., 2015), resulting in three compositionally diverse subsets derived from these datasets, namely **Banking_CG**, **OOS_CG**, and **StackOverflow_CG**. (Refer to Appendix A for dataset construction in detail.)

3.2 ChatGPT Data Augmentation

The training process involves generating paraphrases for utterances in the training dataset using ChatGPT (Figure 1b). This paraphrasing approach aids in enhancing the model's understanding of language by providing alternative compositions of the same meaning. The incorporation of these paraphrases into the training process not only improves the generalizability of the model but also leads to better performance on unseen compositions. (Refer to Appendix C for ChatGPT's paraphrases in detail.)

To effectively integrate paraphrases into the training process of BERT (Devlin et al., 2019) with **ADB** (**DA-ADB**), three different strategies are evaluated. The first strategy involves synthesizing 10 paraphrases for each instance in the dataset (**GPTAUG-F10**), while the second strategy generates 4 paraphrases for each instance (**GPTAUG-F4**). The third strategy, on the other hand, focuses on instances that the model predicts incorrectly at the current iteration and synthesizes 10 paraphrases for each of these instances (**GPTAUG-WP10**). This targeted approach aims to help address specific weaknesses in the model's understanding. The training process iterates through these strategies until the evaluation score, such as accuracy, no longer exhibits any improvement. This iterative process ensures that the model continues to refine its understanding of language by learning from the generated paraphrases, ultimately resulting in a more robust and capable BERT model.

4 Experiments

4.1 Experimental Setup

In our experimental setup, we have extended the TEXTOIR platform (Zhang et al., 2021a), a toolkit that integrates a variety of state-of-the-art algorithms for open intent detection, to conduct our experiments. To ensure fair comparisons across all tests, we employed the pre-trained BERT-base model from Hugging Face (Wolf et al., 2020) as the foundation of our approach. The optimization of the BERT model with ADB (DA-ADB) was carried out using Python and the PyTorch framework (Paszke et al., 2019) and executed on NVIDIA RTX 2080 TI GPUs for computational efficiency.

4.2 Results and Analysis

Experimental results (Table 1) show that ADB (Zhang et al., 2021b) and DA-ADB (Zhang et al., 2023) are not robust and exhibit poor performance in the compositionally diverse subsets: Banking_CG, OOS_CG, and StackOverflow_CG. These subsets are derived from more extensive datasets, namely Banking, OOS, and StackOverflow. This indicates that these models struggle to achieve compositional generalization in more challenging contexts.

Interestingly, ADB is found to be more robust than DA-ADB, particularly in the OOS_CG subset, where the model has to predict a larger number of intents (151 intents) in the test phase. This is about twice the number of intents in Banking_CG and 7.5

Table 1: Performance of our ChatGPT augmentation approaches (GPTAUG-F4, GPTAUG-F10, and GPTAUG-WP10) and the baselines (ADB and DA-ADB). The best results among each setting are bolded. All results are an average of 10 runs using 10 different seed numbers considering that the selection of known intents is a pseudo-random process. (Refer to Appendix D in more detail.)

	Methods	Banking_CG				OOS_CG				StackOverflow_CG			
		F1-IND	F1-OOD	F1-All	Acc-All	F1-IND	F1-OOD	F1-All	Acc-All	F1-IND	F1-OOD	F1-All	Acc-All
25%	ADB	53.49	81.10	54.87	72.31	49.13	90.65	50.19	83.96	58.37	79.04	61.82	71.35
	DA-ADB	53.33	**86.15**	54.97	**78.43**	38.27	91.70	39.64	85.45	**62.32**	**84.84**	**66.08**	**77.68**
	ADB+GPTAUG-F4	56.73	83.37	58.06	75.51	53.54	91.93	54.52	86.23	60.94	82.62	64.55	75.32
	ADB+GPTAUG-F10	**57.58**	84.04	**58.90**	76.46	**54.26**	**92.07**	**55.23**	**86.48**	58.99	80.34	62.55	72.66
	ADB+GPTAUG-WP10	50.04	70.47	51.06	61.47	48.03	88.57	49.07	80.83	51.62	63.54	53.60	56.17
	DA-ADB+GPTAUG-F4	54.58	84.82	56.09	77.11	43.98	91.85	45.21	85.89	59.97	78.03	62.98	70.79
	DA-ADB+GPTAUG-F10	53.52	84.00	55.04	76.00	44.20	91.74	45.42	85.70	59.82	75.31	62.40	70.10
	DA-ADB+GPTAUG-WP10	54.72	82.89	56.13	74.38	43.18	91.55	44.42	85.33	54.61	64.87	56.32	59.22
50%	ADB	59.93	69.63	60.18	65.38	52.32	83.99	52.73	75.66	71.45	76.14	71.88	73.58
	DA-ADB	54.57	74.45	55.08	67.77	33.66	83.31	34.31	73.37	**75.97**	**81.75**	**76.49**	**79.14**
	ADB+GPTAUG-F4	**62.55**	73.20	**62.83**	69.24	55.36	85.39	55.76	78.07	71.58	77.03	72.08	74.37
	ADB+GPTAUG-F10	62.28	73.23	62.56	69.36	**55.40**	**85.57**	**55.80**	**78.44**	70.97	77.56	71.57	74.52
	ADB+GPTAUG-WP10	59.87	61.11	59.90	60.27	53.25	83.06	53.64	74.61	67.04	64.13	66.78	65.37
	DA-ADB+GPTAUG-F4	57.06	**74.67**	57.52	**69.41**	38.85	84.00	39.45	74.96	72.28	74.07	72.44	73.88
	DA-ADB+GPTAUG-F10	56.52	74.42	56.98	69.09	39.02	83.94	39.61	74.90	70.32	74.78	70.72	73.27
	DA-ADB+GPTAUG-WP10	58.63	70.33	58.93	65.30	40.26	83.99	40.84	74.81	69.91	64.58	69.43	66.65
75%	ADB	64.30	53.36	64.12	62.82	53.87	76.24	54.07	68.33	76.13	61.56	75.22	71.58
	DA-ADB	54.74	52.46	54.70	56.94	29.58	71.76	29.96	59.91	**78.57**	**65.80**	**77.77**	**74.51**
	ADB+GPTAUG-F4	**66.65**	**54.82**	**66.45**	**64.89**	**55.99**	**77.36**	**56.18**	**70.70**	75.72	61.68	74.84	71.08
	ADB+GPTAUG-F10	66.22	54.61	66.02	64.54	55.64	77.04	55.83	70.54	75.35	61.15	74.46	70.61
	ADB+GPTAUG-WP10	65.22	47.98	64.93	62.22	54.91	75.78	55.10	67.97	73.86	49.92	72.37	67.67
	DA-ADB+GPTAUG-F4	55.87	51.59	55.80	57.67	33.50	72.40	33.85	61.81	76.87	60.79	75.86	71.51
	DA-ADB+GPTAUG-F10	54.86	50.66	54.78	56.65	33.81	72.48	34.15	62.04	73.65	54.81	72.48	68.10
	DA-ADB+GPTAUG-WP10	62.31	53.33	62.15	61.87	40.21	74.07	40.51	64.11	77.77	60.62	76.70	72.52

times that of StackOverflow_CG. However, DA-ADB outperforms ADB in the StackOverflow_CG subset, which is more balanced and has far fewer intents to predict.

In the Banking_CG subset, it was observed that the overall F1 scores of ADB with ChatGPT data augmentation were consistently higher (by about 2 to 4%) than those of ADB and DA-ADB. A similar trend was seen in the OOS_CG subset, where the F1 scores of ADB with ChatGPT data augmentation were 2 to 5% better than ADB and DA-ADB. These results demonstrate that data augmentation can indeed help bridge the gap between the training and test sets, even when they exhibit compositional dissimilarity.

ADB with ChatGPT data augmentation outperforms DA-ADB with augmentation in both Banking_CG and OOS_CG. Interestingly, GPTAUG-WP10, a more sophisticated data augmentation method (which paraphrases wrongly predicted instances), underperforms when compared to simply incorporating all ChatGPT paraphrases into the training process (GPTAUG-F4 and GPTAUG-F10).

Finally, DA-ADB performs best in StackOverflow_CG, considering that this subset is relatively more balanced and has fewer intents to predict.

5 Conclusion

In conclusion, this paper addresses the challenge of compositional generalization in open intent detection by leveraging the capabilities of ChatGPT, a state-of-the-art large language model. By constructing compositionally diverse datasets (i.e., **Banking_CG**, **OOS_CG**, and **StackOverflow_CG**) and incorporating ChatGPT-generated paraphrases into the training process, we have demonstrated large improvements in model performance on unseen compositions.

Future research should focus on developing more advanced data augmentation approaches that can generate more diverse compositions. One possible direction involves designing better-instructed prompts for ChatGPT to encourage more diverse paraphrases that can help improve compositional generalization even further. Additionally, exploring alternative strategies for incorporating augmented data and refining the iterative training process may lead to further performance improvements.

References

Iñigo Casanueva, Tadas Temčinas, Daniela Gerz, Matthew Henderson, and Ivan Vulić. 2020. Efficient intent detection with dual sentence encoders. In *Proceedings of the 2nd Workshop on Natural Language Processing for Conversational AI*, pages 38–45, Online. Association for Computational Linguistics.

Jacob Devlin, Ming-Wei Chang, Kenton Lee, and Kristina Toutanova. 2019. BERT: Pre-training of deep bidirectional transformers for language understanding. In *Proceedings of the 2019 Conference of the North American Chapter of the Association for Computational Linguistics: Human Language Technologies, Volume 1 (Long and Short Papers)*, pages 4171–4186, Minneapolis, Minnesota. Association for Computational Linguistics.

Stefan Larson, Anish Mahendran, Joseph J. Peper, Christopher Clarke, Andrew Lee, Parker Hill, Jonathan K. Kummerfeld, Kevin Leach, Michael A. Laurenzano, Lingjia Tang, and Jason Mars. 2019. An evaluation dataset for intent classification and out-of-scope prediction. In *Proceedings of the 2019 Conference on Empirical Methods in Natural Language Processing and the 9th International Joint Conference on Natural Language Processing (EMNLP-IJCNLP)*, pages 1311–1316, Hong Kong, China. Association for Computational Linguistics.

Chin-Yew Lin. 2004. ROUGE: A package for automatic evaluation of summaries. In *Text Summarization Branches Out*, pages 74–81, Barcelona, Spain. Association for Computational Linguistics.

Yutao Mou, Keqing He, Pei Wang, Yanan Wu, Jingang Wang, Wei Wu, and Weiran Xu. 2022a. Watch the neighbors: A unified k-nearest neighbor contrastive learning framework for OOD intent discovery. In *Proceedings of the 2022 Conference on Empirical Methods in Natural Language Processing*, pages 1517–1529, Abu Dhabi, United Arab Emirates. Association for Computational Linguistics.

Yutao Mou, Pei Wang, Keqing He, Yanan Wu, Jingang Wang, Wei Wu, and Weiran Xu. 2022b. UniNL: Aligning representation learning with scoring function for OOD detection via unified neighborhood learning. In *Proceedings of the 2022 Conference on Empirical Methods in Natural Language Processing*, pages 7317–7325, Abu Dhabi, United Arab Emirates. Association for Computational Linguistics.

Adam Paszke, Sam Gross, Francisco Massa, Adam Lerer, James Bradbury, Gregory Chanan, Trevor Killeen, Zeming Lin, Natalia Gimelshein, Luca Antiga, et al. 2019. Pytorch: An imperative style, high-performance deep learning library. *Advances in neural information processing systems*, 32.

Thomas Wolf, Lysandre Debut, Victor Sanh, Julien Chaumond, Clement Delangue, Anthony Moi, Pierric Cistac, Tim Rault, Rémi Louf, Morgan Funtowicz, Joe Davison, Sam Shleifer, Patrick von Platen, Clara Ma, Yacine Jernite, Julien Plu, Canwen Xu, Teven Le Scao, Sylvain Gugger, Mariama Drame, Quentin Lhoest, and Alexander M. Rush. 2020. Transformers: State-of-the-art natural language processing. In *Proceedings of the 2020 Conference on Empirical Methods in Natural Language Processing: System Demonstrations*, pages 38–45, Online. Association for Computational Linguistics.

Jiaming Xu, Peng Wang, Guanhua Tian, Bo Xu, Jun Zhao, Fangyuan Wang, and Hongwei Hao. 2015. Short text clustering via convolutional neural networks. In *Proceedings of the 1st Workshop on Vector Space Modeling for Natural Language Processing*, pages 62–69, Denver, Colorado. Association for Computational Linguistics.

Hanlei Zhang, Xiaoteng Li, Hua Xu, Panpan Zhang, Kang Zhao, and Kai Gao. 2021a. TEXTOIR: An integrated and visualized platform for text open intent recognition. In *Proceedings of the 59th Annual Meeting of the Association for Computational Linguistics and the 11th International Joint Conference on Natural Language Processing: System Demonstrations*, pages 167–174.

Hanlei Zhang, Hua Xu, and Ting-En Lin. 2021b. Deep open intent classification with adaptive decision boundary. *Proceedings of the AAAI Conference on Artificial Intelligence*, 35(16):14374–14382.

Hanlei Zhang, Hua Xu, Shaojie Zhao, and Qianrui Zhou. 2023. Learning discriminative representations and decision boundaries for open intent detection. *IEEE/ACM Transactions on Audio, Speech, and Language Processing*.

A Dataset Construction in Detail

Banking_CG, OOS_CG, and StackOverflow_CG are subsets derived from Banking, OOS, and Stack-Overflow by pruning compositionally-similar pairs of utterance instances between their training and test/development sets. Rouge-L score is adopted to identify overlap common subsequences in a pair of utterance instances. The larger Rouge-L score usually indicates that more common compositions (n-grams) are shared among the pair of utterances.

In Banking_CG and OOS_CG, we used a Rouge-L threshold of 0.3 to detect a similar pair of utterance instances between their training and test/development sets, while in StackOverflow_CG, a threshold of 0.2 is adopted. (Refer to Appendix B for more about Rouge score and the corresponding utterance pairs.)

Once the compositionally-similar pair of utterance instances are identified, a graph is created by connecting these instances with edges, then highest-degree nodes (instances) and their edges are pruned iteratively. Considering that training and test/development sets had significantly different numbers of instances, the node degree is multiplied by the weight (the number of remaining instances in the set) to readjust if the node to prune should be from the training or test/development set.

The pruning process iterates until a certain condition is met. In Banking_CG and OOS_CG, we stopped the process when the maximum node degree of the test/development sets reached a number of 5, while in StackOverflow_CG, the process wasn't stopped until all similar pairs were pruned, considering that StackOverflow_CG is relatively more balanced and has fewer intents to predict.

In Banking_CG, 6231, 183, and 1184 utterance instances were pruned from the corresponding training, development and test sets, while in OOS_CG, 11317, 1306, and 2068 were pruned, and in StackOverflow_CG, 9209, 578, and 3095 instances were removed from their training, development and test sets, respectively. Detailed statistics of Banking_CG, OOS_CG, and StackOverflow_CG can be found in Tables 2 to 10.

B Examples of Rouge Scores and Corresponding Utterance Pairs

The compositional similarity of a pair of utterances can be told by Rouge-L score. In the second row of Table 11, given that the Rouge-L score is greater than 0.3, a long span (4-gram) "be using my card" is shared by both the training and test utterance instances. When the Rouge-L score is not greater than 0.3, the first row and the third row of Table 11, literally those pairs are compositionally dissimilar and only a short span (bigram) "my card" is found common between training and test instances.

C Examples of ChatGPT's Paraphrases

Table 12 demonstrates that ChatGPT's paraphrases introduce diverse compositions from the original utterances. For example, in the first row of Table 12b, the bigram "equivalent of" is replaced with a trigram "corresponding phrase for" of the same meaning. In the first row of Table12a, the original sentence "i have a pending top-up" is put into its passive voice structure. The diversities brought by ChatGPT's paraphrases eventually bridge the gap between compositionally dissimilar training and test sets.

D Experimental Results in Detail

For a fair comparison, all settings are evaluated using the seed numbers 0 to 9 for known intent sampling. All settings are built on the BERT-base backbone and are optimized using the ADAM gradient descent algorithm. Full experimental results are shown in Tables 13 to 20.

Table 2: **Banking_CG** training dataset statistics

Intent	#Instance	Intent	#Instance
Refund_not_showing_up	54	get_physical_card	18
activate_my_card	49	getting_spare_card	29
age_limit	31	getting_virtual_card	16
apple_pay_or_google_pay	28	lost_or_stolen_card	22
atm_support	25	lost_or_stolen_phone	24
automatic_top_up	31	order_physical_card	29
balance_not_updated_after_bank_transfer	65	passcode_forgotten	26
balance_not_updated_after_cheque_or_cash_deposit	69	pending_card_payment	51
beneficiary_not_allowed	37	pending_cash_withdrawal	41
cancel_transfer	49	pending_top_up	44
card_about_to_expire	29	pending_transfer	45
card_acceptance	13	pin_blocked	33
card_arrival	51	receiving_money	22
card_delivery_estimate	32	request_refund	49
card_linking	34	reverted_card_payment?	45
card_not_working	33	supported_cards_and_currencies	38
card_payment_fee_charged	85	terminate_account	34
card_payment_not_recognised	64	top_up_by_bank_transfer_charge	20
card_payment_wrong_exchange_rate	68	top_up_by_card_charge	20
card_swallowed	10	top_up_by_cash_or_cheque	21
cash_withdrawal_charge	60	top_up_failed	35
cash_withdrawal_not_recognised	43	top_up_limits	21
change_pin	26	top_up_reverted	39
compromised_card	14	topping_up_by_card	20
contactless_not_working	15	transaction_charged_twice	57
country_support	34	transfer_fee_charged	55
declined_card_payment	40	transfer_into_account	21
declined_cash_withdrawal	54	transfer_not_received_by_recipient	63
declined_transfer	44	transfer_timing	26
direct_debit_payment_not_recognised	89	unable_to_verify_identity	15
disposable_card_limits	25	verify_my_identity	27
edit_personal_details	24	verify_source_of_funds	22
exchange_charge	25	verify_top_up	24
exchange_rate	21	virtual_card_not_working	5
exchange_via_app	24	visa_or_mastercard	37
extra_charge_on_statement	51	why_verify_identity	30
failed_transfer	33	wrong_amount_of_cash_received	67
fiat_currency_support	37	wrong_exchange_rate_for_cash_withdrawal	53
get_disposable_virtual_card	12		

Table 3: **Banking_CG** development dataset statistics

Intent	#Instance	Intent	#Instance
Refund_not_showing_up	13	get_physical_card	8
activate_my_card	12	getting_spare_card	10
age_limit	9	getting_virtual_card	6
apple_pay_or_google_pay	9	lost_or_stolen_card	6
atm_support	9	lost_or_stolen_phone	10
automatic_top_up	11	order_physical_card	9
balance_not_updated_after_bank_transfer	14	passcode_forgotten	5
balance_not_updated_after_cheque_or_cash_deposit	15	pending_card_payment	15
beneficiary_not_allowed	15	pending_cash_withdrawal	11
cancel_transfer	12	pending_top_up	13
card_about_to_expire	10	pending_transfer	14
card_acceptance	4	pin_blocked	7
card_arrival	11	receiving_money	8
card_delivery_estimate	8	request_refund	17
card_linking	10	reverted_card_payment?	14
card_not_working	7	supported_cards_and_currencies	10
card_payment_fee_charged	18	terminate_account	9
card_payment_not_recognised	17	top_up_by_bank_transfer_charge	9
card_payment_wrong_exchange_rate	12	top_up_by_card_charge	8
card_swallowed	4	top_up_by_cash_or_cheque	10
cash_withdrawal_charge	16	top_up_failed	13
cash_withdrawal_not_recognised	16	top_up_limits	8
change_pin	11	top_up_reverted	14
compromised_card	9	topping_up_by_card	10
contactless_not_working	3	transaction_charged_twice	16
country_support	12	transfer_fee_charged	17
declined_card_payment	14	transfer_into_account	8
declined_cash_withdrawal	17	transfer_not_received_by_recipient	14
declined_transfer	10	transfer_timing	9
direct_debit_payment_not_recognised	10	unable_to_verify_identity	9
disposable_card_limits	8	verify_my_identity	7
edit_personal_details	7	verify_source_of_funds	7
exchange_charge	10	verify_top_up	11
exchange_rate	7	virtual_card_not_working	3
exchange_via_app	9	visa_or_mastercard	11
extra_charge_on_statement	12	why_verify_identity	9
failed_transfer	13	wrong_amount_of_cash_received	17
fiat_currency_support	9	wrong_exchange_rate_for_cash_withdrawal	15
get_disposable_virtual_card	7		

Table 4: **Banking_CG** test dataset statistics

Intent	#Instance	Intent	#Instance
Refund_not_showing_up	28	get_physical_card	18
activate_my_card	31	getting_spare_card	29
age_limit	23	getting_virtual_card	21
apple_pay_or_google_pay	22	lost_or_stolen_card	16
atm_support	20	lost_or_stolen_phone	24
automatic_top_up	24	order_physical_card	15
balance_not_updated_after_bank_transfer	25	passcode_forgotten	16
balance_not_updated_after_cheque_or_cash_deposit	30	pending_card_payment	26
beneficiary_not_allowed	37	pending_cash_withdrawal	29
cancel_transfer	29	pending_top_up	25
card_about_to_expire	31	pending_transfer	34
card_acceptance	20	pin_blocked	21
card_arrival	24	receiving_money	26
card_delivery_estimate	23	request_refund	36
card_linking	28	reverted_card_payment?	35
card_not_working	20	supported_cards_and_currencies	24
card_payment_fee_charged	17	terminate_account	11
card_payment_not_recognised	20	top_up_by_bank_transfer_charge	20
card_payment_wrong_exchange_rate	20	top_up_by_card_charge	19
card_swallowed	17	top_up_by_cash_or_cheque	31
cash_withdrawal_charge	34	top_up_failed	30
cash_withdrawal_not_recognised	34	top_up_limits	19
change_pin	18	top_up_reverted	27
compromised_card	18	topping_up_by_card	17
contactless_not_working	20	transaction_charged_twice	35
country_support	18	transfer_fee_charged	33
declined_card_payment	32	transfer_into_account	27
declined_cash_withdrawal	35	transfer_not_received_by_recipient	27
declined_transfer	26	transfer_timing	26
direct_debit_payment_not_recognised	16	unable_to_verify_identity	30
disposable_card_limits	21	verify_my_identity	21
edit_personal_details	27	verify_source_of_funds	26
exchange_charge	24	verify_top_up	29
exchange_rate	22	virtual_card_not_working	9
exchange_via_app	22	visa_or_mastercard	20
extra_charge_on_statement	36	why_verify_identity	22
failed_transfer	27	wrong_amount_of_cash_received	29
fiat_currency_support	23	wrong_exchange_rate_for_cash_withdrawal	28
get_disposable_virtual_card	23		

Table 5: **OOS_CG** training dataset statistics

Intent	#Instance	Intent	#Instance	Intent	#Instance
accept_reservations	50	greeting	33	reset_settings	6
account_blocked	21	how_busy	20	restaurant_reservation	22
alarm	13	how_old_are_you	47	restaurant_reviews	47
application_status	22	improve_credit_score	11	restaurant_suggestion	23
apr	27	income	52	rewards_balance	15
are_you_a_bot	20	ingredient_substitution	42	roll_dice	11
balance	22	ingredients_list	26	rollover_401k	19
bill_balance	18	insurance	29	routing	29
bill_due	15	insurance_change	26	schedule_maintenance	19
book_flight	19	interest_rate	26	schedule_meeting	21
book_hotel	17	international_fees	16	share_location	24
calculator	53	international_visa	33	shopping_list	24
calendar	34	jump_start	10	shopping_list_update	16
calendar_update	17	last_maintenance	14	smart_home	19
calories	41	lost_luggage	28	spelling	33
cancel	30	make_call	20	spending_history	17
cancel_reservation	19	maybe	26	sync_device	7
car_rental	12	meal_suggestion	29	taxes	24
card_declined	16	meaning_of_life	17	tell_joke	26
carry_on	32	measurement_conversion	23	text	27
change_accent	23	meeting_schedule	45	thank_you	25
change_ai_name	15	min_payment	23	time	29
change_language	33	mpg	26	timer	14
change_speed	27	new_card	24	timezone	39
change_user_name	47	next_holiday	17	tire_change	26
change_volume	11	next_song	24	tire_pressure	21
confirm_reservation	25	no	25	todo_list	12
cook_time	24	nutrition_info	28	todo_list_update	21
credit_limit	17	oil_change_how	17	traffic	16
credit_limit_change	13	oil_change_when	15	transactions	26
credit_score	6	order	49	transfer	17
current_location	18	order_checks	20	translate	24
damaged_card	17	order_status	21	travel_alert	55
date	31	pay_bill	23	travel_notification	27
definition	62	payday	22	travel_suggestion	29
direct_deposit	14	pin_change	10	uber	14
directions	40	play_music	42	update_playlist	27
distance	57	plug_type	12	user_name	23
do_you_have_pets	19	pto_balance	7	vaccines	23
exchange_rate	33	pto_request	35	w2	18
expiration_date	13	pto_request_status	18	weather	21
find_phone	11	pto_used	14	what_are_your_hobbies	26
flight_status	29	recipe	37	what_can_i_ask_you	6
flip_coin	13	redeem_rewards	19	what_is_your_name	26
food_last	43	reminder	52	what_song	28
freeze_account	23	reminder_update	26	where_are_you_from	23
fun_fact	18	repeat	14	whisper_mode	23
gas	13	replacement_card_duration	16	who_do_you_work_for	32
gas_type	12	report_fraud	11	who_made_you	43
goodbye	43	report_lost_card	25	yes	47

Table 6: **OOS_CG** development dataset statistics

Intent	#Instance	Intent	#Instance	Intent	#Instance
accept_reservations	15	greeting	13	reset_settings	13
account_blocked	11	how_busy	15	restaurant_reservation	10
alarm	14	how_old_are_you	11	restaurant_reviews	9
application_status	12	improve_credit_score	9	restaurant_suggestion	19
apr	6	income	6	rewards_balance	9
are_you_a_bot	10	ingredient_substitution	13	roll_dice	13
balance	14	ingredients_list	12	rollover_401k	9
bill_balance	11	insurance	11	routing	4
bill_due	9	insurance_change	9	schedule_maintenance	16
book_flight	18	interest_rate	9	schedule_meeting	8
book_hotel	15	international_fees	15	share_location	14
calculator	10	international_visa	5	shopping_list	5
calendar	9	jump_start	17	shopping_list_update	13
calendar_update	16	last_maintenance	11	smart_home	18
calories	5	lost_luggage	15	spelling	11
cancel	18	make_call	14	spending_history	16
cancel_reservation	19	maybe	18	sync_device	13
car_rental	11	meal_suggestion	14	taxes	11
card_declined	11	meaning_of_life	15	tell_joke	13
carry_on	18	measurement_conversion	15	text	9
change_accent	15	meeting_schedule	8	thank_you	15
change_ai_name	13	min_payment	8	time	3
change_language	8	mpg	12	timer	14
change_speed	14	new_card	7	timezone	8
change_user_name	14	next_holiday	11	tire_change	8
change_volume	15	next_song	9	tire_pressure	11
confirm_reservation	12	no	15	todo_list	12
cook_time	9	nutrition_info	11	todo_list_update	5
credit_limit	4	oil_change_how	4	traffic	11
credit_limit_change	12	oil_change_when	8	transactions	14
credit_score	5	order	13	transfer	9
current_location	11	order_checks	16	translate	15
damaged_card	11	order_status	16	travel_alert	11
date	10	pay_bill	8	travel_notification	12
definition	12	payday	9	travel_suggestion	14
direct_deposit	6	pin_change	13	uber	11
directions	10	play_music	16	update_playlist	6
distance	6	plug_type	11	user_name	11
do_you_have_pets	14	pto_balance	9	vaccines	8
exchange_rate	14	pto_request	9	w2	11
expiration_date	9	pto_request_status	10	weather	16
find_phone	5	pto_used	12	what_are_your_hobbies	6
flight_status	7	recipe	11	what_can_i_ask_you	12
flip_coin	16	redeem_rewards	6	what_is_your_name	8
food_last	11	reminder	9	what_song	10
freeze_account	4	reminder_update	12	where_are_you_from	19
fun_fact	18	repeat	13	whisper_mode	12
gas	10	replacement_card_duration	10	who_do_you_work_for	9
gas_type	11	report_fraud	14	who_made_you	9
goodbye	16	report_lost_card	8	yes	12

Table 7: **OOS_CG** test dataset statistics

Intent	#Instance	Intent	#Instance	Intent	#Instance
accept_reservations	17	how_busy	22	restaurant_reservation	17
account_blocked	15	how_old_are_you	16	restaurant_reviews	20
alarm	30	improve_credit_score	8	restaurant_suggestion	21
application_status	19	income	17	rewards_balance	12
apr	11	ingredient_substitution	19	roll_dice	17
are_you_a_bot	17	ingredients_list	20	rollover_401k	11
balance	15	insurance	11	routing	5
bill_balance	17	insurance_change	11	schedule_maintenance	12
bill_due	10	interest_rate	17	schedule_meeting	11
book_flight	15	international_fees	22	share_location	22
book_hotel	17	international_visa	6	shopping_list	5
calculator	14	jump_start	11	shopping_list_update	17
calendar	12	last_maintenance	18	smart_home	22
calendar_update	19	lost_luggage	24	spelling	15
calories	15	make_call	20	spending_history	14
cancel	23	maybe	20	sync_device	12
cancel_reservation	20	meal_suggestion	17	taxes	16
car_rental	15	meaning_of_life	23	tell_joke	15
card_declined	9	measurement_conversion	21	text	18
carry_on	22	meeting_schedule	16	thank_you	25
change_accent	14	min_payment	24	time	10
change_ai_name	18	mpg	25	timer	29
change_language	17	new_card	5	timezone	12
change_speed	15	next_holiday	21	tire_change	8
change_user_name	14	next_song	8	tire_pressure	12
change_volume	16	no	23	todo_list	18
confirm_reservation	14	nutrition_info	25	todo_list_update	10
cook_time	8	oil_change_how	9	traffic	13
credit_limit	10	oil_change_when	11	transactions	20
credit_limit_change	21	oos	1200	transfer	15
credit_score	28	order	17	translate	23
current_location	21	order_checks	17	travel_alert	13
damaged_card	16	order_status	20	travel_notification	14
date	15	pay_bill	6	travel_suggestion	15
definition	17	payday	13	uber	20
direct_deposit	19	pin_change	13	update_playlist	8
directions	19	play_music	21	user_name	7
distance	15	plug_type	18	vaccines	12
do_you_have_pets	25	pto_balance	9	w2	23
exchange_rate	21	pto_request	15	weather	26
expiration_date	17	pto_request_status	15	what_are_your_hobbies	13
find_phone	9	pto_used	20	what_can_i_ask_you	18
flight_status	19	recipe	19	what_is_your_name	15
flip_coin	24	redeem_rewards	19	what_song	13
food_last	16	reminder	14	where_are_you_from	21
freeze_account	9	reminder_update	17	whisper_mode	22
fun_fact	11	repeat	22	who_do_you_work_for	13
gas	16	replacement_card_duration	11	who_made_you	12
gas_type	15	report_fraud	15	yes	16
goodbye	22	report_lost_card	15		
greeting	21	reset_settings	14		

Table 8: **StackOverflow_CG** training dataset statistics

Intent	#Instance	Intent	#Instance	Intent	#Instance	Intent	#Instance	Intent	#Instance
ajax	158	drupal	132	linq	105	osx	139	spring	154
apache	143	excel	106	magento	112	qt	147	svn	116
bash	104	haskell	126	matlab	132	scala	135	visual-studio	200
cocoa	233	hibernate	130	oracle	124	sharepoint	140	wordpress	155

Table 9: **StackOverflow_CG** development dataset statistics

Intent	#Instance	Intent	#Instance	Intent	#Instance	Intent	#Instance	Intent	#Instance
ajax	74	drupal	70	linq	78	osx	91	spring	67
apache	80	excel	70	magento	66	qt	83	svn	75
bash	80	haskell	71	matlab	73	scala	72	visual-studio	42
cocoa	66	hibernate	68	oracle	63	sharepoint	75	wordpress	58

Table 10: **StackOverflow_CG** test dataset statistics

Intent	#Instance	Intent	#Instance	Intent	#Instance	Intent	#Instance	Intent	#Instance
ajax	160	drupal	128	linq	131	osx	193	spring	151
apache	170	excel	140	magento	132	qt	172	svn	149
bash	139	haskell	122	matlab	164	scala	124	visual-studio	106
cocoa	161	hibernate	128	oracle	127	sharepoint	171	wordpress	137

Table 11: Examples of Rouge scores and corresponding utterance pairs

Training instance	Someone might be using my card that is not me.
Test instance	I don't recognize some of the transactions on my card, I think someone must have gotten my card info and used it.
Rouge-L score	0.13
Training instance	Someone might be using my card that is not me.
Test instance	What should I do if I think that someone else may be using my card.
Rouge-L score	0.33
Training instance	Someone might be using my card that is not me.
Test instance	I think someone got my card details and used it because there are transactions i don't recognize. What do I do now?
Rouge-L score	0.13

Table 12: Examples of ChatGPT's Paraphrases

(a) Banking_CG Dataset

Original utterance	i have a pending top-up
ChatGPT's paraphrase	A top-up transaction is still being processed.
Original utterance	What are the currency types that I can keep money in.
ChatGPT's paraphrase	Which currencies are allowed for me to keep my finances?
Original utterance	I think my card is broken or something. I tried using it and it wouldn't go through, please help.
ChatGPT's paraphrase	It appears that my card may be broken or faulty, as I tried to use it but it didn't work. Could you provide me with some assistance, please?

(b) OOS_CG Dataset

Original utterance	what is the equivalent of, 'life is good' in french
ChatGPT's paraphrase	What is the corresponding phrase for 'life is good' in French?
Original utterance	how many inches and centimeters would i need if i had 10 feet of something
ChatGPT's paraphrase	How many inches and centimeters would be needed for 10 feet of an object?
Original utterance	please put taco night on the house calendar date of january 6
ChatGPT's paraphrase	Kindly mark January 6th as the date for taco night on the house calendar.

(c) StackOverflow_CG Dataset

Original utterance	Why this keyboard intercepting kernel extension doesn't work?
ChatGPT's paraphrase	Can you provide an answer for the non-functionality of the keyboard interception kernel extension?
Original utterance	NSColor with calibrated values works differently than regular color??
ChatGPT's paraphrase	Calibrated NSColor showcases a diverse behavior from a typical color.
Original utterance	Tips for using CVS or Subversion as a backup framework for office documents
ChatGPT's paraphrase	Guidelines for utilizing CVS or Subversion as a backup solution for office documents.

Table 13: ADB experimental results in detail

	Seed	Banking_CG				OOS_CG				StackOverflow_CG			
		F1-IND	F1-OOD	F1-All	Acc-All	F1-IND	F1-OOD	F1-All	Acc-All	F1-IND	F1-OOD	F1-All	Acc-All
25%	0	54.32	81.06	55.66	71.10	45.65	91.86	46.83	85.63	66.48	88.37	70.13	82.55
	1	54.36	79.78	55.63	70.94	52.36	91.18	53.35	84.77	60.63	80.47	63.94	72.94
	2	53.99	79.04	55.24	71.10	49.16	91.46	50.24	84.64	59.12	80.55	62.69	72.87
	3	53.55	80.15	54.88	71.78	49.81	89.61	50.83	82.57	59.95	85.19	64.16	78.04
	4	59.76	81.31	60.84	73.31	54.07	91.97	55.04	85.68	58.86	78.74	62.17	70.67
	5	49.72	81.85	51.33	72.52	50.03	90.73	51.07	84.03	55.42	69.00	57.68	61.17
	6	48.92	78.28	50.39	68.88	55.00	89.41	55.88	82.74	59.18	81.67	62.93	73.22
	7	50.79	83.28	52.41	74.21	44.05	89.56	45.22	82.46	61.03	84.09	64.88	76.90
	8	52.18	83.82	53.76	75.11	40.09	89.34	41.35	81.75	53.36	81.30	58.02	72.60
	9	57.33	82.40	58.58	74.10	51.07	91.41	52.11	85.32	49.71	61.01	51.59	52.56
50%	0	57.44	72.01	57.82	66.51	51.47	83.75	51.89	75.55	75.71	82.67	76.34	80.07
	1	62.04	68.92	62.22	65.72	52.52	83.81	52.93	75.30	70.56	73.05	70.78	70.60
	2	61.66	70.50	61.89	66.93	50.64	85.10	51.09	76.29	70.76	78.05	71.42	74.18
	3	58.88	69.09	59.14	64.98	54.26	84.22	54.65	76.35	70.45	74.29	70.80	71.70
	4	62.11	69.96	62.31	66.30	55.06	84.01	55.44	75.63	68.29	71.15	68.55	69.12
	5	58.56	72.02	58.91	66.30	52.78	84.17	53.20	75.69	74.22	77.70	74.54	76.01
	6	55.92	67.11	56.21	62.08	51.95	83.97	52.37	75.94	73.29	80.95	73.99	77.45
	7	57.74	66.71	57.97	61.87	49.92	83.73	50.37	74.83	70.24	75.19	70.69	72.70
	8	60.93	71.71	61.21	67.41	49.19	82.40	49.62	73.49	69.59	73.54	69.95	71.53
	9	63.98	68.29	64.09	65.66	55.37	84.78	55.75	77.53	71.41	74.80	71.72	72.46
75%	0	65.47	56.31	65.31	64.50	53.11	75.08	53.30	66.82	77.73	68.20	77.13	74.97
	1	66.17	51.73	65.93	63.71	53.75	76.63	53.95	68.83	74.97	57.43	73.87	69.60
	2	64.73	52.93	64.53	63.08	52.09	76.01	52.30	67.21	75.13	65.37	74.52	71.94
	3	63.41	49.66	63.18	61.50	55.98	75.57	56.15	68.86	75.72	57.86	74.60	69.98
	4	64.99	52.81	64.79	63.24	56.38	76.64	56.56	69.49	76.82	61.84	75.88	72.87
	5	64.98	59.67	64.89	64.87	51.57	78.20	51.81	68.78	78.43	59.41	77.24	72.25
	6	62.19	53.26	62.04	60.86	53.56	76.88	53.77	68.89	74.44	58.53	73.44	68.74
	7	59.66	51.17	59.51	59.02	52.58	76.27	52.79	68.01	78.70	66.63	77.95	75.22
	8	65.18	54.89	65.00	63.87	52.86	74.40	53.05	66.33	75.25	57.61	74.15	69.81
	9	66.26	51.22	66.01	63.50	56.87	76.72	57.05	70.10	74.12	62.73	73.40	70.43

Table 14: DA-ADB experimental results in detail

	Seed	Banking_CG				OOS_CG				StackOverflow_CG			
		F1-IND	F1-OOD	F1-All	Acc-All	F1-IND	F1-OOD	F1-All	Acc-All	F1-IND	F1-OOD	F1-All	Acc-All
25%	0	51.66	88.27	53.49	80.01	33.93	92.54	35.43	86.62	70.98	90.81	74.29	85.96
	1	55.33	84.21	56.77	76.21	37.62	91.84	39.01	85.55	66.88	87.19	70.26	81.03
	2	50.86	84.62	52.55	77.16	35.91	91.44	37.33	84.91	60.42	82.93	64.17	74.84
	3	55.55	85.63	57.05	78.22	39.84	91.12	41.16	84.61	66.89	88.05	70.41	82.03
	4	58.68	86.10	60.05	79.06	45.06	92.47	46.27	86.81	60.39	84.17	64.35	76.76
	5	51.81	86.97	53.57	78.96	44.04	92.12	45.27	86.29	62.54	81.87	65.76	74.22
	6	46.76	83.06	48.57	74.47	44.73	91.67	45.93	85.71	63.63	87.01	67.52	80.07
	7	49.18	87.05	51.08	78.74	35.03	90.76	36.46	83.92	64.84	86.87	68.51	80.45
	8	54.86	87.38	56.49	80.33	30.67	91.08	32.22	84.33	52.25	83.31	57.43	74.63
	9	58.64	88.16	60.11	81.17	35.87	91.93	37.31	85.74	54.41	76.14	58.04	66.85
50%	0	49.77	75.22	50.42	66.72	31.77	84.11	32.46	74.15	80.15	86.31	80.71	84.17
	1	52.47	71.43	52.96	65.19	34.71	83.17	35.34	73.24	77.32	81.37	77.69	78.93
	2	57.29	74.85	57.74	69.30	31.49	83.23	32.17	72.91	72.93	81.07	73.67	77.18
	3	53.55	72.26	54.03	66.14	34.22	83.41	34.86	73.82	74.07	77.89	74.42	75.52
	4	55.62	73.03	56.07	66.77	37.00	82.77	37.60	72.96	74.59	81.62	75.23	78.66
	5	52.39	76.15	53.00	68.57	37.80	83.32	38.40	73.68	75.76	80.38	76.18	78.18
	6	50.45	77.04	51.13	67.93	35.98	83.47	36.61	73.84	79.23	85.97	79.84	83.17
	7	55.90	74.81	56.38	68.04	32.06	83.22	32.73	72.80	76.72	83.76	77.36	81.31
	8	58.98	77.10	59.44	71.20	31.04	82.92	31.72	72.60	71.85	77.45	72.36	74.87
	9	59.34	72.63	59.68	67.83	30.50	83.46	31.19	73.68	77.05	81.71	77.47	79.38
75%	0	54.14	56.52	54.18	58.97	28.11	72.94	28.51	60.71	81.00	71.38	80.40	78.00
	1	55.05	51.20	54.99	56.75	28.66	71.49	29.04	59.55	75.19	63.00	74.43	71.46
	2	54.38	49.80	54.30	55.85	29.51	72.10	29.89	60.27	77.36	67.09	76.72	74.04
	3	55.38	48.25	55.26	55.27	28.06	71.12	28.44	59.36	78.03	61.71	77.01	72.74
	4	55.04	48.45	54.93	55.49	30.00	71.20	30.37	59.00	81.17	69.09	80.41	77.80
	5	52.59	55.11	52.63	56.80	29.10	73.25	29.49	60.79	79.46	62.63	78.40	74.01
	6	54.04	56.19	54.07	58.02	30.41	71.54	30.77	59.80	76.96	62.10	76.04	71.57
	7	51.78	51.07	51.77	54.32	29.22	71.38	29.59	59.42	81.15	70.17	80.47	77.97
	8	55.68	55.04	55.67	58.23	30.14	70.19	30.50	58.73	77.66	62.87	76.74	72.94
	9	59.35	52.95	59.24	59.70	32.61	72.40	32.97	61.43	77.73	67.98	77.12	74.56

Table 15: ADB+GPTAUG-F4 experimental results in detail

	Seed	Banking_CG				OOS_CG				StackOverflow_CG			
		F1-IND	**F1-OOD**	**F1-All**	**Acc-All**	**F1-IND**	**F1-OOD**	**F1-All**	**Acc-All**	**F1-IND**	**F1-OOD**	**F1-All**	**Acc-All**
25%	0	58.04	85.27	59.40	77.48	52.90	92.93	53.92	87.78	66.07	87.09	69.58	80.90
	1	57.11	81.53	58.33	73.63	56.85	92.69	57.77	87.33	63.04	83.53	66.46	76.56
	2	59.83	83.40	61.01	76.53	54.62	92.73	55.60	87.22	62.06	83.26	65.59	76.11
	3	58.91	83.93	60.16	76.74	53.28	90.81	54.24	84.64	59.22	84.74	63.48	77.52
	4	61.81	82.72	62.86	74.79	56.91	92.21	57.82	86.48	58.39	78.63	61.76	70.50
	5	53.76	84.91	55.31	77.00	56.47	92.70	57.40	87.47	57.87	71.56	60.15	63.86
	6	49.84	78.68	51.28	69.57	59.21	91.51	60.04	86.10	63.44	86.24	67.24	79.14
	7	51.00	84.02	52.65	75.37	45.39	89.72	46.53	82.76	61.32	84.23	65.14	77.11
	8	57.43	84.96	58.81	77.37	44.15	91.12	45.35	84.64	59.58	86.30	64.03	79.14
	9	59.54	84.31	60.78	76.58	55.61	92.91	56.56	87.89	58.38	80.57	62.08	72.36
50%	0	59.88	72.93	60.21	67.99	55.53	85.53	55.92	78.30	74.80	82.30	75.48	79.48
	1	64.52	71.24	64.69	68.72	56.29	84.85	56.67	77.56	73.32	79.95	73.93	76.63
	2	64.21	72.72	64.43	69.67	53.62	85.84	54.04	77.92	69.22	78.59	70.07	74.04
	3	60.36	71.55	60.65	67.77	55.85	85.28	56.24	78.19	70.77	76.59	71.30	73.43
	4	65.22	74.51	65.46	70.62	58.56	85.23	58.91	78.14	66.06	64.09	65.88	64.27
	5	60.60	75.58	60.98	70.15	55.21	85.54	55.60	77.97	73.83	77.12	74.13	75.32
	6	60.24	76.12	60.65	71.10	57.29	86.50	57.68	79.90	73.91	82.90	74.72	79.17
	7	61.76	72.72	62.04	68.04	54.12	85.37	54.53	77.75	71.47	76.16	71.90	73.94
	8	63.54	73.68	63.80	70.31	51.68	84.15	52.11	76.21	68.46	72.63	68.84	70.43
	9	65.21	70.97	65.35	67.99	55.47	85.59	55.87	78.77	73.98	79.95	74.53	77.01
75%	0	68.56	57.90	68.38	67.09	57.04	78.70	57.23	71.92	77.32	67.80	76.72	74.32
	1	68.72	53.37	68.46	65.98	58.07	77.79	58.25	71.45	76.73	62.79	75.86	72.43
	2	65.97	55.15	65.79	64.66	54.59	77.05	54.79	69.60	73.05	63.29	72.44	69.57
	3	65.24	50.29	64.98	62.97	56.72	76.96	56.90	71.01	75.24	59.45	74.25	69.64
	4	64.58	51.19	64.36	62.39	58.43	77.49	58.60	71.56	76.35	61.50	75.42	72.01
	5	66.94	58.90	66.81	65.88	53.77	78.05	53.98	70.43	77.68	59.26	76.53	71.60
	6	64.75	56.67	64.61	63.98	53.65	76.91	53.86	69.71	73.96	57.14	72.91	67.78
	7	67.40	55.04	67.19	65.72	53.77	77.22	53.98	70.04	78.29	65.85	77.51	74.60
	8	66.09	54.49	65.89	64.08	55.79	76.08	55.97	69.77	75.00	56.65	73.86	68.95
	9	68.24	55.17	68.02	66.14	58.04	77.31	58.21	71.48	73.54	63.11	72.88	69.91

Table 16: ADB+GPTAUG-F10 experimental results in detail

	Seed	**Banking_CG**				**OOS_CG**				**StackOverflow_CG**			
		F1-IND	**F1-OOD**	**F1-All**	**Acc-All**	**F1-IND**	**F1-OOD**	**F1-All**	**Acc-All**	**F1-IND**	**F1-OOD**	**F1-All**	**Acc-All**
25%	0	58.71	86.00	60.07	78.59	53.03	92.85	54.05	87.67	66.19	86.48	69.58	80.17
	1	57.87	81.50	59.05	73.68	57.33	92.70	58.24	87.42	62.82	83.08	66.19	75.97
	2	60.23	82.65	61.35	75.74	55.26	92.90	56.22	87.50	58.46	78.12	61.74	70.19
	3	58.84	83.84	60.09	76.64	52.85	91.08	53.83	84.99	53.44	76.63	57.30	68.26
	4	63.74	85.02	64.80	78.01	58.23	92.79	59.11	87.56	58.66	80.21	62.25	72.22
	5	54.81	85.70	56.36	78.11	58.45	92.92	59.33	87.91	53.65	67.25	55.92	59.66
	6	50.23	79.56	51.70	70.73	59.61	91.42	60.43	85.90	58.26	81.54	62.14	73.18
	7	52.00	84.93	53.65	76.58	46.39	89.63	47.49	82.63	60.53	83.16	64.30	75.73
	8	57.18	85.03	58.57	77.43	45.55	91.60	46.73	85.46	58.85	85.62	63.31	78.18
	9	62.15	86.17	63.36	79.06	55.95	92.81	56.90	87.75	59.03	81.32	62.75	73.08
50%	0	59.45	73.31	59.81	68.51	56.05	86.22	56.45	79.32	74.30	82.36	75.03	79.35
	1	64.61	72.94	64.82	70.09	57.44	84.34	57.79	76.98	71.94	78.66	72.55	75.25
	2	63.61	73.12	63.85	69.99	53.01	86.08	53.45	78.61	68.62	78.56	69.52	74.11
	3	60.49	71.53	60.77	67.77	55.27	85.53	55.67	78.58	69.86	76.45	70.45	73.05
	4	65.83	74.73	66.06	71.26	58.02	85.55	58.38	78.69	67.31	68.90	67.45	67.37
	5	59.64	74.90	60.03	69.67	56.20	86.01	56.59	78.83	73.22	78.02	73.66	75.80
	6	60.02	76.72	60.45	71.62	56.64	86.21	57.03	79.71	74.21	83.34	75.04	79.62
	7	61.61	72.19	61.88	67.62	54.29	85.35	54.70	77.75	71.85	80.04	72.59	76.83
	8	62.66	74.10	62.95	70.57	51.47	84.50	51.90	76.82	69.22	75.75	69.81	72.87
	9	64.91	68.75	65.01	66.51	55.60	85.85	56.00	79.13	69.23	73.57	69.62	70.95
75%	0	68.27	57.05	68.08	66.51	56.60	78.20	56.80	71.50	77.85	68.49	77.27	74.91
	1	68.10	53.69	67.86	65.56	56.99	77.18	57.17	70.90	76.53	60.94	75.56	71.29
	2	65.71	56.59	65.56	64.98	53.54	76.59	53.74	69.71	72.94	62.67	72.30	69.36
	3	65.29	52.34	65.07	63.55	57.20	76.27	57.37	70.46	74.57	58.22	73.55	68.74
	4	64.32	50.80	64.09	62.24	58.62	77.76	58.79	72.00	76.26	62.65	75.41	72.08
	5	65.75	57.27	65.60	64.61	54.58	77.99	54.79	70.65	77.08	59.47	75.97	71.33
	6	64.39	54.56	64.22	63.13	52.86	76.82	53.07	69.63	73.89	59.24	72.98	68.40
	7	66.59	54.30	66.38	65.08	53.26	76.52	53.47	69.36	77.40	64.11	76.56	73.56
	8	64.78	54.95	64.62	63.66	54.11	75.50	54.30	69.27	75.57	56.72	74.40	69.12
	9	68.97	54.48	68.72	66.03	58.63	77.61	58.80	71.94	71.42	59.03	70.64	67.33

Table 17: ADB+GPTAUG-WP10 experimental results in detail

	Seed	Banking_CG				OOS_CG				StackOverflow_CG			
		F1-IND	F1-OOD	F1-All	Acc-All	F1-IND	F1-OOD	F1-All	Acc-All	F1-IND	F1-OOD	F1-All	Acc-All
25%	0	53.68	74.20	54.71	63.82	42.78	88.54	43.95	80.23	55.82	55.25	55.72	50.26
	1	51.63	71.00	52.59	61.60	46.34	86.13	47.36	77.18	52.86	61.73	54.34	55.11
	2	50.59	67.94	51.46	60.44	47.38	89.55	48.46	81.55	50.06	60.37	51.78	53.56
	3	54.12	74.17	55.12	65.98	49.64	87.59	50.62	79.71	49.37	70.08	52.83	61.55
	4	58.30	77.65	59.27	69.57	54.61	91.64	55.56	85.27	56.11	74.04	59.10	65.92
	5	45.41	72.00	46.74	61.81	50.45	90.10	51.47	83.20	53.80	68.79	56.30	61.27
	6	47.58	67.77	48.59	58.54	57.17	89.23	58.00	82.65	50.65	68.32	53.60	59.35
	7	42.20	54.62	42.82	47.20	42.85	85.61	43.95	76.57	50.25	62.95	52.37	55.59
	8	45.03	72.01	46.38	61.50	41.98	88.94	43.19	81.22	45.41	54.21	46.88	47.13
	9	51.87	73.33	52.94	64.24	47.13	88.34	48.19	80.70	51.82	59.69	53.13	51.91
50%	0	58.94	62.37	59.03	60.13	52.23	82.91	52.64	74.45	71.75	74.91	72.04	73.29
	1	62.10	58.44	62.00	60.07	52.31	82.77	52.71	74.28	70.46	71.96	70.59	70.02
	2	61.63	65.70	61.73	63.61	51.46	84.34	51.89	75.39	64.61	65.84	64.73	64.20
	3	59.66	64.29	59.78	62.18	55.36	83.71	55.73	75.74	69.14	70.79	69.29	69.16
	4	62.01	59.84	61.95	60.50	56.44	83.40	56.79	74.72	56.88	29.67	54.41	46.92
	5	56.61	63.18	56.78	60.28	54.38	84.28	54.77	75.94	69.88	65.79	69.51	67.13
	6	56.27	58.66	56.33	57.49	53.58	83.42	53.97	75.33	62.22	55.86	61.64	58.42
	7	58.79	57.53	58.76	57.70	49.73	82.41	50.16	73.32	68.51	69.89	68.64	68.85
	8	60.05	61.67	60.09	60.44	49.75	80.34	50.15	71.23	65.71	64.05	65.56	64.54
	9	62.64	59.46	62.56	60.34	57.26	83.06	57.60	75.66	71.25	72.51	71.36	71.15
75%	0	67.13	55.05	66.93	65.14	53.69	74.77	53.88	66.63	76.61	63.64	75.80	72.98
	1	66.55	45.06	66.19	62.45	55.60	75.61	55.78	67.84	74.09	50.07	72.59	67.37
	2	63.93	47.66	63.66	61.55	53.02	75.63	53.22	67.10	73.16	55.16	72.04	68.19
	3	65.11	46.54	64.80	62.13	57.03	75.30	57.19	68.69	72.96	39.88	70.89	64.89
	4	66.03	46.44	65.70	62.18	56.62	76.20	56.79	68.92	76.12	54.41	74.77	70.71
	5	66.35	55.35	66.16	64.35	52.77	77.94	52.99	68.45	74.51	43.38	72.56	67.02
	6	64.69	50.50	64.45	61.87	55.38	76.83	55.57	68.81	73.15	49.34	71.67	66.16
	7	61.94	46.28	61.68	60.07	52.85	75.50	53.06	67.37	75.28	54.81	74.01	70.22
	8	65.27	47.83	64.98	62.13	53.96	73.84	54.14	66.22	73.53	41.78	71.54	65.34
	9	65.17	39.13	64.73	60.34	58.19	76.18	58.35	69.66	69.21	46.78	67.81	63.79

Table 18: DA-ADB+GPTAUG-F4 experimental results in detail

	Seed	Banking_CG				OOS_CG				StackOverflow_CG			
		F1-IND	**F1-OOD**	**F1-All**	**Acc-All**	**F1-IND**	**F1-OOD**	**F1-All**	**Acc-All**	**F1-IND**	**F1-OOD**	**F1-All**	**Acc-All**
25%	0	55.09	86.53	56.66	78.69	38.42	92.36	39.80	86.43	71.49	90.20	74.61	85.16
	1	57.86	82.82	59.11	75.32	42.45	91.97	43.72	85.82	45.42	44.39	45.25	37.59
	2	50.66	83.60	52.31	76.11	41.85	91.92	43.14	85.85	63.07	84.41	66.63	77.04
	3	56.91	83.70	58.25	76.16	46.46	91.05	47.60	84.75	63.46	87.15	67.41	80.59
	4	62.07	84.82	63.21	77.74	50.34	92.73	51.42	87.47	55.97	80.22	60.01	71.64
	5	51.81	85.38	53.49	77.37	48.41	92.23	49.53	86.65	56.85	54.46	56.45	46.47
	6	47.89	83.49	49.67	75.16	53.37	92.06	54.36	86.65	68.30	88.74	71.71	82.65
	7	47.67	85.26	49.55	76.58	38.10	90.42	39.44	83.54	62.50	86.83	66.55	80.07
	8	56.29	85.71	57.76	78.22	36.07	91.53	37.50	85.19	54.72	84.43	59.68	76.28
	9	59.50	86.93	60.88	79.75	44.37	92.27	45.60	86.51	57.94	79.49	61.53	70.43
50%	0	50.54	73.12	51.12	66.51	35.47	84.41	36.11	75.22	78.31	84.84	78.90	82.48
	1	59.47	75.31	59.88	70.83	40.56	83.88	41.13	74.92	54.14	13.38	50.43	37.56
	2	57.98	75.05	58.42	70.04	38.37	84.00	38.97	74.61	70.96	78.61	71.66	74.53
	3	55.67	72.29	56.10	67.25	38.04	83.84	38.65	74.81	70.70	75.70	71.15	72.87
	4	58.89	73.87	59.27	69.15	40.96	83.27	41.51	74.37	71.34	80.37	72.16	76.63
	5	54.31	74.02	54.81	68.09	39.35	83.48	39.93	74.26	76.41	80.97	76.82	79.00
	6	56.25	77.70	56.80	71.99	43.06	84.56	43.60	76.24	75.68	82.58	76.30	79.38
	7	55.99	74.21	56.46	68.04	37.55	84.02	38.16	74.56	75.92	83.00	76.56	80.34
	8	59.88	76.63	60.31	72.10	38.05	83.97	38.65	74.86	73.36	79.61	73.93	76.97
	9	61.65	74.48	61.98	70.09	37.13	84.52	37.75	75.74	75.95	81.64	76.46	79.04
75%	0	55.25	54.49	55.24	58.97	33.04	73.38	33.40	62.42	80.62	71.23	80.03	77.73
	1	57.69	50.92	57.57	58.18	33.93	72.34	34.27	61.70	78.27	65.96	77.50	74.32
	2	55.24	50.60	55.16	56.96	35.07	72.62	35.41	62.33	76.72	65.31	76.00	72.60
	3	53.68	46.91	53.57	54.17	32.50	72.04	32.85	61.59	77.15	60.04	76.08	71.33
	4	53.99	47.43	53.88	54.96	34.23	72.39	34.57	62.25	78.95	65.26	78.09	74.94
	5	54.30	54.09	54.30	57.81	31.94	73.10	32.30	61.59	78.56	61.99	77.52	73.05
	6	53.14	52.15	53.12	56.70	34.54	72.64	34.87	62.25	75.95	60.29	74.97	70.15
	7	57.41	52.71	57.33	58.91	32.39	71.39	32.73	60.57	73.60	50.75	72.17	66.57
	8	56.93	54.07	56.88	59.39	31.40	70.80	31.75	60.05	75.43	49.51	73.81	67.23
	9	61.08	52.53	60.94	60.60	35.98	73.35	36.31	63.33	73.46	57.54	72.47	67.13

Table 19: DA-ADB+GPTAUG-F10 experimental results in detail

	Seed	Banking_CG				OOS_CG				StackOverflow_CG			
		F1-IND	F1-OOD	F1-All	Acc-All	F1-IND	F1-OOD	F1-All	Acc-All	F1-IND	F1-OOD	F1-All	Acc-All
25%	0	52.79	85.62	54.43	77.58	38.97	92.28	40.34	86.29	65.05	79.99	67.54	71.88
	1	56.34	81.59	57.61	73.73	45.12	92.08	46.32	86.07	58.02	81.47	61.93	72.91
	2	50.23	82.99	51.87	75.32	41.15	91.85	42.45	85.66	54.62	76.51	58.26	66.33
	3	57.28	83.52	58.59	75.95	44.85	90.85	46.03	84.39	70.38	90.84	73.79	85.78
	4	56.53	82.43	57.83	73.95	50.29	92.19	51.36	86.59	59.89	84.56	64.00	76.97
	5	52.06	85.16	53.72	77.06	46.97	92.03	48.13	86.32	58.56	75.63	61.41	66.54
	6	47.94	83.57	49.72	75.26	51.96	91.89	52.99	86.32	71.34	90.61	74.55	85.40
	7	49.23	84.65	51.00	76.00	37.52	90.29	38.87	83.31	63.71	88.52	67.84	82.34
	8	55.30	84.64	56.76	76.90	38.27	91.38	39.63	85.02	56.27	84.82	61.03	76.63
	9	57.45	85.85	58.87	78.22	46.91	92.54	48.08	87.00	40.31	0.17	33.62	16.18
50%	0	50.07	71.87	50.63	65.45	36.62	84.47	37.25	75.36	77.45	85.47	78.18	82.86
	1	58.32	75.07	58.75	70.46	39.97	83.92	40.55	74.86	55.61	27.05	53.01	42.10
	2	59.39	74.99	59.79	70.46	38.79	84.03	39.39	74.64	70.36	80.53	71.29	76.21
	3	53.08	71.80	53.56	66.30	38.38	83.62	38.98	74.56	67.74	76.56	68.54	72.74
	4	56.98	73.86	57.41	68.83	40.59	83.27	41.15	74.34	70.46	77.36	71.09	73.80
	5	53.81	74.10	54.33	67.99	40.70	83.56	41.26	74.42	75.73	81.43	76.25	79.00
	6	56.50	77.59	57.04	71.99	42.66	84.53	43.21	76.16	73.76	83.17	74.61	79.52
	7	55.97	74.49	56.44	68.30	39.05	83.96	39.64	74.70	71.88	81.52	72.76	78.18
	8	59.42	76.05	59.85	71.15	36.42	83.68	37.04	74.34	71.55	78.52	72.18	75.59
	9	61.70	74.40	62.03	69.99	37.01	84.37	37.63	75.58	68.63	76.20	69.32	72.67
75%	0	53.43	53.49	53.43	57.54	34.01	73.64	34.36	63.33	77.10	67.88	76.52	74.25
	1	56.61	49.72	56.49	57.01	34.39	72.33	34.73	61.98	76.49	64.84	75.76	72.91
	2	54.23	50.28	54.16	56.17	36.57	73.04	36.89	63.24	74.02	63.03	73.34	69.95
	3	53.09	45.94	52.97	53.43	31.37	71.57	31.73	60.66	72.03	52.61	70.81	65.47
	4	53.99	46.46	53.86	54.22	33.32	72.17	33.66	61.95	73.55	54.27	72.35	68.50
	5	54.03	53.96	54.02	57.54	32.15	73.15	32.52	61.81	76.89	60.00	75.83	71.19
	6	52.23	52.07	52.22	56.17	34.82	72.76	35.15	62.39	73.87	57.40	72.84	67.54
	7	54.64	50.03	54.56	56.01	33.02	71.70	33.36	60.96	77.18	67.03	76.54	74.35
	8	56.11	52.99	56.06	58.44	32.94	71.29	33.28	60.93	71.23	51.46	70.00	64.75
	9	60.22	51.66	60.07	59.92	35.47	73.15	35.80	63.19	64.18	9.64	60.77	52.05

Table 20: DA-ADB+GPTAUG-WP10 experimental results in detail

	Seed	Banking_CG				OOS_CG				StackOverflow_CG			
		F1-IND	**F1-OOD**	**F1-All**	**Acc-All**	**F1-IND**	**F1-OOD**	**F1-All**	**Acc-All**	**F1-IND**	**F1-OOD**	**F1-All**	**Acc-All**
	0	53.70	86.98	55.37	78.06	38.21	92.80	39.61	87.00	63.39	81.83	66.46	74.73
	1	57.08	81.07	58.28	72.47	44.31	91.58	45.53	85.24	47.28	24.40	43.47	30.12
	2	55.92	81.19	57.18	73.58	39.26	91.75	40.61	85.41	47.71	29.83	44.73	31.57
	3	55.73	82.63	57.08	74.47	45.49	90.52	46.64	83.92	59.70	82.07	63.43	74.60
25%	4	62.46	83.43	63.51	75.79	50.07	92.43	51.15	86.81	58.29	77.75	61.53	69.74
	5	50.26	83.71	51.93	74.42	44.47	91.75	45.69	85.74	52.03	70.83	55.16	62.79
	6	49.43	77.93	50.85	68.78	49.18	91.79	50.28	86.10	60.47	80.97	63.88	73.22
	7	47.37	84.04	49.20	74.37	39.63	91.01	40.95	84.44	52.04	68.82	54.83	60.34
	8	55.20	85.40	56.71	77.74	37.16	90.51	38.53	83.65	47.95	60.58	50.06	52.32
	9	60.03	82.55	61.15	74.16	44.05	91.30	45.26	85.02	57.25	71.67	59.65	62.75
	0	53.41	73.46	53.92	66.09	38.59	84.64	39.20	75.39	77.29	82.41	77.76	80.24
	1	62.07	73.60	62.37	69.30	41.71	83.77	42.27	74.45	64.02	27.95	60.75	43.58
	2	56.87	64.58	57.06	60.60	39.02	84.46	39.62	75.06	57.58	37.95	55.80	47.02
	3	59.00	70.99	59.31	66.09	41.87	83.77	42.42	74.89	68.68	67.71	68.59	67.13
50%	4	60.97	70.86	61.22	66.56	42.25	83.81	42.80	74.64	70.05	73.94	70.40	71.39
	5	57.57	71.68	57.93	65.24	41.63	83.77	42.19	74.72	64.25	40.44	62.09	50.57
	6	52.47	70.47	52.93	63.13	42.35	84.68	42.91	76.21	79.65	85.86	80.21	83.20
	7	58.65	70.89	58.96	65.61	38.17	83.97	38.78	74.26	75.57	82.13	76.17	79.59
	8	60.21	68.56	60.43	64.19	39.95	83.01	40.51	73.54	71.58	74.68	71.86	72.98
	9	65.06	68.23	65.14	66.19	37.06	83.97	37.68	74.97	70.44	72.75	70.65	70.81
	0	61.38	56.01	61.29	62.34	38.23	74.93	38.56	64.34	81.59	71.79	80.98	78.62
	1	63.18	51.87	62.99	62.13	39.36	72.85	39.66	63.02	78.88	62.05	77.83	73.56
	2	61.95	52.63	61.80	61.18	40.57	74.43	40.87	64.26	77.74	65.95	77.01	73.91
	3	63.84	48.10	63.57	60.92	40.33	73.76	40.63	64.40	77.20	54.47	75.78	70.36
75%	4	62.31	49.46	62.10	60.86	41.52	74.05	41.80	64.45	80.47	65.99	79.56	76.49
	5	59.10	55.17	59.03	60.81	38.71	75.38	39.04	64.37	78.20	59.34	77.02	72.46
	6	60.86	56.98	60.80	61.81	40.03	74.08	40.33	64.04	77.30	60.53	76.25	71.81
	7	63.63	55.36	63.49	63.50	40.06	73.70	40.36	63.66	81.28	68.34	80.47	77.52
	8	62.06	55.62	61.95	62.24	39.52	71.95	39.81	62.31	70.73	37.47	68.65	60.83
	9	64.74	52.16	64.52	62.87	43.73	75.61	44.01	66.24	74.30	60.24	73.42	69.60

Beyond Classification: Financial Reasoning in State-of-the-Art Language Models

Guijin Son
OneLineAI
ModuLabs
guijin.son@onelineai.com

Hanearl Jung
OneLineAI
earl@onelineai.com

Moonjeong Hahm
Chung-Ang University
daily6298@cau.ac.kr

Keonju Na
Seoul National University of Science and Technology
keonju2@seoultech.ac.kr

Sol Jin
Seoul National University
jinsol9770@snu.ac.kr

Abstract

Large Language Models (LLMs), consisting of 100 billion or more parameters, have demonstrated remarkable ability in complex multi-step reasoning tasks. However, the application of such generic advancements has been limited to a few fields, such as clinical or legal, with the field of financial reasoning remaining largely unexplored. To the best of our knowledge, the ability of LLMs to solve financial reasoning problems has never been dealt with, and whether it can be performed at any scale remains unknown. To address this knowledge gap, this research presents a comprehensive investigation into the potential application of LLMs in the financial domain. The investigation includes a detailed exploration of a range of subjects, including task formulation, synthetic data generation, prompting methods, and evaluation capability. Furthermore, the study benchmarks various GPT variants with parameter scales ranging from 2.8B to 13B, with and without instruction tuning, on diverse dataset sizes. By analyzing the results, we reveal that the ability to generate coherent financial reasoning first emerges at 6B parameters, and continues to improve with better instruction-tuning or larger datasets. Additionally, the study provides a publicly accessible dataset named sFIOG (Synthetic-Financial Investment Opinion Generation), consisting of 11,802 synthetic investment thesis samples, to support further research in the field of financial reasoning. Overall, this research seeks to contribute to the understanding of the efficacy of language models in the field of finance, with a particular emphasis on their ability to engage in sophisticated reasoning and analysis within the context of investment decision-making. We release our models, dataset, and code [1].

1 Introduction

Large Language Models(100+ billion parameters) have undergone remarkable advancements in recent years, enabling them with the ability to generate coherent and meaningful text (Wei et al., 2022a). These LLMs have demonstrated notable abilities in performing complex multi-step reasoning, either by thinking "step by step" (Kojima et al.) or leveraging Chain-of-Thought(CoT) prompts (Wei et al., 2022b). Various fields have attempted to harness such reasoning ability, and among them, the field of clinical research has made notable progress by developing domain-specific LLMs like Med-Palm (Singhal et al., 2022), re-trained on massive amounts of domain-specific texts and tasks, which achieves performance comparable to that of human clinicians. In situations where data is insufficient to train dedicated language models, researchers have directed their efforts towards developing advanced prompt engineering techniques, such as Legal Prompt Engineering (LPE) (Trautmann et al., 2022), or generation of synthetic data via LLMs and training of smaller language models on such samples (Yunxiang et al., 2023). However, there is a lack of comprehensive investigation for either of the methods in the financial domain, leaving the field of financial reasoning largely unexplored.

The research of natural language processing in the financial domain has predominantly been confined to token or sequence classification tasks (Araci, 2019; Shah et al., 2022). This is likely due to the lack of datasets or tasks suitable for training generative language models. Even dedicated financial language models like BloombergGPT, tend to prioritize tasks such as sentiment analysis, binary classification, and named entity recognition, with limited attention given to numerical reasoning tasks (Wu et al., 2023).

Our research aims to comprehensively investigate the **financial reasoning** capabilities of language models, specifically their ability to generate logically coherent and persuasive investment opinions. The investigation involves both prompt

[1] https://github.com/guijinSON/FIOG/tree/main

Proceedings of the Joint Workshop of the 5th Financial Technology and Natural Language Processing (FinNLP) and 2nd Multimodal AI For Financial Forecasting (Muffin), Macao, August 20, 2023.

engineering and specialized training of smaller language models (Fu et al., 2023), seeking to advance our understanding on the ability of language models to engage in sophisticated reasoning and analysis within the context of investment decision-making. Accordingly, our research introduces an original financial reasoning task called "Financial Investment Opinion Generation (FIOG)", which involves the generation of investment opinions by language models with either parametric or injected knowledge. We then benchmark various GPT variants, ranging in size from 2.7B to 13B, with and without instruction-tuning (Ouyang et al., 2022), on the dataset. Additionally, we propose a novel prompting method called In-Context Question Answering for controlled generation of context. Finally, we investigate the alignment between LLM-based evaluators, such as G-Eval (Liu et al., 2023), and human evaluators for financial texts, in order to gain insights into the efficacy of such evaluators in the financial domain.

To support further research on financial reasoning, we provide a publicly accessible dataset named sFIOG (Synthetic-Financial Investment Opinion Generation), which includes 11,802 synthetic investment opinion samples. This dataset is intended to enable benchmarking and experimentation in the field of financial language modeling and investment opinion generation.

2 Related Work

2.1 Reasoning with Language Models

Language Models (LMs) trained using conventional pre-training objectives have demonstrated the ability to acquire complex reasoning capabilities once they reach a certain scale (Wei et al., 2022a). However, recent research has shown that the parameter requirements for complex reasoning abilities of LMs can be significantly alleviated through a process called instruction tuning (Ouyang et al., 2022). Further research has suggested that narrowing down the model's focus to specialize in a specific field can result in additional alleviation of parameter requirements. This can be achieved by including task-specific Chain-of-Thought (CoT) data in the instruction-tuning process, allowing the model to acquire specialized reasoning capabilities (Fu et al., 2023). Some researchers have adopted this approach, leveraging domain-specific CoT data, which is often generated by the LLMs themselves, to enable domain-specific reasoning abilities (Yunxiang et al., 2023). However, the effectiveness of this approach across different domains and the potential variability in parameter and data requirements for specific domains remain relatively unexplored. Accordingly, it is plausible that domains characterized by complex nomenclature and reasoning steps, which significantly deviate from general, widely applicable patterns, may necessitate higher parameter and data requirements.

2.2 Financial Natural Language Processing

The financial domain has been quick to adopt advancements in generic natural language processing research. Notably, BloombergGPT, a language model with 50 billion parameters specifically dedicated for finance, stands out as a significant development in this field (Wu et al., 2023).However, despite its significance, BloombergGPT and recent research of the field have limitations in terms of their investigation in reasoning abilities, which have been left out of the scope of research. The focus of predominant research in the financial domain has largely been limited to token or sequence classification tasks (Araci, 2019; Shah et al., 2022), likely due to the scarcity of suitable datasets or tasks for training generative language models. For instance, corpora containing financial reasoning steps, which are essential for training language models for tasks such as investment opinion generation, are mostly confidential in nature and therefore excluded from the training data of publicly available language models (Scao et al., 2022; Black et al., 2022; Touvron et al., 2023). This limitation poses challenges for developing language models with specialized reasoning capabilities in the financial domain.

Though this study does not involve the development of a finance-native LM of its own, it distinguishes itself from previous research as it comprehensively investigates the circumstances under which specialized financial reasoning capabilities can be enabled.

3 Task Formulation

In this paper we introduce a novel task called Financial Investment Opinion Generation(FIOG), the term encompasses all tasks aiming to train or prompt language models to generate investment opinions in the context of finance, leveraging either parametric or injected knowledge. Our variant of the FIOG task involves providing language models with the necessary information as part of the input. The input information in our variant is provided in two types: full-text and question-and-answer (Q&A). In the full-text type, the input consists of complete text passages, while in the Q&A type, the input comprises pairs of questions and corresponding answers. The Q&A type is used to train and prompt our model via In-Context Question Answering, which will be explained later in the paper. Incorporating investment decision-relevant information as part of the input, enables us to investigate the ability of Language Models (LMs) as reasoning engines, rather than knowledge databases, and allows for a more targeted and effective training process.

4 Dataset Creation

To support further research on financial reasoning, we provide a publicly accessible dataset named sFIOG (Synthetic-Financial Investment Opinion Generation). The sFIOG dataset is generated through the following steps.

1. Collection of expert-written analyst reports: We gathered 1,087 analyst reports from various sources, including J.P Morgan, Truist Financial Corp, and Oppenheimer & Co. These reports cover 752 companies in the U.S stock market.

2. Expert-Written investment thesis set construction: We extracted the "Investment Thesis" and "Related Risk" sections from each analyst report, resulting in a set of expert-written investment theses.

3. Full-Text type input construction: We constructed the Full-Text type input by collecting the abstract from each analyst report.

4. Q&A type input question generation: Using the GPT3.5-Turbo API, we fed the Full-Text type input and required it to generate questions addressing important information.

5. Dummy answer generation: We used the GPT3.5-Turbo API to generate dummy answers for the questions generated in step 4. Human annotators were hired to eliminate answers that deviated greatly from reality.

6. Investment opinion generation: The GPT3.5-Turbo API was employed to generate investment opinions for both types of inputs.

In step 4, we extract questions from a given text rather than relying solely on a LLM to few-shot generate questions on a given topic. This approach is expected to generate questions that inquire about information deemed important by human experts rather than generating random questions. For comparison, we also construct a set of few-shot generated questions. To assess the lexical and syntactic diversity of each method, we use three metrics: Mass and HD-D for lexical diversity, and Syntactic Sim. for syntactic diversity. Mass and HD-D are established metrics for measuring lexical richness and have been shown to be reliable across texts of different lengths (Torruella and Capsada, 2013; McCarthy and Jarvis, 2010). A higher HD-D score indicates greater lexical richness, while a higher Mass score indicates the opposite. For syntactic diversity, we use Syntactic Sim., which measures the average pairwise similarity of the dependency tree across generated samples (Oya, 2020). A higher Syntactic Sim. value indicates greater similarity in syntactic structures across generated samples. As presented in Table 2, our approach resembling question extraction yields synthetic data with a higher degree of both lexical and syntactic diversity.

Step 5, adds multiple dummy answers for the questions generated in the prior step. These dummy answers were carefully screened by a human annotator to eliminate those that deviate greatly from reality. We expect this process to add to the diversity of the dataset aiding the fine-tuning of complex reasoning, similar to diverse reasoning (Ho et al., 2022).

Table 1 includes the statistics for the constructed sFIOG dataset. Our dataset encompasses three types of investment thesis. First, we have 1,087 expert-written investment theses. Second, we have 4,386 investment theses generated with full-text type input. It is noteworthy that the investment thesis generated with the full-text type input exhibits a balanced distribution of buy, hold, and sell opinions, with 1,462 samples for each. Finally, we have 11,802 samples generated with Q&A type input. Each sample was generated with 13 or more Q&A pairs, ensuring that a sufficient amount and diversity of information was provided for the language models to formulate comprehensive investment opinions. More than one sample was generated for each set of Q&A pairs to add to the diversity of the dataset.

The publicly accessible sFIOG dataset is limited

Investment Opinion		(RE) Full-Text Type		(RE) Q&A Type		
Coverage	Investment Thesis	Full-Text	Investment Thesis	Question	Q&A Pair	Investment Thesis
752	1,087	1,087	4,386	10,437	26,138	11,802

Table 1: Dataset Overview. (RE) denotes that the set has been regenerated.

Generation	Few-Shot	Step 4.
HD-D	0.811	0.873
Mass	0.034	0.025
Syntactic Sim.	0.578	0.42

Table 2: Quantitative assessment of questions generated via few-shot generation against ours (step 4).

to the Q&A type input subset of the dataset due to the restriction of third-party sharing of the expert-written analyst reports collected from the web. To the best of our knowledge, the publicly accessible version of the sFIOG dataset is comprised only of synthetically generated questions, answers, and investment opinions.

5 In-Context Question Answering

Both LLM or their smaller variants have been pointed out to hallucinate, or generate context unfaithful from real-world information (Ji et al., 2023). Even if these LMs manage to accurately retrieve real-world information that they have memorized during the pre-training stage, there are still risks of the information being outdated or non-stationary (Son et al., 2023). To address this issue, we propose In-Context Question Answering, where a list of question-and-answer pairs is provided instead of full-text contexts. Through experiments, we demonstrate that our approach has several advantages compared to previous full-text in-context learning approaches when zero-shot prompting LLMs. A sample of the questions used is presented in A.1.

First, our findings indicate that generations grounded on Q&A pairs exhibit a higher degree of controlled behavior, or a lower likelihood to generate unintended context, compared to conventional in-context learning generations. For instance, approximately 11.12% of the samples generated with conventional in-context learning included analysis on the pandemic, even though the investment opinion was intended for the post-pandemic era. In contrast, when using in-context question answering, the chances of generated samples to discuss pandemic-related issues, despite their absence in the provided Q&A sets, was merely 1.63%. This suggests that the proposed in-context question answering may be a more effective approach to zero-shot prompt LLMs to generate controlled outputs, making it more suitable for specific contexts and scenarios, such as post-pandemic era financial analysis. We speculate that such behavior is because in-context question answering delivers a refined version of information with most of the irrelevant text removed, resulting in a more concise and focused input. Language models are susceptible to distraction from irrelevant text (Shi et al., 2023), and the provision of context in a Q&A format allows them to concentrate on the core information without being influenced by unnecessary or irrelevant sentences. This conciseness and absence of irrelevant text in the Q&A format may enable language models to better align with the intended task, leading to improved performance and controlled behavior in generating contextually relevant and accurate content.

Second, we conducted a survey with hired human annotators using a subset of 1,000 samples from each type. In order to assess the performance of our LLM-based evaluators in comparison to human annotators, we also conducted the identical survey using GPT-4 as a respondent, following previous research on G-Eval (Liu et al., 2023). The survey presented respondents with three samples at a time, one from each of the expert-written, full-text type, and Q&A type. They were then required to answer two questions:

1. *Which investment thesis contains the most investment helpful information?*
2. *Which investment thesis presents a more logically structured and reasonable argumentation?*

Figure 1, indicates that human evaluators perceived Q&A type generation to contain the most investment-helpful information in 61.2% of cases and demonstrated the most coherent argumentation in 48% of cases. In contrast, Full-Text type generation was found to have relatively fewer investment-helpful information, which may be attributed to the presence of irrelevant text that could disrupt the language model's output. Notably, the generated samples in either full-text or Q&A type were preferred by human annotators over the expert-written samples for both questions. We speculate that this preference for generated samples over expert-written thesis may be due to the fact that expert-written thesis are tailored for professionals with domain-specific expertise, and may omit explanations or assumed background knowledge, potentially affecting their comprehensibility to human evaluators. An investigation of the inter-annotator agreement was conducted on a subset of 350 samples for each question, revealing a decent Krippendorff's alpha of 0.63 for question 1 and 0.68 for question 2.

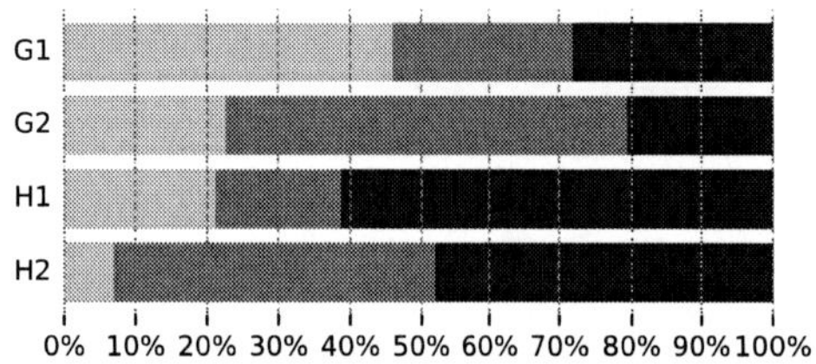

Figure 1: Qualitative Evaluation of Collected Investment Theses: Green denotes expert-written, blue represents full-text type, and dark blue indicates Q&A type. G1 and G2 refer to GPT-4 answers for Question1 and Question2, respectively. H1 and H2 denote human answers for Question1 and Question2, respectively.

Furthermore, we conduct the identical survey using GPT-4, following G-Eval, we use the following prompt:

> *You are a professional financial researcher. You will be given an investment thesis. Your task is to rate the thesis on the following metric. Please make sure you read and understand these instructions carefully. Please keep this document open while reviewing, and refer to it as needed.*
>
> *Evaluation Criteria:*
>
> *Investment-Helpfulness (1-5) - the quality and diversity of financial facts provided in the passage. The investment thesis should provide a diverse set of quantitative information. Quantitative information must include numerical values. Concentrate on the diversity and amount of facts provided. Ignore the argumentation for the moment.*
>
> *Financial Argumentation (1-5) - the quality of the financial reasoning and supporting evidence in the passage. This includes the logical coherence of the financial argument, the strength of the financial evidence provided, and the overall persuasiveness of the financial argument. Specifically, this criterion evaluates the effectiveness of the financial analysis and the quality of the financial data used to support the investment thesis.*

The responses from LLMs were compared with the decision of human annotators to investigate the efficacy of LLM applications for the evaluation of financial reasoning. Unlike previous research (Gilardi et al., 2023), our study found a notable disparity between GPT-4 and human judgments, with low correlation observed regardless of the presence of CoT explanations. Figure 2 displays the confusion matrix comparing the decisions of human and LLM evaluators. The results indicate that the agreement rate between the two evaluators was only 29.26%, and 34.6% for each question correspondingly. Moreover, the Spearman correlation coefficients between human and LLM decisions were -0.07 for question one and -0.073 for question two, significantly lower than that of previous research that reported 0.514 (Liu et al., 2023). This disparity may be attributed to two key factors. First, unlike prior research that focused on LLMs' evaluation of summarization quality or zero-shot classification of tweets, our study required the LLMs to evaluate financial reasoning, which is a more intricate and complex task. Additionally, LLMs were never trained for such tasks, which may have impacted their performance in evaluating the quality of financial reasoning. Secondly, the financial domain poses unique complexities, including diverse nomenclature and domain-specific knowledge, which may present a challenge for generic LLMs to fully comprehend and accurately evaluate the coherence of financial reasoning. Following our findings, LLMs are no longer used as evaluators in this paper.

Overall, the aforementioned experiments yield two important findings. Firstly, the results discover that LLMs are inadequate as evaluators for financial reasoning tasks, given the limited alignment observed between LLMs and human evaluators. Secondly, the proposed In-Context Question Answering method represents a promising alternative

Base Model	Instruction-Tuning	ROUGE-L				BERTScore			
		type#1	type#2	type#3	average	type#1	type#2	type#3	average
LLama	✓	**0.283**	**0.178**	**0.359**	**0.273**	0.830	**0.849**	**0.855**	**0.845**
Galactica	✓	0.108	0.028	0.114	0.083	0.794	0.807	0.799	0.800
GPT-J	✓	0.159	0.023	0.183	0.122	**0.836**	0.692	0.836	0.788
Pythia(2.8B)	✓	0.022	0.000	0.023	0.015	0.731	0.769	0.735	0.745
LLama	✗	0.080	0.123	0.180	0.128	0.592	0.778	0.723	0.698
Galactica	✗	0.086	0.027	0.097	0.070	0.777	0.804	0.773	0.785
GPT-J	✗	0.054	0.023	0.139	0.072	0.773	0.692	0.818	0.761
Pythia(2.8B)	✗	0.017	0.012	0.018	0.016	0.729	0.795	0.728	0.751

Table 3: Results for LLama, Galactica, GPT-J, and Pythia (2.8B), both with and without instruction-tuning, obtained on the sFIOG test dataset. The evaluation was carried out across three distinct subsets. Type#1 consisted of companies and questions from the training set with new corresponding answers. Type#2 featured companies from the training set paired with new, previously unencountered question-and-answer combinations. Lastly, Type#3 introduced companies not present in the training set, accompanied by new question-and-answer pairs.

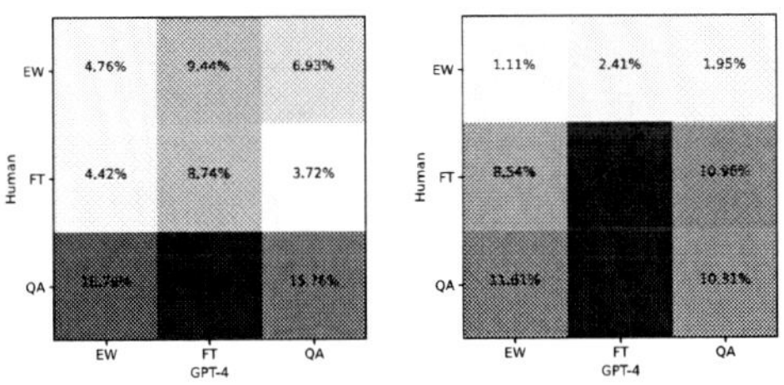

Figure 2: Left for Q1, Right for Q2.

Base Model	Instruction-Tuned	Param.
Pythia	dolly-v2-3b	2.8B
GPT-J	dolly-v1-6b	6B
Galactica	galpaca-6.7b	6.7B
LLama	vicuna-13b-delta-v1.1	13B

Table 4: Summary of GPT variants employed in the experiments, detailing their parameter sizes and whether they underwent instruction tuning. Checkpoints for instruction-tuned models were imported from HuggingFace.

to traditional prompting methods, exhibiting improved controlledness and generating better-quality reports. Notably, this method could be applicable to a broader range of fields beyond finance, wherever controlled generation of information-rich texts is required.

6 Experiments

6.1 Experimental Setup

In this research, we assessed four GPT variants (2.8B to 13B parameters) with and without instruction tuning, as detailed in Table 4. This comparison aimed to identify the point at which the ability to generate financial reasoning emerges. An example of the generation is presented in A.3.

Models in this study were trained using Lora (Hu et al., 2021) and quantization for enhanced hardware efficiency, with a maximum token length of 2048 and an AdamW optimizer. Each model was trained in three epochs on the full sFIOG dataset, which is consisted of 11,802 samples. During the test phase, decoding settings were configured to enhance the quality and diversity of generated outputs, while ensuring a fair comparison across models. The parameters were set as follows: top_k=50, top_p=0.95, no_repeat_ngram_size=3, and max_new_tokens=512. By setting a fixed maximum number of tokens, we prevented models that generate longer sequences from appearing to outperform others in the evaluation.

The test dataset for this study is comprised of three distinct subsets to evaluate the performance of the GPT variants in different settings. The first subset included companies and questions that appeared in the training set but with new corresponding answers. The second subset featured companies from the training set but paired with new, previously unencountered question-and-answer combinations. Lastly, the third subset introduced companies that did not appear in the training set, accompanied by new question-and-answer pairs. Through this dataset split we assess the models' capabilities in generating financial reasoning across varying degrees of familiarity and novelty.

To evaluate the generated context, we used both automated metrics and human evaluations. Automated metrics included rouge-2 and rougeL (Lin, 2004), measuring text overlap, and BERTScore (Zhang et al., 2019), assessing semantic similarity. As mentioned previously, we excluded LLM-based evaluators due to their misalignment with human judgments.

6.2 Model Scale and Financial Reasoning

In Table 3, we present the results for LLama (Touvron et al., 2023), Galactica (Taylor et al., 2022), GPT-J, and Pythia (2.8B) (Biderman et al., 2023), with and without instruction-tuning, on the sFIOG test dataset. Our findings indicate that the ability to generate coherent investment opinions emerges in models with sizes between 2.8B $\sim$ 6B and continues to improve as the model scales. For instance, LLama demonstrates superior performance, achieving the highest average scores in ROUGE-L (0.217) and BERTScore (0.821). There are two possible explanations for the scaling behavior of financial reasoning abilities in these models: (1) larger models are typically trained on more tokens, thereby accumulating a greater amount of knowledge essential for generating well-informed investment theses, and (2) the architecture of larger models inherently allows for improved reasoning capabilities, enabling them to better analyze and synthesize the information they have learned. Consequently, as model size expands, it leads to a stronger ability to effectively generate financial reasoning, as demonstrated by the superior performance of the LLama model in our experiments. An exception in the scaling behavior is observed between GPT-J and Galactica, with GPT-J surpassing Galactica in performance, despite its smaller size. We posit that this discrepancy may arise from two factors: (1) GPT-J is trained on a substantially larger corpus of tokens (402 billion) from a general domain, while Galactica has been trained on a smaller, science-specific corpus (106 billion); (2) The size difference between the two models is relatively minimal, at just 0.7B. This observation is consistent with recent research, suggesting that training smaller models with an increased number of tokens beyond the chinchilla optimal point can yield improved performance (Touvron et al., 2023). Furthermore, this finding emphasizes the potential trade-offs of domain-specific training, which could compromise a model's robustness across broader contexts.

6.3 Instruction-Tuning and Financial Reasoning

We observe that instruction-tuning plays a significant role in enhancing the performance of all models across both evaluation metrics. However, the degree of improvement varies among models, which may be due to the difference of instruction-tuning datasets used to fine-tune each model. It is noteworthy that Pythia (2.8B), the smallest model employed in our experiments, failed to demonstrate the ability to generate coherent financial reasoning, even when instruction-tuning was applied. This finding implies that the ability to generate financial reasoning could be an emergent property that becomes evident as the model size exceeds a specific threshold.

6.4 Dataset and Financial Reasoning

In examining the performance of the models across each subset of the dataset, we find that the models exhibit their weakest performance in type#2 questions, which involve companies included in the training set but are accompanied by new question-and-answer pairs. This observation departs from the authors' initial assumption that type#3 questions, featuring companies not present in the training set, would pose the greatest challenge. The results demonstrate that generating financial opinions for novel question-answer pairs concerning familiar companies is a more demanding task for the models. This finding aligns with past research, suggesting that the non-stationary knowledge acquired during the training process may hinder the models' capacity to generalize their knowledge effectively and apply it to novel situations involving known entities (Son et al., 2023).

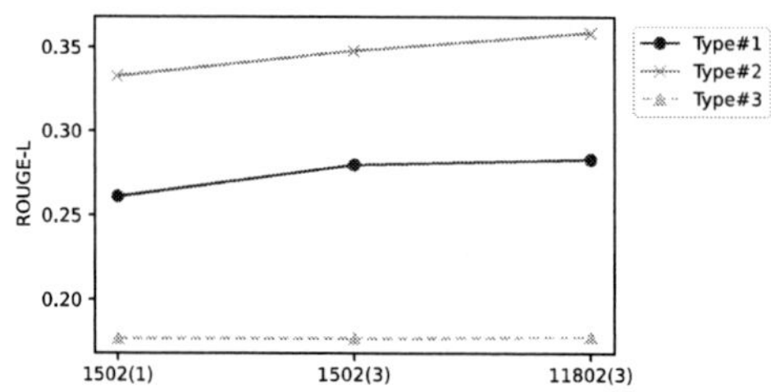

Figure 3: Performance of Vicuna across varying training steps. The x-axis denotes the training step, presented in the format sample_size(epoch). The y-axis displays the corresponding ROUGE-L scores.

Furthermore, we evaluate the financial reasoning abilities of the best-performing model, instruction-tuned LLama 13B, across different dataset sizes and training steps. Specifically, we conducted experiments by training the model for (1) 3 epochs on an 11,802-sample dataset, (2) 3 epochs on a smaller 1,502-sample dataset, and (3) 1 epoch on the same 1,502-sample dataset, where each company in the full dataset was represented by 2 samples. Our results reveal that LLama's performance improved with an increasing number of training steps. However, even the model trained on the smallest configuration exhibited superior performance compared to the instruction-tuned GPT-J, which was the second-best model trained on the full dataset. These findings suggest that model size may be a critical factor in generating coherent financial reasoning, while dataset size may not be as significant.

6.5 Human Preference

To comprehensively evaluate the performance of each instruction-tuned model, a human preference test was conducted on their generated outputs. A panel of human evaluators was presented with four texts, each from one of the models, namely LLama, Galactica, GPT-J, and Pythia(2.8B), and asked to indicate their preference based on several factors, including coherence, relevance, and fluency. The results of the human preference test, depicted in Figure 4, reveal that the LLama model was the most preferred choice, followed by the GPT-J model. This outcome is consistent with the findings of our previous investigation, which utilized automated metrics.

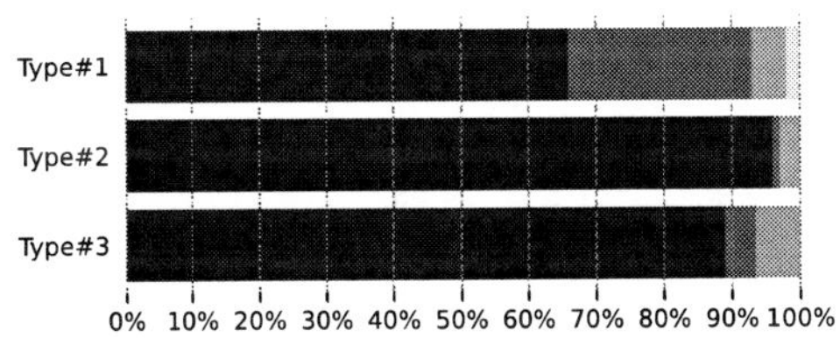

Figure 4: Human preference on generated samples. Dark Blue for LLama, Green for Galactica, Blue for GPT-J, and Yellow for Pytha(2.8B)

7 Limitations and Future Work

It is worth noting that due to hardware constraints, we were unable to investigate the emergent characteristic of financial reasoning ability on models beyond 13B parameters. Additionally, we do not open-source expert-written samples due to copyright issues. Nevertheless, this work still represents the most comprehensive investigation to date on the behavior of language models for financial reasoning generation and the first to make a dataset for financial reasoning publicly available. Going forward, we encourage the financial natural language processing community for collaborative efforts to create larger datasets for financial reasoning tasks and to experiment with larger language models. We believe that such efforts will enable more comprehensive evaluations of language models and their potential for financial reasoning generation, ultimately advancing the state of the art in this field.

8 Conclusion

To the best of our knowledge, this work represents the first public effort to investigate the financial reasoning ability of language models. Our research seeks to contribute to the understanding of the efficacy of language models in the field of finance, with a particular emphasis on their ability to engage in sophisticated reasoning and analysis within the context of investment decision-making. We confirm that the ability to generate coherent investment opinions first emerges in models with 6B parameters and scales as the model gets larger until 13B parameters. Additionally, this study introduced a novel prompting method, In-Context Question-Answering, truth-faithful generation of LLMs. The research also identified the limitations of LLMs in aligning with human evaluators for evaluating financial texts. Finally, we make a valuable contribution to the field by open-sourcing sFIOG, a dataset consisting of 11,802 synthetic investment thesis samples.

9 Acknowledgments

This work was supported by the Ministry of Employment and Labor and HRD Korea's K-Digital Platform project.

References

Dogu Araci. 2019. Finbert: Financial sentiment analysis with pre-trained language models. *arXiv preprint arXiv:1908.10063*.

Stella Biderman, Hailey Schoelkopf, Quentin Anthony, Herbie Bradley, Kyle O'Brien, Eric Hallahan, Mohammad Aflah Khan, Shivanshu Purohit, USVSN Sai Prashanth, Edward Raff, et al. 2023. Pythia: A suite for analyzing large language models across training and scaling. *arXiv preprint arXiv:2304.01373*.

Sid Black, Stella Biderman, Eric Hallahan, Quentin Anthony, Leo Gao, Laurence Golding, Horace He, Connor Leahy, Kyle McDonell, Jason Phang, et al.

2022. Gpt-neox-20b: An open-source autoregressive language model. *arXiv preprint arXiv:2204.06745*.

Yao Fu, Hao Peng, Litu Ou, Ashish Sabharwal, and Tushar Khot. 2023. Specializing smaller language models towards multi-step reasoning. *arXiv preprint arXiv:2301.12726*.

Fabrizio Gilardi, Meysam Alizadeh, and Maël Kubli. 2023. Chatgpt outperforms crowd-workers for text-annotation tasks. *arXiv preprint arXiv:2303.15056*.

Namgyu Ho, Laura Schmid, and Se-Young Yun. 2022. Large language models are reasoning teachers. *arXiv preprint arXiv:2212.10071*.

Edward J Hu, Yelong Shen, Phillip Wallis, Zeyuan Allen-Zhu, Yuanzhi Li, Shean Wang, Lu Wang, and Weizhu Chen. 2021. Lora: Low-rank adaptation of large language models. *arXiv preprint arXiv:2106.09685*.

Ziwei Ji, Nayeon Lee, Rita Frieske, Tiezheng Yu, Dan Su, Yan Xu, Etsuko Ishii, Ye Jin Bang, Andrea Madotto, and Pascale Fung. 2023. Survey of hallucination in natural language generation. *ACM Computing Surveys*, 55(12):1–38.

Takeshi Kojima, Shixiang Shane Gu, Machel Reid, Yutaka Matsuo, and Yusuke Iwasawa. Large language models are zero-shot reasoners. In *Advances in Neural Information Processing Systems*.

Chin-Yew Lin. 2004. ROUGE: A package for automatic evaluation of summaries. In *Text Summarization Branches Out*, pages 74–81, Barcelona, Spain. Association for Computational Linguistics.

Yang Liu, Dan Iter, Yichong Xu, Shuohang Wang, Ruochen Xu, and Chenguang Zhu. 2023. Gpteval: Nlg evaluation using gpt-4 with better human alignment. *arXiv preprint arXiv:2303.16634*.

Philip M McCarthy and Scott Jarvis. 2010. Mtld, vocd-d, and hd-d: A validation study of sophisticated approaches to lexical diversity assessment. *Behavior research methods*, 42(2):381–392.

Long Ouyang, Jeffrey Wu, Xu Jiang, Diogo Almeida, Carroll Wainwright, Pamela Mishkin, Chong Zhang, Sandhini Agarwal, Katarina Slama, Alex Ray, et al. 2022. Training language models to follow instructions with human feedback. *Advances in Neural Information Processing Systems*, 35:27730–27744.

Masanori Oya. 2020. Syntactic similarity of the sentences in a multi-lingual parallel corpus based on the euclidean distance of their dependency trees. In *Proceedings of the 34th pacific Asia conference on language, information and computation*, pages 225–233.

Teven Le Scao, Angela Fan, Christopher Akiki, Ellie Pavlick, Suzana Ilić, Daniel Hesslow, Roman Castagné, Alexandra Sasha Luccioni, François Yvon, Matthias Gallé, et al. 2022. Bloom: A 176b-parameter open-access multilingual language model. *arXiv preprint arXiv:2211.05100*.

Raj Sanjay Shah, Kunal Chawla, Dheeraj Eidnani, Agam Shah, Wendi Du, Sudheer Chava, Natraj Raman, Charese Smiley, Jiaao Chen, and Diyi Yang. 2022. When flue meets flang: Benchmarks and large pre-trained language model for financial domain. *arXiv preprint arXiv:2211.00083*.

Freda Shi, Xinyun Chen, Kanishka Misra, Nathan Scales, David Dohan, Ed Chi, Nathanael Schärli, and Denny Zhou. 2023. Large language models can be easily distracted by irrelevant context. *arXiv preprint arXiv:2302.00093*.

Karan Singhal, Shekoofeh Azizi, Tao Tu, S Sara Mahdavi, Jason Wei, Hyung Won Chung, Nathan Scales, Ajay Tanwani, Heather Cole-Lewis, Stephen Pfohl, et al. 2022. Large language models encode clinical knowledge. *arXiv preprint arXiv:2212.13138*.

Guijin Son, Hanwool Lee, Nahyeon Kang, and Moonjeong Hahm. 2023. Removing non-stationary knowledge from pre-trained language models for entity-level sentiment classification in finance. *arXiv preprint arXiv:2301.03136*.

Ross Taylor, Marcin Kardas, Guillem Cucurull, Thomas Scialom, Anthony Hartshorn, Elvis Saravia, Andrew Poulton, Viktor Kerkez, and Robert Stojnic. 2022. Galactica: A large language model for science. *arXiv preprint arXiv:2211.09085*.

Joan Torruella and Ramón Capsada. 2013. Lexical statistics and tipological structures: a measure of lexical richness. *Procedia-Social and Behavioral Sciences*, 95:447–454.

Hugo Touvron, Thibaut Lavril, Gautier Izacard, Xavier Martinet, Marie-Anne Lachaux, Timothée Lacroix, Baptiste Rozière, Naman Goyal, Eric Hambro, Faisal Azhar, et al. 2023. Llama: Open and efficient foundation language models. *arXiv preprint arXiv:2302.13971*.

Dietrich Trautmann, Alina Petrova, and Frank Schilder. 2022. Legal prompt engineering for multilingual legal judgement prediction. *arXiv preprint arXiv:2212.02199*.

Jason Wei, Yi Tay, Rishi Bommasani, Colin Raffel, Barret Zoph, Sebastian Borgeaud, Dani Yogatama, Maarten Bosma, Denny Zhou, Donald Metzler, et al. 2022a. Emergent abilities of large language models. *arXiv preprint arXiv:2206.07682*.

Jason Wei, Xuezhi Wang, Dale Schuurmans, Maarten Bosma, Ed Chi, Quoc Le, and Denny Zhou. 2022b. Chain of thought prompting elicits reasoning in large language models. *arXiv preprint arXiv:2201.11903*.

Shijie Wu, Ozan Irsoy, Steven Lu, Vadim Dabravolski, Mark Dredze, Sebastian Gehrmann, Prabhanjan Kambadur, David Rosenberg, and Gideon Mann. 2023.

Bloomberggpt: A large language model for finance. *arXiv preprint arXiv:2303.17564*.

Li Yunxiang, Li Zihan, Zhang Kai, Dan Ruilong, and Zhang You. 2023. Chatdoctor: A medical chat model fine-tuned on llama model using medical domain knowledge. *arXiv preprint arXiv:2303.14070*.

Tianyi Zhang, Varsha Kishore, Felix Wu, Kilian Q Weinberger, and Yoav Artzi. 2019. Bertscore: Evaluating text generation with bert. *arXiv preprint arXiv:1904.09675*.

A Sample Prompt, Q-A Pair, and Generation Example

We present a sample prompt, corresponding Q-A pair, and a generation example from our experiments, focusing on Nvidia Corporation.

A.1 Prompt

In our experiment, we use the following template for generations.

```
prompt = f"Assume you are a
    professional financial analyst.
    Read the provided question
    and answer pair about {company
    } and write an investment
    thesis be logical and
    argumentative. \n QA: {QApair}
    Please write in English
    language. \n ### Investment
    Thesis:"
```

A.2 Sample Question and Answer Pair

Here we present an example of a question-and-answer pair. For better visibility, we display ten questions out of the fifteen used in our experiments.

Q1: What are the primary business segments of Nvidia Corporation?

A1: Nvidia operates through two segments: GPU and Tegra Processor.

Q2: How does the Tegra brand contribute to Nvidia's portfolio?

A2: The Tegra brand integrates an entire computer onto a single chip, and incorporates GPUs and multi-core CPUs to drive supercomputing for mobile gaming and entertainment devices, as well as autonomous robots, drones, and cars.

Q3: What markets does Nvidia address with its processor platforms?

A3: Nvidia's processor platforms address four markets: Gaming, Professional Visualization, Datacenter, and Automotive.

Q4: What is the predicted earnings improvement for Nvidia in 2021 and 2022?

A4: Nvidia earnings are expected to improve to $9.50 a share in 2021, and anticipate a +15% increase into 2022.

Q5: What trends are causing increased demand for Nvidia's products?

A5: Nvidia is at the confluence of a couple of macro trends in the chip space, including the growth of need for data and cloud computing and the widespread surge in gaming, both accelerated by COVID-19.

Q6: How is Nvidia's acquisition of Mellanox contributing to its growth story?

A6: The Mellanox acquisition contributes to Nvidia's long term growth, despite having a negative impact on near-term margin numbers.

Q7: What is the predicted gross margin for Nvidia for FY 21 and FY 22?

A7: InSight is forecasting a gross margin of over 65% for FY 21 and 66% for FY 22 for Nvidia.

Q8: How do Nvidia's partnerships in machine learning and self-driving contribute to its growth prospects?

A8: NVDA's partnerships in machine learning and self-driving could become consumer worthy in the coming decade and provide an additional growth driver not currently factored into the price target.

Q9: What is Nvidia's current stance on dividends?

A9: The dividend is currently at $0.16 and raising it is not a priority.

Q10: How is Nvidia involved in the Medical Devices sector?

A10: Nvidia chips are being increasingly used in the healthcare diagnostic and equipment groups, adding to the company's growth.

A.3 Generation Example

The following section presents a sample output from the instruction-tuned LLama 13B model, our top performer in the evaluations conducted. The text was generated with a single decoding option: a maximum token limit of 512. Below, we demonstrate the model's generated investment thesis for Nvidia Corporation:

```
Nvidia is a leading player in the semiconductor and computer technology industry, with a strong presence in the gaming, professional visualization, datacenter, and automotive markets. The company's primary business segments are GPU and Tegra Processor, which are designed to address the growing demand for data and cloud computing, as well as the increasing popularity of gaming and entertainment devices.

The acquisition of Mellanox is expected to contribute to Nvidia's long-term growth, despite having a negative impact on near-term margin numbers. The company's partnerships in machine learning and self-driving also hold significant growth potential, as these technologies are expected to become consumer worthy in the coming decade.

Nvidia is committed to producing energy-efficient chipsets and has set a goal to source 65% of its global power usage from renewable sources by 2025, making a positive contribution to the fight against climate change. The company's corporate governance is considered disciplined and transparent, with a diverse board of directors and few flags in accounting or reporting practices.

Overall, Nvidia is well-positioned to benefit from the growth in demand for data and cloud computing, as well as the increasing popularity of gaming and entertainment devices. The company's acquisition of Mellanox and partnerships in machine learning and self-driving are expected to drive long-term growth, and the company's commitment to sustainability is a positive factor. Given these factors, we believe that Nvidia is a strong investment opportunity, with a potential for a high ROI.
```

Textual Evidence Extraction for ESG Scores

Naoki Kannan[1] and **Yohei Seki**[2]
[1]Graduate School of Comprehensive Human Sciences, University of Tsukuba
[2]Institute of Library, Information and Media Science, University of Tsukuba
s2321684@u.tsukuba.ac.jp
yohei@slis.tsukuba.ac.jp

Abstract

With the growing importance of environmental, social, and governance (ESG) information, ESG scores, which have been rated and published by various institutions, are used for investment decisions or corporate evaluation. The evidence for rating high or low ESG scores, however, is often vague and unclear. In this paper, we propose a method to extract the textual evidence of ESG scores by automatically labeling sentences with information related to ESG. Specifically, we constructed two labeling models for ESG and ESG sentiment, and extracted sentences with high confidence levels using the two models. At first, to label ESG-related information, we developed the annotation corpus using Japanese annual securities reports. Then, we constructed the labeling models by fine-tuning a large language model that was pre-trained on financial documents. The experimental results showed that the macro average F1 scores using the BERT model pre-trained on Japanese financial documents, were 0.874 for ESG labeling and 0.797 for ESG sentiment labeling respectively. These values were higher than those obtained using the comparative models that were pre-trained on Wikipedia documents only. We also confirmed that textual evidence for the ESG scores can be effectively extracted for the companies not included in the training dataset.

1 Introduction

In recent years, the global investment and corporate governance community has become increasingly interested in ESG (Environmental, Social and Governance), the three perspectives necessary for a company's long-term growth. The ESG score is an assessment of a company's level of commitment to ESG and is used by investors to determine the extent to which a company takes ESG factors into account when investing. ESG scores are provided to investors by various rating agencies. Recently, companies with higher ESG scores have been prioritised for investment, and the amount of assets under management for sustainable investments worldwide was expected to increase by 55% between 2016 and 2020 (Global Sustainable Investment Alliance (GSIA), 2021).

Despite this increase in investments taking ESG factors into account, many existing ESG scores are not open and unclear about how they are derived. They are also not consistently evaluated across rating agencies (Christensen et al., 2022). They are also incomplete, opaque and subject to considerable uncertainty (Avramov et al., 2022).

In this paper, we proposes a method for consistently extracting textual evidence from each text in the annual securities reports to assess ESG scores. Annual securities reports contain many general texts that are not related to company initiatives. Therefore, our method, which extracts only the textual evidence, can be used to help investors make decisions. This will help ESG-conscious investors to make decisions when investing in green assets.

Furthermore, "social capital" and "human capital" has become more important in assessing the social dimension ("S" in ESG) of corporate sustainability (Muñoz-Torres et al., 2019). In addition, in many ESG scores, social capital and human capital are evaluated as separate concepts in the assessment of sociability (International Sustainability Standards Board (ISSB), 2021; Toyo Keizai Inc., 2021; MSCI ESG Research LLC., 2023; FTSE Russell, 2022). On the other hand, to the best of authors' knowledge, no computational approach has been found that evaluates sociability separately into social and human capital perspectives. Therefore, we use pre-trained language models to automatically classify the sentences in annual securities reports describing a company's ESG efforts as separate labels for social and human capital, in addition to E and G, and extract textual evidence for rating the ESG score.

We specify the combination of ESG labels and their sentiment labels as the query to extract tex-

Proceedings of the Joint Workshop of the 5th Financial Technology and Natural Language Processing (FinNLP) and 2nd Multimodal AI For Financial Forecasting (Muffin), Macao, August 20, 2023.

tual evidence for ESG scores. For example, to extract textual evidence for a high social capital score, we specify the attributes "social capital (S-1)" and "positive" as queries. Similarly, to extract evidence indicating a low human capital score, we specify the attribute "human capital (S-2)" and "negative" as a query. We also propose a method for extracting textual evidence of ESG scores using the confidence level in assessing ESGs and their sentiments. As confidence levels, the predicted probabilities of the ESG classifier and the ESG sentiment classifier are used. We regard sentences with high confidence levels as textual evidence for the ESG score. In this way, the textual evidence of ESG scores can be extracted from noisy securities reports to support investment decisions.

The contributions of this work can be summarized as follows:

1. We propose our method to extract textual evidence for ESG scores based on labeling ESG and ESG sentiment with their confidence levels from Japanese annual securities reports.
2. We distinguished the "S" in ESG labelling into social capital and human capital, and clarified that textual evidence on corporate social capital and human capital initiatives can be extracted respectively.
3. We also clarified that the pre-trained model on financial documents was effective in the ESG and ESG sentiment labeling tasks.

Our research revealed a strong correspondence between ESG scores and their textual evidence. This finding will be helpful in future works on automatic estimation of ESG scores from textual resources.

The structure of this paper is as follows. Section 2 presents relevant research on automatic labeling of ESG and ESG sentiment. In Section 3, we propose a method for extracting texts as evidence for rating ESG scores. Section 4 describes our dataset for labeling ESG information. In Section 5, we verify the effectiveness of large language models for labeling ESG information. In Section 6, we describe the experiment to verify the effectiveness of the proposed method in terms of extracting textual evidence. Section 7 discusses the results of the evaluation experiments. Finally, Section 8 summarizes the findings of our work.

2 Related Work

In recent years, computational approaches for analyzing ESG ratings have gradually intensified in response to the growing interest in ESG corporate activities.

2.1 ESG Labeling

Goel et al. (2022) achieved 2% higher accuracy than traditional BERT (Devlin et al., 2019) by combining various linguistic and semantic features. Dakle et al. (2022) collected a list of concepts and terms related to ESG issues in the financial domain and constructed a dataset of positive and negative term and concept pairs using a Sentence-BERT-based paraphrase detector. By fine-tuning BERT and RoBERTa (Liu et al., 2019) on this dataset, they achieved 96% accuracy on the validation set and 92.3% accuracy on the test set. Kiriu et al. (2020) analyzed corporate CSR reports and used Word2vec to obtain word-specific embedded representations and classify these words into three values: environmental, social, and governance. They then defined the quantity score and the specificity score and attempted to rate the ESG activities of the companies based on the qualitative information.

In this study, we extract textual evidence to help investors evaluate ESG scores. In contrast to the related works, we created a dataset manually annotated with ESG labels and fine-tuned several Transformer-based models, including BERT, which is pre-trained on a Japanese financial corpus. Also, to retrieve textual evidence for scores such as sociality score and human capital utilization score (Toyo Keizai Inc., 2021), this work defines S (social) concept as S-1 (social capital) and S-2 (human capital) instead of the E, S, and G three-valued classification. This approach follows the trend that human capital has recently become more important in evaluating corporate sociality.

2.2 ESG Sentiment Classification

Pasch et al. (2022) combined S&P Global's ESG score and text from annual reports to train an ESG sentiment model. Among the companies targeted, they labeled those with ESG scores above the median as "positive" and those with scores below the median as "negative" and fine-tuned based on their text. In this study, we performed labeling on a per-sentence basis using manually annotated labels and fine-tuned them to classify the sentiment of ESG-related sentences. Furthermore, by combining ESG labels and their sentiment labels, we extracted textual evidence for ESG scores. We defined the labeling strategy in Section 3.1 and demonstrated that the annotators annotated labels consistently even if they were not ESG or economic experts.

Aue et al. (2022) calculated a company's ESG rating by classifying news into sentiment categories and subtracting the percentage of negative news from the percentage of positive news. Fischbach et al. (2022) proposed ESG-Miner, a tool for analyzing the sentiment of a company's ESG-related news. By contrast, we extract textual evidence for ESG scores based on the assumption that the texts with positive (or negative) sentiments contain the reasons for high (or low) ESG scores.

The methods for fine-tuning pre-trained language models using small amounts of task-specific data are well known in the field of natural language processing in recent years (Howard and Ruder, 2018). These methods are effective in certain domains that contain many specialized words that do not appear often in general documents, such as sentences relevant to ESG. In this work, we performed automatic ESG sentiment classification by fine-tuning with BERT, RoBERTa, or ELECTRA, which have shown high performance in many natural language processing tasks, including sentiment classification.

3 Proposed Method

In this section, we describe our method for extracting textual evidence for rating ESG scores. In Section 3.1, we introduce the definition of the labeling attributes to be assigned to the texts. In Section 3.2, we describe the labeling model for each attribute to extract the evidence text of ESG scores.

3.1 Definition of ESG related attributes

We introduce and define two attributes to create the experimental dataset: ESG sentence type and ESG sentiment.

3.1.1 ESG sentence type

This attribute corresponds to the ESG type of content of the sentence. We define five labels: "Environmental (E)," "Social Capital (S-1)," "Human Capital (S-2)," "Corporate Governance (G)," "ESG General (All)," and "Other." The specific conditions for classification are defined in Table 1, referring to the SASB Standard[1], an international framework for ESG information disclosure, and actual sentences.

3.1.2 ESG sentiment

We defined three labels: "positive," "negative," and "neutral." This attribute indicates the sentiment of the sentence with respect to ESG. In addition, the annotation standards are defined so that non-experimental collaborators who are not experts in economics or investing can evaluate the annotation criteria. Table 2 shows the annotation standards, which are defined by focusing on the most commonly used phrases.

[1]https://www.sasb.org/standards/materiality-map/

Table 1: ESG Sentence Type Requirements

Environmental (E)	• Contains expressions that consider greenhouse gases. • Contains climate-friendly phrases. • Contains phrases that consider the impact on the natural environment. • Contains other environmentally friendly phrases.
Social Capital (S-1)	• Contains statements related to product safety and user health. • Contains expressions related to privacy or information security. • Contains language about managing suppliers or trading partners (supply chain). • Contains other expressions of social responsibility outside the company.
Human Capital (S-2)	• Contains expressions related to employee recruitment, evaluation systems, and training that are not based on the old values. • Contains expressions of concern for workers' human rights and labor standards. • Contains other language that addresses the company's internal social responsibilities.
Governance (G)	• Contains expressions related to the structure of directors, executive officers, and auditors that could be considered relevant to the fairness and transparency of management. • Contains expressions of preparedness for serious risks that may affect the company's survival, compliance with laws and regulations, and ethical conduct. • Contains other language that reflects governance considerations.

Table 2: ESG Sentiment Requirements

Positive	• Contains phrases stating that the company is improving or is likely to improve in the future its long-term values. • Contains other phrases that are considered positive from an ESG perspective.
Negative	• Contains phrases that could be viewed as potentially detrimental to the long-term value of the company. • Contains other phrases that could be considered negative from an ESG perspective.
Neutral	• Contains statements about actions to be taken in the future for which it is not known whether they will actually be taken. • Contains ideas or actions of the company that cannot always be said to be generally true. • Contains statements that cannot be assessed as positive or negative from an ESG perspective.

3.2 Classifiers and Ranking Model

In this work, we classify ESG-relevant sentences by fine-tuning the pre-trained language models: BERT (Devlin et al., 2019), RoBERTa (Liu et al., 2019), and ELECTRA (Clark et al., 2020). These transformer-based machine learning models are capable of acquiring context-aware embedded representations of words, allowing the same word to acquire different vector representations in different contexts.

The overall scheme of the proposed method is shown in Figure 1. First, we use the ESG dataset described in Section 4 and fine-tuned the pre-trained models for predicting ESG sentence type and ESG sentiment labels.

Next, we take sentences from the annual securities reports for the companies under evaluation and perform label prediction. The output is predicted labels and their probabilities for each classification model. The prediction probability is the output value of the Softmax function of the prediction label in the linear transformation layer of the pre-trained language model. This module extracts and ranks the sentences where the probabilities are above a certain threshold. They provide textual evidence for ESG scores.

In this paper, we use Japanese annual securities reports as a source of information to obtain a company's ESG initiatives because of the existence of uniform standards for disclosure, easy comparison with other companies in the same industry, and high machine readability of the data. We also use ESG scores provided by Toyo Keizai Inc. (2021) for major Japanese companies since 2007.

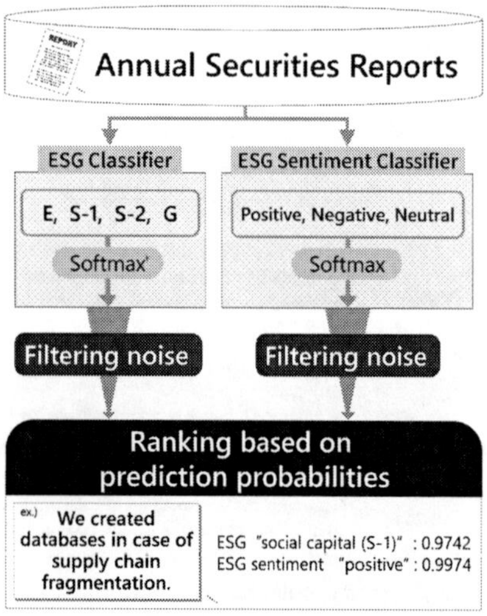

Figure 1: Proposed Method

4 ESG Label Classification Dataset

We created an ESG label classification dataset with sentences and annotated labels using annual securities reports collected from the electronic disclosure system EDINET[2].

4.1 Collection of annual securities reports (ASR)

The dataset was created by analyzing the XBML data from the annual securities reports (Financial Services Agency of Japan (JFSA), 2020) and removing unnecessary characters such as subheadings and symbols. We selected the actual companies for the dataset from Toyo Keizai Inc.'s ESG score ranking for 2021 (2021). Sentences were automatically split into sentence units at each punctuation point, and the output results were checked and corrected by the first author. The statistics of the dataset are as follows.

- Submission period: 2020/4/1 - 2021/3/31
- Data format: XBML
- Total number of sentences: 1,813 in total
- Target companies: 17 companies in 2 industries
  - Automobile manufacturers: 8 companies
  - Electrical manufacturers: 9 companies
- Target chapters in ASR
  - "Management policy, management environment, issues to address"
  - "Business risks"
  - "Research and development activities"
  - "Overview of corporate governance"

4.2 Annotation strategy for each attribute

To construct the ESG label classification dataset, the data described in Section 4.1 are manually annotated with the attributes defined in Section 3. This is done only for 744 sentences out of a total of 1,813 collected sentences. The remaining 1,069 sentences are used in Section 6 to evaluate the proposed method. At first, 562 of the 744 sentences were annotated by five annotators (the first author and four collaborators). Therefore, each of the 562 sentences has five annotations. The labels were determined by a majority vote. In cases in which we could not decide the results by majority vote because the votes were tied, we discussed until agreeing on a final decision. If all annotations for a sentence were different, it was chosen by discussion. Table 3 shows the Fleiss' κ coefficients (1971) for the five annotators as the annotator agreement degree. The κ values for all attributes were greater than 0.8 (almost perfect (Landis and Koch, 1977)).

[2]https://disclosure.edinet-fsa.go.jp/

From these results, we confirmed that there was no significant difference in the annotation results between the annotators. Based on these results, the first author annotated the remaining 182 sentences.

Table 3: Agreement for Each Attribute (Fleiss' κ)

Attribute	κ
ESG Sentence Type	0.89
ESG Sentiment	0.87

5 Language Models for Labeling Attributes

5.1 Objective

Here, we evaluate the accuracy of the proposed method for each attribute of the ESG label classification dataset created in section 4.2, and verify the effectiveness of the method. We describe comparative experiments using large language models pre-trained with different source data.

5.2 Method

First, we evaluate the classification accuracy of all 744 sentences in the ESG label classification dataset in Section 4.2 by predicting each attribute using the five-fold cross-validation method based on the model described in Section 3.2. The values used for the evaluation are precision, recall, $F1$ score, and accuracy, each of which is the macro average of each fold and each label.

The five pre-trained language models for comparison were as follows: BERT (wiki)[3], RoBERTa (wiki+CC100)[4], ELECTRA-base (wiki)[5], BERT (wiki+fin)[6], and ELECTRA-small (wiki+fin)[7]. The latter three models were developed by Suzuki et al. (2023) Note that the characters inside the brackets are the corpus name for pre-training. The hyperparameters were set as follows. The maximum token length was 128, the batch size was 32, the learning rate was $1e^{-5}$, and the maximum number of epochs was 100. Learning was stopped when the loss function did not decrease for more than five epochs.

[3]https://huggingface.co/cl-tohoku/bert-base-japanese-v2

[4]https://huggingface.co/rinna/japanese-roberta-base

[5]https://huggingface.co/izumi-lab/electra-base-japanese-discriminator

[6]https://huggingface.co/izumi-lab/bert-base-japanese-fin-additional

[7]https://huggingface.co/izumi-lab/electra-small-paper-japanese-fin-discriminator

5.3 Results

Tables 4 and 5 show the classification results for ESG sentence types and ESG sentiment, respectively. The number of attribute labels for ESG sentence types used in the five-fold cross-validation is 111 for E, 162 for S-1, 70 for S-2, and 401 for G, respectively. The number of attribute labels for ESG sentiment is 566 for positive, 61 for negative, and 99 for neutral, respectively. Because BERT (wiki+fin) showed the best classification accuracy for all labels, we focus on BERT (wiki+fin) and BERT (wiki) for comparison.

Tables 6 and 7 show the F1 scores for the ESG sentence type and for the ESG sentiment label using BERT (wiki+fin) and BERT (wiki), respectively. In Table 6, the F1 scores of Social Capital (S-1) and Human Capital (S-2) are significantly improved compared to the other labels. Table 7 shows that the F1 scores of positive and neutral are significantly improved compared to the other labels.

Table 4: ESG Sentence Type Classification Results

Pre-trained Language Model	F1 score	Precision	Recall	Accuracy
BERT (wiki)	0.849	0.849	0.856	0.891
BERT (wiki+fin)	**0.874**	**0.870**	**0.885**	**0.906**
RoBERTa (wiki+CC100)	0.845	0.837	0.863	0.882
ELECTRA-base (wiki)	0.685	0.711	0.695	0.786
ELECTRA-small (wiki+fin)	0.175	0.135	0.250	0.539

Table 5: ESG Sentiment Classification Results

Pre-trained Language Model	F1 score	Precision	Recall	Accuracy
BERT (wiki)	0.785	0.807	0.778	0.885
BERT (wiki+fin)	**0.797**	**0.823**	**0.789**	**0.888**
RoBERTa (wiki+CC100)	0.783	0.802	0.774	0.876
ELECTRA-base (wiki)	0.628	0.711	0.627	0.819
ELECTRA-small (wiki+fin)	0.291	0.258	0.334	0.773

Table 6: Comparison Results of ESG Sentence Types Classification Using BERT (wiki+fin) and BERT (wiki) by Label Types

Label (Count)	F1 score	
	BERT (wiki+fin)	BERT (wiki)
Environmental (E - 111)	0.883	**0.887**
Social Capital (S-1 - 162)	**0.825**	0.796
Human Capital (S-2 - 70)	**0.832**	0.763
Governance (G - 401)	**0.955**	0.948

Table 7: Comparison Results of ESG Sentiment Classification Using BERT (wiki+fin) and BERT (wiki) by Label Types

Label (Count)	F1 score	
	BERT (wiki+fin)	BERT (wiki)
positive (566)	**0.879**	0.865
negative (61)	0.939	**0.942**
neutral (99)	**0.574**	0.553

6 Experiment: Extracting Textual Evidence for Rating ESG Scores of Companies

6.1 Objective

The purpose of this experiment is to verify whether the proposed method can extract textual evidence for rating the ESG scores of the companies. Note that the evaluation data for the companies are not used for fine-tuning BERT in Section 5.

6.2 Method

The text used in the experiment consists of 1,069 sentences from two industries and four companies that were not used in model training, as mentioned in Section 4.2 (Financial Services Agency of Japan (JFSA), 2020). Of these, we will refer to two companies as Electrical Manufacturer A and Automobile Manufacturer B for evaluation and two companies as Electrical Manufacturer α and Automobile Manufacturer β for verification.

Table 8 shows the ESG scores of Electrical Manufacturer A and Automobile Manufacturer B, which were extracted from the top 500 companies in the ESG Corporate Ranking in Japan (Toyo Keizai Inc., 2021). When ESG scores are above the mean with a large deviation from the mean, they are underlined. The scores that are below the mean with a large deviation are double-underlined. We evaluate our method to extract the textual evidence for the scores from the annual securities reports. At first, we took all 1,069 sentences into the proposed classifier and assign attributes to each sentence. The prediction probabilities of both classifiers are used as the confidence level of the sentence, and the sentences with high confidence levels are regarded as textual evidence of ESG scores. When the assigned attributes are a combination of "Environmental (E)," "Social Capital (S-1)," "Human Capital (S-2)," or "Governance (G)" and "Positive," then the sentences are textual evidence for high ESG scores, whereas when they are combined with "Negative," they serve as textual evidence for low ESG scores.

Next, we filter the noisy sentences for textual evidence. The filtering is done by setting thresholds for the prediction probabilities of the ESG classifier and the ESG sentiment classifier as the confidence level of the sentence, respectively, as described in Section 3.2. The thresholds were decided by actually checking the sentences as the positive cases with the lowest prediction probabilities in the verification data.

From the evaluation scores of the sentences of the electronics manufacturer α, we decided the threshold for electronics manufacturers, and from the evaluation scores of the sentences of the automobile manufacturer β, we decided the threshold for automobile manufacturers. Attributes for which no sentences were extracted from the verification data were given 0 as a threshold.

Finally, the extracted sentences were evaluated by three experiment participants, including the first author, to decide whether they actually served as textual evidence for the ESG scores. We used the precision at the top 1, 5, 10, and 20 ranks as the evaluation measure.

6.3 Results

The evaluation results for Electrical Manufacturer A and for Automobile Manufacturer B are shown in Tables 9 and 10. From these results, we found that we could extract the textual evidence for the companies rated as having high ESG scores. We also found that there were still challenges in extracting the textual evidence for the companies rated as having low ESG scores.

7 Discussion

In this section, we discuss the effectiveness of our proposed method based on the validity of extracted sentences as textual evidence, the effect of the distinction of S-1 (social capital) and S-2 (human capital), and the validity of the model pre-trained on the financial corpus. We also discuss failure analysis.

7.1 Textual evidence for rating ESG scores

In Figures 2 and 3, we show two example sentences that were extracted as textual evidence for high ESG scores from the annual securities reports

Table 8: ESG Scores of Companies for Evaluation

	ESG Score (Average: 320.4)	E Score (Average: 76.32)	S1 Score (Average: 77.11)	S2 Score (Average: 77.91)	G Score (Average: 88.96)
Electrical Manufacturer A (Rank 46)	372.2	97.4	93.1	85.9	93.8
Automobile Manufacturer B (Rank 336)	300.4	74.4	85.2	60.6	80.2

Table 9: Results of Ranking Textual Evidence for Rating ESG Scores of Electrical Manufacturer A

Query	Threshold		# of textual evidence		Precision@k			
Specified attribute label	ESG classification	ESG sentiment classification	judged by humans	extracted	k=1	k=5	k=10	k=20
"Environmental (E)" and "positive"	0.8456	0.9969	13	16	1.000	1.000	0.900	–
"Social Capital(S-1)" and "positive"	0.9285	0.9963	11	22	1.000	0.400	0.600	0.500
"Human Capital (S-2)" and "positive"	0.8796	0	9	12	1.000	1.000	0.800	–

Table 10: Results of Ranking Textual Evidence for Rating ESG Scores of Automobile Manufacturer B

Query	Threshold		# of textual evidence		Precision@k	
Specified attribute label	ESG classification	ESG sentiment classification	judged by humans	extracted	k=1	k=5
"Social Capital(S-1)" and "positive"	0.9902	0.9967	6	7	1.000	0.800
"Human Capital (S-2)" and "negative"	0	0	0	1	0.000	–

of Electrical Manufacturer A and Automobile Manufacturer B[1], respectively. For Electrical Manufacturer A, we extracted sentences describing that they were building facilities and creating new training curricula for talent development. For Automobile Manufacturer B, we extracted sentences describing that they were creating supply chain databases for each part to prepare for emergencies and manage the supply chain.

Munoz et al. (Muñoz-Torres et al., 2019) examined the rating methodologies used by the eight major ESG rating agencies and analyzed the criteria and their strength (frequency of occurrence) for each environmental, social, and governance dimension. According to their analysis of the ESG rating agencies' evaluation processes in 2017, the main social responsibility criteria, especially those related to human capital, were the quality of working conditions, health and safety, labor management, and human rights. These criteria emphasize responsibility toward employees as stakeholders. In fact, looking at the actual text, the provision of sufficient training programs for employees is considered to contribute to the human capital criteria mentioned for Electronics Manufacturer A. Therefore, the extracted text here corresponds to the addition of ESG scores from a human capital perspective and is considered evidence based on the text of the ESG scores. Similarly, for Automobile Manufacturer B, it can be said that implementing supply chain management to prepare for emergencies fulfills the company's responsibility to society by minimizing the impact on production in the event of a crisis, allowing production to continue. Therefore, the extracted text here corresponds to the addition of ESG scores from a social capital perspective and is considered evidence based on the text of the ESG scores.

[1]Note that we omitted proper nouns that identified the company.

Label: "Human Capital (S-2)"; "Positive"
Value: 0.9968

"We built the Academy Training Center as part of our centennial project to develop the people who will drive our growth. We also reformed personnel development programs, such as the introduction of new curricula, with focusing on the development for highly skilled technicians and professionals."

Figure 2: Textual Evidence for ESG Scores for Electrical Manufacturer A (Original Text in Japanese)

Label: "Social Capital (S-1)"; "Positive"
Value: 0.9974

"In addition, in case of an emergency, we have also performed maintenance to keep the supply chain database of our current core and secondary suppliers to mitigate the impact of supply chain disruptions. This helped us to identify potentially affected suppliers and parts at an early stage, to identify required stocks, to propose alternative manufacturing, and to support the restoration of production facilities. "

Figure 3: Textual Evidence for ESG Scores for Automobile Manufacturer B (Original Text in Japanese)

7.2 Effect of S-1 and S-2 distinction in ESG

We investigate the effect of extracting textual evidence using S-1 (social capital) and S-2 (human capital) by comparing the labeling results using "S" without distinguishing the two attributes.

We compare the classification results of the 4-value classifier for E, S-1, S-2, and G with those of the 3-value classifier for E, S, and G using the same test data. We took 1,069 sentences from the two automobile manufacturers and two electronics manufacturers used in Section 6 as input data into both the ESG 4-value classifier and the ESG 3-value classifier, respectively. Then, we checked which labels are predicted by the 4-value classifier for the top 20 sentences with the highest prediction probability in the 3-value classifier among the sentences classified as "S" in the 3-value classifier.

Table 11: ESG Sentence Examples Correctly Classified as S-1 / S-2 with BERT (wiki+fin)

Input (Original Text in Japanese)	Prediction Labels	
	BERT (wiki+fin)	BERT (wiki)
We used universal design for our products for wheelchair users to operate easily.	S-1	E
In the United States, our 2020 models were rated as *TOP SAFETY PICK+* from the IIHS (Insurance Institute for Highway Safety) in its 2020 safety survey.	S-1	E
We, the management team, aim to be a company where everything is communicated openly and honestly. We also take the initiative in promoting continuous improvement of our organizational environment.	S-2	G

The results showed that many of the sentences classified as "S" by the ternary classifier were actually S-1 (social capital). We examined 80 sentences, 20 sentences from each of the four companies, and found that 57 (71%) of them were S-1 (social capital). This implied that the proposed method using a 3-value classifier cannot extract enough textual evidence of S-2 (human capital). In addition, as shown in Table 6, the annotated dataset was skewed, with 162 sentences for S-1 and 70 sentences for S-2, which might have led to this result. Thus, we conclude that the proposed method using a 4-value classifier allows us to effectively extract textual evidence for both social and human capital sentences.

7.3 Effect of pre-training using financial documents

We investigate the classification results using BERT (wiki+fin), a model retrained on Japanese financial texts by comparing with BERT (wiki), a model not retrained on Japanese financial texts. It should be noted that we omitted proper nouns that could identify the company. From Table 6, the F1 scores of S-1 (Social Capital) and S-2 (Human Capital) were improved using BERT (wiki+fin). There were a certain number of sentences that were correctly classified as S-1 or S-2 in BERT (wiki+fin) but were incorrectly classified as E or G in BERT (wiki). Examples of such sentences are shown in Table 11. All of these sentences are considered to be positive promotional phrases by the company itself, which are specific to annual securities reports. As described, depending on pre-training using financial texts, we identified several contexts that were well captured by BERT (wiki+fin).

7.4 Failure Analysis

We confirmed that textual evidence for rating ESG scores can be extracted with our proposed method. However, some extracted sentences were not used as the textual evidence for ESG scores. We discuss some typical failure cases as follows.

An example of misclassification is the sentence: "AI predicts Chemical Oxygen Demand in 2 hours." It is difficult to consider this sentence as the textual evidence for rating the environmental score, but it may have been misclassified because of the inclusion of phrases such as "oxygen," which are often used in the context of environmental protection.

Another example is the following sentence: "We have added a range of composite environmental sensors." This sentence was also misclassified because of the inclusion of the word "environment." This is because of the fact that sentences annotated with labels such as "Social Capital (S-1)," "Human Capital (S-2)," and "Governance (G)" did not contain many phrases related to "social" or "governance," whereas sentences annotated with the label "Environmental (E)" often contained many phrases related to "environment."

8 Conclusion

In this work, we annotated the sentences in annual securities reports and created classification models by fine-tuning large language models pre-trained on financial documents. We proposed a method for extracting the textual evidence for ESG scores by automatically assigning both ESG sentence type labels (E, S-1, S-2, and G) and ESG sentiment labels to the sentences in annual securities reports and ranking them with their prediction probabilities as the confidence levels to filter out noisy sentences. Through experimentation, we have confirmed that it is possible to extract the textual evidence of companies rated as having a high ESG score.

In the future, we plan to automatically estimate ESG scores from textual resources based on the strong correspondence between ESG scores and their textual evidence.

Ethical sentence

This research was conducted with the approval of the Ethics Review Committee of the Institute of Library, Information and Media Science, the University of Tsukuba. The participants in the corpus creation experiment were asked to sign a consent form in advance and were allowed to quit the experiment at any time.

Acknowledgments

This work was partially supported by the Japanese Society for the Promotion of Science Grant-in-Aid for Scientific Research (B) (#23H03686), and Grant-in-Aid for Challenging Exploratory Research (#22K19822).

References

Tanja Aue, Adam Jatowt, and Michael Färber. 2022. Predicting Companies' ESG Ratings from News Articles Using Multivariate Timeseries Analysis. *arXiv preprint arXiv:2212.11765*.

Doron Avramov, Si Cheng, Abraham Lioui, and Andrea Tarelli. 2022. Sustainable investing with esg rating uncertainty. *Journal of Financial Economics*, 145(2, Part B):642–664.

Dane M. Christensen, George Serafeim, and Anywhere Sikochi. 2022. Why is corporate virtue in the eye of the beholder? The case of ESG ratings. *The Accounting Review*, 97(1):147–175.

Kevin Clark, Minh-Thang Luong, Quoc V Le, and Christopher D Manning. 2020. Electra: Pre-training text encoders as discriminators rather than generators. *arXiv preprint arXiv:2003.10555*.

Parag Pravin Dakle, Shrikumar Patil, Sai Krishna Rallabandi, Chaitra Hegde, and Preethi Raghavan. 2022. Using transformer-based models for taxonomy enrichment and sentence classification. In *Proceedings of the Fourth Workshop on Financial Technology and Natural Language Processing (FinNLP)*, pages 250–258, Abu Dhabi, United Arab Emirates (Hybrid). Association for Computational Linguistics.

Jacob Devlin, Ming-Wei Chang, Kenton Lee, and Kristina Toutanova. 2019. BERT: Pre-training of Deep Bidirectional Transformers for Language Understanding. In *Proceedings of the 2019 Conference of the North American Chapter of the Association for Computational Linguistics: Human Language Technologies, Volume 1 (Long and Short Papers)*, pages 4171–4186. Association for Computational Linguistics.

Financial Services Agency of Japan (JFSA). 2020. Annual Securities Report (*Yuuka Shoken Houkokusho* in Japanese).

Jannik Fischbach, Max Adam, Victor Dzhagatspanyan, Daniel Mendez, Julian Frattini, Oleksandr Kosenkov, and Parisa Elahidoost. 2022. Automatic ESG Assessment of Companies by Mining and Evaluating Media Coverage Data: NLP Approach and Tool.

Joseph L. Fleiss. 1971. Measuring nominal scale agreement among many raters. *Psychological bulletin*, 76(5):378–382.

FTSE Russell. 2022. Esg-ratings-overview.pdf. https://research.ftserussell.com/products/downloads/ESG-ratings-overview.pdf. (Accessed on 04/23/2023).

Global Sustainable Investment Alliance (GSIA). 2021. "GLOBAL SUSTAINABLE INVESTMENT REVIEW 2020". https://www.gsi-alliance.org/wp-content/uploads/2021/08/GSIR-20201.pdf. (Accessed 04/21/2023).

Tushar Goel, Vipul Chauhan, Suyash Sangwan, Ishan Verma, Tirthankar Dasgupta, and Lipika Dey. 2022. TCS WITM 2022@FinSim4-ESG: Augmenting BERT with linguistic and semantic features for ESG data classification. In *Proceedings of the Fourth Workshop on Financial Technology and Natural Language Processing (FinNLP)*, pages 235–242, Abu Dhabi, United Arab Emirates (Hybrid). Association for Computational Linguistics.

Jeremy Howard and Sebastian Ruder. 2018. Universal language model fine-tuning for text classification. *Proceedings of the 56th Annual Meeting of the Association for Computational Linguistics (Volume 1: Long Papers)*, pages 328–339.

International Sustainability Standards Board (ISSB). 2021. Materiality map screenshot). https://www.sasb.org/wp-content/uploads/2021/11/MMap-2021.png. (Accessed on 04/23/2023).

Takuya Kiriu and Masatoshi Nozaki. 2020. A Text Mining Model to Evaluate Firms' ESG Activities: An Application for Japanese Firms. *Asia-Pacific Financial Markets*, 27(4):621–632.

J Richard Landis and Gary G Koch. 1977. The Measurement of Observer Agreement for Categorical Data. *Biometrics. International Biometric Society*, pages 159–174.

Yinhan Liu, Myle Ott, Naman Goyal, Jingfei Du, Mandar Joshi, Danqi Chen, Omer Levy, Mike Lewis, Luke Zettlemoyer, and Veselin Stoyanov. 2019. RoBERTa: A Robustly Optimized BERT Pretraining Approach. *arXiv preprint arXiv:1907.11692*.

MSCI ESG Research LLC. 2023. Esg ratings methodology - msci esg ratings methodology.pdf. https://www.msci.com/documents/1296102/34424357/MSCI+ESG+Ratings+Methodology+%28002%29.pdf. (Accessed on 04/23/2023).

María Jesús Muñoz-Torres, María Ángeles Fernández-Izquierdo, Juana M. Rivera-Lirio, and Elena Escrig-Olmedo. 2019. Can environmental, social, and governance rating agencies favor business models that promote a more sustainable development? *Corporate Social Responsibility and Environmental Management*, 26(2):439–452.

Pasch Stefan and Ehnes Daniel. 2022. NLP for Responsible Finance: Fine-Tuning Transformer-Based Models for ESG. In *2022 IEEE International Conference on Big Data (Big Data)*, pages 3532–3536.

Masahiro Suzuki, Hiroki Sakaji, Masanori Hirano, and Kiyoshi Izumi. 2023. Constructing and analyzing domain-specific language model for financial text mining. *Information Processing & Management*, 60(2):103194.

Toyo Keizai Inc. 2021. *CSR Corporate Social Responsibility White Paper 2021 (in Japanese).* Toyo Keizai Inc.

A Scalable and Adaptive System to Infer the Industry Sectors of Companies: Prompt + Model Tuning of Generative Language Models

Lele Cao*, **Vilhelm von Ehrenheim**, **Astrid Berghult**, **Cecilia Henje**, **Richard Anselmo Stahl**, **Joar Wandborg**, **Sebastian Stan**, **Armin Catovic**, **Erik Ferm** and **Hannes Ingelhag**
Motherbrain, EQT Group, Stockholm, Sweden
{lele.cao, vilhelm.vonehrenheim, astrid.berghult, cecilia.henje, richard.stahl}@eqtpartners.com
{joar.wandborg, sebastian.stan, armin.catovic, erik.ferm, hannes.ingelhag}@eqtpartners.com

Abstract

The Private Equity (PE) firms operate investment funds by acquiring and managing companies to achieve a high return upon selling. Many PE funds are thematic, meaning investment professionals aim to identify trends by covering as many industry sectors as possible, and picking promising companies within these sectors. So, inferring sectors for companies is critical to the success of thematic PE funds. In this work, we standardize the sector framework and discuss the typical challenges; we then introduce our sector inference system addressing these challenges. Specifically, our system is built on a medium-sized generative language model, finetuned with a prompt + model tuning procedure. The deployed model demonstrates a superior performance than the common baselines. The system has been serving many PE professionals for over a year, showing great scalability to data volume and adaptability to any change in sector framework and/or annotation.

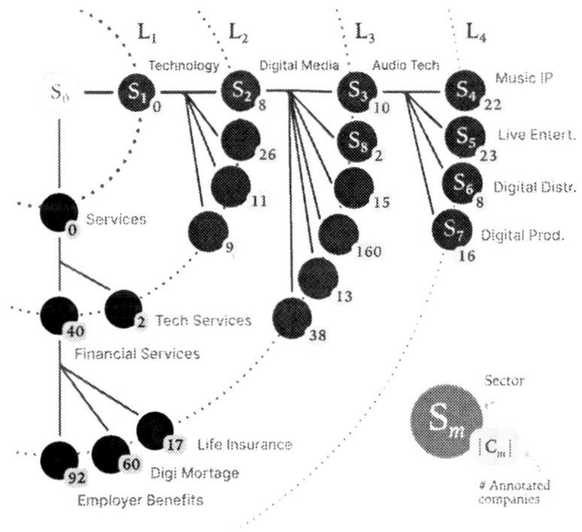

Figure 1: A PE sector framework defined as a tree with a depth L=4. Each non-root node represents a sector (i.e., $\mathsf{s}_1 \sim \mathsf{s}_M$) that is numbered in a depth-first order. The integer attached to the m-th sector/node indicates the number of companies $|\mathsf{C}_m|$ annotated for s_m.

1 Introduction

Private Equity (PE), as a fast-growing branch of the investment industry, operates investment funds on behalf of institutional and accredited investors by acquiring and managing companies before selling them to achieve high, risk adjusted returns. The common PE investment strategies, according to (Block et al., 2019), include venture capital, growth capital, and leveraged buyouts. The majority of PE funds strive to be "thematic" (Bérubé et al., 2014), aiming to identify macro-level trends by covering a variety of relevant sectors and picking promising companies within these sectors. In order to do that, any company should be put into a sector that best describes its main business activity. The sectors are often defined hierarchically (cf. the sector framework in Section 2), where the sectors higher up in the hierarchy tend to have a broader scope (hence usually fewer in number) and be more stable, while the ones lower down (a.k.a. "industries") are more fine-grained and prone to change. A well-defined sector framework enables investment professionals to conduct a deeper analysis of the economy within each individual sector.

There are currently hundreds of millions of companies worldwide, and thousands of new companies are founded daily. Realistically, human professionals can only evaluate a limited number of companies to determine their belonging sectors. In order to significantly increase the coverage of sector mapping, practitioners have begun resorting to predictive systems to infer the belonging sectors of companies. Due to the reasons discussed in Section 2, there has not been any effective system that is generic enough to drive the wide adoption in PE operations. In this paper, we standardize the sector framework and discuss the typical challenges; we then introduce our sector inference system ad-

*Corresponding author.

Proceedings of the Joint Workshop of the 5th Financial Technology and Natural Language Processing (FinNLP) and 2nd Multimodal AI For Financial Forecasting (Muffin), Macao, August 20, 2023.

dressing these challenges. Our system has been successfully serving hundreds of PE professionals for over a year. The highlight is three fold:

- We propose to co-tune the PLM (pretrained language model) starting from a later stage of prompt tuning, attempting to leverage the capability of medium-sized PLMs to an extreme using scarce annotation.
- We implement an autonomous system, which effectively handles the dynamic sector framework, evolving annotation, data imbalance, noisy features, and high inference volume.
- We experimentally show the superior performance of our approach in comparison to the common baselines, and justify many design choices such as model paradigm and size.

2 The Problem and Challenges

Let c_n denote the n-th company ($n=1,2,\ldots,N$) in the scope of a PE firm; the total number of companies N usually reaches the order of millions. Most of the time, PE professionals maintain a hierarchical sector framework containing M different sectors represented as nodes ($\mathsf{s}_1 \sim \mathsf{s}_M$) in a tree with L layers, as illustrated in Figure 1. In practice, the value of L is mostly less than 4, and the total number of sectors (i.e., M) tracked by a large PE firm may reach up to a few hundred. The problem is **how to assign each company c_n to the most relevant sector s_m**. Solving such a problem requires addressing several **challenges** (abbreviated as **Chall.**) that will be discussed below.

Chall.1: scarce, imbalanced and evolving annotation. One might notice there are some public datasets such as G2 and Pitchbook[1] that contain sector annotations, i.e., $\mathsf{c}_n \rightarrow \mathsf{s}_m$. In reality, they can not be directly used to train the sector inferring model, which is the consequence of two main facts: (1) PE firms almost always maintain their own version of sector framework that are drastically different from the ones from public datasets. (2) PE funds may annotate companies differently; for example, Klarna[2] might fall into any sector of *payment method*, *digital bank* and *financial service* depending on the preference of investment professionals or the fund specifications. To that end, we allow professionals to select a sector for any company via the investment platform developed in-house. Formally, we use C_m to denote the set of companies annotated for sector s_m, and the total number of companies in C_m is $|\mathsf{C}_m|$; taking node s_3 in Figure 1 for example, its subscript $\boxed{10}$ contains the value of $|\mathsf{C}_3|$, i.e., $|\mathsf{C}_3|=10$. In reality, the sector annotation is scarce (an intrinsic limitation of manual annotation), imbalanced ($|\mathsf{C}_m|$ can vary greatly among sectors) and ever-evolving (the mapping $\mathsf{c}_n \rightarrow \mathsf{s}_m$ may change frequently).

Chall.2: dynamic sector framework with varying granularity. Due to shifting market trends, the sector framework is rarely fixed for extended periods of time. Instead, the sector framework is really a dynamic one, where one of the three changes[3] can occur: adding new layers, adding new nodes, and removing nodes. Another observation is that PE professionals will pick concepts they think are important and define them as sectors, leading to sectors with varying granularity even on the same layer. For instance, a sector could be anything from a new technology (e.g., block chain), an environmental concern (e.g., water shortage), to an emerging market demand (e.g., Coronavirus test).

Chall.3: availability and quality of features. Intuitively, the most informative feature is probably the textual description about a company, which can be gathered from various data sources such as Pitchbook and Crunchbase[4]. Given an example description "*We develop security analytical tools to identify web-app vulnerabilities. Contact us for a demo of our award-winning product*", one could guess a "*cyber security*" sector just by reading the first sentence, yet many texts look more like the second sentence, which severely lacks context. Moreover, a significant number of companies simply do not have textual descriptions available from popular data sources[5].

Chall.4: high inference frequency and volume. As soon as the textual feature of a company is changed, we need to re-infer its sector. Besides, any change around the sector framework or company annotation may trigger model update, which

[1] https://www.g2.com and https://pitchbook.com

[2] https://www.klarna.com

[3] Note that changing the definition of an existing sector is achieved by altering the associated company annotations; and merging/splitting existing sector(s) can be done via combining operations of adding and removing sector(s). Currently, only a system superuser can modify the sector framework through backend configuration files. However, our future plans involve facilitating this process via a web-based graphical user interface (GUI) integrated to EQT's Motherbrain platform – https://eqtgroup.com/motherbrain.

[4] https://www.crunchbase.com

[5] Cao et al. (2022) present a summary of data sources.

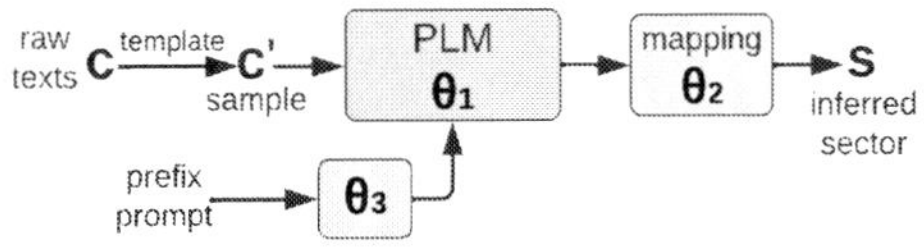

Figure 2: Three paradigms of generative NLP models: prompting $P(\text{s}|\mathbf{c};\boldsymbol{\theta}_2)$, model tuning $P(\text{s}|\mathbf{c};\boldsymbol{\theta}_1,\boldsymbol{\theta}_2)$, and prompt tuning $P(\text{s}|\mathbf{c};\boldsymbol{\theta}_2,\boldsymbol{\theta}_3)$.

requires a re-inference for all N companies. With the current data volume in our data warehouse, the daily amount of re-inference can easily exceed 100 million, which may grow into a bottleneck.

3 The Core Model

Inferring the industry sector of companies can be naturally addressed by a supervised NLP approach, where we **input** the textual description of a company (denoted as $\mathbf{c}$), and **output** a sector s based on a $\boldsymbol{\theta}$-parameterized model $P(\text{s}|\mathbf{c};\boldsymbol{\theta})$; note that we omit the subscripts n and m hereafter for the sake of simplicity. To find the optimal $\boldsymbol{\theta}$, we use the annotated mappings $\mathbf{c} \to \text{s}$ to fit this conditional probability. The prediction target s can be either raw text (e.g., "*cyber security*") or the encoded M-dim one hot vector, where the former is a **generative** approach and the latter is **discriminative**. It is crucial to highlight that generative methods offer two primary advantages over discriminative techniques (such as supervised classification): (1) generative models are capable of predicting sectors beyond those predefined, and (2) since these models output natural words, they can more effectively harness pre-learned knowledge in LM, thus avoiding overfitting on smaller training datasets.

Nowadays, generative approaches dominate the domains of computer vision (e.g., Stable Diffusion by Rombach et al., 2022) and NLP (e.g., GPT-3 (Brown et al., 2020) and GPT-4 (OpenAI, 2023)). Particularly, the language model (LM) is often pretrained following a generative approach, such as predicting the masked words. To address **Chall.1&2**, we need to exploit the capability of a pretrained LM (PLM). We start with designing a template for samples:

> [NAME], concerns [TAGS], is [c]. Sector: [s].

For a certain company, [NAME] is its legal name, [TAGS] is the concatenated tags/keywords[6] that are

[6]Many data sources, such as Pitbook and Crunchbase, have some keywords tagged for each company.

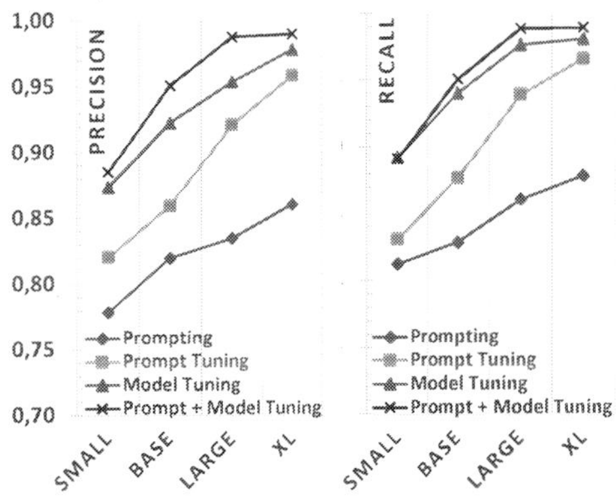

(a) Average precision. (b) Average recall.

Figure 3: Performance comparison over different model paradigms (legend) and sizes (x-axis): the validation (a) precision and (b) recall averaged over 84 sectors.

added to address **Chall.3**. For example, the filled input for company "Klarna" may look like

> *Klarna Bank AB, concerns buy-now-pay-later and shopping, is an online payment platform designed to facilitate cashless payments. Sector:* [s].

As the prediction target, [s] remains unreplaced, thus it is an unanswered sample. Model optimization essentially attempts to make the predicted [s] closer to the annotated sector text, and in this example s = "*financial service*". We use $\mathbf{c}'$ to denote the filled sample for company c.

3.1 Prompt and Model Tuning

Despite minor differences, the generative NLP models largely adhere to one of three paradigms: prompting, model tuning, or prompt tuning. Seen from Figure 2, **prompting** (Liu et al., 2023) freezes the PLM weights $\boldsymbol{\theta}_1$ while learning a mapping function (parameterized with $\boldsymbol{\theta}_2$) to transform the raw PLM output into the sector space. **Model tuning** allows finetuning $\boldsymbol{\theta}_1$, which is the de facto way of leveraging large PLM for downstream tasks (Li and Liang, 2021). **Prompt tuning** prepends some soft prompts, which are essentially learnable virtual tokens, into the input sequence $\mathbf{c}'$ and only trains them (corresponding to parameter $\boldsymbol{\theta}_3$) while keeping $\boldsymbol{\theta}_1$ fixed (Su et al., 2022). PLM can have billions of parameters making model tuning paradigm expensive, while the prompt-based approach (Liu et al., 2023) has only thousands of tunable parameters (Lester et al., 2021).

Following the generative "text-to-text" T5 PLM (Raffel et al., 2020), we compared the performance of these paradigms towards the PE sector inferring

Algorithm 1: Prompt + model tuning

Input: Sector annotations in the form of $\mathsf{c} \rightarrow \mathsf{s}$, a generative NLP model $P(\mathsf{s}|\mathbf{c}; \boldsymbol{\theta}_1, \boldsymbol{\theta}_2, \boldsymbol{\theta}_3)$, PLM freezing steps t', learning rates ϵ_1 and ϵ_2

Output: The optimal parameters $\boldsymbol{\theta}_1^*$, $\boldsymbol{\theta}_2^*$ and $\boldsymbol{\theta}_3^*$

Initialize $\boldsymbol{\theta}_1$ by loading the pretrained T5 model;
Initialize $\boldsymbol{\theta}_2$ and $\boldsymbol{\theta}_3$ randomly;
for $(t = 1; t \leq T; t++)$ **do**
  Sample a mini-batch from the annotations;
  Transform each c into a filled template $\mathbf{c}'$;
  Forward propagate $\mathbf{c}'$ to obtain the prediction $\hat{\mathsf{s}}$;
  Calculate the T5 cross entropy loss $\mathcal{L}(\hat{\mathsf{s}}, \mathsf{s})$;
  if $t \leq t'$ **then**
    $\epsilon = \epsilon_1$;
  else
    $\epsilon = \epsilon_2$ and $\boldsymbol{\theta}_1 := \boldsymbol{\theta}_1 - \epsilon \frac{\partial \mathcal{L}(\hat{\mathsf{s}}, \mathsf{s})}{\partial \boldsymbol{\theta}_1}$;
  $\boldsymbol{\theta}_2 := \boldsymbol{\theta}_2 - \epsilon \frac{\partial \mathcal{L}(\hat{\mathsf{s}}, \mathsf{s})}{\partial \boldsymbol{\theta}_2}$ and $\boldsymbol{\theta}_3 := \boldsymbol{\theta}_3 - \epsilon \frac{\partial \mathcal{L}(\hat{\mathsf{s}}, \mathsf{s})}{\partial \boldsymbol{\theta}_3}$;
$\boldsymbol{\theta}_1^* = \boldsymbol{\theta}_1$, $\boldsymbol{\theta}_2^* = \boldsymbol{\theta}_2$ and $\boldsymbol{\theta}_3^* = \boldsymbol{\theta}_3$;
return $\boldsymbol{\theta}_1^*$, $\boldsymbol{\theta}_2^*$ and $\boldsymbol{\theta}_3^*$;

task. Figure 3 shows the average precision and recall in relation to different paradigms and model sizes (`Small`, `Base`, `Large` and `XL`)[7]. We observe that model tuning of T5 achieves stronger performance than prompting and prompt tuning. Prompt tuning catches up with model tuning as model size increases, which coincide the conclusion drawn by Lester et al. (2021). Intuitively, the label scarcity (**Chall.1**) and varying granularity of sector framework (**Chall.2**) could be better addressed by prompt tuning, since it is supposed to keep the learned knowledge in PLM untouched; meanwhile, we also want to replicate the superior performance of model tuning when using a smaller model. To that end, we propose a model $P(\mathsf{s}|\mathbf{c}; \boldsymbol{\theta}_1, \boldsymbol{\theta}_2, \boldsymbol{\theta}_3)$ that carries out t' steps of prompt tuning (only optimize $\boldsymbol{\theta}_2$ and $\boldsymbol{\theta}_3$) before jointly tune the PLM weights $\boldsymbol{\theta}_1$, as presented in Algorithm 1. Seen from Figure 3, this "Prompt + Model Tuning" approach outperforms all compared methods by a large margin, which is the case even when the PLM size is relatively small.

According to Figure 3, the performance of our approach increase with the size of PLM and plateau (>98%) when reaching a "Large" size. Hence, we initialize our model with the T5-`Large` PLM and train for $T = 1 \times 10^6$ steps with a mini-batch size of 50. The prompt tuning phase is trained for $t' = 3 \times 10^3$ steps with a learning rate of $\epsilon_1 = 0.1$, where the first 1×10^3 steps utilize a linear learning rate warm-up (Goyal et al., 2017). Afterwards, the joint prompt and model tuning begins with a warm-up of 1.5×10^3 steps until reaching a learning rate of $\epsilon_2 = 5 \times 10^{-3}$. Checkpoints are selected via early stopping with respect to the validation accuracy. All these hyper-parameters are determined by an empirical grid search, and the implementation is built upon OpenPrompt (Ding et al., 2022).

[7]We did not manage to experiment the `XXL` T5 model due to our restriction of computing and human resources. The T5 PLMs can be found in `https://huggingface.co/google`.

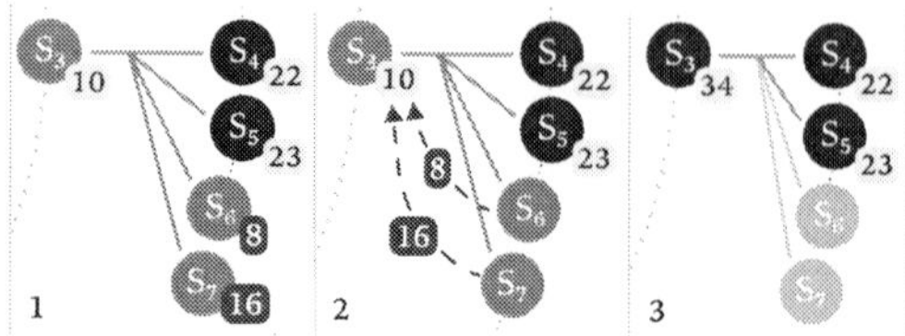

Figure 4: Demonstration of annotation (label) attribution process using s_3 sub-tree from Figure 1 as an example. Darker colored nodes are eligible for modeling.

3.2 Annotation attribution

We empirically regulate that only the sectors with at least 20 annotated companies can be included in the modeling, which implies that some sectors, such as s_3, s_6 and s_7 in Figure 1, are not eligible directly. Since sector annotation is scarce (**Chall.1**), we try to utilize every annotation to predict as much sectors as possible. Subsequently, we run a depth-first (bottom-up) annotation attribution algorithm to collect the eligible sectors s_m and their annotated set of companies C_m. Figure 4 demonstrates this procedure in three steps assuming the annotation attribution algorithm is currently processing the s_3 sub-tree in Figure 1. Initially, only the child sectors s_4 and s_5 are eligible (cf. (s4)[22] and (s5)[23] in Figure 4) because they have more than 20 annotated companies. When it comes to s_6 and s_7, they have insufficient annotations, thus are not eligible. However, their annotations will move up and contribute to the parent sector s_3, enabling s_3 to be included in the training dataset due to $|\mathsf{C}_3|$=10+8+16=34>20.

Despite our best-effort annotation attribution procedure, it is possible that some sectors may still be excluded from training. However, in practice, the trained generative model is capable of producing sector names that are not within the eligible sector set. We believe this occurrence represents scenarios where the sectors are not covered by the labels, yet they are still significant in terms of their inherent business implications. This feature is particularly desirable as it facilitates better understanding and refinement of the sector framework.

Algorithm 2: Sample balancing via EDA

Input: The eligible sectors $\mathsf{s}_1, \ldots, \mathsf{s}_M$ and their corresponding company sets $\mathsf{C}_1, \ldots, \mathsf{C}_M$
Output: The balanced company sets $\mathsf{C}'_1, \ldots, \mathsf{C}'_M$
Initialize: $\mathsf{C}'_1 = \mathsf{C}_1, \ldots, \mathsf{C}'_M = \mathsf{C}_M$;
Calculate $\zeta = 2 \cdot \max\{|\mathsf{C}_1|, \ldots, |\mathsf{C}_M|\}$;
for $(m = 1; m \leq M; m++)$ **do**
  for *each* c *in* C_m **do**
    Augment c for $\lfloor \zeta / \mathsf{C}_M \rfloor - 1$ times with EDA (Wei and Zou, 2019), producing set c';
    $\mathsf{C}'_m = \mathsf{C}'_m \cup \mathsf{c}'$;
return $\mathsf{C}'_1, \ldots, \mathsf{C}'_M$;

3.3 Sample balancing via augmentation

As a part of **Chall.1** discussed in Section 2, the value of $|\mathsf{C}_m|$ can vary from merely 20 all the way to a few hundred. Thus, the aforementioned annotation attribution will produce a heavily imbalanced training dataset. The overall idea is augmenting the samples for minority sectors to achieve inter-sector balance. There is a whole spectrum of text augmentation methods: from rule-based to model-based techniques (Feng et al., 2021), from which we adopt the EDA (easy data augmentation) approach (Wei and Zou, 2019) because of its simplicity and universality. For individual `[NAME]`, `[TAGS]` and `[c]` from our sample template, we perform synonym replacement, insertion, swapping and deletion at random choice with random intensity. Algorithm 2 has the details of the entire balancing procedure.

3.4 Performance analysis

As of December 2022, there are 84 eligible sectors after the annotation attribution procedure as introduced in Section 3.2. We collect all samples manually annotated under one of these 84 sectors, thereby creating a dataset that exhibits imbalance in terms of the number of samples annotated for each sector. The dataset is then balanced via the augmentation procedure introduced in Section 3.3. This results in a final dataset containing 7,260 samples, where each sector has ~86 annotated samples in average. We reserve 15% of the dataset for validation and report the accuracy of different baselines in Table 1. Our approach (i.e., "Prompt + Model Tuning") manages to achieve an accuracy of over 80% on the validation set. In contrast, its discriminative counterpart (cf. Section 5), which employs an M-way classification output head, achieves only 70% accuracy (largely on par with prompt tuning), likely due to the scarcity of labels.

Then we dig down to understand the error contribution from each sectors and find that sectors on low levels (e.g., L3 and L4 in Figure 1) have an accuracy of over 90% except two L3 sectors named *horizontal software* and *vertical software*, as reflected in Figure 5. A horizontal software company caters to a wide and broad ranging market of consumers, and a vertical one provides a solution for a particular line of business or industry. Because of the way they are defined, many businesses in horizontal/vertical software sector might fit in other sectors as well. For example, a company providing bot-based customer service could be part of the horizontal market of any customer support scenario, while also targeting vertically to game publishers. The complete list of predicted sectors is considered to be sensitive proprietary information and therefore we only show the confusion matrix for seven sectors (two from L2 and five from L3) in Figure 5. Since L3 sectors are more fine-grained requiring less (than L2) annotations, a generally better inference performance is observed for L3 than L2, which encourages us to run a bottom-up annotation

Model	Accuracy (%)
M-Way Classification	70.02
Prompting	64.63
Prompt Tuning	70.91
Model Tuning	76.44
Prompt + Model Tuning (Ours)	**80.25**

Table 1: Performance comparison of various baselines, all employing "T5 Large" as the PLM. The reported accuracies have been obtained (in December 2022) using the same random seed for consistency. The highest performing result is highlighted in bold.

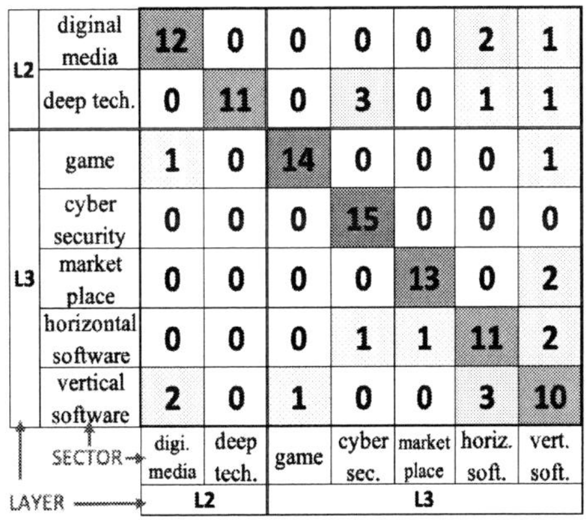

Figure 5: The confusion matrix for seven sectors picked from the 84 (as of December 2022) predicted sectors.

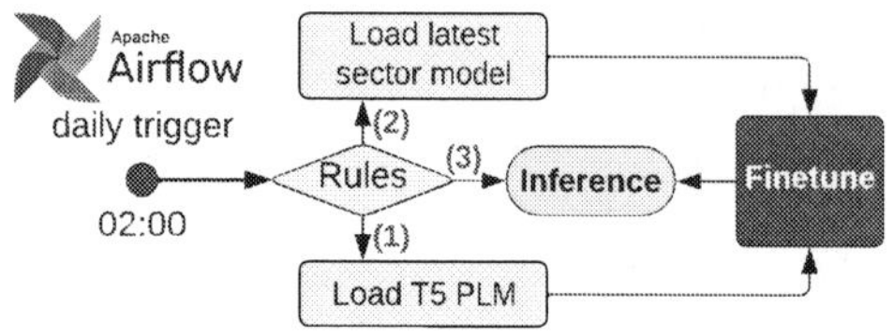

Figure 6: The full system diagram with three scenarios (1∼3) controlled by a rule-based inspection operator.

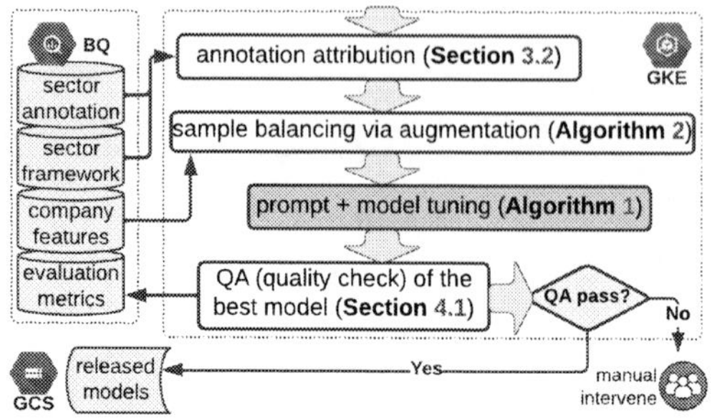

Figure 7: The finetune workflow. BQ: BigQuery, GCS: Google Cloud Storage, GKE: Google Kubernetes Engine.

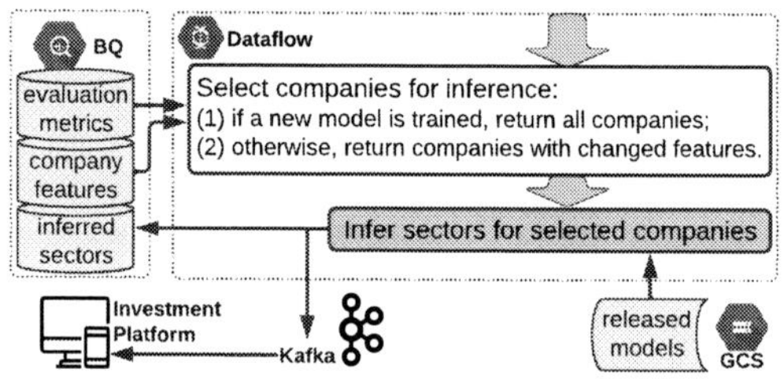

Figure 8: The (differentiated) inference workflow that starts with a rule-based company selection step.

attribution (cf. Section 3.2) to prioritize lower-level sectors.

4 The Full System

The evolving annotation (**Chall.1**) and dynamic sector framework (**Chall.2**) both demand constant model iteration; and any model update would require a full-scale re-inference. As a result, triggering model iteration upon any change in annotation or sector framework will be computationally expensive and hard to scale. Instead, We trigger a rule-based inspection only once every day (e.g., at about `02:00` as exemplified in Figure 6) through Airflow[8]. The inspection rules lead to three scenarios:

(1) **Finetune on T5 PLM** when the sector framework is changed or the annotation for any existing sector has evolved significantly[9]; it takes about 7 hours on 2 × Nvidia P100 GPU.

(2) **Finetune on the latest sector model** when the sector annotation only changed marginally[9]; but the first scenario will be enforced after 90 days since its last execution.

(3) **Skip finetune** otherwise and run incremental inference introduced in Section 4.2.

The second scenario takes less than 1/7 of the effort of the first scenario. We continue to present the key ingredients of finetune and inference.

4.1 Finetune

Figure 7 shows the finetune pipeline which is encapsulated in a docker[10] image run by Google Kubernetes Engine (GKE)[11]. From our data warehouse managed by BigQuery[12] (Melnik et al., 2010), the annotation attribution (Section 3.2) collects all eligible sectors $s_1, \ldots, s_M$ together with their corresponding company sets $C_1, \ldots, C_M$, which are balanced via augmentation (Algorithm 2). The balanced dataset is then split (with a ratio of 9:1) into training and validation sets that are used for prompt + model tuning following Algorithm 1.

The validation metrics (sector-wise precision and recall calculated from a confusion matrix like Figure 5) of the finetuned model will go through a QA (quality check) step to determine if this model is good enough to be automatically released in GCS (Google Cloud Storage)[13]. QA constitutes a series of assertions such as "*The* **precision** *of* **vertical software** *should be greater than* **75%**" and so on. If any of these assertions fails, it will send an alarm to our data scientists via Slack[14] to request a manual interference to take appropriate actions.

4.2 Inference

The inference workflow starts with a selection step (cf. Figure 8) to determine a subset of companies that need re-inference. The selection step greatly reduce the daily inference load (by 95% at least after the system stabilizes), hence it tackles **Chall.4**.

[8]Apache Airflow: `https://airflow.apache.org`

[9]For sector s_m that originally has $|C_m|$ annotated companies, the number of newly added/removed companies is Δ_m, then $\Delta_m/|C_m| \geq 0.75$ is regarded as **significant**, and $0.75 > \Delta_m/|C_m| \geq 0.1$ is a **marginal** change.

[10]`https://www.docker.com`

[11]`https://cloud.google.com/kubernetes-engine`

[12]`https://cloud.google.com/bigquery`

[13]`https://cloud.google.com/storage`

[14]`https://slack.com`

Next, the latest trained model is loaded to infer the sectors for the selected companies, where two facts could relieve **Chall.4** further: (1) being able to use a medium-sized PLM, and (2) job parallelization by Dataflow[15]. The inferred sectors are stored in BigQuery and simultaneously published to Kafka[16] so that our investment platform can further leverage those predictions in many PE analytical use cases.

5 Related Work

As discussed in Section 3, the most relevant approach is M-way classification using either word or sentence level features as input. But the features are usually pre-learned with a fundamentally different setup and target (e.g., MLM: Masked Language Model, cf. Devlin et al., 2019), which makes it potentially difficult to continue finetuning towards a classification target (Gururangan et al., 2020). There is a recent trend of unifying all downstream tasks as a text generation problem (Lester et al., 2021), i.e., a generative NLP paradigm. In fact, using prompt has become the symbol of this paradigm. For example, we can potentially ask a GPT-3 Brown et al., 2020 or InstructGPT (Ouyang et al., 2022): "*Klarna is a company that provide an cashless online payment platform. What is Klarna's industry sector?*" The likely answer would be something that generally make sense, yet will not be mapped directly towards the predefined sector framework. As a result, prompting (Liu et al., 2023) and prompt tuning (Su et al., 2022) emerge to fill this gap. However, Lester et al. (2021) discover that model tuning still prevails when the size of PLM is relatively small, which inspires us to jointly tune small PLM and prompt, as explained in Section 3.1.

6 Conclusion

In order to support thematic PE fund operations, we design and deploy a scalable and adaptive system to infer customized industry sectors for millions of companies. We empirically show that a generative NLP model is superior to its discriminative counterpart, leading to a solution of model + prompt tuning that guarantees superior performance even using scarce annotation and medium-sized PLM. The prompt template is designed to cope with noisy input textual features. To address the ever-changing sector framework and annotation, the system automatically triggers and determines the most appropriate scenario by quantifying the change. Moreover, the system also incorporates best-effort annotation attribution, sample balancing, and incremental inference. Hundreds of PE professionals has benefited from this system for over a year. Last but not least, our solution can be directly generalized to many similar scenarios such as e-commerce product tagging.

[15] `https://cloud.google.com/dataflow`
[16] `https://kafka.apache.org`

Acknowledgements

We are grateful to the support from the entire EQT organization. We also thank the constructive feedbacks from the reviewers of FinNLP@IJCAI 2023. This work is also reviewed by EQT's compliance, communication and legal department prior to publication.

References

Vincent Bérubé, Sacha Ghai, and Jonathan Tétrault. 2014. From indexes to insights: The rise of thematic investing. *McKinsey Invest*, 1:51–56.

Joern Block, Christian Fisch, Silvio Vismara, and René Andres. 2019. Private equity investment criteria: An experimental conjoint analysis of venture capital, business angels, and family offices. *Journal of corporate finance*, 58:329–352.

Tom Brown, Benjamin Mann, Nick Ryder, Melanie Subbiah, Jared D Kaplan, Prafulla Dhariwal, Arvind Neelakantan, Pranav Shyam, Girish Sastry, Amanda Askell, et al. 2020. Language models are few-shot learners. *Advances in neural information processing systems*, 33:1877–1901.

Lele Cao, Vilhelm von Ehrenheim, Sebastian Krakowski, Xiaoxue Li, and Alexandra Lutz. 2022. Using deep learning to find the next unicorn: A practical synthesis. *arXiv preprint arXiv:2210.14195*.

Jacob Devlin, Ming-Wei Chang, Kenton Lee, and Kristina Toutanova. 2019. BERT: Pre-training of deep bidirectional transformers for language understanding. In *Proceedings of the 2019 Conference of the North American Chapter of the Association for Computational Linguistics: Human Language Technologies, Volume 1 (Long and Short Papers)*, pages 4171–4186, Minneapolis, Minnesota. Association for Computational Linguistics.

Ning Ding, Shengding Hu, Weilin Zhao, Yulin Chen, Zhiyuan Liu, Haitao Zheng, and Maosong Sun. 2022. Openprompt: An open-source framework for prompt-learning. In *Proceedings of the 60th Annual Meeting of the Association for Computational Linguistics: System Demonstrations*, pages 105–113.

Steven Y. Feng, Varun Gangal, Jason Wei, Sarath Chandar, Soroush Vosoughi, Teruko Mitamura, and Eduard Hovy. 2021. A survey of data augmentation approaches for NLP. In *Findings of the Association for Computational Linguistics: ACL-IJCNLP 2021*, pages 968–988, Online. Association for Computational Linguistics.

Priya Goyal, Piotr Dollár, Ross Girshick, Pieter Noordhuis, Lukasz Wesolowski, Aapo Kyrola, Andrew Tulloch, Yangqing Jia, and Kaiming He. 2017. Accurate, large minibatch SGD: Training ImageNet in 1 hour. *arXiv preprint arXiv:1706.02677*.

Suchin Gururangan, Ana Marasović, Swabha Swayamdipta, Kyle Lo, Iz Beltagy, Doug Downey, and Noah A. Smith. 2020. Don't stop pretraining: Adapt language models to domains and tasks. In *Proceedings of the 58th Annual Meeting of the Association for Computational Linguistics*, pages 8342–8360, Online. Association for Computational Linguistics.

Brian Lester, Rami Al-Rfou, and Noah Constant. 2021. The power of scale for parameter-efficient prompt tuning. In *Proceedings of the 2021 Conference on Empirical Methods in Natural Language Processing*, pages 3045–3059, Online and Punta Cana, Dominican Republic. Association for Computational Linguistics.

Xiang Lisa Li and Percy Liang. 2021. Prefix-tuning: Optimizing continuous prompts for generation. In *Proceedings of the 59th Annual Meeting of the Association for Computational Linguistics and the 11th International Joint Conference on Natural Language Processing (Volume 1: Long Papers)*, pages 4582–4597, Online. Association for Computational Linguistics.

Pengfei Liu, Weizhe Yuan, Jinlan Fu, Zhengbao Jiang, Hiroaki Hayashi, and Graham Neubig. 2023. Pre-train, prompt, and predict: A systematic survey of prompting methods in natural language processing. *ACM Computing Surveys*, 55(9):1–35.

Sergey Melnik, Andrey Gubarev, Jing Jing Long, Geoffrey Romer, Shiva Shivakumar, Matt Tolton, and Theo Vassilakis. 2010. Dremel: interactive analysis of web-scale datasets. *Proceedings of the VLDB Endowment*, 3(1-2):330–339.

OpenAI. 2023. GPT-4 technical report. *arXiv preprint arXiv:2303.08774*.

Long Ouyang, Jeffrey Wu, Xu Jiang, Diogo Almeida, Carroll Wainwright, Pamela Mishkin, Chong Zhang, Sandhini Agarwal, Katarina Slama, Alex Ray, et al. 2022. Training language models to follow instructions with human feedback. *Advances in Neural Information Processing Systems*, 35:27730–27744.

Colin Raffel, Noam Shazeer, Adam Roberts, Katherine Lee, Sharan Narang, Michael Matena, Yanqi Zhou, Wei Li, and Peter J. Liu. 2020. Exploring the limits of transfer learning with a unified text-to-text transformer. *Journal of Machine Learning Research*, 21(140):1–67.

Robin Rombach, Andreas Blattmann, Dominik Lorenz, Patrick Esser, and Björn Ommer. 2022. High-resolution image synthesis with latent diffusion models. In *Proceedings of the IEEE/CVF Conference on Computer Vision and Pattern Recognition*, pages 10684–10695.

Yusheng Su, Xiaozhi Wang, Yujia Qin, Chi-Min Chan, Yankai Lin, Huadong Wang, Kaiyue Wen, Zhiyuan Liu, Peng Li, Juanzi Li, Lei Hou, Maosong Sun, and Jie Zhou. 2022. On transferability of prompt tuning for natural language processing. In *Proceedings of the 2022 Conference of the North American Chapter of the Association for Computational Linguistics: Human Language Technologies*, pages 3949–3969, Seattle, United States. Association for Computational Linguistics.

Jason Wei and Kai Zou. 2019. EDA: Easy data augmentation techniques for boosting performance on text classification tasks. In *Proceedings of the 2019 Conference on Empirical Methods in Natural Language Processing and the 9th International Joint Conference on Natural Language Processing (EMNLP-IJCNLP)*, pages 6382–6388, Hong Kong, China. Association for Computational Linguistics.

Using Deep Learning to Find the Next Unicorn: A Practical Synthesis on Optimization Target, Feature Selection, Data Split and Evaluation Strategy

Lele Cao[1], **Vilhelm von Ehrenheim**[1], **Sebastian Krakowski**[2], **Xiaoxue Li**[3], **Alexandra Lutz**[1]
[1] Motherbrain, EQT Group, Stockholm, Sweden
[2] House of Innovation, Stockholm School of Economics, Stockholm, Sweden
[3] Department of Political Science, Stockholm University, Stockholm, Sweden
{lele.cao, vilhelm.vonehrenheim, alexandra.lutz}@eqtpartners.com
sebastian.krakowski@hhs.se, xiaoxue.li@statsvet.su.se

Abstract

Startups represent newly established business models associated with disruptive innovation and high scalability, hence strongly propel the economic and social development. Meanwhile, startups are heavily constrained by many factors such as limited financial funding and human resources. Therefore, the chance for a startup to succeed is rare like "finding a unicorn in the wild". Venture Capital strives to identify and invest in unicorn startups as early as possible, hoping to gain a high return. This work is traditionally manual and empirical, making it inherently biased and hard to scale. Recently, the rapid growth of data volume and variety is quickly ushering in deep learning (DL) as a potentially superior approach in this domain. In this work, we carry out a literature review and synthesis on DL-based approaches, emphasizing four key aspects: optimization target, feature selection, data split, and evaluation strategy. For each aspect, we summarize our in-depth understanding and practical learning.

1 Introduction

Startup is a dynamic, flexible, high risk, and newly created company that typically represents a reproducible and scalable business model. It provides innovative products and/or services, and has limited financial funds and human resources (Santisteban et al., 2021; Skawińska and Zalewski, 2020; Blank, 2013). Since startups stimulate growth, generate jobs and tax revenues, and promote many other socioeconomically beneficial factors (Acs and Szerb, 2007), they are commonly regarded as powerful engines for economic and social development. As the startups continue to develop, they often increasingly rely on external funds (as opposed to internal funds from founders and co-founders), from either domestic or foreign capital markets, to unlock a high rate of growth (Marmer et al., 2011). Up till this date, the dominating external fund source has been Venture Capital (VC).

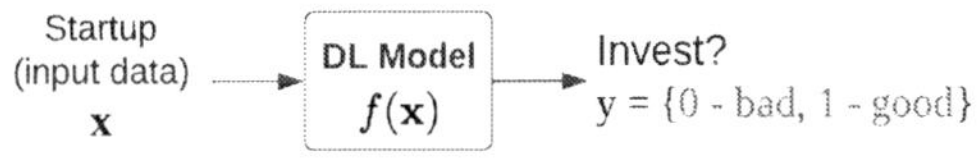

Figure 1: High-level overview of DL (deep learning) based startup sourcing: the model is trained to approximate a function $f(\cdot)$ so that the input $\mathbf{x}$ describing a startup is mapped to an output y indicating the recommended investment propensity that can be either discrete (good vs. bad) or continuous (success probability).

As an industry, VC seeks opportunities to invest in startups with great potential (in the sense of financial returns) to grow and successfully exit. The risk-return trade-off tells us that the potential return rises with a corresponding increase in risk[1]. As a consequence, VC firms strive to mitigate this risk by improving their 1) *deal sourcing* and 2) *value-add* process (Teten et al., 2013). In this survey, we will focus on the published work around the former approach, i.e., finding the *startup unicorn*[2] as accurately as possible. However, this task is a complex one with great uncertainty because of many factors such as vague/immature business ideas, forcing VC firms to make investment decisions based on insufficient information. Therefore a VC's deal sourcing process traditionally turns out to be manual and empirical, leaving estimations of the ROI (return on investment) heavily dependent on the human investors' decisions, which are inherently biased and hard to scale (Cumming and Dai, 2010).

With the rapid growth of data size and diversity (origin and modality), DL (deep learning) methods caught the eyes of increasing number of researchers hunting for unicorns. DL, by definition, represents a subset of ML (machine learning) methods, and is implemented (entirely or partly) with

[1] Statistics revealing the high risk of startups: on average, only about 60% of the startups survive for over 3 years since founded (Hyytinen et al., 2015); top 2% of VCs receive 95% of the returns in the entire industry (Bai and Zhao, 2021); VC has only 10% rate of achieving an ROI (return on investment) of 100% or more (Shane, 2012; Ünal and Ceasu, 2019).

[2] Unicorn startups are private, VC-backed firms with a valuation of at least $500 million (Chernenko et al., 2021).

Proceedings of the Joint Workshop of the 5th Financial Technology and Natural Language Processing (FinNLP) and 2nd Multimodal AI For Financial Forecasting (Muffin), Macao, August 20, 2023.

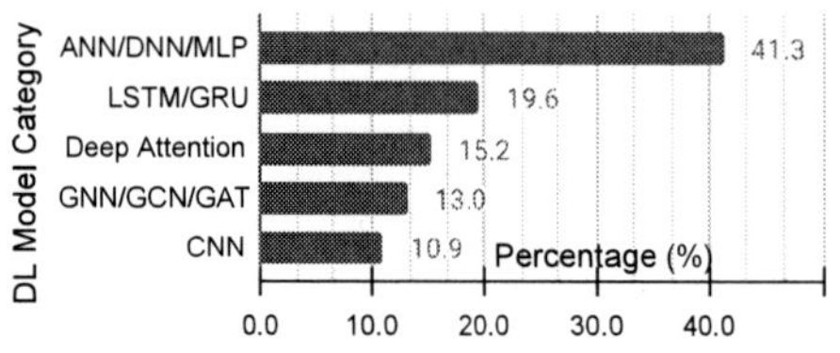

Figure 2: The the adoption percentage of DL models.

ANNs (artificial neural networks) that utilize at least two hidden layers of neurons. As shown in Figure 1, DL-based approaches require practitioners to define the input data $\mathbf{x}$ and label y (indicating good or bad investment according to some criteria) before training a model $f(\cdot)$ that maps $\mathbf{x}$ to y, i.e., $y{=}f(\mathbf{x})$. As a well-known international investment firm practicing data-driven approaches to find startup unicorns, we strive to 1) obtain a thorough and in-depth understanding of the methodologies for startup evaluation using DL, and 2) distil important and actionable learning for practitioners.

Therefore, we carry out a literature survey[3] on using DL to evaluate startups. According to Figure 2, over 40% of the surveyed papers adopt an ANN/DNN/MLP[4] due to its wide applicability to many data types. LSTM/GRU[5] almost dominates the cases when time-series are used. Deep attention (Vaswani et al., 2017) and graph based models (GNN/GCN/GAT)[6] have a rising trend of adoption due to increasing introduction of text and graph input. Lastly, images and videos are relatively least used (Figure 4), leading to only around 10% adoption rate for CNN (convolutional NN). We discover that **the innovation mostly lies in how an existing DL model is applied, rather than in the model itself**. Particularly, we present our literature synthesis and practical learnings from four key aspects: **optimization target**, **feature selection**, **data split**, and **evaluation strategy**. To the best of our knowledge so far, our work is the first of this kind.

2 Optimization Target

Identifying potential unicorns relies on accurate prediction of startup success. So far there is no universally agreed definition of "true success"; most of the existing definitions commonly focus on "growth" which can be measured from different perspectives like revenue, employees, and valuation, to name a few. We summarize the definitions adopted by the reviewed literature, showing each criterion's popularity among researchers. All *success criteria* are quantities in relation to a predefined duration since the time point of evaluation.

1. **Fulfill the preset fundraising goal** (Lee et al., 2018; Yu et al., 2018; Cheng et al., 2019; Yeh and Chen, 2020; Shi et al., 2021; Kaminski and Hopp, 2020; Wu et al., 2022; Tang et al., 2022): the goal (the expected amount of money) of the fund-raise campaign or plan is reached or surpassed, which is common among crowdfunding projects. The readers should be cautious not to confuse with the fund-raise goal of investors.
2. **Future funding** (Chen et al., 2021; Ross et al., 2021; Stahl, 2021; Yin et al., 2021; Garkavenko et al., 2022): any future funding raised above a low-bar amount.
3. **Acquired** (Ang et al., 2022; Ferrati et al., 2021; Kim et al., 2020; Lyu et al., 2021): one company purchases and takes over the operations and assets of the startup.
4. **IPO** (initial public offering) (Ang et al., 2022; Ferrati et al., 2021; Yin et al., 2021): it offers shares to the public in a new stock issuance for the first time; IPO allows the company to raise equity capital from public investors.
5. **Series A** (Zhang et al., 2021; Dellermann et al., 2021): the startup receives the first VC funding round after the seed and angel rounds.
6. N**-year survival** (Ghassemi et al., 2020; Ross et al., 2021): the firm still operates after N years.
7. **Experts view** (Bai and Zhao, 2021; Kinne and Lenz, 2021): the quantified review from human experts.
8. **Upround** (Ang et al., 2022): the valuation after a future funding round becomes higher than the current valuation.
9. **VC-backed** (Garkavenko et al., 2021): the startup is funded by one or more VC firms.
10. **Total raised funding** (Kim and Park, 2017): the accumulated amount of funding received (the higher the better), which is often used as a regression target.

[3]There are 29 English papers/theses sourced (with no restriction of year, type or geo-location) from 1) investment professionals and researchers, 2) keywords searching in Google, Google Scholar, IEEE, ACM, Scopus, Wiley, Springer and Web of Science, and 3) cross reference among papers/theses.

[4]In this paper, ANN, DNN (deep NN) and MLP (multilayer perceptron) refer to a NN with at least two hidden layers.

[5]LSTM: long short term mem.; GRU:gated recurrent unit.

[6]GNN (graph NN), GCN (graph convolution net) and GAT (graph attention net) are three graph based DL models.

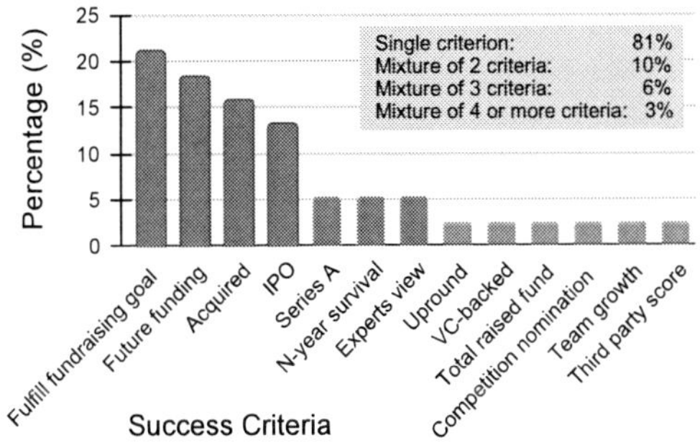

Figure 3: Distribution of the adopted startup success criteria (i.e., optimization objective); the upper-right panel shows the percentage of combining different number of criteria together.

11. **Competition nomination** (Ghassemi et al., 2020): the startup's business idea wins (or nominated by the committee of) a entrepreneurial competition.
12. **Team growth** (Horn, 2021): whether the team size has experienced a fast growth or not, such as "$\geq x\%$ *increase from at least 10 initial employees*".
13. **3rd-party score** (Allu and Padmanabhuni, 2022): some data sources provide certain firm evaluation scores[7].

While the first 12 criteria are intuitively sound, we question the effectiveness of the last criterion of taking the 3rd-party (algorithmic) scores as ground truth to train the DL model, because it is guaranteed to obtain a model inferior to the 3rd-party method. Additionally, there is no financial based success criteria[8] adopted in the DL-based work, which is a consequence of missing rich operating data (Gompers et al., 2020) before exiting the startup phase and entering the *growth phase* (Skawińska and Zalewski, 2020). Although the definition of a successful startup has many versions, for investors, it is relatively straightforward: a profitable exit, often in the form of acquisition or IPO, which incur high ROI (Ang et al., 2022). Practically, short-term events like funding rounds have a higher adoption rate than longer-term acquisition/IPO; the reason is twofold: 1) acquisition/IPO is extremely scarce as very few startups achieve these milestones; and 2) it occurs very late in startup's trajectory, hence potentially weakening the correlation between early data and late success (Stahl, 2021). In most cases,

[7]For example, Crunchbase (`www.crunchbase.com`) provides a so called "trend score" score.

[8]Only a few ML-based (instead of DL-based) work (Lussier and Pfeifer, 2001; Lussier and Halabi, 2010) have investigated using financial based success criteria.

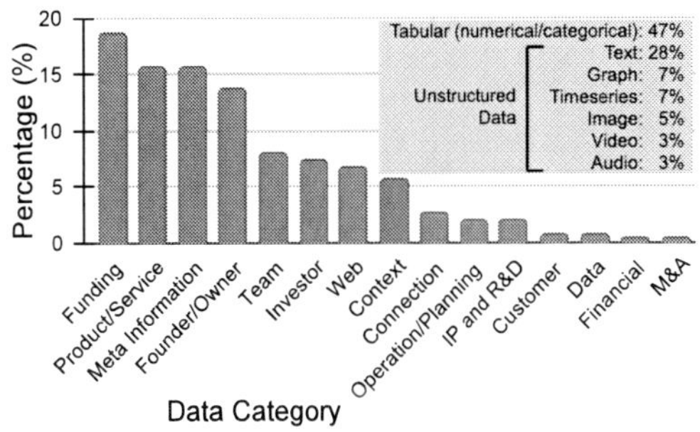

Figure 4: The distribution of data category sorted by the their occurrences; the upper-right panel shows a snapshot (to the date when this paper is written) of the utilized data modalities: numerical, categorical, text, graph, time-series, image, video and audio.

different success criteria do not conflict with each other, implying the possibility to combine multiple criteria; but this kind of *criteria mixture* is still under-investigated as illustrated in the upper-right panel of Figure 3. Generally speaking, one can combine multiple criteria with logical operators (i.e., `OR` and `AND`) (Yin et al., 2021; Ang et al., 2022), or use each criterion separately in a multi-task training setup (Shi et al., 2021).

3 Feature Selection

DL models need data input to make predictions. Before we start gathering input data for model, we might be able to benefit from understanding what input(s) humans use to make decisions. When investment professionals (i.e., humans) try to forecast the success of early stage startups, they make use of two cognitive modes: *intuitive* and *analytical*. The *intuitive mode* is characterized by processing "soft" signals (e.g., innovativeness and personality of entrepreneur) that are mostly *qualitative*; and humans are still the "golden standard" for this mode (Baer and McKool, 2014). The *analytical mode*, on the other hand, deals with "hard" facts (e.g., industry and team size) that are often *quantitative* (Dellermann et al., 2021). The majority of the work we reviewed incorporate both modes into the model input, but they have to quantify the "soft" information via either approximation or questionnaire. Data is often fed into DL models in the form of *features*. **Feature** (a.k.a. "factor" in the scope of financial research) is an individual measurable property or characteristic of a phenomenon, which is sometimes aggregated from raw data. When we try to map out the large number of features used the literature, we found that features tend to cluster into

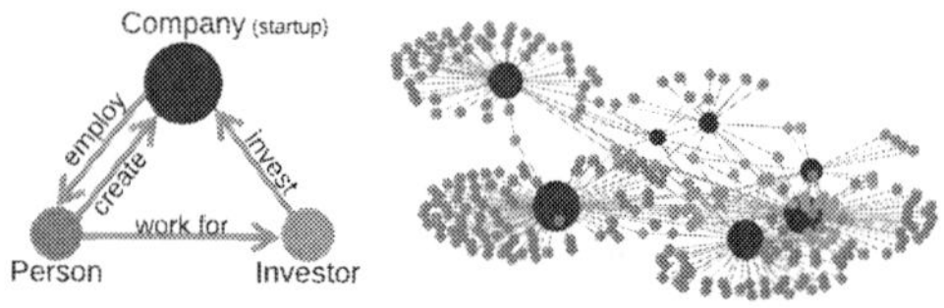

(a) Entity connections. (b) An example graph.

Figure 5: Illustration of the connection feature category, from which a graph can be built: (a) the graph comprises many nodes (denoting company, person or investor) and edges (representing investing/employment/founding relations between nodes); (b) an example company-person-investor graph using (a) as a legend.

different categories, describing different aspects of the startup in scope. We identified 15 feature categories detailed below and visualize their adoption percentage in Figure 4. Refer to Table 1 for the concrete features adopted in each category.

- **Funding**: historical fund received by the startup is direct recognition from other investors, thus it is the most popular category in the literature.
- **Product/Service**: the core value that early startups have to offer is reflected in the product and/or service they aim to create, which makes this category widely adopted.
- **Meta Information**: the general attributes of startups, which seldomly change since creation.
- **Founder/Owner**: the attributes of founding teams and the individuals that comprise them contribute to both the short-term success and longer-term survival (Ghassemi et al., 2020) of the startup; this category is available from many data sources and entrepreneurial competitions.
- **Team**: complementary to the founder/owner feature, the team features capture the statistics of the employees.
- **Investor**: the statistics of investors that have funded the startup can be informative about its early attractiveness.
- **Web**: any feature extracted from web pages.
- **Context**: besides *intrinsic*[9] features, more and more researchers have realized the importance of *extrinsic* factors that may be (but not limited to) competition, environmental, cultural, economical and tax-based.
- **Connection** features, as illustrated in Figure 5, are usually extracted from a graph that encodes connections between different entities: startup, person and investor.
- **Operation/Planning** concerns operational matters such as sales, localization, marketing, supply chain, digitization, advisory, company culture and legal regulation.
- **IP and R&D**: IP (intellectual property) and R&D (research and development) can approximate the startups' originality and innovativeness.
- The **customer**, **financial** and **M&A**[10] features are, most of the time, unavailable publicly, which resonates with their scarcity in Figure 4.

3.1 Noticeable Trends

The surveyed literature reflects several trends, summarized below, concerning selecting the input features for DL models.

Single-modal→multi-modal: although the *tabular (aggregated numerical/categorical data)* form still dominates, we see other emerging data modalities: *text*, *graph*, *time-series*, *image*, *video* and *audio*. The relative adoption of different modalities is shown in Figure 4. Especially, a few recent work (e.g., (Shi et al., 2021; Cheng et al., 2019)) has looked into combining multiple input modalities (i.e., multi-modal).

Structured(aggregated)→unstructured(raw): the modalities excluding "tabular" in Figure 4 are unstructured, which become increasingly important as a complement to the structured data (Lyu et al., 2021; Chen et al., 2021; Gastaud et al., 2019), or as a standalone input to the model (Zhang et al., 2021; Tang et al., 2022). Since raw, unstructured data often has a large scale and contains intact-yet-noisy signal, it may bring forward superior performance as long as a proper DL approach is applied (Garkavenko et al., 2022).

Proprietary→paid→free: all data sources utilized in DL-based methods are sorted in Figure 6 according to their occurrences. The traditional proprietary sources are not favored any more due to the limitation of scale and shareability. Paid data sources (e.g., Crunchbase and Pitchbook) are still very popular, because they are mostly quite affordable and well organized. However, neither paid or proprietary data is up-to-date or fine-grained, leading to the increasing adoption of free sources like web page scraping (Garkavenko et al., 2022).

[9]While intrinsic features act from within a company, extrinsic ones wield their influence from the outside. The former often can be controlled by the startup, but the latter can not.

[10]M&A (merger and acquisition) refers to a business transaction in which the ownership of companies (or their operating units) are transferred to or consolidated with another company.

Category	Description of Common Features	The Reference[ref] of Example Work	#ref
Funding	Total number of funding rounds and amount raised	(Allu and Padmanabhuni, 2022; Yin et al., 2021; Horn, 2021; Stahl, 2021) ...	10
	Funding type (e.g., angel and series A/B/C)	(Dellermann et al., 2021; Stahl, 2021; Yeh and Chen, 2020; Sharchilev et al., 2018) ...	8
	Elapsed time since latest funding	(Garkavenko et al., 2022; Ang et al., 2022; Gastaud et al., 2019) ...	6
	Size and type of the latest funding	(Ang et al., 2022; Garkavenko et al., 2022; Ross et al., 2021; Gastaud et al., 2019)	4
	Size and type of seed funding	(Dellermann et al., 2021; Bai and Zhao, 2021; Lyu et al., 2021)	3
	Average per-round statistics	(Garkavenko et al., 2022; Ang et al., 2022; Garkavenko et al., 2021)	3
	Average time between consecutive rounds	(Ross et al., 2021; Garkavenko et al., 2021; Sharchilev et al., 2018)	3
	The raw time-series of funding rounds	(Chen et al., 2021; Stahl, 2021; Horn, 2021)	3
	Accumulated amount for different funding types	(Ross et al., 2021; Sharchilev et al., 2018)	2
	Total amount raised from VC	(Dellermann et al., 2021; Ross et al., 2021)	2
	Post-money valuation of rounds	(Garkavenko et al., 2021)	1
Product/ Service	Industry/sector/sub-sector	(Ang et al., 2022; Ghassemi et al., 2020; Sharchilev et al., 2018; Yu et al., 2018) ...	11
	Textual product description	(Chen et al., 2021; Kim et al., 2020; Cheng et al., 2019; Lee et al., 2018) ...	9
	Project specification on crowdfunding platforms	(Yeh and Chen, 2020; Cheng et al., 2019; Yu et al., 2018; Kim and Park, 2017) ...	7
	Image, video or audio of the product/service	(Tang et al., 2022; Shi et al., 2021; Kaminski and Hopp, 2020; Cheng et al., 2019) ...	5
	Time to market, novelty and differentiation	(Bai and Zhao, 2021; Dellermann et al., 2021; Sharchilev et al., 2018)	3
	Technology maturity, novelty and differentiation	(Allu and Padmanabhuni, 2022; Dellermann et al., 2021; Bai and Zhao, 2021)	3
	Customer focus (e.g., B2B/B2C/B2B2C)*	(Stahl, 2021; Dellermann et al., 2021)	2
	Quality, market penetration and traction	(Bai and Zhao, 2021)	1
	Business models† and scalability	(Dellermann et al., 2021)	1
	The number of product varieties	(Sharchilev et al., 2018)	1
	Textual product review and comment	(Lee et al., 2018)	1
Meta Info.	Founded date and geographical location	(Chen et al., 2021; Garkavenko et al., 2021; Sharchilev et al., 2018; Yu et al., 2018) ...	16
	Has Facebook/Linkedin/Twitter account	(Shi et al., 2021; Dellermann et al., 2021; Ross et al., 2021; Kim and Park, 2017) ...	5
	Domain name or homepage URL	(Ross et al., 2021; Srinivasan et al., 2020; Kim and Park, 2017)	3
	Company legal name and aliases	(Ross et al., 2021; Srinivasan et al., 2020)	2
	Office count and age	(Garkavenko et al., 2022; Sharchilev et al., 2018)	2
	Registered address, email and phone number	(Ross et al., 2021)	1
	Incubator or accelerator support	(Dellermann et al., 2021)	1
Founder Owner	Founding team size (number of co-founders)	(Garkavenko et al., 2021; Ross et al., 2021; Gastaud et al., 2019) ...	11
	Founders' (successful) founding/industry experience	(Bai and Zhao, 2021; Shi et al., 2021; Yeh and Chen, 2020; Srinivasan et al., 2020) ...	11
	Gender, ethnicity or education (uni., major and year)	(Lyu et al., 2021; Ross et al., 2021; Kaiser and Kuhn, 2020; Corea, 2019) ...	8
	Founder ID and score from 3rd-party data sources	(Shi et al., 2021; Yeh and Chen, 2020; Srinivasan et al., 2020; Sharchilev et al., 2018)	4
	Skill (e.g., leadership, sales, law, finance, marketing)	(Bai and Zhao, 2021; Ghassemi et al., 2020; Pasayat et al., 2020; Bento, 2018)	4
	Social capital‡	(Shi et al., 2021; Srinivasan et al., 2020)	2
	Founders' biography (text) and photo	(Srinivasan et al., 2020; Kim and Park, 2017)	2
	Founders' entrepreneurial vision and dedication	(Bai and Zhao, 2021; Dellermann et al., 2021)	2
Team	Team size of all or different functions	(Ang et al., 2022; Garkavenko et al., 2022; Ross et al., 2021; Kim et al., 2020) ...	6
	Completeness and capability of managers and board	(Garkavenko et al., 2021; Bai and Zhao, 2021; Sharchilev et al., 2018)	3
	The time-series of team size	(Stahl, 2021; Horn, 2021)	2
	Statistics of new hire or leavers	(Garkavenko et al., 2021; Sharchilev et al., 2018)	2
	Team composition (e.g., diversity and gender)	(Ross et al., 2021; Sharchilev et al., 2018)	2
	Educational degrees, vocational skill and experience	(Garkavenko et al., 2021; Ross et al., 2021)	2
	3rd-party team score and person ID	(Ghassemi et al., 2020; Sharchilev et al., 2018)	2
	Employees from renowned organizations	(Chen et al., 2021)	1
	Balance/empowerment/competence of the project team	(Yeh and Chen, 2020)	1
Investor	The number of total/distinct investors	(Ferrati et al., 2021; Chen et al., 2021; Kim et al., 2020; Sharchilev et al., 2018) ...	8
	Investor rank by reputation, experience and performance	(Stahl, 2021; Yin et al., 2021; Ferrati et al., 2021; Sharchilev et al., 2018)	4
	VC syndicate (e.g., advantage, diversity and centrality)	(Gastaud et al., 2019; Shin, 2019; Hochberg et al., 2007; Nahata, 2008)	4
	Share and involvement time of each investor	(Sharchilev et al., 2018)	1
Web	Rank/count/duration/bounce rate of website visit	(Garkavenko et al., 2022; Dellermann et al., 2021; Stahl, 2021) ...	5
	The count (aggregated or **timeseries**) of published news	(Yin et al., 2021; Garkavenko et al., 2021; Gastaud et al., 2019; Sharchilev et al., 2018)	4
	Topic or sentiment of **news/articles**	(Garkavenko et al., 2022; Kim et al., 2020; Sharchilev et al., 2018)	3
	Twitter statistics (e.g., followers, tweets and sentiment)	(Garkavenko et al., 2022, 2021; Dellermann et al., 2021)	3
	Count of web pages and domain names	(Garkavenko et al., 2022; Dellermann et al., 2021; Sharchilev et al., 2018)	3
Context	The number of direct competitors	(Allu and Padmanabhuni, 2022; Pasayat and Bhowmick, 2021; Xiang et al., 2012) ...	8
	Funding raised by competitors	(Stahl, 2021; Gastaud et al., 2019)	2
	Per-industry prosperity of the hosting geo-location	(Yin et al., 2021; Gastaud et al., 2019)	2
	Country/state/sector economy and financing env.	(Ross et al., 2021; Yin et al., 2021)	2
	Market/industry size and growth rate	(Allu and Padmanabhuni, 2022)	1
Connection	**The raw company-person-investor graph**	(Allu and Padmanabhuni, 2022; Pasayat and Bhowmick, 2021; Xiang et al., 2012)	3
	Pre-calculated graph features (e.g., betweenness)	(Bonaventura et al., 2020; Liang and Yuan, 2016; Hochberg et al., 2007)	3
Operation/ Planning	Planned revenue model	(Allu and Padmanabhuni, 2022; Dellermann et al., 2021; Bai and Zhao, 2021)	3
	Global exposure and internationalization	(Sharchilev et al., 2018)	1
	Market positioning and go-to-market strategy	(Bai and Zhao, 2021)	1
	Technological surveillance	(Allu and Padmanabhuni, 2022)	1
IP and/ R&D	The number, category and growth of patents	(Kinne and Lenz, 2021; Ferrati et al., 2021; Ross et al., 2021; Kim et al., 2020)	4
	University partnership	(Dellermann et al., 2021)	1
Customer	Customer satisfaction/loyalty	(Chen et al., 2021)	1
	The number of pilot customers	(Dellermann et al., 2021)	1
Financial	Revenue and/or turnover	(Kim et al., 2020; Cao et al., 2022a)	2
M&A	The number of acquisitions	(Ross et al., 2021)	1
Data	The total number of events/records	(Kim et al., 2020)	1

* Common types of customer focus: B2B: business-to-business. B2C: business-to-consumer. B2B2C: business-to-business-to-consumer, where businesses access customers via a 3rd-party.
† Business models include many, such as subscription centric, freemium, cross selling, hidden revenue, no frills, and layer player.
‡ Social capital is a positive product of human interactions, which comprises two aspects: bonding (intra group) and bridging (inter groups). Nowadays, it is increasingly represented by activities on social media and applications (Shi et al., 2021).

Table 1: The feature categories and the commonly adopted features within each categy. Due to limited space, we can not list all publications that adopt the corresponding feature, but the right-most "#ref" column indicates the total number of occurrences for each feature. Most of the features are structured numerical/categorical input, and we use **boldface** to emphasize the unstructured features.

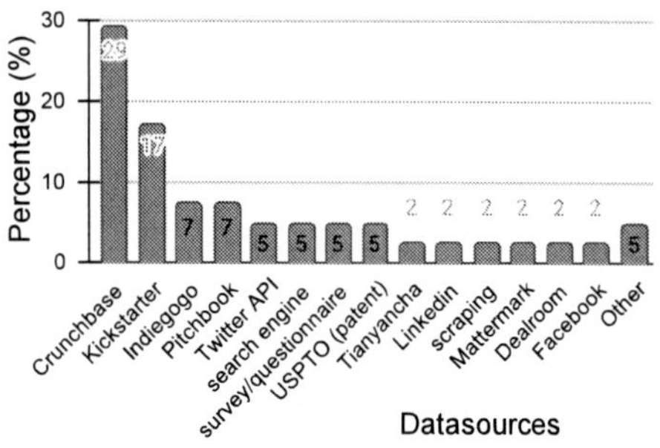

Figure 6: The occurrences of common data sources: **paid** sources are Crunchbase, Pitchbook, Tianyancha, Linkedin, Mattermark, Dealroom; **free** sources are Kickstarter/Indiegogo/scraping, Twitter API, search engines (e.g., Google), USPTO (United States Patent and Trademark Office, Facebook (the pages about startups); **proprietary** data are usually only accessible from investment firms (in "Other" category), governmental/administrative departments or survey/questionnaire.

About dataset size: to understand how many samples (the number of companies) researchers use for training their DL models, we plot the distribution/histogram of dataset size in Figure 8. It shows a median and average size of 35,621 and 107,694 respectively, which is expected to continue to grow.

Intrinsic(independent)→extrinsic(contextual): classically, most factors driving investors' decisions would be only *independent and intrinsic*[9] to the startup, most notably at the expense of *extrinsic and contextualized*[9] features (Gastaud et al., 2019). The community has started steering towards using more context and connection features.

4 Data Split

Splitting the dataset is a mandatory step before training any ML/DL model, yet it is often discussed very lightly (sometimes even neglected) in the literature on startup success prediction. It is generally recommended to divide the dataset into non-overlapping *training* ($\mathbf{x}_{\text{train}}$), *evaluation* ($\mathbf{x}_{\text{eval}}$) and *test* ($\mathbf{x}_{\text{test}}$) subsets. The model will be trained solely on $\mathbf{x}_{\text{train}}$. Hyper-parameters are searched using $\mathbf{x}_{\text{eval}}$. In the simplest form, the training will be run for N times with different hyper-parameters, resulting in N trained models, each of which is evaluated on $\mathbf{x}_{\text{eval}}$. The best performing model on $\mathbf{x}_{\text{eval}}$ should be tested on $\mathbf{x}_{\text{test}}$ before deployment.

4.1 Company-Centric vs. Investor-Centric

To predict the success of startups, the appropriate way to split the dataset is not as straightforward as it appears in ML/DL researches for other domains. We visualize a minimal example in Figure 7 to facilitate our discussion; there are three startups (A, B and C) founded at different dates over the timeline. According to some success criteria (Section 2), A and B are labeled as positive (i.e., promising investing targets: $y^{(A)}=y^{(B)}=1$) some time after they are founded. The majority become unfavourable (e.g., the label of C is $y^{(C)}=0$) to VC, if no sign of success some years after their founding dates.

With a **company-centric** view, one can choose some event types (e.g., seed and pre-A rounds), the dates of which are *feature snapshot dates*. We can then compute one sample using data before each snapshot date. As shown in Figure 7, there are three snapshot dates on the timeline of startup A, leading to three samples (i.e., $\mathbf{x}_1^{(A)}$, $\mathbf{x}_2^{(A)}$ and $\mathbf{x}_3^{(A)}$) that are all labeled positive (i.e., $y_1^{(A)}=y_2^{(A)}=y_3^{(A)}=1$). In a sense, startup A is augmented by generating three ⟨sample, label⟩ pairs: $\langle \mathbf{x}_1^{(A)}, y_1^{(A)} \rangle$, $\langle \mathbf{x}_2^{(A)}, y_2^{(A)} \rangle$ and $\langle \mathbf{x}_3^{(A)}, y_3^{(A)} \rangle$. Similarly, B and C create another four pairs: $\langle \mathbf{x}_1^{(B)}, y_1^{(B)} \rangle$, $\langle \mathbf{x}_2^{(B)}, y_2^{(B)} \rangle$, $\langle \mathbf{x}_1^{(C)}, y_1^{(C)} \rangle$ and $\langle \mathbf{x}_2^{(C)}, y_2^{(C)} \rangle$. The company-centric split will randomly allocate these pairs into one of the sets (training, evaluation or test), as in work such as (Ang et al., 2022; Yeh and Chen, 2020).

With an **investor-centric** view, as in work like (Wu et al., 2022; Ferrati et al., 2021), the feature snapshot dates are randomly sampled (before the corresponding label date), therefore they do not represent any event(s). More importantly, the global timeline is fragmented (from earliest startup founding date to now) into three periods, i.e., training, evaluation and test period, as illustrated in Figure 7. For a startup, the period that its label belongs determines the dataset split it should go to. Applying this rule, we can see (cf. Figure 7) that the three ⟨sample, label⟩ pairs from A should go to the training set; the two pairs from B belong to the test set; and lastly, the two pairs from C will head to the evaluation set. (Sharchilev et al., 2018) claims that **investor-centric view is preferred**, since it better resembles the real-world scenario of how investment professionals predict the success of startups.

4.2 Data Generation Process Matters

When assembling the samples (i.e., $\mathbf{x}_i^{(\cdot)}$ in Figure 7) using data up till the snapshot dates, one should make sure that no future information is leaked into $\mathbf{x}_i^{(\cdot)}$. This requires in-depth understanding of not only the data itself (*know-what*) but also the data generation process (*know-how*), which we found

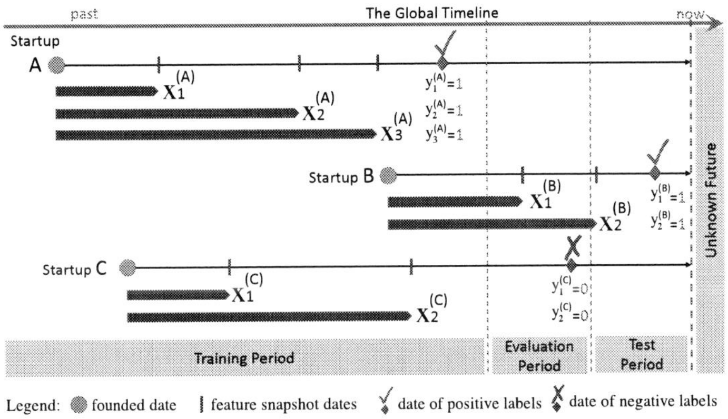

Figure 7: Visualization of investor-centric split using three example startups.

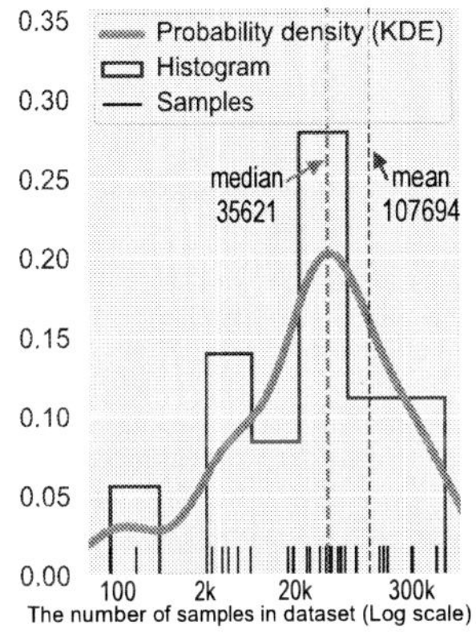

Figure 8: Dataset size distribution.

is seldomly addressed by the literature. We hereby give a concrete example out of many: a startup in the dataset has an annual revenue data point (from BvD[11]) with a timestamp 2020-12-31; but this data point should be ignored when predicting on 2021-06-01. The reason is that fiscal reports (the source of revenue data) often have a delay of about 12 months, causing the 2020-12-31 data point unavailable until (earliest) 2021-12-31. Without examining such matters, the model performance in production may fail catastrophically.

5 Evaluation Strategy

The decision of deploying any model is often made by looking at the evaluation results. To achieve that, some *evaluation metrics* are employed to measure the quality of predictions y by comparing to the ground-truth labels $\hat{y}$. The metric values computed over the evaluation set (i.e., $\mathbf{x}_{\text{eval}}$) are used to determine which model (among many trained using different hyper-parameters) will be deployed for production eventually. This process also fulfills the objective of hyper-parameter search. It has been discussed in Section 4 that the evaluation metrics should also be calculated on the test set $\mathbf{x}_{\text{test}}$ as an indication of the model's generalization capability.

The evaluation metrics adopted in the DL literature include (ordered by their occurrences as shown in Figure 9 with an example citation) *precision* (Zhang et al., 2021), *ROC-AUC* (*area under the receiver operating characteristics*) (Ross et al., 2021), *accuracy* (Bai and Zhao, 2021), *FPR* (*false-positive rate*) (Ghassemi et al., 2020), *TPR* (*true-positive rate*) (Garkavenko et al., 2022), *hit rate* (Allu and Padmanabhuni, 2022), *NDCG* (*normalized discounted cumulative gain*) (Chen et al., 2021), *portfolio simulation* (Yin et al., 2021), *RMSE* (*root mean square deviation*) (Wu et al., 2022), *AUPR* (*area under the precision-recall curve*) (Zhang et al., 2021), *average precision* (Lyu et al., 2021), *confusion matrix* (Ross et al., 2021), *F0.1 score* (Sharchilev et al., 2018), *MAE* (*mean absolute error*) (Wu et al., 2022), *MCC* (*Matthews correlation coefficient*) (Dellermann et al., 2021), *PR* (*precision-recall*) *curve* (Stahl, 2021), and R^2 (Garkavenko et al., 2021).

Most trained models are expected to serve as a decision-support system for VC deal sourcing. Realistically, human professionals are only able to assess a limited amount of startups. Further, because of fund size limitation, investors can only fund a very small fraction of startups (Stahl, 2021). As a result, the **evaluation metric should aim for high-precision** (corresponding to high-certainty and low-recall)[12] (Sharchilev et al., 2018), which explains the popularity of *precision*, *TPR*, *FPR*, *hit rate* and *F0.1 score* in Figure 9.

5.1 Portfolio Simulation

There are four key questions to answer concerning any model trained to facilitate VC deal sourcing: **Q1** What is the expected success ratio (or ROI) of the portfolio (with different sizes) constructed according to model predictions? **Q2** How will the model-driven portfolio perform in relation to the historical records of renowned investment firms? **Q3** Is the model significantly superior than a random policy? **Q4** How far does the model fall be-

[11] Bureau van Dijk: `www.bvdinfo.com`

[12] In the scope of VC deal sourcing, high-precision means the rate of "correct" prediction within the top-N list (i.e., TPR) should be high. According to the typical PR curve, precision tends to be higher for smaller N; yet recall suffers from it.

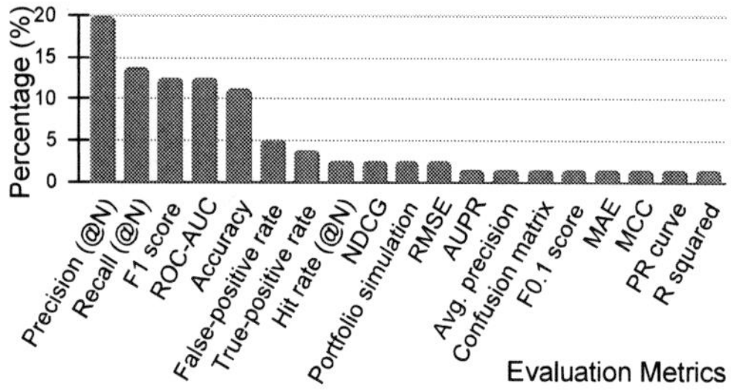

Figure 9: The distribution of adopted evaluation metrics. The notation "@N" implies the corresponding metric is calculated over a top-N list. Precision, hit rate, and F0.1 score are popular metrics with a focus of high-precision. Portfolio simulation suited particularly well to startup success prediction, while others are general-purpose metrics for evaluating ML/DL models.

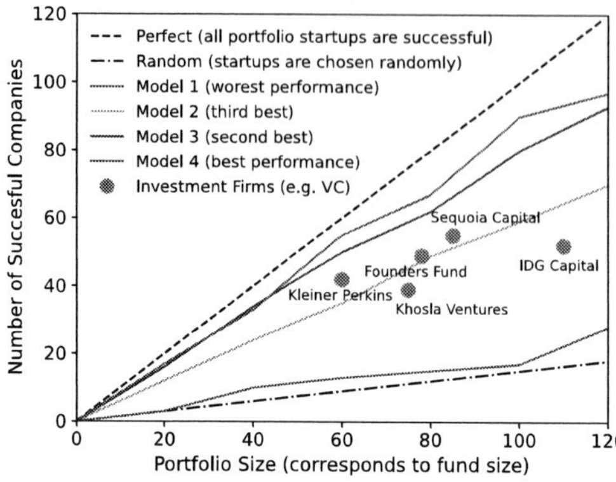

Figure 10: Portfolio simulation. The trained DL model is used to form portfolios of size $k \in \{20, 40, \ldots, 120\}$ (x-axis); the number of eventually successful startups is plotted against the corresponding k, resulting in a performance curve (cf. the colored curves). The perfect/random cases (dashed lines) and performance of investment firms (red dots) can be plotted as well for comparison. It is adapted from (Halvardsson, 2023).

hind a theoretical perfect portfolio with 100% success ratio? Answering all questions simultaneously using any single general-purpose ML/DL metric is challenging and sometimes far-fetched. To that end, some recent works (Ross et al., 2021; Yin et al., 2021) (though still far from a wide adoption according to Figure 9) have emerged proposing to **evaluate via portfolio simulations**. Recall that in Section 4, we recommended the investor-centric dataset split demonstrated in Figure 7. With that split, we make the trained models to predict the conditional success probability of each startup in evaluation/test subset, using the end date of training period as the feature snapshot date. Then, we construct an investment portfolio of size k by selecting top-k startups with the highest predicted probabilities. As an indication of portfolio performance, we count the number of startups that eventually obtain a positive label. The portfolio size k should be varied, so that we can plot one performance curve (the four colored curves in Figure 10) for each model. To answer **Q1**, a steeper curve corresponds to a better model. The performance of a perfect model is a diagonal line, implying all portfolio startups will succeed. To address **Q2**, one just needs to measure the angular distance to diagonal. The simplest possible model is a random policy, the performance of which is represented by the flattest straight-dashed line in Figure 10; the angular distance between this "random" line to any model's curve answers **Q3**. Finally, the historical fund performance of investment firms can be easily plotted as individual points, the vertical distances from which to models' curves give insights for **Q4**. In practice, the investment firms are more constrained than simulation: they can not invest in any startup due to many reasons like founders preference, portfolio conflict and investment mandate. This constraint becomes more prominent when investors compete to invest in startups with great success potential.

6 Conclusion

Finding the rare unicorn startups is a challenging task, hence often regarded as the holy grail for early-stage investors like Venture Capital firms. To avoid entirely relying on human domain expertise and intuition, investors usually employ data-driven approaches to forecast the success probability of startups. The rapid growth of data volume and variety makes deep learning (DL) a potentially superior approach to address this task. To the best of our knowledge till this date, there has not been any comprehensive survey on this topic. According to our synthesis of carefully selected literature, the innovation mostly lies in how an off-the-shelf DL model is applied, rather than in the model itself. So we focus on summarizing our understanding and learning concerning four key aspects:

- Optimization target: consider a mixture of criteria, while prioritizing the short-term event.
- Feature selection: scale the dataset with multi-modal, unstructured, free and extrinsic features.
- Data split: apply the investor-centric split with the knowledge of data generation process.
- Evaluation strategy: pick the metrics aiming for high-precision and perform portfolio simulation.

Finally, authors' outlook of DL adoption in startup success prediction is three fold: (1) more easy-to-use software tools will be developed to promote good practices and lower the barrier to entry; (2) the majority of the available data is unlabeled and small scaled, hence more data/label efficient DL models will be proposed; (3) data privacy and model security will gain more emphasis in the coming years.

Acknowledgments

We are especially grateful to Alex Patow, Anton Ask Åström, Armin Catovic, Ashley Lundström, Dhiana Deva, Drew McCornack, Richard Stahl and Sofie Grant from EQT Group for the discussion and feedback on a more comprehensive and detailed version of this study (Cao et al., 2022b). We also thank the interest and input from Celine Xu (H&M×AI & McKinsey), Daniel Wroblewski (CPPIB), Fenni Kang (AntAlpha & Barclays), Gustaf Halvardsson (KTH & EQT), Rockie Yang (Knock Data) and Wenbing Huang (Tsinghua Uni.). This work is also generally supported by the entire EQT Motherbrain team.

References

Zoltan J Acs and Laszlo Szerb. 2007. Entrepreneurship, economic growth and public policy. *Small business economics*, 28(2):109–122.

Ramakrishna Allu and Venkata Nageswara Rao Padmanabhuni. 2022. Predicting the success rate of a start-up using lstm with a swish activation function. *Journal of Control and Decision*, 9(3):355–363.

Yu Qian Ang, Andrew Chia, and Soroush Saghafian. 2022. Using machine learning to demystify startups' funding, post-money valuation, and success. In *Innovative Technology at the Interface of Finance and Operations*, pages 271–296. Springer.

John Baer and Sharon S McKool. 2014. The gold standard for assessing creativity. *International Journal of Quality Assurance in Engineering and Technology Education (IJQAETE)*, 3(1):81–93.

Sarah Bai and Yijun Zhao. 2021. Startup investment decision support: Application of venture capital scorecards using machine learning approaches. *Systems*, 9(3):55.

Francisco Ramadas da Silva Ribeiro Bento. 2018. *Predicting start-up success with machine learning*. Ph.D. thesis, Universidade NOVA de Lisboa.

Steve Blank. 2013. Why the lean start-up changes everything. *Harvard business review*, 91(5):63–72.

Moreno Bonaventura, Valerio Ciotti, Pietro Panzarasa, Silvia Liverani, Lucas Lacasa, and Vito Latora. 2020. Predicting success in the worldwide start-up network. *Scientific Reports*, 10(1):1–6.

Lele Cao, Sonja Horn, Vilhelm von Ehrenheim, Richard Anselmo Stahl, and Henrik Landgren. 2022a. Simulation-informed revenue extrapolation with confidence estimate for scaleup companies using scarce time series data. In *Proceedings of the 31st ACM International Conference on Information and Knowledge Management (CIKM '22), October 17–21, 2022, Atlanta, GA, USA*, page 12 pages, New York, NY, USA. Association for Computing Machinery (ACM).

Lele Cao, Vilhelm von Ehrenheim, Sebastian Krakowski, Xiaoxue Li, and Alexandra Lutz. 2022b. Using deep learning to find the next unicorn: A practical synthesis. *arXiv preprint arXiv:2210.14195*.

Miao Chen, Chao Wang, Chuan Qin, Tong Xu, Jianhui Ma, Enhong Chen, and Hui Xiong. 2021. A trend-aware investment target recommendation system with heterogeneous graph. In *Intl. Joint Conf. on Neural Networks*, pages 1–8.

Chaoran Cheng, Fei Tan, Xiurui Hou, and Zhi Wei. 2019. Success prediction on crowdfunding with multimodal deep learning. In *International Joint Conference on Artificial Intelligence*, pages 2158–2164.

Sergey Chernenko, Josh Lerner, and Yao Zeng. 2021. Mutual funds as venture capitalists? evidence from unicorns. *The Review of Financial Studies*, 34(5):2362–2410.

Francesco Corea. 2019. AI and venture capital. In *An introduction to data*, pages 101–110. Springer.

Douglas Cumming and Na Dai. 2010. Local bias in venture capital investments. *Journal of empirical finance*, 17(3):362–380.

Dominik Dellermann, Nikolaus Lipusch, Philipp Ebel, Karl Michael Popp, and Jan Marco Leimeister. 2021. Finding the unicorn: Predicting early stage startup success through a hybrid intelligence method. In *International Conference on Information Systems*.

Francesco Ferrati, Haiquan Chen, and Moreno Muffatto. 2021. A deep learning model for startups evaluation using time series analysis. In *European Conf. on Innovation and Entrepreneurship*, page 311. Academic Conferences limited.

Mariia Garkavenko, Eric Gaussier, Hamid Mirisaee, Cédric Lagnier, and Agnès Guerraz. 2022. Where do you want to invest? predicting startup funding from freely, publicly available web info. *arXiv preprint arXiv:2204.06479*.

Mariia Garkavenko, Hamid Mirisaee, Eric Gaussier, Agnès Guerraz, and Cédric Lagnier. 2021. Valuation of startups: A machine learning perspective. In *European Conference on Information Retrieval*, pages 176–189. Springer.

Clement Gastaud, Theophile Carniel, and Jean-Michel Dalle. 2019. The varying importance of extrinsic factors in the success of startup fundraising: competition at early-stage and networks at growth-stage. *arXiv preprint arXiv:1906.03210*.

M Ghassemi, C Song, and T Alhanai. 2020. The automated venture capitalist: Data and methods to predict the fate of startup ventures. In *AAAI Workshop on Knowledge Discovery from Unstructured Data in Financial Services*.

Paul A Gompers, Will Gornall, Steven N Kaplan, and Ilya A Strebulaev. 2020. How do venture capitalists make decisions? *Journal of Financial Economics*, 135(1):169–190.

Gustaf Halvardsson. 2023. A transformer-based scoring approach for startup success prediction. Master's thesis, KTH Royal Institute of Technology & EQT Partners.

Yael V Hochberg, Alexander Ljungqvist, and Yang Lu. 2007. Whom you know matters: Venture capital networks and investment performance. *The Journal of Finance*, 62(1):251–301.

Sonja Horn. 2021. Deep learning models as decision support in venture capital investments: Temporal representations in employee growth forecasting of startup companies. Master's thesis, KTH Royal Institute of Technology & EQT Partners.

Ari Hyytinen, Mika Pajarinen, and Petri Rouvinen. 2015. Does innovativeness reduce startup survival rates? *Journal of business venturing*, 30(4):564–581.

Ulrich Kaiser and Johan M Kuhn. 2020. The value of publicly available, textual and non-textual information for startup performance prediction. *Journal of Business Venturing Insights*, 14:e00179.

Jermain C Kaminski and Christian Hopp. 2020. Predicting outcomes in crowdfunding campaigns with textual, visual, and linguistic signals. *Small Business Economics*, 55(3):627–649.

Hyoung J Kim, Tae San Kim, and So Y Sohn. 2020. Recommendation of startups as technology cooperation candidates from the perspectives of similarity and potential: A deep learning approach. *Decision Support Systems*, 130:113229.

Jongho Kim and Jiyong Park. 2017. Does facial expression matter even online? an empirical analysis of facial expression of emotion and crowdfunding success. In *International Conference on Information Systems*.

Jan Kinne and David Lenz. 2021. Predicting innovative firms using web mining and deep learning. *PloS One*, 16(4):e0249071.

SeungHun Lee, KangHee Lee, and Hyun-chul Kim. 2018. Content-based success prediction of crowdfunding campaigns: A deep learning approach. In *Companion of the ACM Conference on Computer Supported Cooperative Work and Social Computing*, pages 193–196.

Yuxian E Liang and Soe-Tsyr D Yuan. 2016. Predicting investor funding behavior using Crunchbase social network features. *Internet Research: Electronic Networking Applications and Policy*, 26(1):74–100.

Robert N Lussier and Claudia E Halabi. 2010. A three-country comparison of the business success versus failure prediction model. *Journal of Small Business Management*, 48(3):360–377.

Robert N Lussier and Sanja Pfeifer. 2001. A crossnational prediction model for business success. *Journal of Small Business Management*, 39(3):228–239.

Shiwei Lyu, Shuai Ling, Kaihao Guo, Haipeng Zhang, Kunpeng Zhang, Suting Hong, Qing Ke, and Jinjie Gu. 2021. Graph neural network based VC investment success prediction. *arXiv preprint arXiv:2105.11537*.

Max Marmer, Bjoern L Herrmann, Ertan Dogrultan, Ron Berman, Cuck Eesley, and Steve Blank. 2011. Startup genome report extra: premature scaling. *Startup Genome*, 10:1–56.

Rajarishi Nahata. 2008. Venture capital reputation and investment performance. *Journal of Financial Econ.*, 90(2):127–151.

Ajit Kumar Pasayat and Bhaskar Bhowmick. 2021. An evolutionary algorithm-based framework for determining crucial features contributing to the success of a start-up. In *IEEE Technology and Engineering Management Conference-Europe (TEMSCON-EUR)*, pages 1–6. IEEE.

Ajit Kumar Pasayat, Bhaskar Bhowmick, and Ritik Roy. 2020. Factors responsible for the success of a startup: A meta-analytic approach. *IEEE Transactions on Engineering Management*.

Greg Ross, Sanjiv Das, Daniel Sciro, and Hussain Raza. 2021. CapitalVX: A machine learning model for startup selection and exit prediction. *The Journal of Finance and Data Science*, 7:94–114.

José Santisteban, David Mauricio, Orestes Cachay, et al. 2021. Critical success factors for technology-based startups. *International Journal of Entrepreneurship and Small Business*, 42(4):397–421.

Scott Shane. 2012. The importance of angel investing in financing the growth of entrepreneurial ventures. *The Quarterly Journal of Finance*, 2(02):1250009.

Boris Sharchilev, Michael Roizner, Andrey Rumyantsev, Denis Ozornin, Pavel Serdyukov, and Maarten de Rijke. 2018. Web-based startup success prediction. In *International Conference on Information and Knowledge Management*, pages 2283–2291.

Jiatong Shi, Kunlin Yang, Wei Xu, and Mingming Wang. 2021. Leveraging deep learning with audio analytics to predict the success of crowdfunding projects. *The Journal of Supercomputing*, 77(7):7833–7853.

Sang Yoon Shin. 2019. Network advantage's effect on exit performance: examining venture capital's inter-organizational networks. *International Entrepreneurship and Management Journal*, 15(1):21–42.

Eulalia Skawińska and Romuald I Zalewski. 2020. Success factors of startups in the EU - a comparative study. *Sustainability*, 12(19):8200.

Arvind Srinivasan et al. 2020. An ensemble deep learning approach to explore the impact of enticement, engagement and experience in reward based crowdfunding. Working paper, Department of Computer Science and Engineering, SRM Institute of Science and Technology.

Richard Hermann Anselmo Stahl. 2021. Leveraging time-series signals for multi-stage startup success prediction. Master's thesis, ETH Zurich & EQT Partners.

Zhe Tang, Yi Yang, Wen Li, Defu Lian, and Lixin Duan. 2022. Deep cross-attention network for crowdfunding success prediction. *IEEE Transactions on Multimedia*.

David Teten, Adham AbdelFattah, Koen Bremer, and Gyorgy Buslig. 2013. The lower-risk startup: how venture vapitalists increase the odds of startup success. *The Journal of Private Equity*, 16(2):7–19.

Cemre Ünal and Ioana Ceasu. 2019. A machine learning approach towards startup success prediction. IRTG 1792 Discussion Paper 2019-022, Berlin.

Ashish Vaswani, Noam Shazeer, Niki Parmar, Jakob Uszkoreit, Llion Jones, Aidan N Gomez, Łukasz Kaiser, and Illia Polosukhin. 2017. Attention is all you need. *Advances in neural information processing systems*, 30.

Likang Wu, Zhi Li, Hongke Zhao, Qi Liu, and Enhong Chen. 2022. Estimating fund-raising performance for start-up projects from a market graph perspective. *Pattern Recognition*, 121:108204.

Guang Xiang, Zeyu Zheng, Miaomiao Wen, Jason Hong, Carolyn Rose, and Chao Liu. 2012. A supervised approach to predict company acquisition with factual and topic features using profiles and news articles on TechCrunch. In *Proceedings of the International AAAI Conference on Web and Social Media*, volume 6, pages 607–610.

Jen-Yin Yeh and Chi-Hua Chen. 2020. A machine learning approach to predict the success of crowdfunding fintech project. *Journal of Enterprise Information Management*.

Dafei Yin, Jing Li, and Gaosheng Wu. 2021. Solving the data sparsity problem in predicting the success of the startups with machine learning methods. *arXiv preprint arXiv:2112.07985*.

Pi-Fen Yu, Fu-Ming Huang, Chuan Yang, Yu-Hsin Liu, Zi-Yi Li, and Cheng-Hung Tsai. 2018. Prediction of crowdfunding project success with deep learning. In *International Conference on E-Business Engineering*, pages 1–8. IEEE.

Shengming Zhang, Hao Zhong, Zixuan Yuan, and Hui Xiong. 2021. Scalable heterogeneous graph neural networks for predicting high-potential early-stage startups. In *ACM SIGKDD Conference on Knowledge Discovery and Data Mining*, pages 2202–2211.

Breaking the Bank with ChatGPT: Few-Shot Text Classification for Finance

Lefteris Loukas[1,2] and **Ilias Stogiannidis**[1,2] and **Prodromos Malakasiotis**[2] and **Stavros Vassos**[1]
[1]Helvia.ai
[2]Department of Informatics, Athens University of Economics and Business, Greece
{lefteris.loukas, ilias.stogiannidis, stavros}@helvia.ai

Abstract

We propose the use of conversational GPT models for easy and quick few-shot text classification in the financial domain using the Banking77 dataset. Our approach involves in-context learning with GPT-3.5 and GPT-4, which minimizes the technical expertise required and eliminates the need for expensive GPU computing while yielding quick and accurate results. Additionally, we fine-tune other pre-trained, masked language models with SetFit, a recent contrastive learning technique, to achieve state-of-the-art results both in full-data and few-shot settings. Our findings show that querying GPT-3.5 and GPT-4 can outperform fine-tuned, non-generative models even with fewer examples. However, subscription fees associated with these solutions may be considered costly for small organizations. Lastly, we find that generative models perform better on the given task when shown representative samples selected by a human expert rather than when shown random ones. We conclude that a) our proposed methods offer a practical solution for few-shot tasks in datasets with limited label availability, and b) our state-of-the-art results can inspire future work in the area.

1 Introduction

Virtual agents have become increasingly popular in recent years, with conversational models like GPT-3.5 (Ouyang et al., 2022) and its successor ChatGPT[1] garnering attention worldwide. While the intent detection task, as seen in the customer assistance domain, has been a well-known problem in academia for many years, it is under-explored in the financial industry due to the limited availability of datasets (Galitsky and Ilvovsky, 2019; Casanueva et al., 2020). This study aims to bridge the gap between the financial industry and the latest developments in academia.

Financial Intent	Label
It declined my transfer.	Declined Transfer
How can I trade currencies with this app?	Exchange Via App
How do your exchange rates factor in?	Exchange Rate
I just topped up, and the app denied it.	Top-up Failed
There has been a red flag on my top up.	Top-up Failed
Tell me how to replace my expired card.	Card About to Expire
...	...
My card is needed soon.	Card Delivery Estimate
What caused my transfer to fail?	Failed Transfer

Table 1: Example financial intents and their labels from the Banking77 dataset. In total, there are 77 different labels in the dataset.

In this paper, we use Banking77 (Casanueva et al., 2020), a real-life dataset of customer service intents and their classification labels. Unlike many datasets in the intent detection literature, Banking77 covers the niche of a single domain, contains a large number of labels (77), and many of the classes have tight overlaps between them, making it perfect for a business use-case scenario. Previous works have focused on fixing labeling errors (Ying and Thomas, 2022) or exploring pre-training intent representations (Li et al., 2022), which require a high level of technical expertise.

First, we demonstrate how well (and quickly) we can solve a few-shot financial text classification task using conversational GPT models. Secondly, we fine-tune other, non-generative, pre-trained models, based on MPNet (Song et al., 2020), with SetFit (Tunstall et al., 2022), a recent contrastive learning technique developed by HuggingFace which minimizes the time and samples needed to fine-tune a pre-trained model.

Our contributions include demonstrating a clever use of in-context learning with GPT-3.5 and GPT-4 to solve a challenging intent classification task. This solution is a) especially handy when rapid and accurate results are needed for few-shot tasks in financial datasets with limited label availability, and b) requires no GPUs and minimizes the need for technical expertise, which is often lacking in the banking industry. We also show that in-context

[1]https://chat.openai.com/

Proceedings of the Joint Workshop of the 5th Financial Technology and Natural Language Processing (FinNLP) and 2nd Multimodal AI For Financial Forecasting (Muffin), Macao, August 20, 2023.

learning can perform better than fine-tuned masked language models (MLMs), even when presented with fewer examples. However, such solutions may be costly for small organizations due to subscription fees and often have limited token capacity, which only allows us to show the model 3 samples, for example. Lastly, we report state-of-the-art results by fine-tuning pre-trained models both when using the whole training dataset (Full-Data setting) and in a few-shot setting where only 10 training instances per class were used (10-shot setting) by employing SetFit and selecting representative samples after hiring a human expert.

2 Related Work

2.1 Studies on Banking77

Previous research papers provide important insights into improving the performance of financial intent classification models on the Banking77 dataset through the correction of label errors, the pre-training of intent representations, and the use of unattended tokens and example-driven training to improve utterance classification models. Initially, Casanueva et al. (2020) established a baseline accuracy of 93.66% by fine-tuning BERT (Devlin et al., 2019) for the Full-Data setting, and an 85.19% for the 10-shot setting by using a Universal Sentence Encoder (Cer et al., 2018) and efficient Transformer representations (Henderson et al., 2020).

Ying and Thomas (2022) aimed at reducing label errors in the Banking77 dataset through a confident learning framework (Northcutt et al., 2017, 2021) and a cosine similarity approach. Their classifiers achieved an 88.2% accuracy and 87.8% F1-Score on the original dataset, increasing to 92.4% accuracy and 92.0% F1-Score on the refined dataset.

Li et al. (2022) demonstrated that pre-training intent representations can improve intent classification, achieving an 82.76% accuracy and 87.35% Macro-F1 Score on the Banking77 benchmark. The strategy involved prefix-tuning and only fine-tuning the last layer of an LLM.

Lastly, Mehri and Eric (2021) proposed to enhance text classification models in dialog systems using observer tokens and example-driven training. The combination of these approaches resulted in an 85.95% accuracy in the 10-shot setting and 93.83% in the Full-Data setting.

Banking77 Statistics	Train	Test
Number of examples	10,003	3,080
Minimum length in characters	13	13
Average length in characters	59.5	54.2
Maximum length in characters	433	368
Minimum word count	2	2
Average word count	11.9	10.9
Maximum word count	79	69

Table 2: Dataset statistics for the Banking77 dataset. The dataset contains 10,003 examples for training and 3,080 examples for testing, with 77 different intents. Text length statistics are also provided.

2.2 Few-Shot Text Classification

Learning from just a few training instances is crucial when data collection is difficult. Interestingly, the predominant training paradigm of fine-tuning LMs exhibits poor performance in few-shot scenarios (Dodge et al., 2020), while the growing size of LMs often makes their use in this paradigm prohibitive. An alternative is to use in-context learning (Brown et al., 2020), where a generative LLM is prompted with a context and is asked to solve NLP tasks without any fine-tuning. The context typically contains a short description of the task, a few demonstrations (the context), and the instance to be classified. The intuition behind in-context learning is that the LLM has already learned several tasks during its pre-training and the prompt tries to locate the appropriate one (Reynolds and McDonell, 2021). Selecting the appropriate prompt is not trivial, though; LLMs are unable to understand the meaning of the prompt (Webson and Pavlick, 2022). This phenomenon was somewhat alleviated by fine-tuning LLMs to follow human instructions (Ouyang et al., 2022; OpenAI, 2023). Nonetheless, in-context learning is still correlated with term frequencies encountered during pre-training (Razeghi et al., 2022), while instruct-based LLMs like GPT-3.5 and GPT-4 carry the biases of the human annotators that provided the training instructions. To further deal with the difficulties of in-context learning, prompt-tuning has emerged as a promising research direction (Lester et al., 2021; Zhou et al., 2021; Jia et al., 2022).

3 Task and Dataset

Intent detection is a special case of text classification, and it has a crucial role in task-oriented conversational systems in various domains. It reflects the complexity of real-world financial and commercial systems which can be attributed to the partially overlapping intent categories, the need for fine-grained decisions, and the usual lack of data in finance (Casanueva et al., 2020; Loukas et al., 2021, 2022; Zavitsanos et al., 2022).

However, publicly available intent detection datasets are limited, and existing datasets oversimplify the task and do not reflect the complexity of real-world industrial systems (Braun et al., 2017; Coucke et al., 2018). Following the recent trends towards building robust datasets for industry-ready systems (Larson et al., 2019; Liu et al., 2019a, 2021), Banking77 (Casanueva et al., 2020) was created by PolyAI[2] as part of their study on a new intent classifier using pre-trained dual sentence encoders based on fixed Universal Sentence Encoders (Cer et al., 2018) and ConveRT (Henderson et al., 2020). In contrast to other multi-domain and broad-intent datasets, which may not capture the full complexity of each domain, Banking77 is a single-domain dataset that contains a large number (77) of fine-grained intents related to banking. Casanueva et al. believe that the dataset's single-domain focus and the large number of intents make the intent detection task more realistic and challenging. However, some intent categories partially overlap with others, requiring fine-grained decisions that cannot rely solely on the semantics of individual words, indicating the tasks's difficulty.

The dataset comprises 13,083 annotated customer service queries labeled with 77 intents and is split into two subsets: train (10,003 examples) and test (3,080 samples) (Table 2). The label distribution is heavily imbalanced in the training subset (Figure 1), demonstrating the challenge in developing classifiers in the Full-Data setting.

4 Methodology

4.1 In-Context Learning

For in-context learning, we use **GPT-3.5** (Ouyang et al., 2022) and **GPT-4** (OpenAI, 2023), which are based on the Generative Pre-trained Transformer (GPT) (Radford et al., 2018, 2019) and further trained with Reinforcement Learning from Human Preferences (RLHF) (Christiano et al., 2017) to follow instructions. GPT-3.5 is a 175B-parameter model able to consume a context o 4,096 tokens, while GPT-4 is a multi-modal model able to consume 32,768 tokens.

4.2 Fine-tuning MLMs

MPNet (Song et al., 2020) is a family of models based on the transformer architecture (Vaswani et al., 2017; Devlin et al., 2019), which adopts a novel pre-training objective that leverages the dependency among predicted tokens through permuted language modeling and takes auxiliary position information as input. MPNet is pre-trained on 160GB text corpora and outperforms other models like BERT (Devlin et al., 2019), XLNet (Yang et al., 2019), and RoBERTa (Liu et al., 2019b) on various downstream tasks. We use a variation of MPNet, establishing it as a prominent method for our task. We use two variants of MPNet, dubbed **S-MPNet-v2**[3] and **P-MPNet-v2**.[4] Both variants were trained to identify similarities between pairs of texts which we believe allows the model to learn representations that encapsulate the more salient semantic details of the texts. Also, P-MPNet-v2 was trained with a more strict objective than S-MPNet-v2, which required both texts in the pair to have the exact same meaning.

4.3 Few-Shot Contrastive Learning

SetFit (Tunstall et al., 2022) is a few-shot learning methodology that fine-tunes a pre-trained Sentence Transformer (like S-MPNet-v2) on a small number of text pairs with contrastive learning (Chen et al., 2020). Tunstall et al. showed that using SetFit and 8 training examples has comparable performance to training models on the complete dataset.

4.4 Human Expert Annotation

Casanueva et al. (2020) identified class overlaps during the creation of Banking77. To address these challenges, we curated a subset of Banking77 for few-shot text classification with the help of a human expert who reviewed a sample of 10 examples per class and selected the top 3 examples based on their relevance to the intent they represent. This approach provided a light curation that helped avoid overlaps and ensured that each example was highly relevant to its intended intent. We expect these training instances to lead to better performance than randomly selecting training instances per class in the few-shot setting.

[2] https://github.com/PolyAI-LDN/task-specific-datasets

[3] https://huggingface.co/sentence-transformers/all-mpnet-base-v2

[4] https://huggingface.co/sentence-transformers/paraphrase-mpnet-base-v2

5 Experimental Setup

Fine-tuning: For all of our methods, we use TensorFlow (Abadi et al., 2015) and HuggingFace (Wolf et al., 2020). For the Few-shot Experiments, we use SetFit following the developers' recommended practises.[5]

Prompt Engineering: We experimented with different prompt settings, as found in Appendix B.

In-context Learning: We utilize the OpenAI API when employing GPT-3.5.[6] Due to maximum token limitations, we use the 1-Shot setting for GPT-3.5 and the 3-shot setting for GPT-4. The prompt we use can be broken down into three parts. The first contains the description of the task and the available classes, the second provides a few examples, and the third presents the text to be classified. The prompt can be found in the Appendix A.

Note that although models like GPT-3.5 or GPT-4 can provide a quick solution without the need for technical expertise, they come at a cost as they are only accessed behind a paywall. Our experiments cost around 60$ when using GPT-3.5 ($0.002 per 1K tokens) and 1,480$ when using GPT-4 ($0.03 per 1K tokens for the 8K context model).[7]

6 Results

To understand the model's performance, we report micro-F1 (μ-F_1) and macro-F1 (m-F_1). Table 3 shows that S-MPNet-v2 achieves competitive results across all few-shot settings using SetFit. When trained on only 3 samples, it achieves scores of 76.3 μ-F_1 and 75.6 m-F_1. As we increase the number of samples, the performance improves, reaching a 91.2 micro-F1 and 91.3 macro-F1 score with 20 samples. This is only 3 percentage points (pp) lower than fine-tuning the model with all the data. Lastly, S-MPNet-v2 outperforms the previous state-of-the-art (Mehri and Eric, 2021), both in the 10-shot setting (by 2.2 pp) and in the Full-Data setting (by 0.2 pp). P-MPNet-v2 has a similar but slightly worse behavior than S-MPNet-v2.

GPT-3.5 achieves competitive results despite that it is presented with only 1 sample per class (either representative or random). It outperforms S-MPNet-v2 and P-MPNet-v2 by a large margin (over 17 pp) in the 1-shot setting, while being comparable in the 3-shot setting. As expected, using our human-curated representative samples leads to better in-context learning results. GPT-4 also shows potential for few-shot classification, outperforming all other models on the 3-shot setting by more than 6 pp. Similarly to GPT-3.5, its performance drops substantially (approximately 9 pp) when trained on random samples as opposed to when trained on the human-curated representative ones.

Methods	Setting	μ-F_1	m-F_1
Mehri and Eric (2021)	Full-Data	93.8	NA
Mehri and Eric (2021)	10-shot	85.8	NA
Ying and Thomas (2022)	Full-Data	NA	92.0
S-MPNet-v2 (ours)	Full-Data	**94.0**	**93.9**
P-MPNet-v2 (ours)	Full-Data	93.0	93.0
S-MPNet-v2	1-shot	57.4	55.9
P-MPNet-v2	1-shot	50.6	48.7
GPT-3.5 (representative samples)	1-shot	**75.2**	**74.3**
GPT-3.5 (random samples)	1-shot	74.0	72.3
S-MPNet-v2	3-shot	76.3	75.6
P-MPNet-v2	3-shot	71.4	70.9
GPT-4 (representative samples)	3-shot	**83.1**	**82.7**
GPT-4 (random samples)	3-shot	74.2	73.7
S-MPNet-v2	5-shot	83.5	83.3
S-MPNet-v2	10-shot	88.0	87.9
S-MPNet-v2	15-shot	90.6	90.5
S-MPNet-v2	20-shot	91.2	91.3
P-MPNet-v2	5-shot	79.2	79.1
P-MPNet-v2	10-shot	85.7	85.8
P-MPNet-v2	15-shot	88.4	88.4
P-MPNet-v2	20-shot	90.1	90.0

Table 3: Classification results for all models on the test data, with N-Shot indicating the number of samples used during training. All MPNet variants are fine-tuned without the `SetFit` method on the Full-Data setting.

7 Conclusion

We presented a few-shot text classification study on the financial domain. Experimenting with Banking77, a financial intent classification dataset, we showed that in-context learning with conversational LLMs can be a straightforward solution when one needs fast and accurate results in few-shot settings. In addition, we demonstrated that generative LLMs, like GPT-3.5 and GPT-4, can perform better than MLM models, even with fewer examples. While LLMs minimize the technical expertise needed or omit GPU training times, they can be considered costly for small organizations, given that LLMs can be only accessed behind a paywall (approximately 1,600$ for GPT-3.5 and GPT-4). On the other side, by fine-tuning S-MPNet-v2 with SetFit, we surpassed the previous state-of-the-art in the 10-shot setting by 2 pp. The same model also achieved state-of-the-art results in the Full-Data setting with standard fine-tuning.

[5] `https://github.com/huggingface/setfit`

[6] We use the `gpt-3.5-turbo` variant.

[7] `https://openai.com/pricing`

References

Martín Abadi, Ashish Agarwal, Paul Barham, Eugene Brevdo, Zhifeng Chen, Craig Citro, Greg S. Corrado, Andy Davis, Jeffrey Dean, Matthieu Devin, Sanjay Ghemawat, Ian Goodfellow, Andrew Harp, Geoffrey Irving, Michael Isard, Yangqing Jia, Rafal Jozefowicz, Lukasz Kaiser, Manjunath Kudlur, Josh Levenberg, Dandelion Mané, Rajat Monga, Sherry Moore, Derek Murray, Chris Olah, Mike Schuster, Jonathon Shlens, Benoit Steiner, Ilya Sutskever, Kunal Talwar, Paul Tucker, Vincent Vanhoucke, Vijay Vasudevan, Fernanda Viégas, Oriol Vinyals, Pete Warden, Martin Wattenberg, Martin Wicke, Yuan Yu, and Xiaoqiang Zheng. 2015. TensorFlow: Large-scale machine learning on heterogeneous systems. Software available from tensorflow.org.

Daniel Braun, Adrian Hernandez Mendez, Florian Matthes, and Manfred Langen. 2017. Evaluating natural language understanding services for conversational question answering systems. In *Proceedings of the 18th Annual SIGdial Meeting on Discourse and Dialogue*, pages 174–185, Saarbrücken, Germany. Association for Computational Linguistics.

Tom B. Brown, Benjamin Mann, Nick Ryder, Melanie Subbiah, Jared Kaplan, Prafulla Dhariwal, Arvind Neelakantan, Pranav Shyam, Girish Sastry, Amanda Askell, Sandhini Agarwal, Ariel Herbert-Voss, Gretchen Krueger, Tom Henighan, Rewon Child, Aditya Ramesh, Daniel M. Ziegler, Jeffrey Wu, Clemens Winter, Christopher Hesse, Mark Chen, Eric Sigler, Mateusz Litwin, Scott Gray, Benjamin Chess, Jack Clark, Christopher Berner, Sam McCandlish, Alec Radford, Ilya Sutskever, and Dario Amodei. 2020. Language models are few-shot learners. In *Proceedings of the 34th International Conference on Neural Information Processing Systems*, NIPS'20, Red Hook, NY, USA. Curran Associates Inc.

Iñigo Casanueva, Tadas Temčinas, Daniela Gerz, Matthew Henderson, and Ivan Vulić. 2020. Efficient intent detection with dual sentence encoders. In *Proceedings of the 2nd Workshop on Natural Language Processing for Conversational AI*, pages 38–45, Online. Association for Computational Linguistics.

Daniel Cer, Yinfei Yang, Sheng-yi Kong, Nan Hua, Nicole Limtiaco, Rhomni St. John, Noah Constant, Mario Guajardo-Cespedes, Steve Yuan, Chris Tar, Brian Strope, and Ray Kurzweil. 2018. Universal sentence encoder for English. In *Proceedings of the 2018 Conference on Empirical Methods in Natural Language Processing: System Demonstrations*, pages 169–174, Brussels, Belgium. Association for Computational Linguistics.

Ting Chen, Simon Kornblith, Mohammad Norouzi, and Geoffrey Hinton. 2020. A simple framework for contrastive learning of visual representations. In *Proceedings of the 37th International Conference on Machine Learning*, ICML'20. JMLR.org.

Paul F Christiano, Jan Leike, Tom Brown, Miljan Martic, Shane Legg, and Dario Amodei. 2017. Deep reinforcement learning from human preferences. In *Advances in Neural Information Processing Systems*, volume 30. Curran Associates, Inc.

Alice Coucke, Alaa Saade, Adrien Ball, Théodore Bluche, Alexandre Caulier, David Leroy, Clément Doumouro, Thibault Gisselbrecht, Francesco Caltagirone, Thibaut Lavril, Maël Primet, and Joseph Dureau. 2018. Snips voice platform: an embedded spoken language understanding system for private-by-design voice interfaces. *ArXiv*, abs/1805.10190.

Jacob Devlin, Ming-Wei Chang, Kenton Lee, and Kristina Toutanova. 2019. BERT: Pre-training of deep bidirectional transformers for language understanding. In *Proceedings of the 2019 Conference of the North American Chapter of the Association for Computational Linguistics: Human Language Technologies, Volume 1 (Long and Short Papers)*, pages 4171–4186, Minneapolis, Minnesota. Association for Computational Linguistics.

Jesse Dodge, Gabriel Ilharco, Roy Schwartz, Ali Farhadi, Hannaneh Hajishirzi, and Noah Smith. 2020. Fine-tuning pretrained language models: Weight initializations, data orders, and early stopping.

Boris Galitsky and Dmitry Ilvovsky. 2019. On a chatbot conducting a virtual dialogue in financial domain. In *Proceedings of the First Workshop on Financial Technology and Natural Language Processing*, pages 99–101, Macao, China.

Matthew Henderson, Iñigo Casanueva, Nikola Mrkšić, Pei-Hao Su, Tsung-Hsien Wen, and Ivan Vulić. 2020. ConveRT: Efficient and accurate conversational representations from transformers. In *Findings of the Association for Computational Linguistics: EMNLP 2020*, pages 2161–2174, Online. Association for Computational Linguistics.

Menglin Jia, Luming Tang, Bor-Chun Chen, Claire Cardie, Serge Belongie, Bharath Hariharan, and Ser-Nam Lim. 2022. Visual prompt tuning. In *Computer Vision – ECCV 2022*, pages 709–727, Cham. Springer Nature Switzerland.

Stefan Larson, Anish Mahendran, Joseph J. Peper, Christopher Clarke, Andrew Lee, Parker Hill, Jonathan K. Kummerfeld, Kevin Leach, Michael A. Laurenzano, Lingjia Tang, and Jason Mars. 2019. An evaluation dataset for intent classification and out-of-scope prediction. In *Proceedings of the 2019 Conference on Empirical Methods in Natural Language Processing and the 9th International Joint Conference on Natural Language Processing (EMNLP-IJCNLP)*, pages 1311–1316, Hong Kong, China. Association for Computational Linguistics.

Brian Lester, Rami Al-Rfou, and Noah Constant. 2021. The power of scale for parameter-efficient prompt tuning. In *Proceedings of the 2021 Conference on Empirical Methods in Natural Language Processing*, pages 3045–3059, Online and Punta Cana, Dominican Republic. Association for Computational Linguistics.

Xianzhi Li, Will Aitken, Xiaodan Zhu, and Stephen W. Thomas. 2022. Learning better intent representations for financial open intent classification. In *Proceedings of the Fourth Workshop on Financial Technology and Natural Language Processing (FinNLP)*, pages 68–77, Abu Dhabi, United Arab Emirates (Hybrid). Association for Computational Linguistics.

Xingkun Liu, Arash Eshghi, Pawel Swietojanski, and Verena Rieser. 2019a. Benchmarking natural language understanding services for building conversational agents. In *Increasing Naturalness and Flexibility in Spoken Dialogue Interaction - 10th International Workshop on Spoken Dialogue Systems, IWSDS 2019, Syracuse, Sicily, Italy, 24-26 April 2019*, volume 714 of *Lecture Notes in Electrical Engineering*, pages 165–183. Springer.

Xingkun Liu, Arash Eshghi, Pawel Swietojanski, and Verena Rieser. 2021. *Benchmarking Natural Language Understanding Services for Building Conversational Agents*, pages 165–183. Springer Singapore, Singapore.

Yinhan Liu, Myle Ott, Naman Goyal, Jingfei Du, Mandar Joshi, Danqi Chen, Omer Levy, Mike Lewis, Luke Zettlemoyer, and Veselin Stoyanov. 2019b. Roberta: A robustly optimized bert pretraining approach. *ArXiv*, abs/1907.11692.

Lefteris Loukas, Manos Fergadiotis, Ion Androutsopoulos, and Prodromos Malakasiotis. 2021. EDGAR-CORPUS: Billions of tokens make the world go round. In *Proceedings of the Third Workshop on Economics and Natural Language Processing*, pages 13–18, Punta Cana, Dominican Republic. Association for Computational Linguistics.

Lefteris Loukas, Manos Fergadiotis, Ilias Chalkidis, Eirini Spyropoulou, Prodromos Malakasiotis, Ion Androutsopoulos, and Georgios Paliouras. 2022. FiNER: Financial numeric entity recognition for XBRL tagging. In *Proceedings of the 60th Annual Meeting of the Association for Computational Linguistics (Volume 1: Long Papers)*, pages 4419–4431, Dublin, Ireland. Association for Computational Linguistics.

Shikib Mehri and Mihail Eric. 2021. Example-driven intent prediction with observers. In *Proceedings of the 2021 Conference of the North American Chapter of the Association for Computational Linguistics: Human Language Technologies*, pages 2979–2992, Online. Association for Computational Linguistics.

Curtis G. Northcutt, Lu Jiang, and Isaac L. Chuang. 2021. Confident learning: Estimating uncertainty in dataset labels. *Journal of Artificial Intelligence Research (JAIR)*, 70:1373–1411.

Curtis G. Northcutt, Tailin Wu, and Isaac L. Chuang. 2017. Learning with confident examples: Rank pruning for robust classification with noisy labels. In *Proceedings of the Thirty-Third Conference on Uncertainty in Artificial Intelligence*, UAI'17. AUAI Press.

OpenAI. 2023. Gpt-4 technical report.

Long Ouyang, Jeffrey Wu, Xu Jiang, Diogo Almeida, Carroll Wainwright, Pamela Mishkin, Chong Zhang, Sandhini Agarwal, Katarina Slama, Alex Ray, John Schulman, Jacob Hilton, Fraser Kelton, Luke Miller, Maddie Simens, Amanda Askell, Peter Welinder, Paul F Christiano, Jan Leike, and Ryan Lowe. 2022. Training language models to follow instructions with human feedback. In *Advances in Neural Information Processing Systems*, volume 35, pages 27730–27744. Curran Associates, Inc.

Alec Radford, Karthik Narasimhan, Tim Salimans, and Ilya Sutskever. 2018. Improving language understanding with unsupervised learning. Accessed: 06 May 2023.

Alec Radford, Jeff Wu, Rewon Child, David Luan, Dario Amodei, and Ilya Sutskever. 2019. Language models are unsupervised multitask learners. *OpenAI Blog*, 1(8):9.

Yasaman Razeghi, Robert L Logan IV, Matt Gardner, and Sameer Singh. 2022. Impact of pretraining term frequencies on few-shot numerical reasoning. In *Findings of the Association for Computational Linguistics: EMNLP 2022*, pages 840–854, Abu Dhabi, United Arab Emirates. Association for Computational Linguistics.

Laria Reynolds and Kyle McDonell. 2021. Prompt programming for large language models: Beyond the few-shot paradigm. In *Extended Abstracts of the 2021 CHI Conference on Human Factors in Computing Systems*, CHI EA '21, New York, NY, USA. Association for Computing Machinery.

Kaitao Song, Xu Tan, Tao Qin, Jianfeng Lu, and Tie-Yan Liu. 2020. Mpnet: Masked and permuted pretraining for language understanding. In *Proceedings of the 34th International Conference on Neural Information Processing Systems*, NIPS'20, Red Hook, NY, USA. Curran Associates Inc.

Lewis Tunstall, Nils Reimers, Unso Eun Seo Jo, Luke Bates, Daniel Korat, Moshe Wasserblat, and Oren Pereg. 2022. Efficient few-shot learning without prompts. *ArXiv*, abs/2209.11055.

Ashish Vaswani, Noam M. Shazeer, Niki Parmar, Jakob Uszkoreit, Llion Jones, Aidan N. Gomez, Lukasz Kaiser, and Illia Polosukhin. 2017. Attention is all you need. pages 5998–6008.

Albert Webson and Ellie Pavlick. 2022. Do prompt-based models really understand the meaning of their prompts? In *Proceedings of the 2022 Conference of the North American Chapter of the Association for Computational Linguistics: Human Language Technologies*, pages 2300–2344, Seattle, United States. Association for Computational Linguistics.

Thomas Wolf, Lysandre Debut, Victor Sanh, Julien Chaumond, Clement Delangue, Anthony Moi, Pierric Cistac, Tim Rault, Remi Louf, Morgan Funtowicz, Joe Davison, Sam Shleifer, Patrick von Platen,

Clara Ma, Yacine Jernite, Julien Plu, Canwen Xu, Teven Le Scao, Sylvain Gugger, Mariama Drame, Quentin Lhoest, and Alexander Rush. 2020. Transformers: State-of-the-art natural language processing. In *Proceedings of the 2020 Conference on Empirical Methods in Natural Language Processing: System Demonstrations*, pages 38–45, Online. Association for Computational Linguistics.

Zhilin Yang, Zihang Dai, Yiming Yang, Jaime Carbonell, Ruslan Salakhutdinov, and Quoc V. Le. 2019. *XLNet: Generalized Autoregressive Pretraining for Language Understanding*. Curran Associates Inc., Red Hook, NY, USA.

Cecilia Ying and Stephen Thomas. 2022. Label errors in BANKING77. In *Proceedings of the Third Workshop on Insights from Negative Results in NLP*, pages 139–143, Dublin, Ireland. Association for Computational Linguistics.

Elias Zavitsanos, Dimitris Mavroeidis, Konstantinos Bougiatiotis, Eirini Spyropoulou, Lefteris Loukas, and Georgios Paliouras. 2022. Financial misstatement detection: A realistic evaluation. In *Proceedings of the Second ACM International Conference on AI in Finance*, ICAIF '21, New York, NY, USA. Association for Computing Machinery.

Kaiyang Zhou, Jingkang Yang, Chen Change Loy, and Ziwei Liu. 2021. Learning to prompt for vision-language models. *International Journal of Computer Vision*, 130:2337 – 2348.

A In-context Learning Prompt

You are an expert assistant in the field of customer service. Your task is to help workers in the customer service department of a company. Your task is to classify the customer's question in order to help the customer service worker to answer the question. In order to help the worker, you MUST respond with the number and the name of one of the following classes you know. If you cannot answer the question, respond: "-1 Unknown". In case you reply with something else, you will be penalized.

The classes are:
0 activate_my_card
1 age_limit
.. ..
75 wrong_amount_of_cash_received
76 wrong_exchange_rate_for_cash_withdrawal

Here are some examples of questions and their classes:
How do I top-up while traveling? automatic_top_up
How do I set up auto top-up? automatic_top_up
... ...
It declined my transfer. declined_transfer

How do I locate my card?

B Prompt Engineering

We experiment with two different prompt settings using GPT-4 in a 3-shot setting on a held-out validation subset.[8] In the first setting, we present the few-shot examples as the previous chat history. In the second setting, the few-shot examples are presented as a message from the `system`, which is one of the roles in the conversational setting of OpenAI. The second setting yielded the best results (Table 4), and we proceed to use it for the rest of our experiments. As seen in Table 4, by presenting the few-shot examples to the OpenAI API via previous chat history, we score a 77.5 μ-F_1 and a 74.4 m-F_1 score. However, presenting the examples as a `system` message hyperparameter to the API, which sets the assistant behavior, we achieve an improved μ-F_1 of 77.7 and a m-F_1 of 77.0.

Thus, we present the few-shot examples as `system` in the OpenAI later in our prompt-tuning methods (GPT-3.5 and GPT-4).

[8]We used 5% of the training data.

Few shot examples given as	μ-F_1	m-F_1
Previous chat history	75.5	74.4
System context	**77.7**	**77.0**

Table 4: Validation Micro-F1 and Macro-F1 scores for our two prompt settings with GPT-4 in the 3-Shot scenario.

C Class Distribution

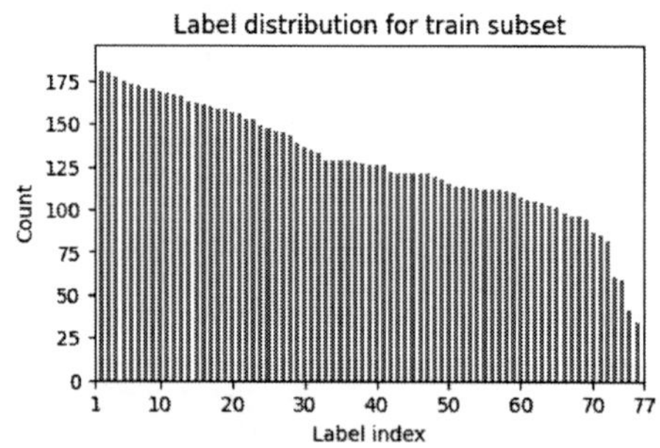

Figure 1: Class distribution of the 77 intents used over the training subset. Intent indices are shown instead of tag names for brevity.

DeRisk: An Effective Deep Learning Framework for Credit Risk Prediction over Real-World Financial Data

Yancheng Liang[13*] **Jiajie Zhang**[1*] **Hui Li**[2] **Xiaochen Liu**[2]
Yi Hu[2] **Yong Wu**[2] **Jinyao Zhang**[2] **Yongyan Liu**[2] **Yi Wu**[13]
[1] Tsinghua University [2] Fintopia Group [3] Shanghai Qi Zhi Institute

Abstract

Despite the tremendous advances achieved over the past years by deep learning techniques, the latest risk prediction models for industrial applications still rely on highly hand-tuned stage-wised statistical learning tools, such as gradient boosting and random forest methods. Different from images or languages, real-world financial data are high-dimensional, sparse, noisy and extremely imbalanced, which makes deep neural network models particularly challenging to train and fragile in practice. In this work, we propose *DeRisk*, an effective deep learning risk prediction framework for credit risk prediction on real-world financial data. *DeRisk* is the first deep risk prediction model that outperforms statistical learning approaches deployed in our company's production system. We also perform extensive ablation studies on our method to present the most critical factors for the empirical success of *DeRisk*.

1 Introduction

Credit risk is the risk of loan default or loan delinquency when a borrower fails to repay on time. Credit risk prediction is an analytical problem that is vital for financial institutions when they are formulating lending strategies for loan applications. It helps make lending decisions by assessing the solvency of the applicants from their credit information. Accurate prediction keeps bad debts at a low level, which directly saves substantial financial loss for the multi-billion dollar credit loan industry (Malekipirbazari and Aksakalli, 2015; Tan et al., 2018). As credit risk is one major threat to financial institutions (Buehler et al., 2008; Li et al., 2015; Ma et al., 2018; Tan et al., 2018), better credit risk prediction also improves the risk management capacity of banks and financial technology companies.

Although credit scores, such as FICO Score, have been widely used as mainstream risk indicators by many financial institutions, data-driven methods have recently shown their great potential and superior practical performances (Xu et al., 2021). Deep learning (DL), the dominating modeling technique in various domains such as computer vision, natural language processing, and recommendation system, has been a promising and increasingly popular tool considered to tackle financial problems. Recent attempts include market prediction (Ding et al., 2015; Minh et al., 2018), stock trading (Sezer et al., 2017) and exchange rate prediction (Shen et al., 2015). Despite the recent trend of using deep models, non-DL methods, such as XGBoost and logistic regression, remain the most effective techniques so far for credit risk prediction in the financial industry. Many existing studies have shown that neural network models lead to similar or even worse performances than non-DL methods (Fu, 2017; Kvamme et al., 2018; Varmedja et al., 2019; Li et al., 2020; Moscato et al., 2021).

Credit risk prediction can be formulated as a binary classification problem, where the goal is to learn a function $f_\theta : \mathcal{X} \rightarrow [0, 1]$ to map the credit information $x \in \mathcal{X}$ of an applicant to a risk score $y \in [0, 1]$ that represents the probability of default.

Despite such a simple problem formulation, credit risk prediction can be particularly challenging. Existing deep-learning-based solutions mainly focus on e-commerce consumer data (Liang et al., 2021), which typically include dense features and highly frequent user activities, such as clicks and payments, on e-commerce platforms. However, these fine-grained data are not commonly available to financial institutions. Specifically, in our application, we adopt the official credit reports provided by the Credit Reference Center (CRC) of the People's Bank of China. These financial data are of much lower quality, i.e., containing much higher dimensions (over 4k) with a large portion of missing entries and extreme values, due to low-frequency credit records. End-to-end training neural networks on these data can be substantially more challeng-

* Both authors contributed equally to this research.

Proceedings of the Joint Workshop of the 5th Financial Technology and Natural Language Processing (FinNLP) and 2nd Multimodal AI For Financial Forecasting (Muffin), Macao, August 20, 2023.

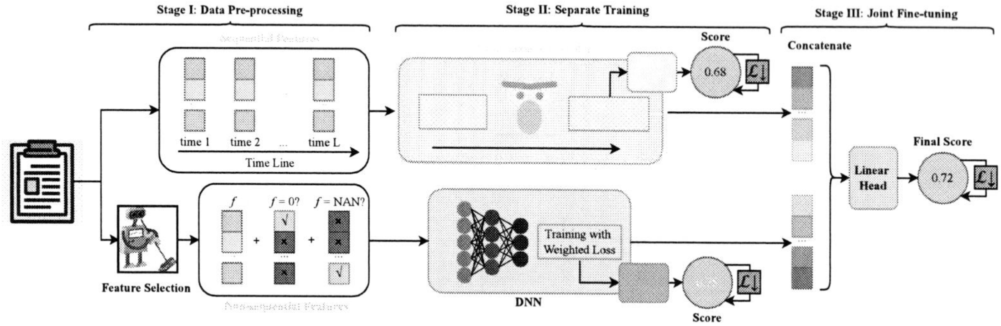

Figure 1: The three-stage pipeline of our *DeRisk* framework. First, in data pre-processing, feature selection and DL-specific data argumentation are adopted to benefit the optimization of DL models. Then we separately train two models for non-sequential data and sequential data, respectively. Finally, we combine them and fine-tune the joint model on the whole multi-format data. In contrast to the end-to-end paradigm in conventional DL applications, we remark the multi-stage process is critical to the overall success of *DeRisk* on real-world financial data.

ing and brittle (Poole et al., 2016; Borisov et al., 2021). Therefore, to the best of our knowledge, most financial institutions (e.g., banks) still adopt non-DL-based methods.

In this work, we present a successful industrial case study by developing an effective deep learning framework, *DeRisk*, which outperforms our production decision-tree-based system, on real-world financial data. Our *DeRisk* framework consists of three major stages including data pre-processing, separate training of non-sequential and sequential models, and joint fine-tuning. We also design a collection of practical techniques to stabilize deep neural network training under the aforementioned challenges. Specifically for the low-quality real-world financial data, we observe that a multi-stage process with feature selection and DL-specific engineering processing can be critical to the overall success of our framework.

Main contributions. (1) We develop a **comprehensive workflow** that *considers all the model training aspects* for risk prediction. (2) We implement *DeRisk*, the *first* deep risk prediction model that **outperforms statistical learning approaches** on *real-world financial data*. (3) We conduct **extensive ablation studies** on the effect of different technical components of *DeRisk*, which *provides useful insights and practical suggestions* for the research community and relevant practitioners.

2 Related Work

There have been extensive studies using machine learning techniques for credit risk prediction, including linear regression (Puro et al., 2010; Guo et al., 2016), SVM (Jadhav et al., 2018; Kim and Cho, 2019), decision tree based methods like Random Forest (RF) (Malekipirbazari and Aksakalli, 2015; Varmedja et al., 2019; Xu et al., 2021) or Gradient Boost Decision Tree (GBDT) (Xia et al., 2017a; He et al., 2018), deep learning (Byanjankar et al., 2015; Kvamme et al., 2018; Yang et al., 2018; Yotsawat et al., 2021), or an ensemble of them (Fu, 2017; Li et al., 2020). Most of these works use data with non-sequential features. Although deep learning is applied, empirical results find that XGBoost or other GBDT approaches usually outperforms deep learning (Fu, 2017; Kvamme et al., 2018; Varmedja et al., 2019; Xu et al., 2021).

On the other hand, deep learning has shown its superiority beyond tabular data through the flexibility of deep neural networks. Convolutional Neural Network (CNN) (Kvamme et al., 2018), Long Short-Term Memory (LSTM) (Yang et al., 2018) and Graph Neural Network (GNN) (Wang et al., 2021a) are adopted for sequential data or graph data since other machine learning techniques like GBDT fail to properly model non-tabular data. According to (Liang et al., 2021), deep learning outperforms conventional methods on multimodal e-commerce data for credit risk prediction.

Many data challenges in financial applications are also common in other machine learning fields. (1) For high-dimensional data, many feature selection methods have been proposed, including filter methods (Gu et al., 2011), wrapper methods (Yamada et al., 2014) and embedded methods (Feng and Simon, 2017). Many risk prediction works have adopted feature selection for better performance (Xia et al., 2017a; Ha et al., 2019; Li et al., 2020) or interpretability (Ma et al., 2018; Xu et al., 2021). (2) Handling multiple data formats and feature types is related to the field of deep learning for tabular data (Gorishniy et al., 2021; Borisov et al., 2021). There are typical three popular deep neural network architectures for tabular data (Klambauer et al., 2017; Huang et al., 2020; Arık and Pfister, 2021), including Multi-Layer Perception (MLP), Residual Network (ResNet) (He et al., 2016) and Transformer (Vaswani et al., 2017). Similar to the financial domain, it is also reported that deep models are not universally superior to GBDT models (Gorishniy et al., 2021) on tabular data. (3) For the out-of-time distribution shift issue, it is common to split training and test data according to the temporal order (Kvamme et al., 2018; Jiang et al., 2021). (4) Furthermore, data imbalance is also a long-standing problem in machine learning research. Among the popular over-sampling and under-sampling strategies (He et al., 2018; Bastani et al., 2019; Mahbobi et al., 2021), Synthetic Minority Over-sampling Technique (SMOTE) (Chawla et al., 2002) is a widespread technique for synthetic minority data, which is also reported be effective for credit risk prediction (Bastani et al., 2019). Generative adversarial networks can also be used to generate additional minority data (Mariani et al., 2018) and this method can be applied to financial data (Liu et al., 2020) for risk prediction. However, these methods are limited to non-sequential data generation, while our financial data has multiple formats. Class-balanced loss is another method to make the model attend more to the minority samples (Lin et al., 2017; Xia et al., 2017b; Cui et al., 2019; Ren et al., 2022). Comparative experiments (Kaur et al., 2019; Moscato et al., 2021) show that all strategies have their pros and cons. In our work, we use a class-balanced loss to mitigate the problem of data imbalance, and different strategies are used for non-sequential data and sequential data thanks to their great difference in data dimension.

3 Preliminary

In this section, we first present the problem statement for the credit risk prediction task, and then introduce the credit information and labels used in the task.

3.1 Task Formulation

The credit risk prediction task aims to decide whether a loan can be granted to the applicant according to his/her credit information. To be more specific, the risk prediction model needs to learn a function $f_\theta : \mathcal{X} \to [0, 1]$, which takes the credit information $x \in \mathcal{X}$ of an applicant as input and produces a risk score $y \in [0, 1]$ that represents the probability of delinquent on the applicant's payments.

3.2 Multi-format Credit Information.

In this work, we adopt the credit information in the credit report data that is generally available in financial institutions. The credit report data of an applicant consists of two parts: non-sequential features and sequential features. Specifically, the non-sequential part usually contains thousands of stable profiles of the applicant, including age, marital status, industry, property status, etc. We remark that the non-sequential data of a credit report can be extremely high-dimensional and sparse, which requires further processing to successfully train deep neural network models. The sequential part contains dozens of features and consists of three components of the applicant's financial behavior organized by time: (1) applicant's past loan information (**loan**), including the date of loan issuing, type of lending institution, loan amount, etc.; (2) the records that applicant's credit report was inquired in the past (**inquiry**), including inquiry time, inquiry institutions, inquiry reasons, etc.; (3) applicant's credit card information (**card**), including card application date, credit card type, currency, etc. Note that the number of sequential features is much smaller than non-sequential features.

3.3 Multiple Labels and Imbalanced Data

Loan repayments naturally generate multiple labels because of installment (e.g., the first or the second month to pay back) and different degrees of delinquency (e.g., one-week or one-month delay). These labels are roughly categorized into short-term labels (e.g., the first/second/third installment is more than 30 days overdue) and long-term labels (e.g., any installment in recent 12 months is more than 5/15/30 days overdue). Due to the general priority of short-term benefits and the convenience of subsequent collection, financial institutions typically use short-term labels for evaluation. However, directly using this short-term evaluation label as the training label can be suboptimal. The choice of training label needs careful consideration for the best practice. Note that all these labels are particularly imbalanced (10% or even 1% for minority samples) because applicants who pay on time are much more than applicants who are overdue. Therefore, different choices of labels may lead to drastically different model performances in practice, as shown in our ablation study in Section 7.2.

4 Methodology

4.1 Overall Pipeline

The overall pipeline of our *DeRisk* framework is shown in Figure 1. Firstly, we apply careful data processing to turn noisy and irregular input features into a neatly structured format, which is indispensable for training deep networks. Secondly, to well utilize both sequential and non-sequential features, we design two main sub-models: a DNN model for processing non-sequential features and a Transformer-based model $\mathcal{M}_{\text{S}}$ for processing sequential features. We train them separately in the second stage. In the last stage, we fuse $\mathcal{M}_{\text{NS}}$ and $\mathcal{M}_{\text{S}}$ by concatenating the final hidden layers from both models and applying another linear head to give the final prediction score. We jointly fine-tune this whole model to get improved performance.

4.2 Selection of Training Label

As we mentioned in Sec. 3, there are multiple labels in risk prediction tasks that record an applicant's repayment behavior in different time periods. Among these labels, we choose a long-term label to train our model for two reasons. First, long-term labels are more balanced than short-term labels. Second, the data distribution (e.g., the ratio of negative and positive data) varies over time (see Appendix A.3) because of economic changes and the continual improvement of our deployed model. The long-term label is less sensitive to these influences and is more stable because it summarizes an applicant's behavior in the last 12 months, conceptually performing a smoothing operator over the timeline. We believe this will make our model more generalizable and perform better on the out-of-time test set, though predicting long-term risk is inherently more difficult.

4.3 Data Pre-Processing

The credit report data, especially the non-sequential data, is extremely complex and noisy, as it contains many missing values and outlier values. This low-quality input can make the learning process unstable and hurts the final performance. Therefore, proper data pre-preprocessing can be significantly beneficial for the optimization of DL models.

Both sequential and non-sequential features can be divided into three types: time features (i.e., features about time such as credit card issue date), real-value features (e.g., age, loan amount), and category features (e.g., industry, type of lending institution). For the time features, we always use a relative date difference to avoid the models memorizing input data according to the date. We also apply normalization for the numerical time features and real-value features, and discard minor classes in the category features.

In addition, we adopt specific techniques for non-sequential features. We found that lots of non-sequential real-value features are useless noise and even harmful for training. Hence we adopt a commonly-used feature selection technique that utilizes XGBoost (Chen et al., 2015) to select the most important 500 features among thousands of non-sequential real-value features and discard the others. Besides, most non-sequential features have many 0s and missing values (NAN) that naturally arise from the financial behaviors and data collection processes, which makes non-sequential data sparse, noisy, and problematic for DL training. These 0s and NANs are not necessarily meaningless, e.g., a NAN in "The time of first application for a mortgage" may imply that this applicant has never applied for a mortgage. Besides, if we simply fill these entries with a constant c, it will influence those true entries close to c and significantly influence the learned model. So, we treat these 0s and NANs carefully. For every category feature, we add a category $\langle\text{NAN}\rangle$, and for every real-value and time feature, besides replacing all NANs with 0s, we also create two indicators that directly tell whether a value is 0 and is NAN. With explicit indicators, DL models can therefore directly utilize the information implied by meaningful 0s and NANs and learn to ignore those 0s and NANs that are harmful to training.

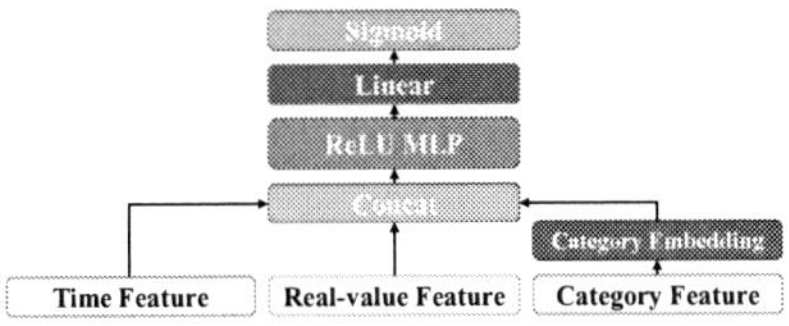

Figure 2: Non-sequential DNN model.

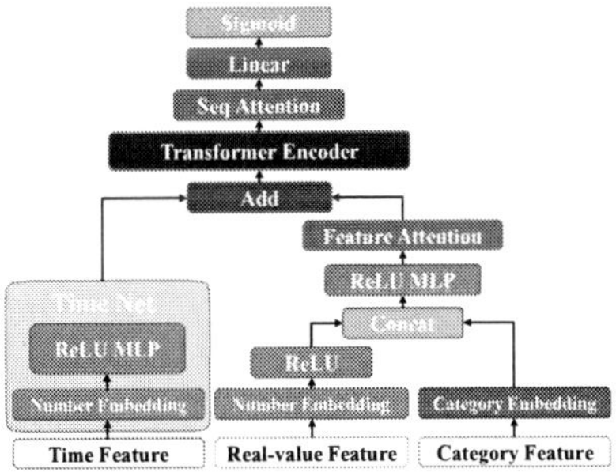

Figure 3: Sequential Transformer-based model.

4.4 Modeling Non-sequential Features

We adopt a simple but effective neural network for non-sequential features. The architecture is shown in Figure 2. Firstly it uses an embedding layer to convert category features into dense vectors and concatenate them with time and real-value features to the dense input $x^{\text{NS}}_{\text{dense}} \in \mathbb{R}^{m_1}$. Then $x^{\text{NS}}_{\text{dense}}$ is fed into a MLP (multi-layer perceptron) with ReLU activation function to get the non-sequential output hidden state $x^{\text{NS}}_{\text{final}} \in \mathbb{R}^{m_2}$. And the final prediction $\hat{y}^{\text{NS}}$ is computed as: $\hat{y}^{\text{NS}} = \sigma((\text{w}^{\text{NS}}_{\text{logit}})^T x^{\text{NS}}_{\text{final}} + \text{b}^{\text{NS}}_{\text{logit}})$, where $\text{w}^{\text{NS}}_{\text{logit}} \in \mathbb{R}^{m_2}$ and $\text{b}^{\text{NS}}_{\text{logit}}$ are the weight vector and bias for the logit, respectively, $z^{\text{NS}} = (\text{w}^{\text{NS}}_{\text{logit}})^T x^{\text{NS}}_{\text{final}} + \text{b}^{\text{NS}}_{\text{logit}}$ is the logit, and $\sigma(x) = 1/(1 + \exp(-x))$ is sigmoid activation.

4.5 Modeling Sequential Features

4.5.1 Architecture

We adopt a Transformer (Vaswani et al., 2017)-based model for its strong modeling capacity. The architecture is shown in Figure 3. Three such models, $\mathcal{M}_{\text{card}}$, $\mathcal{M}_{\text{inquiry}}$, and $\mathcal{M}_{\text{loan}}$, are used for card, inquiry, and loan features, respectively. Suppose the sequence length is l and the embedding size is e. Firstly a time net will convert the time feature into time embedding $E_t \in \mathbb{R}^{l \times e}$, which plays a role of position embedding, and attention is used to merge different feature embeddings into one, i.e., $E_f \in \mathbb{R}^{l \times e}$. Then a Transformer encoder will encode the sequential embeddings $E = E_t + E_f$ into hidden feature $x_h \in \mathbb{R}^{l \times e}$, which will be pooled by another attention into output feature $x^*_{\text{final}} \in \mathbb{R}^e$, where $*$ refer to card, inquiry or loan. We concatenate $x^{\text{card}}_{\text{final}}$, $x^{\text{inquiry}}_{\text{final}}$, and $x^{\text{loan}}_{\text{final}}$ to obtain $x^{\text{S}}_{\text{final}} \in \mathbb{R}^{3e}$. At last, similar to non-sequential case, we have logit $z^{\text{S}} = (\text{w}^{\text{S}}_{\text{logit}})^T x^{\text{S}}_{\text{final}} + \text{b}^{\text{S}}_{\text{logit}}$ and final prediction $\hat{y}^{\text{S}} = \sigma(z^{\text{S}})$. To improve the generalization ability of the sequential model, we share the time net and Transformer encoder among $\mathcal{M}_{\text{card}}$, $\mathcal{M}_{\text{inquiry}}$, and $\mathcal{M}_{\text{loan}}$.

4.5.2 Mask Language Model Pre-training

During training, we found that optimization of the sequential model is much harder than the non-sequential model (the left part of Figure 4) due to the scarcity of sequential features compared with non-sequential features. To ease the training of the sequential model, we adopt mask language model (MLM) pre-training as BERT (Devlin et al., 2019) to make the model first learn informative and general features from sequential data. We randomly mask the input sequential features, where 80% of masked value are replaced with token ⟨MASK⟩ (for category features) or 0 (for time and real-value features), 10% are replaced with a random value, and 10% remain unchanged. The three output hidden features of Transformer encoder, i.e., x^{card}_h, x^{inquiry}_h, and x^{loan}_h, will be input into different classification heads to predict different type of origin value at the masked position. After pre-training, we fine-tune $\mathcal{M}_{\text{NS}}$ on the downstream classification task.

4.6 Weighted BCE Loss

We also adopt weighted BCE loss to deal with data imbalance. Firstly, BCE (binary cross entropy) loss function is commonly used in binary classification tasks:

$$\text{BCE} = -\frac{1}{n}\sum_{i=1}^{n}[y_i \log(\hat{y}_i) + (1 - y_i)\log(1 - \hat{y}_i)].$$

However, when negative samples are much more than positive samples, naive BCE loss will induce the model to output $\hat{y}_i = 0$. To avoid this, we can give more weight to positive samples by using weighted BCE loss:

$$\text{WBCE} = -\frac{1}{|\mathcal{D}^-|}\sum_{i\in\mathcal{D}^-}\log(1-\hat{y}_i) - \frac{1}{|\mathcal{D}^+|}\sum_{i\in\mathcal{D}^+}\log(\hat{y}_i),$$

where $\mathcal{D}^+ = \{i : y_i = 1\}$ is the set of positive samples and $\mathcal{D}^- = \{i : y_i = 0\}$ is the set of negative samples. Another implementation of the

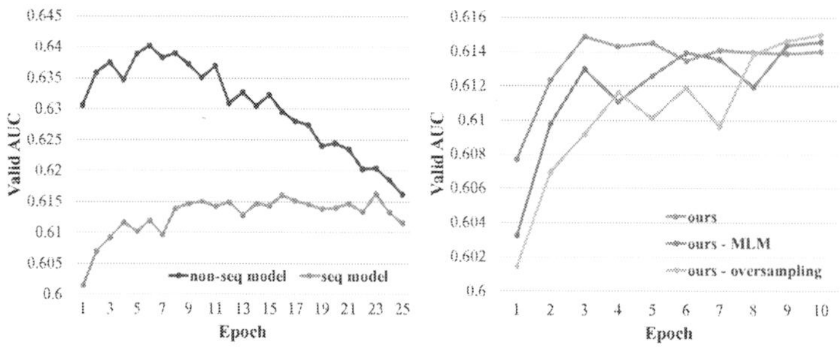

Figure 4: Left: valid AUC of non-sequential and sequential models with training epoch. Right: change of valid AUC of the sequential model with and without MLM pre-training or oversampling.

above-mentioned weighted loss is oversampling, i.e., adjusting the ratio $|\mathcal{D}^-| : |\mathcal{D}^+|$ to $1 : 1$ by re-sampling positive samples.

We use oversampling on the sequential model and use normal weighted BCE loss on the non-sequential model and joint fine-tuning stage. This is because the optimization of the non-sequential model is much harder and slower than that of the non-sequential model due to the small number of non-sequential features, while oversampling enables the model to see rare samples multiple times in one epoch and thus accelerates optimization. On the other hand, the number of non-sequential features is large and the optimization of the non-sequential model is already fast enough, oversampling may lead to overfitting on the minority samples instead.

4.7 Separate Training & Joint Fine-tuning

To fuse the sequential and non-sequential features, we use a concatenation layer (**Concat Net**) on the top of them to concatenate their output hidden states and to predict the final score, i.e., $\hat{y} = \sigma((\mathrm{w}_{\text{logit}})^T x_{\text{final}} + \mathrm{b}_{\text{logit}})$, where $x^{\text{NS}}_{\text{final}} = [x^{\text{NS}}_{\text{final}}, x^{\text{S}}_{\text{final}}]$. Note that the hardness of optimization non-sequential and sequential models is different, so if we train them with the concatenation layer together from scratch, the overall model will totally rely on the non-sequential outputs, which are easier to train on, while ignoring the output of the sequential model. To avoid this and to utilize the sequential features better, we adopt a two-stage training strategy: separately train sequential and non-sequential models first and then jointly fine-tune them with the Concat Net.

Data	Time	Real-value	Category
card	1	2	5
inquiry	1	0	2
loan	1	4	5
non-sequential	13	4098	9

Table 1: Number of time, real-value, and category features in each sample of sequential and non-sequential data. The card, inquiry, and loan sequences for each user are clipped with lengths 32, 64, and 128, respectively.

5 Experiment Setup

5.1 Notation

We mainly use a long-term label $\mathcal{Y}_{\text{long}}$ for training and a short-term label $\mathcal{Y}^{\text{eval}}_{\text{short}}$ for evaluation. $\mathcal{Y}^{\text{other1}}_{\text{short}}, \mathcal{Y}^{\text{other2}}_{\text{short}}, \mathcal{Y}^{\text{other3}}_{\text{short}}$, There are also three other short-term labels used in our experiments. The description of these labels are in Sec A.2.

5.2 Dataset Statistics

We sample 582,996 Yanqianguan Users and use their credit report data and repayment behavior from August 2020 to July 2021 as the dataset. To simulate the out-of-time prediction in real business scenarios, we take the 430,865 data pieces from August 2020 to May 2021 as the training set and 152,131 data pieces from June 2021 to July 2021 as the test set. The ratio of negative and positive samples is about $50 : 1$ according to the short-term label used for evaluation and is about $10 : 1$ according to the long-term label used for training.[1] For sequential data, we set the maximum sequence length of card, query, and loan data to be 32, 64, and 128, respectively, according to the distribution

[1]We keep the exact ratio numbers confidential due to commercial and security concerns.

Model	$y_{\text{short}}^{\text{eval}}$	$y_{\text{short}}^{\text{other2}}$	$y_{\text{short}}^{\text{other3}}$
non-seq model over non-seq data only			
XGBoost	0.6418	0.6282	0.6187
DeepFM	0.5700	0.5508	0.5478
SDCN	0.6450	0.6319	0.6236
PDCN	0.6483	0.6343	**0.6254**
AutoInt	0.6454	0.6325	0.6238
DNN	**0.6499**	**0.6349**	**0.6254**
seq model over sqe data only			
Pooled MLP	0.5996	0.5821	0.5749
LSTM	0.6108	0.5936	0.5859
Transformer	0.6132	0.5941	0.5871
Transformer+MLM	**0.6156**	**0.5971**	**0.5885**
joint model over the entire data			
Add-Attn Net	0.6504	0.6369	0.6285
Mul-Attn Net	0.6520	0.6377	0.6278
DeRisk(ours)	**0.6546**	**0.6398**	**0.6297**

Table 2: All models are evaluated by AUC scores on three different short-term labels.

of data length. Only the latest data will be included for training and evaluation. Some statistics are summarized in Table 1.

Note that all above data are definitely authorized by the customers since they hope to apply for loan in our platform and they should provide the access to their credit report. We also anonymized the names of people and organizations on credit reports to protect customers' privacy.

5.3 Evaluation Metric

The metric commonly used to evaluate credit risk prediction models $\mathcal{M}$ is AUC (Area Under the ROC Curve) score. We remark that this is a challenging task and an increment of 0.01 in AUC can be significant in performance as this results in a roughly 5% decrement of real-world bad debts.

6 Main Results

6.1 Baselines

For non-sequential model, the baselines include (1) current popular traditional ML model **XGBoost** (Chen et al., 2015) (main baseline) and several more complicated deep models including (2) **DeepFM** (Guo et al., 2017): the final score is $y^{\text{NS}} = \sigma(z^{\text{NS}}_{\text{DNN}} + z^{\text{NS}}_{\text{FM}})$, where $z^{\text{NS}}_{\text{DNN}}$ is the logit of DNN and $z^{\text{NS}}_{\text{FM}}$ is the logit gotten by a FM (factorization machine (Rendle, 2010)) layer. (3) **DCNv2** (Wang et al., 2021b): use cross-network (multiple cross layers) to obtain high-order cross feature. A DNN can be stacked on top of the cross-network (SDCN); we could also place them in parallel (PDCN). (4) **AutoInt** (Song et al., 2019): use a multi-head self-attention to learn interacted features.

For the sequential model, our baselines are **pooled MLP** (which uses a pooling layer to average hidden states of different times that are individually produced by the MLP) and **LSTM** (Hochreiter and Schmidhuber, 1997).

For the final module that fuses the output of the hidden state by the non-sequential model and sequential model, we compare our simple Concat Net with an additive attention layer (**Add-Attn Net**) and a multiplicative attention layer (**Mul-Attn Net**) that use x^{NS}_{final} as a query vector to pool output hidden feature of Transformer Encoder x_h by additive and multiplicative attention, respectively.

6.2 Evaluation and Analysis

Since our dataset has multiple formats, we first test separated models for single-format data modeling. For non-sequential data, we compare the DNN module in *DeRisk* with XGboost, a widely-used decision-tree model in our production system. We aim to show whether our *DeRisk* system and techniques can make its DNN module outperform other non-DL methods on real-world financial data. Other popular models in recommendation systems like DeepFM, DCN, and AutoInt are also tested as DL competitors. For sequential data, we consider different sequential models including Pooled MLP, LSTM, and Transformer for evaluation. Our *DeRisk* adopts Transformer and additionally adopts MLM-pretraining to accelerate training.

Finally, we consider joint models trained over the entire dataset with both formats by fusing the best non-sequential model, DNN, and the best sequential model MLM-pretrained Transfomer, to obtain joint models for the best evaluation results. With more data, the joint models outperform either separated models, but we also find different fusing techniques lead to different performances. We compare our Concat Net with two different attention-based methods.

Table 2 summarizes the main results. All models are evaluated by three different labels to show consistent results. From the results we can see that:

(1) Our non-sequential model DNN and sequential model

Change	AUC
No (ours)	**0.6546**
w/o Separate Training (end-to-end)	0.6487
w/ Freeze Sub-models	0.6512

Table 3: $\mathcal{Y}_{\text{short}}^{\text{eval}}$ AUC scores with different training strategies.

MLM+Transformer outperform all baselines, respectively. Specifically, compared with current popular XGBoost model, our DNN model $\mathcal{M}_{\text{NS}}$ and best joint model *DeRisk* (with Concat Net) improve $\mathcal{Y}_{\text{short}}^{\text{eval}}$ AUC score by 0.0081 and 0.0128, respectively.

(2) Joint fine-tuning of non-sequential and sequential models can achieve better results than only using a single non-sequential or sequential model.

(3) Complex models do not necessarily perform better: simplest DNN and Concat Net outperform other more complicated models. This indicates that the high-order features created by those additional networks such as FM and cross layers are not that helpful for the credit risk prediction task.

7 Ablation Study

In this section, we conduct a series of experiments to demonstrate the effect of each part of our *DeRisk* framework. We mainly use $\mathcal{Y}_{\text{short}}^{\text{eval}}$ for evaluation since we find it shows a consistent result with other short-term labels as in Table 2. We test the effectiveness of different modules in our multi-stage process, including separate training & joint fine-tuning, feature selection, indicator features, and MLM-pretraining. Many different techniques for data imbalance are also studied in this section. With our ablation studies, we also present best practices for training deep neural network models over real-world financial data.

7.1 Effect of Multi-stage Training

Because the hardness of optimization on non-sequential data and sequential data is different as shown in Figure 4, we first separately train $\mathcal{M}_{\text{NS}}$ and $\mathcal{M}_{\text{S}}$ and then joint fine-tune them. We also tried joint training them from scratch (end-to-end), or freezing $\mathcal{M}_{\text{NS}}$ and $\mathcal{M}_{\text{S}}$ and only tuning the concatenating layer during joint fine-tuning. The results are reported in Table 3. We can see that separate training outperforms the other two training strategies.

Training Label	Test Label	AUC
non-seq model		
$\mathcal{Y}_{\text{long}}$ (Ours)	$\mathcal{Y}_{\text{short}}^{\text{eval}}$	**0.6499**
$\mathcal{Y}_{\text{short}}^{\text{other1}}$	$\mathcal{Y}_{\text{short}}^{\text{eval}}$	0.6392
$\mathcal{Y}_{\text{short}}^{\text{eval}}$	$\mathcal{Y}_{\text{short}}^{\text{eval}}$	0.6363
seq model		
$\mathcal{Y}_{\text{long}}$ (Ours)	$\mathcal{Y}_{\text{short}}^{\text{eval}}$	**0.6156**
$\mathcal{Y}_{\text{short}}^{\text{other1}}$	$\mathcal{Y}_{\text{short}}^{\text{eval}}$	0.6113
$\mathcal{Y}_{\text{short}}^{\text{eval}}$	$\mathcal{Y}_{\text{short}}^{\text{eval}}$	0.6105

Table 4: Experiment results of selecting different training labels on non-sequential and sequential models.

Change	AUC
No (Ours)	**0.6499**
$\lvert\mathcal{F}_R\rvert = 4098$	0.6415
$\lvert\mathcal{F}_R\rvert = 100$	0.6390
w/o Indicator	0.6426
w/ BCE Loss	0.6454
w/ Focal Loss	0.6403
w/ Oversample	0.6458

Table 5: Analysis experiment results on non-sequential DNN model, where $\lvert\mathcal{F}_R\rvert$ is the number of selected features.

Suggestion#1: It is beneficial to first perform separate training and then joint tuning for multi-format data. The additional tunable parameters introduced in the fine-tuning process should be sufficiently large for effective multi-format fusion.

7.2 Effect of Different Training Labels

We tried taking two short-term labels ($\mathcal{Y}_{\text{short}}^{\text{other1}}$ and $\mathcal{Y}_{\text{short}}^{\text{eval}}$) and a long-term label ($\mathcal{Y}_{\text{long}}$) as the training label, respectively. The results in Table 4 demonstrate that the long-term label is the best choice for both non-sequential and sequential models, even when the model is evaluated on a short-term label.

Suggestion#2: It is better to choose a balanced and stable signal that measures the long-term behaviors as the training label.

7.3 Effect of Real-value Feature Selection

To show the effect of selecting real-value features with XGBoost, we compare the following three

Change	AUC
No (Ours)	**0.6156**
w/o MLM Pre-training	0.6132
w/o Oversampling	0.6153

Table 6: Analysis experiment results on sequential Transformer-based model.

cases: no selection, selecting 500 real-value features (Ours), and selecting 100 real-value features. The results in Table 5 show that selecting 500 features performs the best. This indicates that (1) by selecting real-value features with XGBoost, we can drop useful fewer features and improve the performance. (2) dropping too many features would lead to worse predictions.

Suggestion#3: It is important to perform feature selection before deep learning training. The dimension of selected features should be chosen carefully.

7.4 Effect of Indicator Features

To show the effect of NAN and zero indicators, we compare the case with and without them. As shown in Table 5, after removing indicators, the AUC score decreases by 0.0073.

Suggestion#4: Some NANs and 0s can be meaningful and it is better to use indicator features rather than simply filling these missing values with a constant or discarding them.

7.5 Comparison of Different Loss Functions

We compared the performance of using weighted BCE loss (Ours) with using naive BCE loss on the DNN model. In addition, we also tried Focal loss (Lin et al., 2017) which is designed for the data imbalance case, but the result in Table 5 shows that it is not helpful for our task and weight BCE achieves the best performance.

Suggestion#5: Adding more weight to rare positive samples is critical to prevent the model from biasing to the overwhelming negative outputs.

7.6 Effect of Oversampling

We compared the cases with and without oversampling on both the non-sequential model and sequential model to demonstrate the effect of oversampling. We can see from Table 6 and the right of Figure 4 that for sequential model, oversampling (1) improves AUC. (2) accelerates optimization. By enabling the model to see rare positive samples more times in each epoch, oversampling reduces the training difficulty of the sequential model. On the other hand, oversampling also makes the non-sequential model, the one easier to optimize, overfits more quickly on the training data and thus cannot achieve good performance as shown in Table 5. In practice, DNN with oversampling usually overfits after the first epoch.

Suggestion#6: Oversampling makes optimization of the sequential model easier and improves performance. And considering the difference between non-sequential data and sequential data, each separated model should be optimized with different sampling strategies.

7.7 Effect of MLM Pre-training of Sequential Model

From Table 6 and the right of Figure 4 that MLM pre-training of the sequential model (1) improves performance. (2) accelerates optimization. This indicates that the pre-trained model has learned some knowledge of sequential data that are useful for the risk prediction task.

Suggestion#7: MLM pre-training benefits the optimization of the sequential model on credit risk prediction.

8 Conclusion

In this work, we proposed an effective deep learning framework, *DeRisk*, which utilizes both sequential and non-sequential features for credit risk prediction. We apply careful data pre-processing to obtain clean and useful data for deep models, use MLM to pre-train the sequential model, adopt weighted BCE loss and oversampling to deal with the data imbalance problem, and select generalizable and stable training labels for better performance. The overall performance of *DeRisk* largely outperforms existing approaches on real-world financial data. We remark that it is unnecessary that a more complicated network always performs better. In our analysis, every components of the training framework including data pre-processing and a carefully designed optimization process are all critical to make deep learning models perform well on a real-world financial application. We hope our framework and analysis can bring insights for a wide range of important commercial applications and inspire future research on developing more powerful deep learning tools for real-world industrial data.

References

Sercan O Arık and Tomas Pfister. 2021. Tabnet: Attentive interpretable tabular learning. In *AAAI*, volume 35, pages 6679–6687.

Kaveh Bastani, Elham Asgari, and Hamed Namavari. 2019. Wide and deep learning for peer-to-peer lending. *Expert Systems with Applications*, 134:209–224.

Vadim Borisov, Tobias Leemann, Kathrin Seßler, Johannes Haug, Martin Pawelczyk, and Gjergji Kasneci. 2021. Deep neural networks and tabular data: A survey. *arXiv preprint arXiv:2110.01889*.

Kevin Buehler, Andrew Freeman, and Ron Hulme. 2008. The new arsenal of risk management. *Harvard Business Review*, 86(9):93–100.

Ajay Byanjankar, Markku Heikkilä, and Jozsef Mezei. 2015. Predicting credit risk in peer-to-peer lending: A neural network approach. In *2015 IEEE symposium series on computational intelligence*, pages 719–725. IEEE.

Nitesh V Chawla, Kevin W Bowyer, Lawrence O Hall, and W Philip Kegelmeyer. 2002. Smote: synthetic minority over-sampling technique. *Journal of artificial intelligence research*, 16:321–357.

Tianqi Chen, Tong He, Michael Benesty, Vadim Khotilovich, Yuan Tang, Hyunsu Cho, et al. 2015. Xgboost: extreme gradient boosting. *R package version 0.4-2*, 1(4):1–4.

Yin Cui, Menglin Jia, Tsung-Yi Lin, Yang Song, and Serge Belongie. 2019. Class-balanced loss based on effective number of samples. In *Proceedings of the IEEE/CVF conference on computer vision and pattern recognition*, pages 9268–9277.

Jacob Devlin, Ming-Wei Chang, Kenton Lee, and Kristina Toutanova. 2019. BERT: pre-training of deep bidirectional transformers for language understanding. In *Proceedings of the 2019 Conference of the North American Chapter of the Association for Computational Linguistics: Human Language Technologies, NAACL-HLT 2019, Minneapolis, MN, USA, June 2-7, 2019, Volume 1 (Long and Short Papers)*, pages 4171–4186. Association for Computational Linguistics.

Xiao Ding, Yue Zhang, Ting Liu, and Junwen Duan. 2015. Deep learning for event-driven stock prediction. In *Twenty-fourth international joint conference on artificial intelligence*.

Jean Feng and Noah Simon. 2017. Sparse-input neural networks for high-dimensional nonparametric regression and classification. *arXiv preprint arXiv:1711.07592*.

Yijie Fu. 2017. Combination of random forests and neural networks in social lending. *Journal of Financial Risk Management*, 6(4):418–426.

Yury Gorishniy, Ivan Rubachev, Valentin Khrulkov, and Artem Babenko. 2021. Revisiting deep learning models for tabular data. *Advances in Neural Information Processing Systems*, 34.

Quanquan Gu, Zhenhui Li, and Jiawei Han. 2011. Generalized fisher score for feature selection. In *27th Conference on Uncertainty in Artificial Intelligence, UAI 2011*, pages 266–273.

Huifeng Guo, Ruiming Tang, Yunming Ye, Zhenguo Li, and Xiuqiang He. 2017. Deepfm: a factorization-machine based neural network for ctr prediction. In *Proceedings of the 26th International Joint Conference on Artificial Intelligence*, pages 1725–1731.

Yanhong Guo, Wenjun Zhou, Chunyu Luo, Chuanren Liu, and Hui Xiong. 2016. Instance-based credit risk assessment for investment decisions in p2p lending. *European Journal of Operational Research*, 249(2):417–426.

Van-Sang Ha, Dang-Nhac Lu, Gyoo Seok Choi, Ha-Nam Nguyen, and Byeongnam Yoon. 2019. Improving credit risk prediction in online peer-to-peer (p2p) lending using feature selection with deep learning. In *2019 21st International Conference on Advanced Communication Technology (ICACT)*, pages 511–515. IEEE.

Hongliang He, Wenyu Zhang, and Shuai Zhang. 2018. A novel ensemble method for credit scoring: Adaption of different imbalance ratios. *Expert Systems with Applications*, 98:105–117.

Kaiming He, Xiangyu Zhang, Shaoqing Ren, and Jian Sun. 2016. Deep residual learning for image recognition. In *Proceedings of the IEEE conference on computer vision and pattern recognition*, pages 770–778.

Sepp Hochreiter and Jürgen Schmidhuber. 1997. Long short-term memory. *Neural computation*, 9(8):1735–1780.

Xin Huang, Ashish Khetan, Milan Cvitkovic, and Zohar Karnin. 2020. Tabtransformer: Tabular data modeling using contextual embeddings. *arXiv preprint arXiv:2012.06678*.

Swati Jadhav, Hongmei He, and Karl Jenkins. 2018. Information gain directed genetic algorithm wrapper feature selection for credit rating. *Applied Soft Computing*, 69:541–553.

Junxiang Jiang, Boyi Ni, and Chunping Wang. 2021. Financial fraud detection on micro-credit loan scenario via fuller location information embedding. In *Companion Proceedings of the Web Conference 2021*, pages 238–246.

Harsurinder Kaur, Husanbir Singh Pannu, and Avleen Kaur Malhi. 2019. A systematic review on imbalanced data challenges in machine learning: Applications and solutions. *ACM Computing Surveys (CSUR)*, 52(4):1–36.

Aleum Kim and Sung-Bae Cho. 2019. An ensemble semi-supervised learning method for predicting defaults in social lending. *Engineering Applications of Artificial Intelligence*, 81:193–199.

Diederik P Kingma and Jimmy Ba. 2014. Adam: A method for stochastic optimization. *arXiv preprint arXiv:1412.6980*.

Günter Klambauer, Thomas Unterthiner, Andreas Mayr, and Sepp Hochreiter. 2017. Self-normalizing neural networks. *Advances in neural information processing systems*, 30.

Håvard Kvamme, Nikolai Sellereite, Kjersti Aas, and Steffen Sjursen. 2018. Predicting mortgage default using convolutional neural networks. *Expert Systems with Applications*, 102:207–217.

Jianping Li, Xiaoqian Zhu, Cheng-Few Lee, Dengsheng Wu, Jichuang Feng, and Yong Shi. 2015. On the aggregation of credit, market and operational risks. *Review of Quantitative Finance and Accounting*, 44(1):161–189.

Wei Li, Shuai Ding, Hao Wang, Yi Chen, and Shanlin Yang. 2020. Heterogeneous ensemble learning with feature engineering for default prediction in peer-to-peer lending in china. *World Wide Web*, 23(1):23–45.

Ting Liang, Guanxiong Zeng, Qiwei Zhong, Jianfeng Chi, Jinghua Feng, Xiang Ao, and Jiayu Tang. 2021. Credit risk and limits forecasting in e-commerce consumer lending service via multi-view-aware mixture-of-experts nets. In *Proceedings of the 14th ACM international conference on web search and data mining*, pages 229–237.

Tsung-Yi Lin, Priya Goyal, Ross Girshick, Kaiming He, and Piotr Dollár. 2017. Focal loss for dense object detection. In *Proceedings of the IEEE international conference on computer vision*, pages 2980–2988.

Yang Liu, Xiang Ao, Qiwei Zhong, Jinghua Feng, Jiayu Tang, and Qing He. 2020. Alike and unlike: Resolving class imbalance problem in financial credit risk assessment. In *Proceedings of the 29th ACM International Conference on Information & Knowledge Management*, pages 2125–2128.

Xiaojun Ma, Jinglan Sha, Dehua Wang, Yuanbo Yu, Qian Yang, and Xueqi Niu. 2018. Study on a prediction of p2p network loan default based on the machine learning lightgbm and xgboost algorithms according to different high dimensional data cleaning. *Electronic Commerce Research and Applications*, 31:24–39.

Mohammad Mahbobi, Salman Kimiagari, and Marriappan Vasudevan. 2021. Credit risk classification: an integrated predictive accuracy algorithm using artificial and deep neural networks. *Annals of Operations Research*, pages 1–29.

Milad Malekipirbazari and Vural Aksakalli. 2015. Risk assessment in social lending via random forests. *Expert Systems with Applications*, 42(10):4621–4631.

Giovanni Mariani, Florian Scheidegger, Roxana Istrate, Costas Bekas, and Cristiano Malossi. 2018. Bagan: Data augmentation with balancing gan. *arXiv preprint arXiv:1803.09655*.

Dang Lien Minh, Abolghasem Sadeghi-Niaraki, Huynh Duc Huy, Kyungbok Min, and Hyeonjoon Moon. 2018. Deep learning approach for short-term stock trends prediction based on two-stream gated recurrent unit network. *Ieee Access*, 6:55392–55404.

Vincenzo Moscato, Antonio Picariello, and Giancarlo Sperlí. 2021. A benchmark of machine learning approaches for credit score prediction. *Expert Systems with Applications*, 165:113986.

Ben Poole, Subhaneil Lahiri, Maithra Raghu, Jascha Sohl-Dickstein, and Surya Ganguli. 2016. Exponential expressivity in deep neural networks through transient chaos. *Advances in neural information processing systems*, 29.

Lauri Puro, Jeffrey E Teich, Hannele Wallenius, and Jyrki Wallenius. 2010. Borrower decision aid for people-to-people lending. *Decision Support Systems*, 49(1):52–60.

Jiawei Ren, Mingyuan Zhang, Cunjun Yu, and Ziwei Liu. 2022. Balanced mse for imbalanced visual regression. *arXiv preprint arXiv:2203.16427*.

Steffen Rendle. 2010. Factorization machines. In *2010 IEEE International conference on data mining*, pages 995–1000. IEEE.

Omer Berat Sezer, Murat Ozbayoglu, and Erdogan Dogdu. 2017. A deep neural-network based stock trading system based on evolutionary optimized technical analysis parameters. *Procedia computer science*, 114:473–480.

Furao Shen, Jing Chao, and Jinxi Zhao. 2015. Forecasting exchange rate using deep belief networks and conjugate gradient method. *Neurocomputing*, 167:243–253.

Weiping Song, Chence Shi, Zhiping Xiao, Zhijian Duan, Yewen Xu, Ming Zhang, and Jian Tang. 2019. Autoint: Automatic feature interaction learning via self-attentive neural networks. In *Proceedings of the 28th ACM International Conference on Information and Knowledge Management*, pages 1161–1170.

Fei Tan, Xiurui Hou, Jie Zhang, Zhi Wei, and Zhenyu Yan. 2018. A deep learning approach to competing risks representation in peer-to-peer lending. *IEEE transactions on neural networks and learning systems*, 30(5):1565–1574.

Dejan Varmedja, Mirjana Karanovic, Srdjan Sladojevic, Marko Arsenovic, and Andras Anderla. 2019. Credit card fraud detection-machine learning methods. In *2019 18th International Symposium INFOTEH-JAHORINA (INFOTEH)*, pages 1-5. IEEE.

Ashish Vaswani, Noam Shazeer, Niki Parmar, Jakob Uszkoreit, Llion Jones, Aidan N Gomez, Łukasz Kaiser, and Illia Polosukhin. 2017. Attention is all you need. In *Advances in neural information processing systems*, pages 5998–6008.

Daixin Wang, Zhiqiang Zhang, Jun Zhou, Peng Cui, Jingli Fang, Quanhui Jia, Yanming Fang, and Yuan Qi. 2021a. Temporal-aware graph neural network for credit risk prediction. In *Proceedings of the 2021 SIAM International Conference on Data Mining (SDM)*, pages 702–710. SIAM.

Ruoxi Wang, Rakesh Shivanna, Derek Cheng, Sagar Jain, Dong Lin, Lichan Hong, and Ed Chi. 2021b. Dcn v2: Improved deep & cross network and practical lessons for web-scale learning to rank systems. In *Proceedings of the Web Conference 2021*, pages 1785–1797.

Yufei Xia, Chuanzhe Liu, YuYing Li, and Nana Liu. 2017a. A boosted decision tree approach using bayesian hyper-parameter optimization for credit scoring. *Expert Systems with Applications*, 78:225–241.

Yufei Xia, Chuanzhe Liu, and Nana Liu. 2017b. Cost-sensitive boosted tree for loan evaluation in peer-to-peer lending. *Electronic Commerce Research and Applications*, 24:30–49.

Junhui Xu, Zekai Lu, and Ying Xie. 2021. Loan default prediction of chinese p2p market: a machine learning methodology. *Scientific Reports*, 11(1):1–19.

Makoto Yamada, Wittawat Jitkrittum, Leonid Sigal, Eric P Xing, and Masashi Sugiyama. 2014. High-dimensional feature selection by feature-wise kernelized lasso. *Neural computation*, 26(1):185–207.

Zhi Yang, Yusi Zhang, Binghui Guo, Ben Y Zhao, and Yafei Dai. 2018. Deepcredit: Exploiting user cickstream for loan risk prediction in p2p lending. In *Twelfth International AAAI Conference on Web and Social Media*.

Wirot Yotsawat, Pakaket Wattuya, and Anongnart Srivihok. 2021. A novel method for credit scoring based on cost-sensitive neural network ensemble. *IEEE Access*, 9:78521–78537.

A Appendix

A.1 Training Details

For our model and all the deep-learning baselines, we use Adam (Kingma and Ba, 2014) optimizer with learning rate 5×10^{-4} and weight decay 1×10^{-4}. We set the batch size to $1,000$. For non-sequential model DNN, we set the embedding size to 16, use three-layer MLP, and set the hidden size to 1028, 256, and 128, respectively. For sequential models, we use a one-layer Transformer encoder, set the embedding size to 128, the number of heads to 8, and the dropout probability to be 0.1. We adopt a 5-fold cross-validation on the training set and evaluate the ensembled model on the test set.

Both sequential and non-sequential features are composed of time features (i.e., features about time such as date), real-valued features, and category features. For every time feature in date format, we subtract it by the date at which the credit report is used for prediction. That is, the time feature indicates the number of days between when the financial activity happens and when the credit report is called. Then for every time and real-value feature, we do zero-mean and one-std normalization and clip all values into $[-4, 4]$ to make the distribution easier for DL models to learn. For every category feature, we merge all the categories outside the top 30 into one category $\langle$UNK$\rangle$.

We utilize XGBoost (Chen et al., 2015) to select the most important 500 features of the non-sequential real-value features and discard the rest of them. We simply train an XGBoost model on the same task of risk prediction. After that, we choose 500 features with the highest feature importance value to feed the non-sequential DL model. For every category feature, we add a category $\langle$NAN$\rangle$, and for every real-value and time feature, besides replacing all NANs with 0s, we also create two indicators $[x = 0]$ and $[x = NAN]$. Therefore, for every real-value and time feature, there will be three corresponding features after this process. Thus, the 500 features we selected above become 1500 features.

A.2 Label Notation

The dataset mainly contains two types of labels: 1) short-term label i$x$label$y$, which means the user fails to pay back y days after the xth-month's repayment deadline; 2) long-term label overdue$y$, which means the user has at least one y-day overdue behavior in the last year.

In the following experimental parts we mainly use the following labels: $\mathcal{Y}_{\text{long}}$, the long-term label overdue15; $\mathcal{Y}_{\text{short}}^{\text{eval}}$, the main short-term label i1label30 used for evaluation; $\mathcal{Y}_{\text{short}}^{\text{other1}}, \mathcal{Y}_{\text{short}}^{\text{other2}}, \mathcal{Y}_{\text{short}}^{\text{other3}}$, denoting another three short-term labels i1label15, i2label30, i3label30, for training and evaluation.

A.3 Dataset Analysis

We show in Figure 5 that the input data distribution, i.e., the ratio of negative and positive data,

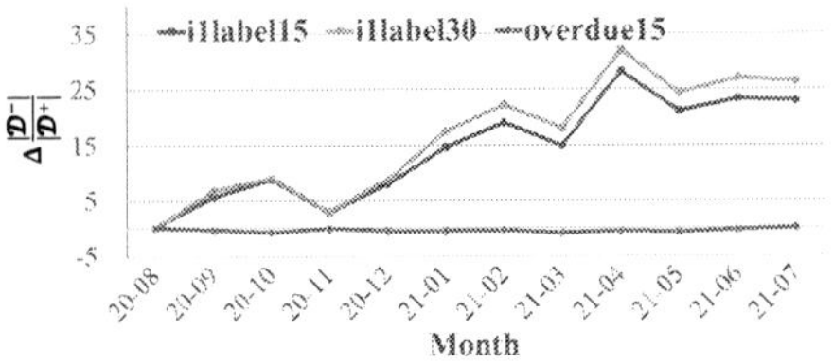

Figure 5: The change of imbalance ratio $\Delta\frac{|\mathcal{D}^-|}{|\mathcal{D}^+|}$ from August 2020 to July 2021. Compared with i1label15 and i1label30, the ratio of overdue15 is more stable.

varies over time. Besides the changes of the economic environment, the data distribution changes also because the consumers are first filtered by a basic decision model in practice, which keeps being optimized over time. As a result of a better filtering process, fewer applicants default and the data becomes more imbalanced. (e.g., see Jan-2021 and May-2021 for i1label15 and i1label30). Empirically, compared to the short-term label, we notice that the long-term label overdue15 is less sensitive to economic environment influence and optimization of the basic decision model. It is more stable because it summarizes a customer's behavior in the last 12 months, which is conceptually performing a smoothing operator over the timeline. In addition, the prediction of long-term risk is more difficult and thus is less affected by the basic decision model.

Reducing tokenizer's tokens per word ratio in Financial domain with T-MuFin BERT Tokenizer

Braulio C. Blanco Lambruschini and **Patricia Becerra-Sanchez** and **Mats Brorsson**
SNT, University of Luxembourg, Esch-sur-Alzette, Luxembourg
{braulio.blanco, patricia.becerra, mats.brorsson}@uni.lu

Maciej Zurad
Yoba S.A., Luxembourg, Luxembourg
maciej.zurad@yoba.com

Abstract

Most domain-specific BERT models are designed to work with short sentences and do not deal with the limitation of 512 tokens in the default BERT tokenizer. This limitation is further exacerbated if the tokenizer has high number of tokens per word ratio (fertility) and thus splits words into several tokens. A term-based multilingual Financial (T-MuFin) BERT tokenizer has been proposed to reduce the fertility of the default BERT tokenizer by extending the base dictionary with the most common financial terms instead of word pieces. One key factor of this proposal is to introduce multiword domain-specific terms without affecting the performance of the BERT models. T-MuFin BERT tokenizer reduces at least 40% of the fertility of long text sequences. T-MuFin BERT improves the fine-tuning of a downstream task by approximately 4% compared to a default fine-tuned model. Hence, by reducing the tokenizer's fertility, the results of explainable methods are more user-friendly.

1 Introduction

The vast amount of available textual information has allowed the development of Natural Language Processing (NLP) models to accelerate in recent years. In 2017, the *Transformer model* was proposed as a big step for NLP models (Vaswani *et al.*, 2017). The Transformer model uses an encoder-decoder architecture. The encoder extracts features from the input and the decoder interprets these features to produce the output. The input is a sequence of numerical vectors that represent the text. These numerical representations of the text are the embeddings. Both blocks take text embeddings as input and parallelize the processing using a self-attention mechanism. This mechanism replaces the sequentially of the existing Recurrent Neural Networks(RNN) processing at once each single *word-piece* and its most related text-pieces. This parallelization sped up the training of bigger models with much more data compared to the RNNs.

In 2018, google published BERT (Devlin *et al.*, 2018). BERT uses the encoder block of the Transformer Architecture for pre-training language models to perform specific eleven NLP tasks like Classification, Named Entity Recognition (NER), Sentiment Analysis (SA), and so on. The input text is divided into word-pieces or tokens and then passed to the BERT's embedding layer, limited to a maximum of 512 tokens.

The resulting pre-trained models contain a high text understanding level and can be fine-tuned for specific tasks and domains. Therefore, this fine-tuning requires less computational resources and less data. Training a BERT model with domain-specific language allows BERT to adapt the general BERT model to the target domain. Two examples of domain adaptation are FinBERT (Araci, 2019) for finance, BioBERT (Lee *et al.*, 2019) for Biomedicine, and so forth. Is important to mention that the BERT model used as the pre-trained model should be in the same language as the domain-specific training corpus. If is required to work with more than one language, a multilanguage BERT version can be used (Google-Research, 2019).

As explained before, BERT is limited to having up to 512 input tokens. The number of tokens depends on the tokenizer's capacity to divide the text into one or several sub-texts. For doing this, BERT uses WordPiece tokenization, which means that the biggest unit is *the word* and *one word can generate one or more tokens*. The measure of this capacity is called *tokenizer's fertility*. The authors in Rust *et al.* (2020) defines the tokenizer's fertility as the measure of the average number of subwords produced per tokenized word. The fertility of one means that each word produces a single token. Higher the fertility, the higher the number of tokens generated per word. Most of the current BERT-based models were trained to understand monolingual domains (English in our examples) and to perform NLP tasks based on short input sequences.

As previously stated, multilingual BERT models can understand several languages, but its drawback is its higher fertility in comparison with monolingual models, consequently less information can be fed into the model. For long text sequences, this can result in choosing which part of the sequence should be fed into the network and which one should be discarded, thus losing information that could be significant for the desired task.

We propose *Term-based Multilingual Financial BERT* or *T-MuFin BERT* Tokenizer. T-MuFin BERT not only fine-tunes the BERT model in the financial domain as FinBERT and similar models, but also, increases the dictionary size with multi-word financial terms, reducing the tokenizer's fertility below one.

T-MuFin BERT tokenizer is based on a multilingual BERT model fine-tuned with a dataset of annexes of Luxembourgish Annual Accounts in three languages (French, German, and English). In contrast with other financial BERT models, we extract the most frequent financial multi-word terms for extending the base dictionary. We use a n-gram terms generation and then we filter and extract the most frequent financial terms.

Besides to the self-discovered multi-word financial terms, we add to the dictionary also the financial terms from the Standardized Accounting Plan of the European Union [1]. This is because there are many financial terms that are not frequent but important in this domain.

T-MuFin BERT tokenizer was fine-tuned using a Masked Model Learning task (MML) and then tested using a classification task (CL) as the downstream task. T-MuFin BERT tokenizer reduces the average fertility of the default BERT tokenizer by 40-50%. Furthermore, it reduced the number of truncated sentences for paragraphs to almost zero in our downstream task.

Another benefit of having tokens at the term level is to have also explanations at this level. Especially in finance, models have to explain the reason for their predictions, promote transparency and adjust models to reduce any kind of bias. At the subword level, we must weigh the contributions of the subtokens that make up each term in order to facilitate the understanding for the end user. With our approach, we get a direct understandable result.

The next steps of our research are aimed at aligning numerical representations of domain-specific terms for a multilingual scenario. Our proposition can be extended to other domains where is important to give complete numerical meaning to multi-word terms and to clarify the explanations of NLP models such as medicine, law, or science.

2 Related Work

Natural Language Processing (NLP) models help machines to understand and process human language, but machines only understand numbers. In consequence, the first difficulty was to express the text in numbers that a machine can understand. As referred by Khurana *et al.* (2022), the initial models like Bag-Of-Words and One-hot-Encoding were very sparse. Later, models like Word2Vec (Mikolov *et al.*, 2013) and GloVe (Pennington *et al.*, 2014) could reduce the sparsity but still, the context was not considered to give a proper meaning for dealing with ambiguity.

BERT (Devlin *et al.*, 2018) made a big step in NLP, using the encoder of the Transformer Architecture and its self-attention mechanism, for parallelizing the processing of the input in contrast to the existing sequential models like Recurrent Neural Network (RNN) (Rumelhart *et al.*, 1986), Long-short Term Memory (LSTM / BiLSTM) (Hochreiter and Schmidhuber, 1997; Schuster and Paliwal, 1997) and Gated Recurrent Units (GRU) (Cho *et al.*, 2014). BERT is a Pre-trained Language Model (PLM), which means that has a vocabulary, relations, and some good level of language understanding in its weights. The smaller BERT model contains 12 encoder layers with 110M parameters. It was trained using Masked Language Model (MLM) and Next Sentence Prediction (NSP) with a corpus with more than 3.3 billion English words in four days using 16 TPU chips. In consequence, we can use the pre-trained model to fine-tune it for specifics downstream tasks, and it will require fewer data and a shorter training time. Some of these NLP downstream tasks are Named Entity Recognition (NER), Classification Task (CL), Sentiment Analysis (SA), Next Sentence Prediction, Machine Translation, Question Answering, and Text Summarization.

A tokenizer converts text into a vector of numbers before feeding into the model. These numeri-

[1] Regulation (EC) No 1606/2002 of the European Parliament and of the Council of 19 July 2002. Source: https://eur-lex.europa.eu/legal-content/EN/TXT/HTML/?uri=CELEX:32002R1606

cal representations are called embeddings. BERT comes with its own tokenizer and using a dictionary of known words, replaces each word into one or several word-pieces or tokens. Is important to focus on the dictionary of words, because based on that, the meanings of the words were going to be defined by the surrounding context (Tripathy *et al.*, 2021). BERT was originally trained with English corpus, and there are many other versions trained for other languages like CamemBERT for French (Martin *et al.*, 2020), GBERT for German (Chan *et al.*, 2020), RoBERTa for Spanish (Liu *et al.*, 2019) and so on. On contrary of these monolingual models, there are also multilingual models which were trained with 104 different languages for use in multilingual scenarios.

BERT tokenizers were trained under the wordPiece paradigm. It means that one word can be composed of several entries in the dictionary and therefore, several tokens. Especially for Multilingual BERT, the average number of generated tokens per word is higher than in monolingual models. Rust *et al.* (2020) defined this ratio as the *tokenizer's fertility*. Higher fertility means more generated tokens per text input and could cause less information provided into a network in long sequences of text. Multilingual BERT models are useful for using a single model to perform a specific task for a multilanguage dataset. But the main drawback of this is the high fertility of the corresponding tokenizer. BERT models are limited to 512 input tokens, and this is the reason why only short sentences can be processed in this model (avoiding using them together with other models like LSTM).

BERT models can vary also with respect to the specific domain, to improve its performance for specific tasks. This domain adaptation is usually a fine-tuning for the desired task with a domain corpus. Most of the published and available BERT-based models work on fine-tuning the weights of the BERT model itself with the default BERT tokenizer dictionary. It means that they do not add new terms to the default dictionary. In other domains different from finance, we can find a few works on extending the BERT's dictionary with new terms like Douka *et al.* (2021), which creates JuriBERT, a fine-tuned BERT Legal french model which appends 32,000 new entries to CamemBERT dictionary. Wang *et al.* (2019) extended the multilingual dictionary of BERT to reduce the out-of-vocabulary (OOV) words. They use existing tokens to provide meaning to the new one-word terms under two approaches *Joint Mapping* and *Mixture Mapping*. This approach is equivalent to sentence embedding methods such as SciBERT (Beltagy *et al.*, 2019) for science and LegalBERT (Chalkidis *et al.*, 2020) for law. In our case, we train the embeddings of the multiword terms together with their components to try to align all the numerical representations.

In the financial domain, there are some fine-tuned BERT models like FinBERT (Araci, 2019), which is based on bert-base-uncased[2], having a total of 30,522 entries in the dictionary and trained for English. FinBERT uses the default BERT tokenizer to avoid extending the main dictionary. This model outperforms the default BERT model in the financial domain using PhraseBank, a database of financial news, for predicting the sentiment of the short text sequence (SA). Despite this improvement, its fertility is the same as the English default BERT model.

In 2022, FINER-139 by Loukas *et al.* (2022) was released, a financial dataset of 1.1 M annotated sentences. These annotations were obtained from company filings using XBRL tags. These tags are been using by many countries and over time are going to be broadly used. This format requires companies to enrich financial reports with tags that can be read easily. Most of these tokens are numeric values associated with financial concepts. They replace these numeric values with concept-based tokens. They created SEC-BERT, a fine-tuned BERT model where they test the new tokens. With SEC-BERT they showed that fragmented tokens (one word is composed of several tokens) harm BERT's performance and in comparison with FinBERT, their results outperform the default BERT and FinBERT models.

Contrasted with the initial numerical representation of words like Word2Vec (Mikolov *et al.*, 2013), where the vector itself represents the meaning of the specific word, BERT's Embedding layer is not enough to represent the meaning of a word. BERT model process the embeddings in 12 Encoder layers. Due to BERT's ability to handle term ambiguities based on its context, the numerical meaning for each word is defined in the lower Encoder layers.

Thus, BERT uses lower Encoder layers for language understanding and the remaining upper layers for performing the specific NLP downstream task. As an example, the word *"bank"*, can be inter-

[2]https://huggingface.co/bert-base-uncased

preted as *"financial institution"*, *"place to sit"*, or *"place alongside the river"*. There is no clear limit to where the language understanding finishes and the task-related understanding starts. It varies from term to term along the 512 input tokens and the 12 Encoder layers.

The current state of the art with respect to financial tokenizers is mostly limited to terms discovered from financial news datasets. Our contribution is to provide a multi-word dictionary with contextualized embeddings for being used in financial BERT-based models. Allowing to reduce the tokenizer's multi-language fertility, keeping financial multi-word terms as a whole without losing performance.

As studied in detail by Yang *et al.* (2023). Other models than BERT which are having even better results are derived from the Transformer architectures that take only the decoder part. These models like GPT-1 and its derivative works such as GPT-3, ChatGPT, Llama, Bard, and many others, are mainly closed sources and require a huge computational architecture to train and fine-tune. Some open-source GPT-derived, and not heavy, models like Alpaca or Vicuna are available only for research purposes, not for commercial, which limits their application.

3 Dataset

The data used in this study was obtained from the Luxembourg Business Registers (LBR) and is publicly available for download [3]. The LBR Annual Accounts consist of Financial Statements, which can contain only Balance Sheets or also Profit and Loss Statements, and Legal Annexes or Appendixes. These annexes use natural language to provide additional information to the Financial Statements. Although the Financial Statements must follow a specific template, there is no set layout for the legal annexes [4]. We have annexes that have a single page or even more than 15 pages.

For the present work, our dataset only considers the last presented Annual Account for a company that can be active or inactive. In this case, we have 74,539 annual accounts that were processed using OCR tools for scanned documents and HTML content extraction for PDF-readable documents. Most of the documents' pages in the LBR dataset are in French ($\approx 84\%$) and the rest are in German ($\approx 7\%$) and English ($\approx 9\%$), as shown in Table 1.

Language	Documents	(%)	Pages	(%)
French	66,114	88.7	426,610	84.4
German	4,924	6.6	33,966	6.7
English	3,501	4.7	45,112	8.9
Total	74,539	100	505,688	100

Table 1: Dataset distribution per language.

4 Proposition

Our main goal is to create a dictionary of financial frequent terms that will have associated vector embeddings trained with a context of words from the Annexes of the Annual Accounts. This will allow us to disambiguate the terms to a finance context and feed the models with more information without increasing the size of the input layer or reducing their performance in comparison with a base model.

4.1 Dictionary extension and embedding's training

We are using *bert-base-multilingual-uncased* [5] as the base model and tokenizer (with a corresponding dictionary D). If a word is not part of the dictionary D the tokenizer splits the word into a set of sub-words and/or characters, in consequence, tokenizing a word can result in a set of one or more tokens. For this reason, we are extending the base dictionary with domain-specific terms and then fine-tuning the model to calculate the vector embeddings. For the fine-tuning, we use Masked Language Model (MLM).

The terms to be added to the dictionary are the result of performing the following steps.

1. *Candidates extraction*: We are using multi-word terms for creating the tokenizer's dictionary. Hereby, the list of candidates is the result of the text extraction in the form of n-grams. We defined empirically n=5, which covers most of the financial terms.

2. *Candidates cleaning*: For each term, we perform a set of cleaning tasks: (A) removing enumerators (like a., note 1.3, iv., etc); (B) removing noisy characters (;-,); (C) using regular expressions identifying and replacing dates

[3] https://www.lbr.lu

[4] https://guichet.public.lu/en/entreprises/gestion-juridique-comptabilite/comptable/enregistrement/methodes-etablissement-comptes-annuels.html

[5] https://huggingface.co/bert-base-multilingual-uncased

and numbers with special *[DATE]* and *[NUMBER]* tags respectively; (D) and replace apostrophes with blank spaces.

3. *Top terms selection*: The cleaned candidates' list is sorted by frequency and then we select the top τ terms by language. This list will be our *base list*.

4. *Financial statements labeled terms*: The tree structure of a financial report like a balance sheet or profit and loss statements are full of multi-word terms that have a semantic relation with their surrounding neighbors in the three. For example *"convertible loans"* with *"non convertible loans"* (sibling) and *"creditors"* (parent). This list is appended in the *base list*.

5. *Terms decomposition*: Each term in the *base list* is decomposed and the main subterms are added to the *base list*. For instance, if the term is "subscribed capital amount", the extracted decomposed terms are *"subscribed capital"*, *"capital amount"*, *"subscribed"*, *"capital"* and *"amount"*. The main terms and their components are going to be inserted into our *base list* v.

For example, with T-MuFin BERT tokenizer, a financial multi-word term like *"capital investment subsidies"* will be considered as a single token because it is a frequent term. Moreover, this term is added to the dictionary as a whole, also we are adding its term components. For instance, for the previous example, the tokenizer also going to generate the following tokens: *"capital investment subsidies"*, *"capital investment"*, *"investment subsidies"*, *"capital"*, *"investment"* and *"subsidies"*. During training, all those tokens are going to be numerically related to each other.

Only the terms t in v that are not part of the dictionary D are included in the dictionary D ($t_{new} \leftarrow t \in v \;\; \& \;\; t \notin v$). The increment in the dictionary size causes a resizing of the embedding layer in the base BERT model before training. For the fine-tuning of the default BERT, we use as well the MLM task.

The training and testing datasets consist in sentences that have at least one t_{new}. For each sentence, the same *Candidates cleaning* step that we use for obtaining the most frequent terms are used. With the cleaned sentence, we identify t_{new} and we extract the context surrounding it. The context consists of the previous κ words and the following κ words to t_{new} (κ: context size). If κ=2, we take two words previous to the frequent term and two words posterior to the new term (if exists). Finally, we replace 20% of context's tokens with the `[MASK]` token, considering that the masked word should have more than five characters (to avoid connectors, negations and so on to be masked) and do not mask tokens that are part of a word. If a term contains n words, we also append to the training and testing dataset each component of t_{new} tokenized. This resulting dataset is shuffled and we use 70 % of the samples for training and the remaining 30% for testing. Additionally, for training the financial statements labeled terms, we add the terms and the training context are the siblings and parents until the first level, this will allow us to create a strong relationship between terms in the same financial category.

Hyper-parameter	Values
σ: dataset size	10, 25, 50, 75 and 100%
ϕ: frozen layers	2, 4, 6, 8 and 10
λ: learning rate	1e-5, 2e-5, 3e-5 and 4e-5
δ: dropout	10s, 15 and 20%
κ: context size	2,3,4 and 5

Table 2: Testing values for each hyper-parameter for training T-MuFin embeddings.

We test different hyper-parameters that lead us to the best-performed model. These hyper-parameters are κ*: context size*; λ*: optimizer's learning rate*; δ*: BERT's dropout percentage*; σ*: dataset size* for (a) extracting the frequent terms and (b) for training the MLM model; and ϕ*: number of BERT encoder layers to freeze*. Table 2 shows the different test case values per each hyperparameter. We use AdamW as the optimizer.

Freezing from 2 to 12 encoder BERT layers of the BERT model during fine-tuning allows us to reduce the memory used in the GPU and make the model put the effort into the embeddings' training and also the upper encoder BERT layers (remaining layers and the final dense layer). We are going to try different numbers of layers to freeze in order to get the best results and take advantage of the memory in the GPU, increasing the batch size. Figure 1 shows the layers to freeze and the corresponding layers to train in the MLM task.

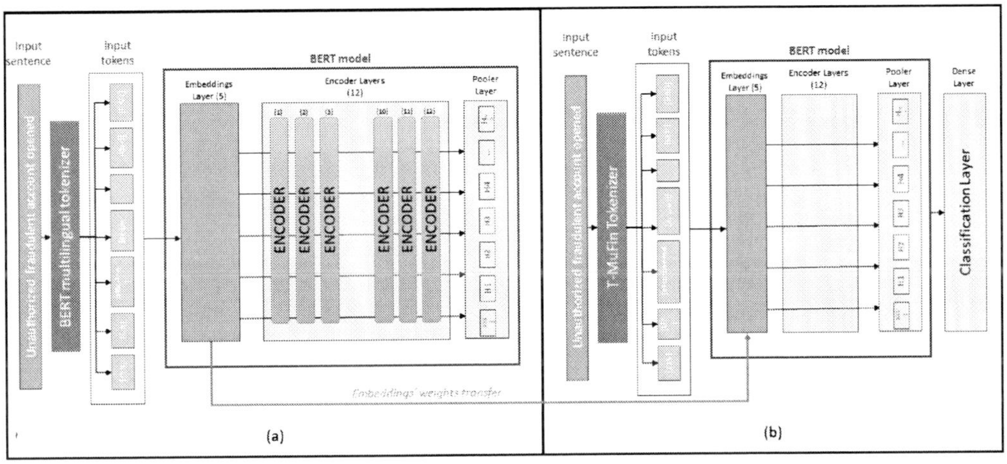

Figure 1: (a) shows the BERT model and tokenizer. The layers to freeze are up to 10 first encoder layers, for each test case, the remaining layers will be training layers; (b) shows the model to test the performance of T-MuFin BERT tokenizer which includes a final dense layer for the specific classification task, transferring the first unfreezed layers from the MLM model

4.2 Classification as Downstream task

To test the performance of T-MuFin BERT tokenizer, we use a Classification Task (CL) as the downstream task. The model will predict nine financial categories based on a text paragraph. For doing this, from each Annual Account Annex, we extracted the last-level subtitles and their corresponding paragraphs. Then we selected the first most frequent subtitles and manually assigned them one of nine financial categories. These categories are (1) Asset, (2) Capital, (3) Deposit, (4) Expenses, (5) Investment, (6) Obligations, (7) Personal, (8) Receivables, and (9) Taxes. The training and testing datasets are obtained from subtitles that have an assigned financial category and also have paragraphs with at least 20 words. The evaluation dataset is composed of 10,000 documents.

The base model is a *bert-base-multilingual-uncased* BertModel with its own default tokenizer. For comparing our tokenizers with respect to the base model we copy the weights from T-MuFin BERT tokenizer (Embedding and unfreezed encoder layers) and train in the Classification task for 5 epochs like the base model. All the hyper-parameters are the same for the base model and T-MuFin-based models.

For these models, we only add a classification layer after BERT model. We take only the first hidden state ([CLS]) of the BERT model as input for our dropout and classification layer (Dense Layer). The dropout percentage of the classification layer

Hyper-parameter	Value
σ: dataset size	34K working samples%
ϕ: frozen layers	embeddings and first 10
λ: learning rate	1e-5
δ: dropout	10%

Table 3: Hyper-parameter for downstream task (CL) evaluation.

and the BERT dropout is the same (δ). We are using CrossEntropyLoss as our loss function, using the class weights to deal with unbalanced datasets.

Table 3 shows the hyperparameters used for this model. Using AdamW as the optimizer and a batch size of 30.

Equation 1 evaluates the tokenizers' fertility ψ, which is the average number of tokens generated per word. Additionally, as shown in Equation 2, we are going to measure the proportion of samples that were truncated because of the 510 tokens limitation (Π), considering reducing two special tokens for [CLS] and [SEP].

$$\psi = \sum_{i=0}^{n} \frac{(Number_{tokens}/Number_{words})}{n} \quad (1)$$

$$\Pi = \sum_{i=0}^{n} \begin{cases} 1 & , Number_{tokens} > 510 \\ 0 & , \text{otherwise.} \end{cases} \quad (2)$$

Moreover, in the results section, we show other

Dataset size (σ)	Time (hr.)	F1 Score Training	F1 Score Testing
10	**6.78**	**85.62%**	**77.65%**
25	11.90	85.64%	76.03%
50	18.37	86.30%	78.19%
75	22.52	87.24%	79.59%

Table 4: Impact of dataset size in tokenizer's training.

Frozen Layer (ϕ)	F1 Score Training	F1 Score Testing
2	85.63%	84.79 %
4	85.78%	84.72 %
6	86.59%	85.07 %
8	87.37%	84.95 %
10	**86.41%**	**85.55%**

Table 5: Evaluation of the number of frozen layers.

Learning rate Layer (λ)	F1 Score Training	F1 Score Testing
1e-5	**84.86 %**	**83.72%**
2e-5	84.52%	83.16%
3e-5	83.66%	82.40%
4e-5	83.53%	82.17%
5e-5	83.54%	82.25%

Table 6: Evaluation of learning rate λ.

Dropout Layer (ϕ)	F1 Score Training	F1 Score Testing
10	**85.37%**	**80.80%**
15	85.22%	80.72%
20	85.40%	80.40%

Table 7: Evaluation of dropout percentage.

statistical measures like the average number of tokens per document, the average number of words per document, and the average number of tokens per word.

To evaluate the explainability results with the default BERT tokenizer and T-MuFin BERT tokenizer, we use the fine-tuned models with Captum.ai [6], which analyze the most important input features that the model takes into consideration for making a single prediction.

5 Experiment and Results

The subsection 5.1 shows the results for training the tokenizer. The best-performed tokenizer has been selected to be evaluated in the CL task (subsection 5.1).

5.1 Tokenizer: Embedding's training

In this section, we train the tokenizer with different hyper-parameters such as κ, λ, δ, and ϕ.

5.1.1 Dataset size selection (σ)

Table 4 shows the impact of the different dataset sizes in the overall F1 Score, having: $\kappa = 2$, $\lambda = 5e - 5$ and $\delta = 10\%$.

We decided to train with only 10% of the data based on the results in Table 4. This is because the impact on the performance is not high and the time required for tokenizer's training is significantly lower.

Once defined the dataset size σ for the tokenizer's training, we execute several test cases with different hyper-parameters: ϕ, λ, δ, and κ. When a hyper-parameter is being evaluated the default values for the others are $\phi = 0$, $\lambda = 5e-5$, $\delta = 10\%$, $\kappa = 2$.

Table 6 shows that the best learning rate λ is 1e-5, with a F1 Score of 83.72%. We also tested others lowers and biggers learning rates whose performance were lower.

Table 7 shows that the best dropout percentage δ is 10%, with a F1 Score of 80.80%. Also, we test bigger values like 20% and 30% but the performance drops drastically.

Table 8 shows that the best context size is $\kappa = 5$, with a F1 Score of 85.05%.

As shown in Table 9 with the best combination of these hyper-parameters, we got the following results in 5 epochs. We use this model for fine-tuning the BertModel for the selected downstream task.

5.2 Tokenizer's Performance evaluation

5.2.1 Establishing CL baseline

For the evaluation of T-MuFin BERT tokenizer, first, we evaluate the performance of BERT baseline model and the parameters specified in Table 3. In Table 10 is shown the performance F1 score for training, testing and also the default fertility and the proportion of samples that did not fit in the model.

As our Classification task is working only with small text to determine if the dictionary extension of the tokenizer affects the downstream tasks, the effect on the tokenizer's fertility is not easy to appreciate. Hence, we use T-MuFin tokenizer to process 1,000 Annual Accounts' Annexes. As we can

[6]https://captum.ai/

Context Size Layer (κ)	F1 Score Training	F1 Score Testing
2	83.54%	82.25%
3	85.10%	84.05%
4	84.85%	83.83%
5	**85.99%**	**85.05%**

Table 8: Evaluation of context size κ.

F1 Score Training	F1 Score Testing
89.87%	89.08%

Table 9: Results for training with the best hyper-parameters

F1 Score Training	F1 Score Testing	Fertility (ψ)	% Truncated samples (Π)
95.08%	94.97%	1.2592	0.79

Table 10: Performance of BERT BaseLine

Metric	Value
Avg. Number of tokens per document	1,182
Avg. Number of words per document	867
Avg. Number of tokens per word	1.37
Avg. fertility per document (ψ)	0.126

Table 11: BaseLine for fertility ratios

F1 Score Training	F1 Score Testing	Fertility (ψ)	% Truncated samples (Π)
98.20%	98.80%	0.8906	0.2

Table 12: Results for training with T-MuFin BERT tokenizer

see in Table 11, on average for feeding a BERT model with complete annexes of Luxembourgish Annual Accounts, we require on average 867 tokens.

5.2.2 T-MuFin BERT Tokenizer results

With the best performed T-MuFin BERT tokenizer from Table 9 and the same hyper-parameters as the baseline in our downstream task, we got an increment of the F1 score for testing from 94.97% to 98.80% as shown in Table 12.

As shown in Table 12, T-MuFin BERT tokenizer could reduce from 1.2592 to 0.8906 ($\approx 41\%$) the fertility ψ with respect to the default BERT tokenizer and reduces almost to zero (0.2%) the truncated sentences Π.

As shown in Table 13, we can see that the number of tokens per word was reduced on average at ≈ 1.0, this is mainly because a big group of multi-term tokens is reducing the average of the words that produce more than one token. The average fertility of the document was improved $\approx 50\%$.

Figure 2 shows the difference in terms of explainable NLP with T-MuFin tokenizer, which makes more easy to understand for the final user and also allows the NLP model to focus on the term as a whole.

6 Discussion

Most of the current NLP projects using BERT-based models are related to domain adaptation while keeping the same default dictionary. However, researchers who are increasing the dictionary are only considering single-word terms. T-MuFin increases its dictionary with multiword terms in finance without affecting the performance of downstream tasks and even increasing them due to the self-nature of the fine-tuning. Adding these domain-specific terms always reduces the fertility of the tokenizer. For T-MuFin, this fertility goes below one, which means that we can feed more information into the BERT-based models.

In our proposed terms discovery method, the discovery of new terms is not only based on including frequent multi-word terms in the new dictionary but also on including their corresponding components and training them together.

Using T-MuFin BERT tokenizer can help explainable models produce more understandable results. This is because financial terms are no longer divided into word-pieces, which can make it more difficult for the user to process at first sight.

This proposed method for terms discovery and training can be applied to any other domain like Medicine, Law, or Science; where most of the multiword terms tend to be understood as a whole.

Is important to mention that in the lasts weeks, the GPT-based model is reaching very good performance for NLP tasks, but unlike BERT-based models, those models can not be used for commercial purposes unless the service is purchased.

7 Conclusion

By training the BERT embeddings with financial data and extending the dictionary with the most common multi-word financial terms, T-MuFin BERT tokenizer can increase the information feed

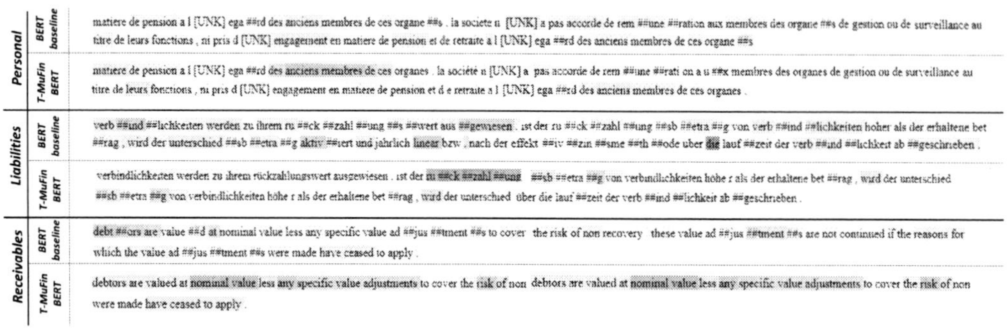

Figure 2: Comparison between NLP explainability using the default BERT multilingual tokenizer for French, German, and English using the Classification fine-tuned model (left), and the fine-tuned model using T-MuFin BERT tokenizer (right).

Table 13: BaseLine for fertility ratios

Metric	Value	Improvement
Avg. number of tokens per document	868	26%
Avg. number of words per document	867	-
Avg. number of tokens per word	1.02	34%
Avg. fertility per document (ψ)	0.065	48.41%

into a BERT model. When we freeze the first 10 layers of BERT to calculate the weights of the embeddings, we force the model to disambiguate the terms at the beginning of the model, in the Embeddings layers. Later these weights are transferred to a default BERT and used for any downstream task. With T-MuFin tokenizer, we could increase the F1 score from 94.97% to 98.80% with respect to the baseline of the downstream task. This means that we are not losing performance with the newly trained multiword terms; on the contrary, we increase it.

On the other hand, we reduced between $\approx 40\%$ and $\approx 50\%$ of the fertility of the default BERT tokenizer for short and long text sentences respectively. We could also reduce almost to zero the truncation of long paragraphs and facilitate explainable AI.

For future steps, we plan to align the numerical representations of the terms along different languages. This means that the same term in different languages should have very similar numerical representation, making it easier to include more languages in the NLP models.

Acknowledgements

This work has been partly funded by the Luxembourg National Research Fund (FNR) under contract number 15403349.

References

Dogu Araci. Finbert: Financial sentiment analysis with pre-trained language models, 2019.

Iz Beltagy, Kyle Lo, and Arman Cohan. SciBERT: A pretrained language model for scientific text. In *Proceedings of the 2019 Conference on Empirical Methods in Natural Language Processing and the 9th International Joint Conference on Natural Language Processing (EMNLP-IJCNLP)*, pages 3615–3620, Hong Kong, China, November 2019. Association for Computational Linguistics.

Ilias Chalkidis, Manos Fergadiotis, Prodromos Malakasiotis, Nikolaos Aletras, and Ion Androutsopoulos. Legal-bert: The muppets straight out of law school, 2020.

Branden Chan, Stefan Schweter, and Timo Möller. German's next language model. In *Proceedings of the 28th International Conference on Computational Linguistics*, pages 6788–6796, Barcelona, Spain (Online), December 2020. International Committee on Computational Linguistics.

Kyunghyun Cho, Bart Van Merrienboer, Caglar Gulcehre, Dzmitry Bahdanau, Fethi Bougares, Holger Schwenk, and Yoshua Bengio. Learning phrase representations using rnn encoder-decoder for statistical machine translation. *arXiv preprint arXiv:1406.1078*, 2014.

Jacob Devlin, Ming-Wei Chang, Kenton Lee, and Kristina Toutanova. Bert: Pre-training of deep bidirectional transformers for language understanding, 2018.

Stella Douka, Hadi Abdine, Michalis Vazirgiannis, Rajaa El Hamdani, and David Restrepo Amariles. Juribert: A masked-language model adaptation for french legal text. *CoRR*, abs/2110.01485, 2021.

Google-Research. Bert: Multilingual models, 2019.

Sepp Hochreiter and Jürgen Schmidhuber. Long short-term memory. *Neural Computation*, 1997.

Diksha Khurana, Aditya Koli, Kiran Khatter, and Sukhdev Singh. Natural language processing: state of the art, current trends and challenges. In Springer, editor, *Multimedia Tools and Applications*, 2022.

Jinhyuk Lee, Wonjin Yoon, Sungdong Kim, Donghyeon Kim, Sunkyu Kim, Chan Ho So, and Jaewoo Kang. BioBERT: a pre-trained biomedical language representation model for biomedical text mining. *Bioinformatics*, 36(4):1234–1240, 09 2019.

Yinhan Liu, Myle Ott, Naman Goyal, Jingfei Du, Mandar Joshi, Danqi Chen, Omer Levy, Mike Lewis, Luke Zettlemoyer, and Veselin Stoyanov. Roberta: A robustly optimized bert pretraining approach, 2019.

Lefteris Loukas, Manos Fergadiotis, Ilias Chalkidis, Eirini Spyropoulou, Prodromos Malakasiotis, Ion Androutsopoulos, and Georgios Paliouras. FiNER: Financial numeric entity recognition for XBRL tagging. In *Proceedings of the 60th Annual Meeting of the Association for Computational Linguistics (Volume 1: Long Papers)*, pages 4419–4431, Dublin, Ireland, May 2022. Association for Computational Linguistics.

Louis Martin, Benjamin Muller, Pedro Javier Ortiz Suá rez, Yoann Dupont, Laurent Romary, Éric de la Clergerie, Djamé Seddah, and Benoît Sagot. CamemBERT: a tasty french language model. In *Proceedings of the 58th Annual Meeting of the Association for Computational Linguistics*. Association for Computational Linguistics, 2020.

Tomas Mikolov, Kai Chen, Greg Corrado, and Jeffrey Dean. Efficient estimation of word representations in vector space, 2013.

Jeffrey Pennington, Richard Socher, and Christopher D. Manning. Glove: Global vectors for word representation. 2014.

David E Rumelhart, Geoffrey E Hinton, and Ronald J Williams. Learning representations by back-propagating errors. *Nature*, 323(6088):533–536, 1986.

Phillip Rust, Jonas Pfeiffer, Ivan Vulić, Sebastian Ruder, and Iryna Gurevych. How good is your tokenizer? on the monolingual performance of multilingual language models, 2020.

Mike Schuster and Kuldip K. Paliwal. Bidirectional recurrent neural networks. *IEEE Transactions on Signal Processing*, 1997.

Jatin Karthik Tripathy, Sibi Chakkaravarthy Sethuraman, Meenalosini Vimal Cruz, Anupama Namburu, Mangalraj P., Nandha Kumar R., Sudhakar Ilango S, and Vaidehi Vijayakumar. Comprehensive analysis of embeddings and pre-training in nlp. *Computer Science Review*, 42:100433, 2021.

Ashish Vaswani, Noam Shazeer, Niki Parmar, Jakob Uszkoreit, Llion Jones, Aidan N Gomez, Łukasz Kaiser, and Illia Polosukhin. Attention is all you need. *Advances in neural information processing systems*, 30, 2017.

Hai Wang, Dian Yu, Kai Sun, Jianshu Chen, and Dong Yu. Improving pre-trained multilingual model with vocabulary expansion. In *Proceedings of the 23rd Conference on Computational Natural Language Learning (CoNLL)*, pages 316–327, Hong Kong, China, November 2019. Association for Computational Linguistics.

Jingfeng Yang, Hongye Jin, Ruixiang Tang, Xiaotian Han, Qizhang Feng, Haoming Jiang, Bing Yin, and Xia Hu. Harnessing the power of llms in practice: A survey on chatgpt and beyond, 2023.

LoKI: Money Laundering Report Generation via Logical Table-to-Text using Meta Learning

Ram Ganesh V*, Harika CM*, Rajesh Kumar Ranjan, Debasmita Das, Siddhartha Asthana
AI Garage, Mastercard, Gurgaon, India
{firstname.secondname}@mastercard.com

Abstract

The submission of Anti-Money Laundering (AML) reports is a key compliance mandate that financial institutions strictly adhere to, which involves a detailed scrutiny of accounts and transactions that may potentially be suspicious. Previous research have explored the automation of report creation via table-to-text generation. Our paper introduces a novel approach utilising table-to-text generation, known as Logical Key Inference (LoKI). Proposed method employs meta-learning to augment the content selection and addresses three salient gaps in logical table-to-text generation: (1) dynamic selection of pertinent table attributes, (2) mitigating hallucination during the attribute-to-value mapping process, and (3) the ability to incorporate newly added attributes without the demand for explicit additional training. Through experiments and ablation studies, we show that LoKI outperforms existing generative methods for compliance reporting.

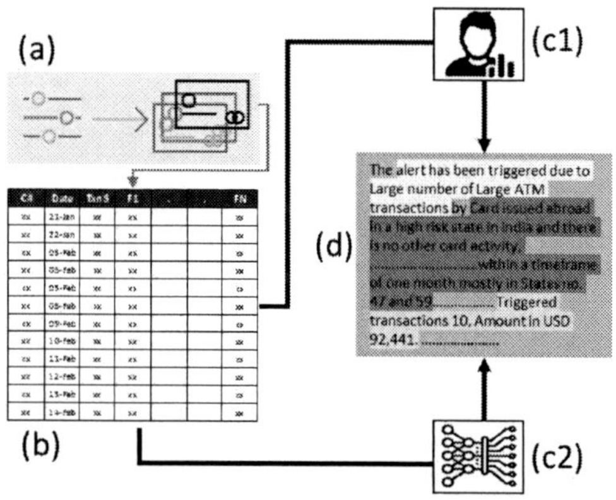

Figure 1: **AML report generation process** (a) Explanatory system to flag suspicious Money Laundering accounts and transactions (b) Tabular data containing historical transactions of the potential suspicious accounts (c) Report generation: (c1) Financial analyst generating AML reports by reviewing the tabular data (c2) Alternatively system-generated AML reports (d) The text report containing factual evidence against each suspicious account.

1 Introduction

Money laundering is a global issue affecting nations in terms of financial health and physical security including terrorism, human trafficking etc. (IMF, 2023). According to an estimate (Kolmar, 2022), 2-5% of global GDP ($2 trillion) is laundered in a single year. Hence, combating money laundering is more urgent than ever, especially for financial institutions like banks and payment networks. Financial institutions are required to provide highly confidential reports that include information on suspicious activities to national law enforcement authorities investigating financial matters. Financial analysts thoroughly review historical transactions regarding potentially risky accounts before scrupulously writing the reports. These reports are often written after analysing data stored in a tabular format containing suspicious accounts and corresponding transaction history (see Figure 1). Research tried to reduce the manual effort by automating the process of report creation using Table-to-text generation methods (Lin et al., 2022).

Table-to-text generation (TTG) is an active area of research aiming to generate text from tabular data. Existing methods for TTG includes static attribute selection (i.e., rule-based (Reiter and Dale, 2000), and template based (Oh and Rudnicky, 2000)), conditional copy of text, (Puduppully et al., 2019), and fine-tuning sequence-to-sequence models (Kale and Rastogi, 2020). Even though the generated text is linguistically fluent, the challenge is that the surface-level spurious correlations are easier to capture than the causal relationship between tabular data and generated text, resulting in hallucination, generation of incorrect facts, and inconsistent content planning and document structuring. There are recent research work that ad-

*These two authors contributed equally to this work

Proceedings of the Joint Workshop of the 5th Financial Technology and Natural Language Processing (FinNLP) and 2nd Multimodal AI For Financial Forecasting (Muffin), Macao, August 20, 2023.

dress content planning by using copy-mechanism (Gehrmann et al., 2018) or neural models based on soft-template (Wiseman et al., 2018). Researchers have also explored training a separate planning module to produce relevant content, which is then fed into a generator (Goldfarb-Tarrant et al., 2020) but the strategies result in a disconnection between planning and generation of high fidelity logically structured summaries. Given how sensitive and confidential nature of this data is using we cannot use the latest models released by OPEN AI like GPT 3.5 and GPT 4 due to privacy concerns.

To address the above gaps, we formulate three objectives in our proposed solution: (1) Dynamic selection of logical key table attributes (i.e. feature selection) to include in the report, (2) Ability to handle hallucination while mapping attributes to values (3) Adaptability of the system when new attributes get added with changing landscape of money laundering, without explicit additional training. Our proposed solution, LoKI, generates high-fidelity, logical, well structured, and insightful reports given the tabular data with significantly high number of attributes. The focal point of LoKI is Logical Key Inference - it adequately selects only the important, logically correlated attributes to generate the final report. LoKI uses Meta-Learning for content selection and explores BART and T5 for TTG. We perform the experiments on a repository of real-world financial transaction data for potential high-risk accounts related to money laundering. We show that the proposed method outperforms existing generative methods through extensive experiments and ablation studies.

2 Related Work

Natural text generation has been a significant focus of research across various fields such as sports(Wiseman et al., 2017), weather(Liang et al., 2009), and health (Lee, 2018) sectors. While advancements(Chen et al., 2020b) have been made, these methods often suffer from imprecision, hallucinations, and lack of proper content planning and structuring. To address these, researchers have proposed architectures (Castro Ferreira et al., 2019) that include multi-step processes (Tian et al., 2019; Puduppully and Lapata, 2021; See et al., 2017; Zeng et al., 2018; Liu and Lapata, 2018) such as discourse ordering, text structuring, and surface realization. However, most of these methods end up restating facts and producing relatively short texts. The introduction of datasets like Logic2Text and LogicNLG shifted the focus towards ensuring the fidelity of logical-level generations. LOGEN(Zhang et al., 2021) and PLOG(Liu et al., 2022a) are two models that operate on these datasets, utilizing logical form and table content to generate target text. Although they improve generation fidelity, they require logic as an input, highlighting the need for selecting the most important logical relationships. A model introduced by (Zhao et al., 2023) in 2023 provided a solution for diversity and faithfulness in Logic2Text by using logical forms as mediators for controllable text generation. Despite the improvement, this model struggled to generate comprehensive paragraph summaries that capture various key perspectives in a table.

In response to these issues, (a) we propose a method to generate high-fidelity logical and insightful summaries given the table without any logic or cells as input (b) our model dynamically selects the significant features to appear in the reports and ignores the irrelevant pieces of information.

3 Proposed Solution

LoKI has three parts as shown in Figure 2. (a) 'Logical Key' attribute selection using Model Meta Learning, (b) TTG Transformers for generating well structured report templates containing selected attributes (c) Replacing the attributes in template with corresponding values to generate final report to minimize hallucination.

3.1 'Logical Key' attribute selection using Meta Learning

First, we dynamically select 'logical key' table attributes for the report using a meta-learning algorithm, where each task governs the selection of a specific attribute. This approach overcomes the limitations of traditional machine learning methods, such as the need for large datasets, long model training time, compromised performance with increased target classes, and high operating costs. Meta-learning optimizes the learning process, enabling faster learning for new tasks with fewer examples. The report generation task involves a table T and a natural language target text Y. Table T, with M rows and C columns, records card profiles with each column representing an aggregated feature at the account level. The target text outlines the potential risk associated with the card.

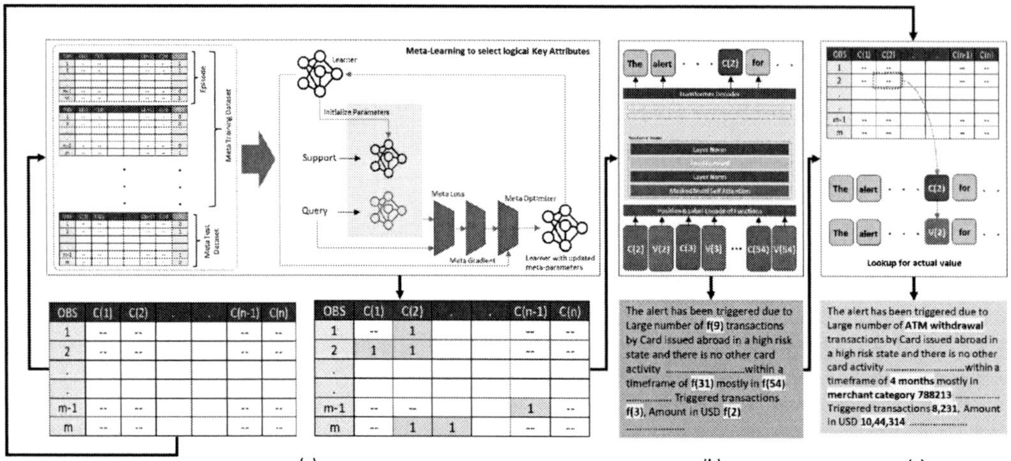

Figure 2: **LoKI has three parts** (a) Logical Key attribute selection using Meta Learning, (b) TTG Transformers for generating well structured report templates containing selected attributes (c) Replacing the attributes in template with corresponding values to generate final report to minimize hallucination.

3.1.1 Defining a Meta Learning Task

Every attribute present in the table is a meta learning task and the number of tasks corrrespond to the number of attributes availabe in the table. We used a supervised approach here. The reports are annotated (refer to methodology section) to create a target variable for every episode. For a specific episode, if the corresponding attribute is included in the report, then the target variable is 1, else it is set to 0. The same process is repeated for all the attributes to create the final set of tasks for meta-learning algorithm

3.1.2 Training a Meta Learning Algorithm

Let us consider a model f parameterized by a parameter θ, and let $p(N)$ represent a distribution over tasks. First, we randomly initialize the model parameter θ and sample a batch of tasks from the task distribution, denoted as $N_i \sim p(N)$. We then sample P different tasks, and the set of tasks can be represented as $N = N_1, N_2, N_3, ..., N_P$.

For each task N_i in the set of tasks N, we sample k data points and prepare our training and test sets as follows:

$$D_i^{train} = (x_1, y_1), (x_2, y_2), ..., (x_k, y_k) \quad (1)$$

$$D_i^{test} = (x_1, y_1), (x_2, y_2), ..., (x_k, y_k) \quad (2)$$

Next, we employ a neural network model to train on the training set D_i^{train} and minimize the loss using gradient descent and obtain the optimal parameters θ'_i.

$$\theta' i = \theta - \alpha \nabla \theta L_{N_i}(f_\theta) \quad (3)$$

where $L_{N_i}(f_\theta)$ denotes the cross-entropy loss function.

So for each of the tasks, we sample k data points and minimize the loss on the train set and get the optimal parameters . As we sampled P tasks we will have P optimal parameters $\{\theta'_1, \theta'_2, \theta'_3, ..., \theta'_P\}$. Now, we perform meta optimization in the test set i.e D_i^{test} here we try to minimize the loss in the test set.We minimize the loss by calculating the gradient with respect to our optimal parameter θ'_i calculated in the previous step and update our randomly θ_i initialized parameter using our test set. It can be mathematically represented as :

$$\theta = \theta - \beta \nabla_\theta \sum_{N_i \sim p(N)} L_{N_i}(f_{\theta'_i}) \quad (4)$$

.

3.1.3 Getting the 'Logical Key' Attributes

The meta-learning algorithm assigns a probability score to each attribute for every account. If the score exceeds a predetermined threshold, we will carry forward that attribute and its respective value to the subsequent stage. Any attributes that do not meet this threshold are eliminated before being processed by the language model. It's worth noting that the number of selected attributes can vary between accounts.

3.2 Table to Text Generation using Transformers

To generate well structured report templates containing selected attributes we have used transformer-based table to text generators. Theoretically any language model can achieve the knowledge transfer from the table-to-text downstream task. To evaluate this, we have included several language model such as GPT-2 ((Radford et al., 2019)), BART-Base ((Lewis et al., 2019b)), BART-Large CNN ((Lewis et al., 2019a)), T5 Base ((Raffel et al., 2020)). The output of this step is saved as template report containing dynamically selected attributes.

3.3 Mitigating Factual Hallucination

In this step, we assign the attributes in the template report, created in the prior stage, to the actual values derived from the aggregated transaction data. This involves conducting a lookup for the original values of the selected attributes. We substitute the function placeholders with these actual values to produce the final report.

4 Methodology

In this section, we provide a synopsis of the different experiments that we have performed followed by analysis of the results for in-depth insights and deliberations.

4.1 Data Description

We conducted experiments on a three-year real-world financial dataset of potentially high-risk accounts tied to money laundering, covering over 20,000 accounts. To ensure privacy, we concealed customers' identities and specific experiment timeframes. We aggregated attributes at the account level, examining merchant, transaction, card, and other features such as origin country, transaction volume, transaction channels, card type, and suspicious activities.

4.2 Annotation

We perform the experiments on historical reports prepared by the analyst. We manually annotate the reports to evaluate the inclusion of specific attributes. The numbers/facts are replaced with their corresponding attributes.

4.3 Experiment Protocols

Our study focuses on generating highly accurate, logically correct and precise, well-structured report generation from tabular data. We evaluated the performance of LoKI (1) quantitatively by comparing it with existing generative methods on metrics like BLEU-4, ROUGE-4 , Precision, Recall, etc and (2) qualitatively with the help of internal experts.

4.4 Implementation Details

This section outlines the baseline models including LLaMa (Touvron et al., 2023), GPT-2 (Radford et al., 2019), BART-Base (Lewis et al., 2019b), BART-Large CNN (Lewis et al., 2019a), T5-Base (Raffel et al., 2020) and our custom models: Meta-learning+BART-Large and Meta-learning+T5-Base in a fully-supervised setting. Using Transformers and PyTorch, we conducted numerous experiments, setting the max length to 6000 for source and 2000 for target sequences. Each model was fine-tuned for ten epochs with the entire training data. We omitted logical table-to-text methods like PLOG and LOFT from our experiments as they require a logical input form. In contrast, our pipeline doesn't require such input and autonomously selects logical statements based on attribute values. We evaluated our models (Liu et al., 2022a; Lin et al., 2022) using surface-level metrics (BLEU-4, ROGUE-4, Precision, Recall) and logic-based metrics (SP-Acc, TAPEX-Large (Liu et al., 2022b)) to ensure logical fidelity in output. Evaluation was based on n-gram matching between model-generated summaries and references. All these were implemented with the Tensorflow and PyTorch.

5 Result

In this section we present, quantitative and qualitative (human) evaluation of 'LoKI'.

(1) Quantitative Evaluation: The experimental results are detailed in Table 1. Despite GPT-2's extensive training, it struggles with numeric data, dates, and logical patterns. Our Meta-learning models outperform both T5-Base and BART-Large, indicating that focusing on selective features enhances output quality and fidelity. The consistent advancement across various models underscores the universal applicability of our approach. (see Table 1).

Surface-Level Evaluation						Logical Fidelity	
Models	**BLEU-4**	**ROUGE-4**	**Precision**	**Recall**	**F1**	**SP-Acc**	**Tapex-Acc**
GPT 2	27.1	23.5	30.1	25.4	27.6	9.4	12.5
Bart-Base	40.5	43.9	54.5	46.7	50.3	42.1	35.7
BART-Large CNN	53.7	54.2	59.5	72.5	65.4	51.9	64.3
T5-Base	58.6	59.2	60.8	63.7	61.8	67.5	59.9
LLaMa	43.1	46.5	58.1	60.5	59.2	65.4	68.1
(ML*+BART) (-Large CNN)	**76.4**	**75.6**	**79.9**	**87.5**	**83.5**	**80.9**	**83.2**
(ML*+T5-Base)	**79.7**	**78.3**	**82.7**	**84.4**	**83.6**	**84.7**	**89.8**

Table 1: Evaluation results for all baselines and our (marked with *) models. We use meta learning and T5 Large as a language model to produce the results

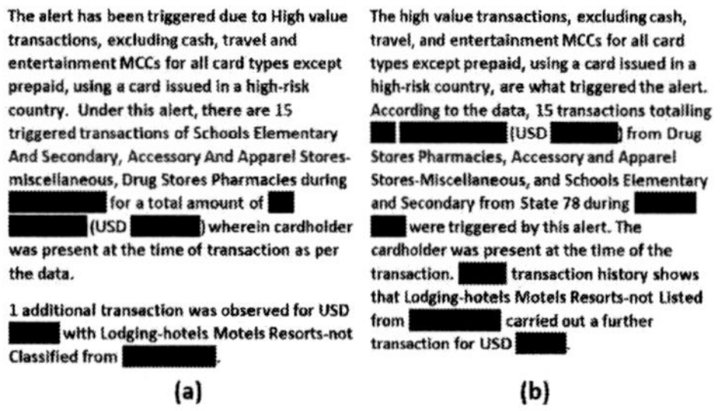
The alert has been triggered due to High value transactions, excluding cash, travel and entertainment MCCs for all card types except prepaid, using a card issued in a high-risk country. Under this alert, there are 15 triggered transactions of Schools Elementary And Secondary, Accessory And Apparel Stores-miscellaneous, Drug Stores Pharmacies during [redacted] for a total amount of [redacted] [redacted] (USD [redacted]) wherein cardholder was present at the time of transaction as per the data.

1 additional transaction was observed for USD [redacted] with Lodging-hotels Motels Resorts-not Classified from [redacted].

(a)

The high value transactions, excluding cash, travel, and entertainment MCCs for all card types except prepaid, using a card issued in a high-risk country, are what triggered the alert. According to the data, 15 transactions totalling [redacted] [redacted] (USD [redacted]) from Drug Stores Pharmacies, Accessory and Apparel Stores-Miscellaneous, and Schools Elementary and Secondary from State 78 during [redacted] [redacted] were triggered by this alert. The cardholder was present at the time of the transaction. [redacted] transaction history shows that Lodging-hotels Motels Resorts-not Listed from [redacted] carried out a further transaction for USD [redacted].

(b)

Figure 3: **Human Evaluation** (a) The report manually generated by the analyst (b) The report generated by LoKI. (Pursuant to internal and legal controls to protect data, confidentiality, and privacy, some of the parts of reports are blackened out, so that the results cannot be traced back to any original transaction or customers.)

(2) Qualitative Evaluation We randomly sampled 400 examples from the test data. Internal experts scored each generated summary in the discrete range between 0 and 4 with the help of according to criteria adopted in (Chen et al., 2020a). Non-sense (0): the sentence suffers with respect to text fluency and logic fidelity, and people need help understanding its meaning. Wrong (1): the sentence is fluent, but it contains factual errors, i.e. accuracy of recalled risk is low. Partially correct (2): the sentence describes multiple facts. Most of them are wrong, but it contains at least one factually correct sentence. Almost Correct (3): the sentence describes multiple facts. Most of them are correct, but it contains at least one factual error. Entirely Correct (4): the sentence is of high quality in fluency and risk accuracy. The evaluation is based on the generated summaries and the tabular input data. From the evaluation results, the proposed models *ML+T5-Base* and *ML+BART - Large* are the highest scorers with 89% and 84% of entirely correct statements, respectively.

6 Conclusion

In this work, we formulate the problem of logical key feature selection from a tabular dataset consisting of significantly large number of attributes to generate a structured, factually accurate and logically correct Anti-Money Laundering report for suspicious accounts. In our case, we emphasized that the facts presented in the report must be unequivocally accurate. Inclusion of incorrect facts in the generated report can potentially lead to legal and reputational harm. To achieve this, we are using the natural language model to learn only the template of the report, unlike previous research where the language model generates the final report. Through our results, we demonstrate that proposed method considerably outperforms the existing state-of-art models. We believe that our work can highly successful in convincing regulators about the applications of AI in related domains as well.

References

Thiago Castro Ferreira, Chris van der Lee, Emiel van Miltenburg, and Emiel Krahmer. 2019. Neural data-to-text generation: A comparison between pipeline and end-to-end architectures. In *Proceedings of the 2019 Conference on Empirical Methods in Natural Language Processing and the 9th International Joint Conference on Natural Language Processing (EMNLP-IJCNLP)*, pages 552–562, Hong Kong, China. Association for Computational Linguistics.

Wenhu Chen, Jianshu Chen, Yu Su, Zhiyu Chen, and William Yang Wang. 2020a. Logical natural language generation from open-domain tables. In *Proceedings of the 58th Annual Meeting of the Association for Computational Linguistics*, pages 7929–7942, Online. Association for Computational Linguistics.

Zhiyu Chen, Harini Eavani, Wenhu Chen, Yinyin Liu, and William Yang Wang. 2020b. Few-shot NLG with pre-trained language model. In *Proceedings of the 58th Annual Meeting of the Association for Computational Linguistics*, pages 183–190, Online. Association for Computational Linguistics.

Sebastian Gehrmann, Falcon Dai, Henry Elder, and Alexander Rush. 2018. End-to-end content and plan selection for data-to-text generation. In *Proceedings of the 11th International Conference on Natural Language Generation*, pages 46–56, Tilburg University, The Netherlands. Association for Computational Linguistics.

Seraphina Goldfarb-Tarrant, Tuhin Chakrabarty, Ralph Weischedel, and Nanyun Peng. 2020. Content planning for neural story generation with aristotelian rescoring. In *Proceedings of the 2020 Conference on Empirical Methods in Natural Language Processing (EMNLP)*, pages 4319–4338, Online. Association for Computational Linguistics.

IMF. 2023. International monetary fund. `https://www.imf.org/en/About/Factsheets/Sheets/2023/Fight-against-money-laundering-and-terrorism-financing`. [Online; accessed 17-feb-2023].

Mihir Kale and Abhinav Rastogi. 2020. Text-to-text pre-training for data-to-text tasks. In *Proceedings of the 13th International Conference on Natural Language Generation*, pages 97–102, Dublin, Ireland. Association for Computational Linguistics.

Chris Kolmar. 2022. 20 MONEY LAUNDERING STATISTICS [2023] FACTS ABOUT MONEY LAUNDERING IN THE U.S. `https://www.zippia.com/advice/money-laundering-statistics/`. [Online; accessed 17-feb-2023].

Scott H Lee. 2018. Natural language generation for electronic health records. *NPJ digital medicine*, 1(1):63.

Mike Lewis, Yinhan Liu, Naman Goyal, Marjan Ghazvininejad, Abdelrahman Mohamed, Omer Levy, Ves Stoyanov, and Luke Zettlemoyer. 2019a. Bart: Denoising sequence-to-sequence pre-training for natural language generation, translation, and comprehension. *arXiv preprint arXiv:1910.13461*.

Mike Lewis, Yinhan Liu, Naman Goyal, Marjan Ghazvininejad, Abdelrahman Mohamed, Omer Levy, Veselin Stoyanov, and Luke Zettlemoyer. 2019b. BART: denoising sequence-to-sequence pre-training for natural language generation, translation, and comprehension. *CoRR*, abs/1910.13461.

Percy Liang, Michael I Jordan, and Dan Klein. 2009. Learning semantic correspondences with less supervision. In *Proceedings of the Joint Conference of the 47th Annual Meeting of the ACL and the 4th International Joint Conference on Natural Language Processing of the AFNLP*, pages 91–99.

Xiexiong Lin, Huaisong Li, Tao Huang, Feng Wang, Linlin Chao, Fuzhen Zhuang, Taifeng Wang, and Tianyi Zhang. 2022. A logic aware neural generation method for explainable data-to-text. In *Proceedings of the 28th ACM SIGKDD Conference on Knowledge Discovery and Data Mining*, pages 3318–3326.

Ao Liu, Haoyu Dong, Naoaki Okazaki, Shi Han, and Dongmei Zhang. 2022a. PLOG: Table-to-logic pretraining for logical table-to-text generation. In *Proceedings of the 2022 Conference on Empirical Methods in Natural Language Processing*, pages 5531–5546, Abu Dhabi, United Arab Emirates. Association for Computational Linguistics.

Qian Liu, Bei Chen, Jiaqi Guo, Morteza Ziyadi, Zeqi Lin, Weizhu Chen, and Jian-Guang Lou. 2022b. TAPEX: Table pre-training via learning a neural SQL executor. In *International Conference on Learning Representations*.

Yang Liu and Mirella Lapata. 2018. Learning structured text representations. *Transactions of the Association for Computational Linguistics*, 6:63–75.

Alice Oh and Alexander Rudnicky. 2000. Stochastic language generation for spoken dialogue systems. In *ANLP-NAACL 2000 Workshop: Conversational Systems*.

Ratish Puduppully, Li Dong, and Mirella Lapata. 2019. Data-to-text generation with content selection and planning. In *Proceedings of the AAAI conference on artificial intelligence*, volume 33, pages 6908–6915.

Ratish Puduppully and Mirella Lapata. 2021. Data-to-text generation with macro planning. *Transactions of the Association for Computational Linguistics*, 9:510–527.

Alec Radford, Jeff Wu, Rewon Child, David Luan, Dario Amodei, and Ilya Sutskever. 2019. Language models are unsupervised multitask learners.

Colin Raffel, Noam Shazeer, Adam Roberts, Katherine Lee, Sharan Narang, Michael Matena, Yanqi Zhou, Wei Li, and Peter J. Liu. 2020. Exploring the limits of transfer learning with a unified text-to-text transformer. *Journal of Machine Learning Research*, 21(140):1–67.

Ehud Reiter and Robert Dale. 2000. Building natural generation systems. *Studies in Natural Language Processing. Cambridge University Press.*

Abigail See, Peter J Liu, and Christopher D Manning. 2017. Get to the point: Summarization with pointer-generator networks. *arXiv preprint arXiv:1704.04368*.

Ran Tian, Shashi Narayan, Thibault Sellam, and Ankur P Parikh. 2019. Sticking to the facts: Confident decoding for faithful data-to-text generation. *arXiv preprint arXiv:1910.08684*.

Hugo Touvron, Thibaut Lavril, Gautier Izacard, Xavier Martinet, Marie-Anne Lachaux, Timothée Lacroix, Baptiste Rozière, Naman Goyal, Eric Hambro, Faisal Azhar, et al. 2023. Llama: Open and efficient foundation language models. *arXiv preprint arXiv:2302.13971*.

Sam Wiseman, Stuart M Shieber, and Alexander M Rush. 2017. Challenges in data-to-document generation. *arXiv preprint arXiv:1707.08052*.

Sam Wiseman, Stuart M Shieber, and Alexander M Rush. 2018. Learning neural templates for text generation. *arXiv preprint arXiv:1808.10122*.

Xiangrong Zeng, Daojian Zeng, Shizhu He, Kang Liu, and Jun Zhao. 2018. Extracting relational facts by an end-to-end neural model with copy mechanism. In *Proceedings of the 56th Annual Meeting of the Association for Computational Linguistics (Volume 1: Long Papers)*, pages 506–514.

Ningyu Zhang, Hongbin Ye, Jiacheng Yang, Shumin Deng, Chuanqi Tan, Mosha Chen, Songfang Huang, Fei Huang, and Huajun Chen. 2021. Logen: few-shot logical knowledge-conditioned text generation with self-training. *arXiv preprint arXiv:2112.01404*.

Yilun Zhao, Zhenting Qi, Linyong Nan, Lorenzo Jaime Yu Flores, and Dragomir Radev. 2023. Loft: Enhancing faithfulness and diversity for table-to-text generation via logic form control. *arXiv preprint arXiv:2302.02962*.

Multi-Lingual ESG Issue Identification

Chung-Chi Chen,[1] Yu-Min Tseng,[2] Juyeon Kang,[3] Anaïs Lhuissier,[3]
Min-Yuh Day,[4] Teng-Tsai Tu,[5] Hsin-Hsi Chen[2]
[1]AIST, Japan
[2]Department of Computer Science and Information Engineering,
National Taiwan University, Taiwan
[3]3DS Outscale (ex Fortia), France
[4]Graduate Institute of Information Management, National Taipei University, Taiwan
[5]Graduate Institute of International Business, National Taipei University, Taiwan

Abstract

This paper introduces an innovative approach for incorporating environmental, social, and governance (ESG) factors into AI-based financial decision-making processes. Recent developments in AI and NLP have predominantly focused on financial outcomes, often disregarding the significant impacts that corporations can have on society and the environment. This perspective overlooks potential business risks associated with environmental and social issues. We propose a task, the Multilingual ESG Issue Identification Task (ML-ESG), that seeks to integrate the ESG paradigm into financial NLP systems. The ML-ESG is designed according to the MSCI ESG rating methodology and requires systems to classify news articles into 35 key ESG issues. Moreover, systems must identify the target company and its industry, as the weighting of each issue varies accordingly. This paper presents an overview of the ML-ESG shared task, implemented as part of the FinNLP-2023 workshop, detailing the datasets, methods, and participant performances.

1 Introduction

Finance often brings to mind a world dominated by monetary transactions and market forecasts. The environmental and social implications of investment decisions, significant factors in today's business environment, have been largely overlooked in machine learning models. For instance, even in scenarios where a corporation is reported to be engaged in environmentally harmful practices, such as improper waste disposal, AI models may still recommend purchasing the corporation's stock following a market overreaction to the news. Such decisions, while potentially profitable in the short-term, can lack foresight into potential long-term risks associated with the corporation's practices.

To address this concern, we introduce the concept of ESG (environmental, social, and governance) into our shared task, aiming to help AI models consider the broader impacts of investment decisions. By integrating insights from the financial domain into NLP research, we hope to promote long-term, value-driven investments that also account for non-monetary factors like environmental and social impacts.

The ESG concept, initially proposed by the UN Global Compact in 2005, has gained increasing attention over the past few years, particularly since 2020. The idea of ESG has matured over time, with a growing body of research analyzing and evaluating these non-monetary factors (Amel-Zadeh and Serafeim, 2018; Matos, 2020). In last year's FinNLP workshop, we proposed the first step towards integrating ESG considerations into NLP with the FinSim-2022 task, which focused on learning semantic similarities. This task aimed to classify given words into ESG-related taxonomies and sentences into sustainable or unsustainable descriptions, thereby evaluating models' understanding of ESG narratives.

Building on this foundation, this year's FinNLP workshop presents a more detailed task: the Multilingual ESG Issue Identification Task (ML-ESG). This task is designed according to the MSCI ESG rating methodology and requires systems to classify news articles into 35 key ESG issues, as depicted in Figure 1. The ESG Industry Materiality Map provides these weights thus, the system's primary task is to identify the topic. In this shared task, we offer multilingual datasets (English, Chinese, French) to identify ESG issues in news articles. This paper provides an overview of the ML-ESG shared task in the FinNLP-2023 workshop, detailing the dataset, participant methods, and performances. Twenty-seven teams registered, ten of which submitted their system outputs for the official evaluation.

2 Dataset and Task Setting

This section outlines the composition of our proposed datasets and elucidates the corresponding

Proceedings of the Joint Workshop of the 5th Financial Technology and Natural Language Processing (FinNLP) and 2nd Multimodal AI For Financial Forecasting (Muffin), Macao, August 20, 2023.

Figure 1: List of the ESG issues and examples of the weighting. This is the screenshot of the ESG Industry Materiality Map.

	English	French	Chinese
Train	1,199	1,200	900
Development	-	-	100
Test	300	300	238
Total	1,499	1,500	1,238

Table 1: Statistics of Datasets

task settings, as depicted in Table 1.

2.1 English and French Datasets

The English and French datasets are collected from ESG-related news articles acquired from ESGToday (English)[1], RSEDATANEWS (French)[2], and Novethic (French)[3]. Given a news article, annotators are asked to select the related issues from the 35 pre-defined ESG Key Issues by MSCI[4], and then label it with the most relevant issues. The English and French datasets are annotated by experts (2 annotators and 1 reviewer) in Fortia's Data & Language Analyst team.

Many events comprise multiple components, including various pillars (e.g., Environment + Social), themes within the same pillar (e.g., Environment > Natural Capital + Pollution & Waste), or even within the same theme (e.g., Environment > Pollution & Waste > Toxic Emissions & Electronic Waste). Although key issues are clearly defined to establish boundaries between somewhat similar themes, real-life events are not always so clear-cut.

For that reason, we have chosen to divide a news article into multiple paragraphs based on the topic. In both the English and French task settings, the objective is to predict one of the ESG issues based on a specific paragraph extracted from a news article.

2.2 Chinese Dataset

Our Chinese dataset is sourced from ESG-related news articles available on ESG-BusinessToday (Chinese)[5]. Seven postgraduate students from the Graduate Institute of Information Management at National Taipei University undertake the annotation of this dataset. To maintain consistency and accuracy in annotation, we organize bi-weekly meetings to address arising issues and ensure a consensus on the guidelines and labels.

Given that Chinese news articles are annotated on an article-based framework, each article may pertain to more than one ESG issue, which calls for a multi-label task setting in the Chinese dataset.

Furthermore, we noted that some articles on the ESG news platform do not truly align with ESG or ESG scoring principles. To account for this discrepancy, we have included an additional label to identify articles that are not related to ESG.

To gain a more comprehensive understanding of ESG issues, we have merged the SASB Standard with MSCI's guidelines, which has yielded 44 issues.[6]

3 Methods

3.1 French and English

Exploring diverse BERT language model strategies, such as SVM (Cortes and Vapnik, 1995) with

[1]https://www.esgtoday.com/category/esg-news/companies/

[2]https://www.rsedatanews.net/

[3]https://www.novethic.fr/actualite/environnement.html

[4]https://www.msci.com/our-solutions/esg-investing/esg-ratings/esg-ratings-key-issue-framework

[5]https://esg.businesstoday.com.tw/

[6]For a more detailed definition, please refer to the following document: https://drive.google.com/file/d/12ia_CF3nrjv_R8$_e44SLnZnNcHH-D0_/view?usp=sharing

Submission	Precision	Recall	F1-Score
NCMU_English_1	0.69	0.70	0.69
TradingCentralLabs_English_1	0.67	0.68	0.67
NCMU_English_2	0.68	0.66	0.66
kaka-ML-ESG_English_Test_gpt	0.67	0.67	0.65
Jetsons_English_1	0.64	0.65	0.64
Jetsons_English_2	0.63	0.64	0.63
LASTI_English_2	0.64	0.63	0.63
NCMU_English_3	0.65	0.63	0.63
HKESG_English_3	0.63	0.63	0.62
Jetsons_English_3	0.63	0.64	0.62
kaka-ML-ESG_English_Test_word2vec_tfidf	0.62	0.63	0.61
LASTI_English_3	0.62	0.62	0.61
TradingCentralLabs_English_2	0.61	0.63	0.61
HKESG_English_1	0.61	0.62	0.60
kaka-ML-ESG_English_Test_roberta	0.62	0.62	0.60
LASTI_English_1	0.61	0.60	0.60
HKESG_English_2	0.59	0.59	0.58
TradingCentralLabs_English_3	0.59	0.59	0.58
HHU_English_3	0.60	0.58	0.57
HHU_English_1	0.55	0.59	0.56
HHU_English_2	0.42	0.36	0.35
LivermoreSXI_English_1	0.36	0.33	0.30
wwy_test_English_1	0.28	0.37	0.30

Table 2: Experimental results in English Dataset.

SBERT embeddings (Reimers and Gurevych, 2019) and RoBERTa, Linhares Pontes et al. (2023) conduct experiments on monolingual and multilingual data. Their findings reveal that RoBERTa performs best on monolingual data for the English dataset, while on the French dataset, RoBERTa excels on multilingual data, achieving superior results. Glenn et al. (2023) generate synthetic data using a large language model - gpt-3.5-turbo - in order to augment the training data which is then used to fine-tune the multilingual BERT for classification. Hanwool et al. (2023) use generative models like Pythia (Biderman et al., 2023), CerebrasGPT (Dey et al., 2023), and OPT (Zhang et al., 2022), along with the zero-shot (Xian et al., 2017), GPT3Mix (Yoo et al., 2021) and translation as augmentation techniques to tackle the data imbalance issue; then, explore encoder models, RoBERTa (Liu et al., 2019), DeBERTa (He et al., 2021), and FinBERT (Araci and Genç, 2020). Mashkin and Chersoni experiment with ESG Transformers (Mukut, 2020), and for classification, Logistic Regression, Random Forests and Support Vector Machine achieving the best results with SVM classifier for both languages. Billert and Conrad introduce adapter modules (Houlsby et al., 2019) to a multilingual base model, mBERT (Devlin et al., 2019), then train it using Masked Language Modeling (MLM) (Pfeiffer et al., 2020).

3.2 Chinese

Wang et al. (2023) leverage MacBERT (Cui et al., 2020)—a contrastive learning framework—enhancing performance using both unlabeled and pseudo-labeled data. Linhares Pontes et al. (2023) explores the performance of SVM (Cortes and Vapnik, 1995) when combined with SentenceBERT's embeddings (Reimers and Gurevych, 2019) (SBERT). Additionally, Glenn et al. (2023) outlines a method for utilizing synthetic data generated by a large language model, ChatGPT,[7] to enhance the performance of multilingual BERT (mBERT).

4 Results

Performance metrics, including precision, recall, and F1-score, were utilized to evaluate the English and French datasets. Given the distinctive task settings of the Chinese dataset, micro-averaged F1, macro-averaged F1, and weighted F1 were adopted for evaluation. Tables 2, 3, and 4 display the experimental results from the participants' system outputs in the official evaluation round.

We find that BERT-like language models with data augmentation by LLMs perform well for the English and French results. NCMU (Hanwool et al., 2023) ranks first and second in these two datasets. Jetsons (Glenn et al., 2023) also uses

[7]gpt-3.5-turbo: https://platform.openai.com/docs/models/gpt-3-5

Submission	Precision	Recall	F1-Score
Jetsons_French_2	0.80	0.79	0.78
NCMU_French_1	0.80	0.79	0.78
HHU_French_3	0.80	0.77	0.77
Jetsons_French_1	0.78	0.78	0.77
HHU_French_1	0.78	0.75	0.75
TradingCentralLabs_French_2	0.76	0.76	0.75
kaka-ML-ESG_French_Test_gpt	0.75	0.75	0.74
HHU_French_2	0.76	0.74	0.73
TradingCentralLabs_French_3	0.74	0.74	0.73
HKESG_French_3	0.72	0.72	0.71
TradingCentralLabs_French_1	0.73	0.72	0.71
Jetsons_French_3	0.70	0.71	0.70
NCMU_French_2	0.71	0.70	0.69
HKESG_French_1	0.69	0.68	0.67
HKESG_French_2	0.65	0.62	0.62
kaka-ML-ESG_French_Test_word2vec_tfidf	0.62	0.61	0.60
LASTI_French_1	0.60	0.59	0.59
LASTI_French_2	0.61	0.60	0.59
LASTI_French_3	0.56	0.56	0.55
LivermoreSXI_French_1	0.32	0.33	0.28
kaka-ML-ESG_French_Test_roberta	0.16	0.25	0.18

Table 3: Experimental results in French Dataset.

Submission	Micro F1	Macro F1	Weighted F1
CheryFS_Chinese_2 (Wang et al., 2023)	0.391	0.180	0.392
TradingCentralLabs_Chinese_3 (Linhares Pontes et al., 2023)	0.279	0.137	0.263
TradingCentralLabs_Chinese_2 (Linhares Pontes et al., 2023)	0.267	0.103	0.233
TradingCentralLabs_Chinese_1 (Linhares Pontes et al., 2023)	0.212	0.073	0.179
Jetsons_Chinese_1 (Glenn et al., 2023)	0.134	0.042	0.102
Jetsons_Chinese_3 (Glenn et al., 2023)	0.134	0.042	0.102
Jetsons_Chinese_2 (Glenn et al., 2023)	0.121	0.038	0.091
CheryFS_Chinese_1 (Wang et al., 2023)	0.089	0.074	0.123

Table 4: Experimental results in Chinese Dataset.

synthetical data to get the best performance in the French dataset.

For the Chinese dataset, the performance is lower due to the multiple-label task setting. The MacBERT with data augmentation method proposed by Wang et al. (2023) gets the best performances.

5 Conclusion

This paper presents the findings of the ML-ESG shared task and highlights the impact of data augmentation methods on performance, regardless of the language employed. It is worth noting, however, that the effectiveness of data generated by LLMs may not always yield favorable outcomes. Selecting the optimal LLM for data augmentation remains an unresolved challenge, with participants opting for a practical approach of utilizing data generated by diverse augmentation methods. Moving forward, our next objective within the ML-ESG initiative is to determine whether a given news event can be classified as an opportunity or risk within the realm of ESG considerations.

Acknowledgments

This research is supported by National Science and Technology Council, Taiwan, under grants 110-2221-E-002-128-MY3, 110-2634-F-002-050-, and 111-2634-F-002-023-. The work of Chung-Chi Chen was supported in part by JSPS KAKENHI Grant Number 23K16956.

References

Amir Amel-Zadeh and George Serafeim. 2018. Why and how investors use esg information: Evidence from a global survey. *Financial Analysts Journal*, 74(3):87–103.

Dogu Araci and Zülküf Genç. 2020. Financial sentiment analysis with pre-trained language models.

Stella Biderman, Hailey Schoelkopf, Quentin Anthony, Herbie Bradley, Kyle O'Brien, Eric Hallahan, Mohammad Aflah Khan, Shivanshu Purohit, USVSN Sai Prashanth, Edward Raff, Aviya Skowron, Lintang Sutawika, and Oskar van der Wal. 2023. Pythia: A suite for analyzing large language models across training and scaling.

Fabian Billert and Stefan Conrad. 2023. Team hhu at the finnlp-2023 ml-esg task: A multi-model approach to esg-key-issue classification. In *Proceedings of the Fifth Workshop on Financial Technology and Natural Language Processing (FinNLP) and the Second Multimodal AI For Financial Forecasting (Muffin)*.

Corinna Cortes and Vladimir Vapnik. 1995. Support-vector networks. *Machine learning*, 20(3):273–297.

Yiming Cui, Wanxiang Che, Ting Liu, Bing Qin, Shijin Wang, and Guoping Hu. 2020. Revisiting pre-trained models for Chinese natural language processing. In *Findings of the Association for Computational Linguistics: EMNLP 2020*, pages 657–668, Online. Association for Computational Linguistics.

Jacob Devlin, Ming-Wei Chang, Kenton Lee, and Kristina Toutanova. 2019. Bert: Pre-training of deep bidirectional transformers for language understanding.

Nolan Dey, Gurpreet Gosal, Zhiming, Chen, Hemant Khachane, William Marshall, Ribhu Pathria, Marvin Tom, and Joel Hestness. 2023. Cerebras-gpt: Open compute-optimal language models trained on the cerebras wafer-scale cluster.

Parker Glenn, Alolika Gon, Nikhil Kohli, Sihan Zha, Parag Pravin Dakle, and Preethi Raghavan. 2023. Jetsons at the finnlp-2023: Using synthetic data and transfer learning for multilingual esg issue classification. In *Proceedings of the Fifth Workshop on Financial Technology and Natural Language Processing (FinNLP) and the Second Multimodal AI For Financial Forecasting (Muffin)*.

Lee Hanwool, Choi Jonghyun, Kwon Sohyeon, and Jung Sungbum. 2023. Easyguide : Esg issue identification framework leveraging abilities of generative large language models. In *Proceedings of the Fifth Workshop on Financial Technology and Natural Language Processing (FinNLP) and the Second Multimodal AI For Financial Forecasting (Muffin)*.

Pengcheng He, Xiaodong Liu, Jianfeng Gao, and Weizhu Chen. 2021. Deberta: Decoding-enhanced bert with disentangled attention.

Neil Houlsby, Andrei Giurgiu, Stanislaw Jastrzebski, Bruna Morrone, Quentin de Laroussilhe, Andrea Gesmundo, Mona Attariyan, and Sylvain Gelly. 2019. Parameter-efficient transfer learning for nlp.

Elvys Linhares Pontes, Mohamed Benjannet, and Lam Kim Ming. 2023. Leveraging bert language models for multi-lingual esg issue identification. In *Proceedings of the Fifth Workshop on Financial Technology and Natural Language Processing (FinNLP) and the Second Multimodal AI For Financial Forecasting (Muffin)*.

Yinhan Liu, Myle Ott, Naman Goyal, Jingfei Du, Mandar Joshi, Danqi Chen, Omer Levy, Mike Lewis, Luke Zettlemoyer, and Veselin Stoyanov. 2019. Roberta: A robustly optimized bert pretraining approach.

Ivan Mashkin and Emmanuele Chersoni. 2023. Hkesg at the ml-esg task: Exploring transformer representations for multilingual esg issue identification. In *Proceedings of the Fifth Workshop on Financial Technology and Natural Language Processing (FinNLP) and the Second Multimodal AI For Financial Forecasting (Muffin)*.

Pedro Matos. 2020. Esg and responsible institutional investing around the world: A critical review.

Mukherjee Mukut. 2020. Esg-bert: Nlp meets sus- tainable investing. In *Towards Data Science Blog*.

Jonas Pfeiffer, Ivan Vulić, Iryna Gurevych, and Sebastian Ruder. 2020. MAD-X: An Adapter-Based Framework for Multi-Task Cross-Lingual Transfer. In *Proceedings of the 2020 Conference on Empirical Methods in Natural Language Processing (EMNLP)*, pages 7654–7673, Online. Association for Computational Linguistics.

Nils Reimers and Iryna Gurevych. 2019. Sentence-BERT: Sentence embeddings using Siamese BERT-networks. In *Proceedings of the 2019 Conference on Empirical Methods in Natural Language Processing and the 9th International Joint Conference on Natural Language Processing (EMNLP-IJCNLP)*, pages 3982–3992, Hong Kong, China. Association for Computational Linguistics.

Weiwei Wang, Wenyang Wei, Qingyuan Song, and Yansong Wang. 2023. Leveraging contrastive learning with bert for esg issue identification. In *Proceedings of the Fifth Workshop on Financial Technology and Natural Language Processing (FinNLP) and the Second Multimodal AI For Financial Forecasting (Muffin)*.

Yongqin Xian, Christoph Lampert, Bernt Schiele, and Zeynep Akata. 2017. Zero-shot learning - a comprehensive evaluation of the good, the bad and the ugly. *IEEE Transactions on Pattern Analysis and Machine Intelligence*, PP.

Kang Min Yoo, Dongju Park, Jaewook Kang, Sang-Woo Lee, and Woomyoung Park. 2021. GPT3Mix: Leveraging large-scale language models for text augmentation. In *Findings of the Association for Computational Linguistics: EMNLP 2021*, pages 2225–2239, Punta Cana, Dominican Republic. Association for Computational Linguistics.

Susan Zhang, Stephen Roller, Naman Goyal, Mikel Artetxe, Moya Chen, Shuohui Chen, Christopher Dewan, Mona Diab, Xian Li, Xi Victoria Lin, Todor Mihaylov, Myle Ott, Sam Shleifer, Kurt Shuster, Daniel Simig, Punit Singh Koura, Anjali Sridhar, Tianlu Wang, and Luke Zettlemoyer. 2022. Opt: Open pre-trained transformer language models.

Leveraging Contrastive Learning with BERT for ESG Issue Identification

Weiwei Wang, Wenyang Wei, Qingyuan Song and **Yansong Wang**
Technology Innovation Center, Chery HuiYin Motor Finance Service Co.,Ltd.
{wangweiwei, weiwenyang, songqingyuan, wangyansong}@cheryfs.cn

Abstract

In this study, we, the CheryFS team, present a model solutions dedicated to the task of "Multi-Lingual ESG Issue Identification" in the Chinese track. The objective is to predict the ESG (Environmental, Social, and Governance) label associated with each news article. Our approach integrates supervised and unsupervised data into a comprehensive contrastive learning framework of a MacBERT model with further pretrained. This innovative methodology has resulted in Micro-F1 score of 0.412 on the validation dataset. Furthermore, we perform a meticulous analysis of the model's optimization strategy, providing valuable insights for future research.

1 Introduction

Natural Language Processing (NLP) harnesses the capability to extract extensive semantic information from copious volumes of unstructured data, demonstrating immense potential for application in the financial services industry. By analyzing diverse types of unstructured data, including data reports, news articles, text chat records, and research reports, NLP can effectively contribute to scenario recognition and risk analysis in various financial contexts. Commonly, individuals express their opinions on financial products, services, investments, and stock markets through news or social media channels. Thus, the strategic mining of such financial sentiments can inform decision-making, offer valuable advice, and shape user or business understanding.

The "Multi-Lingual ESG Issue Identification"(Chen et al., 2023) subtask aims at uncovering themes related to Environmental, Social, and Corporate Governance (ESG) in Chinese, English, and French news articles. The challenge is defined as follows: Given an article derived from an ESG-focused news website, the model is expected to predict its potentially relevant themes. English and French datasets include a single theme per article, while the Chinese dataset may contain multiple themes. Due to the limitation of time, our team engaged with the Chinese track of this task.

In our research, we incorporated labeled data, unlabeled data obtained through web crawlers, and pseudo-labeled data for data augmentation. Our initial model was constructed around the MacBERT(Cui et al., 2020) architecture. We endeavored to enhance its performance by 1) investigating a variety of data augmentation strategies, 2) implementing further pretrained with all accessible data, 3) fusing our pre-trained model from the second stage with contrastive learning(Khosla et al., 2021) to boost sensitivity to disparate topics, and 4) consolidating the results of several analogous models with different parameters through ensemble methods.

2 Related Work

2.1 Data Augmentations

Data augmentation(Feng et al., 2021) has recently attracted heightened interest within the Natural Language Processing (NLP) field due to developments in low-resource domains.

Rule-based strategies are straightforward to implement but typically result in incremental performance improvements. Wei and Zou (2019) proposes EDA, a set of token-level random perturbation operations including random insertion, deletion, and swap. Techniques that leverage trained models may entail higher implementation costs but introduce greater data variability, leading to substantial performance enhancements.

Model-based techniques tailored for downstream tasks can significantly impact performance. The popular method, back translation(Sennrich et al., 2016), translates a sequence into another language and then back into the original language. Kobayashi (2018)(contextual augmentation) feeds

Proceedings of the Joint Workshop of the 5th Financial Technology and Natural Language Processing (FinNLP) and 2nd Multimodal AI For Financial Forecasting (Muffin), Macao, August 20, 2023.

surrounding words to large model like BERT, RoBERTA(Liu et al., 2019) or XLNET(Yang et al., 2020) to inference the most suitable word.

In our research, we employ a combination of rule-based and model-based techniques to generate pseudo-labeled data from labeled data.

2.2 Sentence Representation and Self-supervised

The prevalent paradigm for most NLP research since 2018 entails a two-stage training process. Initially, a neural language model (LM), typically comprising millions of parameters, is trained on extensive unlabeled corpora through various pre-training tasks. Subsequently, the word representations acquired in the pre-trained model are repurposed during fine-tune for a downstream task. Several self-supervised pre-training tasks have been proposed to pre-train language models, such as Masked Language Modeling (MLM) (Devlin et al., 2019), and MAsked Sequence to Sequence pre-training (MASS) (Song et al., 2019). Sun et al. (2020) has proved that further pre-train BERT with masked language model tasks on the domain-specific data can improving the performance of the model.

In our research, we utilize all available data for the further pre-trained of the MacBERT model, which results in a more robust representation.

2.3 Contrastive Learning

Contrastive learning has proven its efficacy in learning robust representations, particularly within the natural language domain. In recent years, multiple studies have investigated the construction of sentence embeddings using contrastive learning. The fundamental concept of contrastive learning involves generating positive and negative sentence pairs, with the aim of drawing positive pair representations closer while distancing the negative ones.

Several strategies have been proposed to realize this objective. Fang et al. (2020) employs contrastive self-supervised learning at the sentence level with back-translation data augmentation. Gao et al. (2022) uses both unsupervised denoising objective and supervised natural language inference signals to learn sentence embeddings.

In our research, we introduce a contrastive loss function that encourages data with similar semantics to cluster together, while carefully avoiding the repulsion of false negatives.

Dataset	**C**	**L**	$\overline{L}$	$\hat{L}$	$\overline{W_c}$
Train	900	45	2.95	59.06	1400
Val	100	37	2.61	7.05	1378
Test	238	42	2.81	15.95	1338
Unlabeled	1000	-	-	-	1410
Pseudo	2000	45	2.95	59.06	1396

Table 1: Details of the datasets. C: the amounts of the dataset; L: the numbers of labels; $\overline{L}$: average labels per instance; $\hat{L}$: average instances per label; $\overline{W_c}$: the average char per instance in content;

3 Dataset and Methods

The ESG dataset comprises columns such as title, content, and corresponding topic labels. The Chinese track training set includes 900 instances, the validation set includes 100 instances, and the test set encompasses 238 instances.

In addition to the labeled data, we have amassed 1000 instances of unlabeled data utilizing website crawlers. The distribution of this unlabeled data aligns with that of the labeled data.

Besides, we implement data augmentation methods such as EDA, back translation, and contextual augmentation yielding 2000 instances of pseudo-labeled data.

The distribution of the dataset is illustrated in Table 1.

3.1 MacBERT with Further Pre-trained

Given the impressive results BERT has achieved across various domains, we utilize the MacBERT model as the backbone of our model. However, while the MacBERT model is pre-trained on a general domain corpus, all training data derives from a specific domain's small corpus. Directly fine-tuning our BERT model could lead to overfitting. To mitigate this, we further pre-trained BERT-Chinese with masked language model tasks on all the labeled and unlabeled data.

Following this additional pre-trained, we input a sentence comprising m different tokens into BERT, extracting token embeddings from the last hidden layer as $[CLS, T1, T2, \cdots, T_m]$, where CLS is a special token denoting the start of the sentence for classification. The sentence representation is then obtained by applying mean-pooling to the token embeddings with a fixed length:

$$u = mean - pooling([CLS, T1, T2, \cdots, T_m]) \quad (1)$$

We place a binary classifier at top of the representation derived from the BERT model.

3.2 Constrastive Learning

We introduce a contrastive learning objective aimed at attracting similar instances and repelling disparate ones within the embedding space to achieve superior classification scores. For additional details, please refer to section 5.2.

In practice, we begin by encoding the instances with the further pre-trained model described earlier. Then, for a given instance x_i, all other instances in the batch sharing the same label y_j with it constitute the positive sample set S_j. The set of positive samples under each label is denoted by $S = S_1, S_2, \cdots, S_q$, where q represents the topic number of instance x_i. We can then define the contrastive learning loss for each instance across the batch as

$$L_{cl} = \frac{-1}{q} \sum_{S_j \in S} \sum_{s \in S_j} \log \frac{func\,(E_i, E_s)}{\sum_{k \in I/\{i\}} func\,(E_i, E_k)} \tag{2}$$

$$func\,(u, v) = \exp\left(sim\,(u, v)\,/\tau\right) \tag{3}$$

where E_i denotes the sentence representation, $sim(\cdot)$ indicates the cosine similarity function, τ is the contrastive learning temperature.

Besides, we combine the constrastive loss with cross-entropy and train them jointly. The overall training objective is calculated as follows:

$$L = \alpha \cdot L_{cl} + (1 - \alpha) \cdot L_{ce} \tag{4}$$

where α is a parameters which determined the importance of the contrastive loss.

3.3 Ensemble

We also construct an ensemble model using various sizes of MacBERT. Specifically, we train two instances of MacBERT-Large and two instances of MacBERT-Base, each with a different seed. We amalgamate all the models' predictions by averaging their probabilities, thereby enhancing the overall accuracy of the prediction.

4 Experiments

4.1 Training Setup

We adopt MacBERT-Large and MacBERT-Base models as our backbone model. For self-supervised pre-training, we employ all the labeled and unlabeled data with a batch size of 32 across 25 epochs, implementing early-stopping validated with a patience of 100 steps. The pre-training learning rate for all models is set to $1e-5$.

When fine-tuning with constrative learning, we utilize all the labeled and pseudo-labeled data with a batch size of 16 for 20 epochs. The learning rate for the BERT-Chinese-Large model is set to $5e-5$, and for the MacBERT-Base model, it's set to $4e-5$. All models are trained across 15 epochs.

Models	Micro-F1	Macro-F1
Base	0.389	0.173
Large	0.407	0.178
Ensemble	0.412	0.181

Table 2: Performance of all the models on the validation set.

4.2 Results

Table 2 shows the appearance on the validation set. The table shows that the MacBERT-Large model with further pretrained performs the best on the validation set for single model with an Micro-F1 score of 0.407. The last submitted ensemble models achieve an Micro-F1 score of 0.412 on the validation set, while achieve 0.3914 on the test set. Unfortunately, due to time constraints, we were unable to record additional results on the test set.

5 Analysis

5.1 Effect of Data Augmentaion Methods

We experimented with three different data augmentation methods: (1) Easy Data Augmentation (EDA); (2) Back-Translation (BT); and (3) Contextual Augmentation (CA). These experiments were built upon the further pre-trained BERT-Chinese-Base model, with the augmented data utilized for contrastive learning.

The results, displayed in Table 3, show that among the single data augmentation methods, CA yielded the highest improvement in model performance, achieving a Micro-F1 score of 0.384. Among the combined augmentation methods, CA and BT had the most significant impact on model performance, securing an increase of 0.389. As a result, we ultimately selected a combination of CA and BT for data augmentation.

We delved into the differences between these three methods and discovered a potential reason for the ineffective EDA data augmentation scheme. It appeared that the key tokens edited by the method

Models	Micro-F1	Macro-F1
EDA	0.378	0.164
BT	0.383	0.168
CA	0.384	0.169
EDA+BT	0.381	0.167
EDA+CA	0.382	0.167
BT+CA	0.389	0.173
EDA+BT+CA	0.386	0.171

Table 3: Performance of all the data augmentaion methods on the validation set.

was not relevant to the topic label corresponding to the original sentence, or some key words were omitted, leading to incorrect annotation. Here are some examples:

Original content: "···但随著全球零排放航空旅行的兴趣增加，···", the related topic label is "E01 - 气候变化|碳排放量(Carbon Emissions)".

BT content: "···但当全球零排放航空旅行的兴趣增加，···"

MG content: "···但随著全球零排放旅游的兴趣增加，···"

EDA content: "···但随著全球航空旅行的增加兴趣，···"

We can observe that the lack of token "零排放" has resulted in a disconnection between sentence semantics and their corresponding topic.

5.2 Effect of Contrastive Learning

We explored three implementations of contrastive learning to determine the most effective method in MacBERT-Base model. For our analysis, let's consider a batch composed of K samples, denoted as $Batch = (X_1, Y_1), (X_2, Y_2), \cdots, (X_K, Y_K)$. For a given sample i, where X_i represents a text sequence and its topic label set is denoted as Y_i, the model's encoding provides us the sentence representation E_i and the topic probability Q_i of X_i. Here, $Q_i = Q_{i1}, Q_{i2}, \cdots, Q_{iL}$, with L representing the total number of topic labels.

We represent Y_i as the one hot encoding of the label, defined as $Y_i = y_1, y_2, \cdots, y_L$. For a given i-th topic label $y_i \in 0, 1, y_i = 0$ signifies the absence of this type of label in the text, while $y_i = 1$ implies its presence.

We tested three implementations of contrastive learning:

(1) strictly contrastive learning(SCL) This approach mandates that a sample can serve as a positive contrastive sample of the anchor point only when their label sets exactly match. SCL is rigorous and does not consider samples that partially overlap with the anchor label set.

Models	Micro-F1	Macro-F1
SCL	0.377	0.168
JSCL	0.385	0.171
SLCL	0.389	0.173

Table 4: Performance of different contrastive learning methods on the validation set.

(2) Jaccard Similarity Contrastive Loss (JSCL)(Li et al., 2022): This method works on samples to varying degrees based on the similarity of their labels. For a given sample, JSCL draws samples with the exact same label as closely as possible, while only slightly pulling in samples that share some labels.

(3) Stepwise Label Contrastive Loss (SLCL): While the previous two methods primarily consider multiple emotions simultaneously, SLCL considers different labels separately, computes the contrast loss independently, and then combines each emotion's losses.

As the result shown in Table 4, SLCL achieve the best score and we choose this method as our contrastive learning method.

6 Conclusion

In this paper, we discussed the methodologies employed for the multi-lingual ESG issue identification (ML-ESG) shared task at FinNLP 2023. Our team's proposed MacBERT model, equipped with further pre-trained and contrastive learning strategies, achieved the highest ranking in the Chinese track. Our experimental results underscored the efficiency of further self-supervised pre-training and contrastive learning approaches. Comprehensive experiments confirmed our method's efficacy and helped discern the aspects contributing to our performance enhancements.

7 Limitations

Despite our promising results, our study was limited by time and resource constraints. Consequently, we could not undertake semi-supervised experiments and few-shot learning experiments. These methodologies present intriguing prospects for future exploration.

References

Chung-Chi Chen, Yu-Min Tseng, Juyeon Kang, Anaïs Lhuissier, Min-Yuh Day, Teng-Tsai Tu, and Hsin-Hsi Chen. 2023. Multi-lingual esg issue identification. In *Proceedings of the Fifth Workshop on Financial Technology and Natural Language Processing (FinNLP) and the Second Multimodal AI For Financial Forecasting (Muffin)*.

Yiming Cui, Wanxiang Che, Ting Liu, Bing Qin, Shijin Wang, and Guoping Hu. 2020. Revisiting pre-trained models for Chinese natural language processing. In *Findings of the Association for Computational Linguistics: EMNLP 2020*, pages 657–668, Online. Association for Computational Linguistics.

Jacob Devlin, Ming-Wei Chang, Kenton Lee, and Kristina Toutanova. 2019. BERT: Pre-training of deep bidirectional transformers for language understanding. In *Proceedings of the 2019 Conference of the North American Chapter of the Association for Computational Linguistics: Human Language Technologies, Volume 1 (Long and Short Papers)*, pages 4171–4186, Minneapolis, Minnesota. Association for Computational Linguistics.

Hongchao Fang, Sicheng Wang, Meng Zhou, Jiayuan Ding, and Pengtao Xie. 2020. Cert: Contrastive self-supervised learning for language understanding.

Steven Y. Feng, Varun Gangal, Jason Wei, Sarath Chandar, Soroush Vosoughi, Teruko Mitamura, and Eduard Hovy. 2021. A survey of data augmentation approaches for nlp.

Tianyu Gao, Xingcheng Yao, and Danqi Chen. 2022. Simcse: Simple contrastive learning of sentence embeddings.

Prannay Khosla, Piotr Teterwak, Chen Wang, Aaron Sarna, Yonglong Tian, Phillip Isola, Aaron Maschinot, Ce Liu, and Dilip Krishnan. 2021. Supervised contrastive learning.

Sosuke Kobayashi. 2018. Contextual augmentation: Data augmentation by words with paradigmatic relations. In *Proceedings of the 2018 Conference of the North American Chapter of the Association for Computational Linguistics: Human Language Technologies, Volume 2 (Short Papers)*, pages 452–457, New Orleans, Louisiana. Association for Computational Linguistics.

Junjie Li, Yixin Zhang, Zilei Wang, and Keyu Tu. 2022. Probabilistic contrastive learning for domain adaptation.

Yinhan Liu, Myle Ott, Naman Goyal, Jingfei Du, Mandar Joshi, Danqi Chen, Omer Levy, Mike Lewis, Luke Zettlemoyer, and Veselin Stoyanov. 2019. Roberta: A robustly optimized bert pretraining approach.

Rico Sennrich, Barry Haddow, and Alexandra Birch. 2016. Improving neural machine translation models with monolingual data. In *Proceedings of the 54th Annual Meeting of the Association for Computational Linguistics (Volume 1: Long Papers)*, pages 86–96, Berlin, Germany. Association for Computational Linguistics.

Kaitao Song, Xu Tan, Tao Qin, Jianfeng Lu, and Tie-Yan Liu. 2019. Mass: Masked sequence to sequence pre-training for language generation.

Chi Sun, Xipeng Qiu, Yige Xu, and Xuanjing Huang. 2020. How to fine-tune bert for text classification?

Jason Wei and Kai Zou. 2019. EDA: Easy data augmentation techniques for boosting performance on text classification tasks. In *Proceedings of the 2019 Conference on Empirical Methods in Natural Language Processing and the 9th International Joint Conference on Natural Language Processing (EMNLP-IJCNLP)*, pages 6382–6388, Hong Kong, China. Association for Computational Linguistics.

Zhilin Yang, Zihang Dai, Yiming Yang, Jaime Carbonell, Ruslan Salakhutdinov, and Quoc V. Le. 2020. Xlnet: Generalized autoregressive pretraining for language understanding.

Leveraging BERT Language Models for Multi-Lingual ESG Issue Identification

Elvys Linhares Pontes and **Mohamed Benjannet**
Trading Central Labs, Trading Central, Paris, France
{elvys.linharespontes,mohamed.benjannet}@tradingcentral.com

Lam Kim Ming
Trading Central, Hong Kong, China

Abstract

Environmental, Social, and Governance (ESG) has been used as a metric to measure the negative impacts and enhance positive outcomes of companies in areas such as the environment, society, and governance. Recently, investors have increasingly recognized the significance of ESG criteria in their investment choices, leading businesses to integrate ESG principles into their operations and strategies. The Multi-Lingual ESG Issue Identification (ML-ESG) shared task encompasses the classification of news documents into 35 distinct ESG issue labels. In this study, we explored multiple strategies harnessing BERT language models to achieve accurate classification of news documents across these labels. Our analysis revealed that the RoBERTa classifier emerged as one of the most successful approaches, securing the second-place position for the English test dataset, and sharing the fifth-place position for the French test dataset. Furthermore, our SVM-based binary model tailored for the Chinese language exhibited exceptional performance, earning the second-place rank on the test dataset.

1 Introduction

Financial markets and investors play a crucial role in advancing the transition towards a more sustainable economy by actively promoting investments in companies that adhere to ESG (Environment, Social, and Governance) principles[1]. In today's landscape, there is a burgeoning interest among investors in assessing the sustainability performance of firms (Kim and Li, 2021). Consequently, it becomes imperative to efficiently identify and extract pertinent information pertaining to companies' ESG strategies.

To facilitate this process, the application of NLP (Natural Language Processing) techniques tailored to the finance and ESG domain can significantly aid in the identification and processing of relevant information. By leveraging these advanced methods, valuable insights can be gleaned from vast amounts of financial data and reports, enabling informed investment decisions aligned with sustainable principles (Armbrust et al., 2020; Mehra et al., 2022).

Indeed, Armbrust et al. (2020) analyzed the impact of a company's environmental performance, on the connection between the company's disclosures and financial performance. The authors, discovered that the textual information in the Management's Discussion and Analysis of Financial Conditions and Results of Operations section alone does not provide insights into the future financial performance of the company. However, they did find evidence that NLP methods can extract information about the environmental performance of the company. Mehra et al. (2022) focused on building a BERT-based model to predict two tasks: determining whether there was a change or no change in environmental scores; and identifying a positive or negative change (if any) in the environmental scores of companies based on ESG-related text found in their 10-Q filings. Their results demonstrated that their model can predict not only environmental risk scores but also assessing Social and Governance risk scores for companies.

The Multi-Lingual ESG Issue Identification (ML-ESG) shared task focus on the classification of ESG issue of news articles (Chen et al., 2023). Based on the MSCI ESG rating guidelines, the organizers created multilingual news articles and categorized them into 35 key ESG issues. The target languages include English, Chinese, and French, enhancing the task's cross-lingual scope and enriching the diversity of the dataset.

The main challenge of this task lies in accurately identifying the ESG issues discussed in each article. To address this challenge, the system must possess comprehensive knowledge about the specific ESG

[1] https://www.investopedia.com/terms/e/environmental-social-and-governance-esg-criteria.asp

Proceedings of the Joint Workshop of the 5th Financial Technology and Natural Language Processing (FinNLP) and 2nd Multimodal AI For Financial Forecasting (Muffin), Macao, August 20, 2023.

issues addressed in each article. In this study, we propose a range of strategies that leverage the capabilities of BERT language models. Among our various approaches, our RoBERTa classifier achieved outstanding results and securing the second-highest scores for the English test set, and sharing the fifth-place position for the French test dataset of the shared task. Additionally, our SVM-based binary model achieved the second-best results on the Chinese test dataset. These findings demonstrate the effectiveness of our proposed strategies in accurately classifying ESG issues in multilingual news articles.

2 Multi-Lingual ESG Issue Identification shared task

The Multi-Lingual ESG Issue Identification (ML-ESG) shared task presents a compelling challenge focused on ESG issue identification. Drawing from the well-established MSCI ESG rating guidelines[2], ESG-related news articles can be categorized into 35 distinct ESG key issues. For this task, participants are expected to devise systems capable of recognizing and classifying the specific ESG issue associated with an article (Chen et al., 2023).

In essence, the objective of the ML-ESG shared task is to develop robust systems that demonstrate awareness of the ESG issues encompassed within each article. By accurately classifying the ESG issues, participants can effectively contribute to the advancement of ESG analysis and understanding within the domain of multi-lingual news articles.

2.1 Datasets

The organizers provided a multilingual datasets for Chinese, English and French languages. They annotated these datasets based on the MSCI ESG rating guidelines. More precisely, these datasets are composed of news articles that were classified into 35 ESG key issues. The English and French datasets contain 1200 articles and the Chinese dataset contains 1000 articles. More details about the datasets are available at (Chen et al., 2023).

3 BERT-based approaches

We applied several strategies to classify the article in the ESG issues classes. As BERT-based models has proved the performance of general and financial applications (Pontes and Benjannet, 2021; Linhares Pontes et al., 2022; Yang et al., 2022), our following strategies are based on the BERT models on their architectures.

3.1 SVM+EE

Inspired by the performance of semantic similarity (Linhares Pontes et al., 2018) and the performance of the Linhares Pontes et al. (2022)'s model in classifying the ESG taxonomies, this approach analyzes the ESG issue classification by considering all articles pertaining to a specific ESG issue as similar, as they inherently share the same underlying semantic information. To facilitate this analysis, we employ the SBERT (Sentence-BERT) model (Reimers and Gurevych, 2019), which projects the articles onto a shared dimensional space.

To classify these paraphrased articles into their respective ESG issue classes, we employ a Support Vector Machine (SVM) model (Platt, 2000). The SVM model is trained to analyze and categorize the articles based on their semantic similarity and the corresponding ESG issue classes.

In our methodology, we further enhance the classification process by incorporating the probability of each class provided by the SVM, along with the cosine distance between the SBERT representation of the article and the SBERT representation of the corresponding ESG issue definition (i.e. Esg issue Embeddings (EE)). This combined approach allows us to capture the semantic relationships between articles and ESG issue classes, enabling more accurate and robust classification results.

3.2 RoBERTa

We present an approach for article classification, leveraging the capabilities of RoBERTa-based language models (Liu et al., 2019) in conjunction with a feed-forward multi-layer perceptron. Our proposed RoBERTa classifier effectively captures contextual information within sentences, enabling accurate classification into distinct ESG issue classes.

To extract sentence context and facilitate classification, we utilize the representation of the special [CLS] token from the final layer of the BERT-based language models. Furthermore, we incorporate a feed-forward layer to enhance the classification process, accurately assigning input articles to their respective ESG issue classes.

[2]https://www.msci.com/our-solutions/esg-investing/esg-ratings

3.3 RoBERTa+EE

Delving deeper into the realm of neural networks, we have extended the RoBERTa classifier by incorporating ESG issue embeddings (EE). More precisely, The architecture of our model integrates RoBERTa-based language models with article embeddings and ESG issue label definition embeddings using SBERT model. This integration enables us to perform a more comprehensive analysis of the article and classify it accurately into one of the ESG issue classes.

To extract the contextual information and aid in classification, we employ the representation of the special [CLS] token from the final layer of the BERT-based language models, along with the incorporation of article and ESG issues representations. By combining these representations, we capture a richer understanding of the article's content and its relationship to all ESG issues. Finally, our model incorporates a feed-forward layer that combines all this information on the classification of input articles into their respective ESG issue classes.

3.4 RoBERTa+CNN+SVM

This architecture leverages the combined strength of the RoBERTa language model, a Convolutional Neural Network (CNN) (O'Shea and Nash, 2015), and a SVM to extract diverse features from articles at various levels. Firstly, the RoBERTa language model generates token embeddings for an input article, taking into account its contextual information. Next, the CNN layer performs five convolutions on these token embeddings, capturing different features within the contextualized tokens. This enables the CNN to extract local patterns and features from the textual data, effectively capturing important information across different scales. The final layer of the neural network consists of a feed-forward layer that classifies the output of the CNN into respective ESG issue classes.

Once the neural network model is trained, we use an SVM model to classify the articles into ESG issue classes. To accomplish this, we feed the representation of the articles, which is generated by the previously described CNN, as input to the SVM model.

4 Experimental setup and evaluation

4.1 Evaluation metrics

All system outputs were evaluated by examining key performance metrics such as precision, recall, and F1-score. Precision represents the number of well predicted positives divided by all the positives predicted. Recall measures the number of well predicted positives divided by the total number of positives. Finally, the F1-score takes into account both precision and recall, providing a balanced assessment of the system's performance in identifying and classifying ESG issues.

4.2 Training procedure

The dataset provided by the organizers was divided into two parts: 70% was allocated for training purposes, while the remaining 30% was set aside for development. To set up the meta-parameters for each approach, we used the development dataset. Our SBERT model uses the pre-trained model '*sentence-transformers/paraphrase-multilingual-mpnet-base-v2*'[3] to generate the embeddings of articles and ESG issue definitions for all languages in the same dimensional space.

For all approaches, we created two models versions with different training datasets. In the first version, our classifier model was trained exclusively on target language data (monolingual). For the second version, we combined English and French training data (multilingual) to train our classifier models. The SVM models were trained using a linear kernel to classify the article embeddings provided by the SBERT model into ESG issue labels. For BERT-based models, the last layer incorporates a dropout of 0.2 to improve the model's generalization ability. Additionally, we used the '*xlm-roberta-large*' for the multilingual training and French and Chinese models, and '*roberta-large*' for the English model.

Once the meta-parameters were defined, we proceeded to train the model using both the train and development datasets.

4.3 Experimental evaluation

In order to select the best models for the ML-ESG shared task, we evaluated all models on the development dataset. For the English dataset, the RoBERTa classifier using only monolingual data achieved the best results. The use of SBERT to represent the article and ESG issue embeddings did not add relevant information to improve the performance of our classifiers. Interestingly, despite the simplest model being the SVM+EE trained on the

[3]https://huggingface.co/sentence-transformers/paraphrase-multilingual-mpnet-base-v2

English dataset, it achieved similar results to the BERT+CNN+SVM model.

Approach	Acc.	MF1	WF1
SVM+EE monolingual	0.66	0.59	0.65
SVM+EE multilingual	0.61	0.57	0.6
RoBERTa monolingual	**0.71**	**0.67**	**0.71**
RoBERTa multilingual	0.69	0.67	0.69
RoBERTa+EE monolingual	0.7	0.63	0.69
RoBERTa+EE multilingual	0.69	0.68	0.69
BERT+CNN+SVM multilingual	0.66	0.61	0.65

Table 1: English results for the development dataset. The best results are highlighted in bold. Acc: accuracy, MF1: macro average f-score, and WF1: weighted averaged f-score.

Differently from the English model, the use of multilingual data to train our models improve the results when compared with their respective monolingual version. The RoBERTa classifier using multilingual data achieved the best results.

Approach	Acc.	MF1	WF1
SVM+EE monolingual	0.66	0.63	0.66
SVM+EE multilingual	0.69	0.69	0.68
RoBERTa monolingual	0.71	0.7	0.71
RoBERTa multilingual	**0.73**	**0.72**	**0.73**
RoBERTa+EE monolingual	0.72	0.72	0.72
RoBERTa+EE multilingual	0.73	0.71	0.72

Table 2: French results for the development dataset. The best results are highlighted in bold. Acc: accuracy, MF1: macro average f-score, and WF1: weighted averaged f-score.

For the Chinese model, we utilized the SVM model trained on the representation provided by the SBERT model. This allowed us to classify the ESG issue classes in a binary mode. We employed a binary classifier for each ESG issue and then selected the ESG issue classes with the highest probabilities as the output of our classifiers.

4.4 Official results

The organizers published the official results for each language. Our models were labeled as TradingCentralLabs (TCL). For the Chinese dataset, we submitted three runs (Table 3). All runs use the same model but the number of ESG issue labels output change for each one of them. More precisely, the run 1 provides only the most probable ESG issue class as answer, the run 2 uses the top 2 most probable classes and run 3 uses the top 3 ESG issue classes.

The superior performance of run 3, compared to other runs, can be attributed to the prevalence of multiple ESG issue classes for each article in the gold data. It is worth noting that many examples in the gold data encompassed multiple classes, with some cases containing up to 8 classes. As the Chinese test data consisted of several examples with multiple ESG issue classes, run 3 achieved the best results by predicting the top 3 ESG issue classes.

This ability to accommodate the presence of multiple classes in certain cases elucidates why run 3 outperformed the others. Finally, our run 3 secured the second position in the official ranking for the Chinese data.

Runs	Mic. F1	Mac. F1	WF1
CheryFS_2	**0.3914**	**0.1799**	**0.3921**
TCL_3	*0.2790*	*0.1367*	*0.2633*
TCL_2	0.2665	0.1032	0.2332
TCL_1	0.2115	0.0730	0.1791

Table 3: Official results for the Chinese test data. The best results are highlighted in bold and our best results are in italic. Micro (Mic.), macro (Mac.) and weighted (WF1) F1-score.

For the English runs, we employed three different approaches (Table 4). The run 1 corresponds to the RoBERTa classifier (monolingual), the run 2 corresponds to the RoBERTa+EE classifier (monolingual) and the run 3 employed the BERT+CNN+SVM classifier (multilingual). As expected, the run 1 outperformed the other runs by generalizing much better ESG issue labels. While the gap in the results on the development data was quite small, the run 1 increased the gap compared to the runs 2 and 3 on test data. The RoBERTa classifier obtained the second-place ranking, achieving a score just 2 points lower than the NCMU_1 model.

Runs	P	R	F1
NCMU_1	**0.69**	**0.70**	**0.69**
TradingCentralLabs_1	*0.67*	*0.68*	*0.67*
TradingCentralLabs_2	0.61	0.63	0.61
TradingCentralLabs_3	0.59	0.59	0.58

Table 4: Official results for the English test data. The best results are highlighted in bold and our best results are in italic. P: precision, R: recall, and F1: f1-score.

We submitted three runs for the French test data as well (Table 5). Run 1 used the SVM+EE model, run 2 employed the RoBERTa classifier, and run 3 utilized RoBERTa+EE. All three runs were trained using both the English and French training datasets.

Our run 2 achieved a commendable fifth place in terms of F1-score, falling just 3 points short of the top position. This highlights its competitive performance and showcases its potential for accurately classifying ESG issue classes in the French language.

Runs	P	R	F1
Jetsons_2	**0.80**	**0.79**	**0.78**
TradingCentralLabs_2	*0.76*	*0.76*	*0.75*
TradingCentralLabs_3	0.74	0.74	0.73
TradingCentralLabs_1	0.73	0.72	0.71

Table 5: Official results for the French test data. The best results are highlighted in bold and our best results are in italic. P: precision, R: recall, and F1: f1-score.

5 Conclusion

This paper presents the participation of Trading Central Labs in the Multi-Lingual ESG Issue Identification evaluation campaign for financial documents. Our objective was to accurately classify financial documents into ESG issue labels, and to achieve this, we proposed several BERT-based models.

Among our models, the one based on the RoBERTa classifier emerged as a standout performer, securing the second-place ranking for the English language. It was just 2 points behind the top-performing model. Additionally, our RoBERTa-based model also demonstrated its capability in the French language, sharing the fifth place, with a slight margin of 3 points from the leading result. Finally, our SVM-based model for the Chinese data claimed the second-place ranking, further illustrating our competitive performance.

These results underscore the competitive edge and potential of our models in accurately classifying ESG issue classes across different languages.

Acknowledgements

This work has been partially supported by the France Relance project (grant agreement number ANR-21-PRRD-0010-01).

References

Felix Armbrust, Henry Schäfer, and Roman Klinger. 2020. A computational analysis of financial and environmental narratives within financial reports and its value for investors. In *Proceedings of the 1st Joint Workshop on Financial Narrative Processing and MultiLing Financial Summarisation*, pages 181–194.

Chung-Chi Chen, Yu-Min Tseng, Juyeon Kang, Anaïs Lhuissier, Min-Yuh Day, Teng-Tsai Tu, and Hsin-Hsi Chen. 2023. Multi-lingual esg issue identification. In *Proceedings of the Fifth Workshop on Financial Technology and Natural Language Processing (FinNLP) and the Second Multimodal AI For Financial Forecasting (Muffin)*.

Sang Kim and Zhichuan (Frank) Li. 2021. Understanding the impact of esg practices in corporate finance. *Sustainability*, 13(7).

Elvys Linhares Pontes, Mohamed Ben Jannet, Jose G. Moreno, and Antoine Doucet. 2022. Using contextual sentence analysis models to recognize ESG concepts. In *Proceedings of the Fourth Workshop on Financial Technology and Natural Language Processing (FinNLP)*, pages 218–223, Abu Dhabi, United Arab Emirates (Hybrid). Association for Computational Linguistics.

Elvys Linhares Pontes, Stéphane Huet, Andréa Carneiro Linhares, and Juan-Manuel Torres-Moreno. 2018. Predicting the semantic textual similarity with Siamese CNN and LSTM. In *Actes de la Conférence TALN. Volume 1 - Articles longs, articles courts de TALN*, pages 311–320, Rennes, France. ATALA.

Yinhan Liu, Myle Ott, Naman Goyal, Jingfei Du, Mandar Joshi, Danqi Chen, Omer Levy, Mike Lewis, Luke Zettlemoyer, and Veselin Stoyanov. 2019. Roberta: A robustly optimized bert pretraining approach. Cite arxiv:1907.11692.

Srishti Mehra, Robert Louka, and Yixun Zhang. 2022. Esgbert: Language model to help with classification tasks related to companies environmental, social, and governance practices. *arXiv preprint arXiv:2203.16788*.

Keiron O'Shea and Ryan Nash. 2015. An introduction to convolutional neural networks. *CoRR*, abs/1511.08458.

J. Platt. 2000. Probabilistic outputs for support vector machines and comparison to regularized likelihood methods. In *Advances in Large Margin Classifiers*.

Elvys Linhares Pontes and Mohamed Benjannet. 2021. Contextual sentence analysis for the sentiment prediction on financial data. In *2021 IEEE International Conference on Big Data (Big Data)*, pages 4570–4577.

Nils Reimers and Iryna Gurevych. 2019. Sentence-bert: Sentence embeddings using siamese bert-networks. In *Proceedings of the 2019 Conference on Empirical Methods in Natural Language Processing*. Association for Computational Linguistics.

Zhengzheng Yang, Le Zhang, Xiaoyun Wang, and Yubo Mai. 2022. Esg text classification: An application of the prompt-based learning approach. *The Journal of Financial Data Science*.

EaSyGuide : ESG Issue Identification Framework leveraging Abilities of Generative Large Language Models

Hanwool Lee, Jonghyun Choi, Sohyeon Kwon, Sungbum Jung
NCSOFT
{albertmade, excelsiorcjh, sohyeonk, successtiger}@ncsoft.com

Abstract

This paper presents our participation in the FinNLP-2023 shared task on multi-lingual environmental, social, and corporate governance issue identification (ML-ESG). The task's objective is to classify news articles based on the 35 ESG key issues defined by the MSCI ESG rating guidelines. Our approach focuses on the English and French subtasks, employing the CerebrasGPT, OPT, and Pythia models, along with the zero-shot and GPT3Mix Augmentation techniques. We utilize various encoder models, such as RoBERTa, DeBERTa, and FinBERT, subjecting them to knowledge distillation and additional training.

Our approach yielded exceptional results, securing the first position in the English text subtask with F1-score 0.69 and the second position in the French text subtask with F1-score 0.78. These outcomes underscore the effectiveness of our methodology in identifying ESG issues in news articles across different languages. Our findings contribute to the exploration of ESG topics and highlight the potential of leveraging advanced language models for ESG issue identification.

1 Introduction

Environmental, Social, and Governance (ESG) factors have gained significant attention in the realm of corporate sustainability in recent years. Companies are increasingly recognizing the profound impact of ESG practices on their long-term success and resilience. Numerous research have highlighted the positive correlation between robust ESG strategies and improved financial performance(Eccles et al., 2019). For instance, a comprehensive meta-analysis of over 2000 empirical studies revealed a positive correlation between ESG and corporate financial performance, indicating the integral role of ESG in value creation(Gunnar et al., 2015). Consequently, understanding and integrating ESG principles into corporate strategies have become crucial for ensuring sustainable and resilient businesses in the modern era.

In parallel, there has been a growing recognition of the importance of leveraging natural language processing (NLP) techniques to incorporate ESG factors effectively. The integration of NLP holds great potential for enhancing our understanding of ESG-related information and its impact on businesses and society. By leveraging NLP, we can effectively analyze and extract insights from vast amounts of textual data, such as news articles, to gain deeper insights into companies' ESG performance and their societal impact.

Motivated by these developments, our team participated in the FinNLP-2023 shared task on multilingual ESG issue identification(ML-ESG)(Chen et al., 2023). The objective was to classify ESG-related news articles into 35 key issues based on the MSCI ESG rating guidelines. To accomplish this, We employed useful techniques such as Zero-shot and GPT3Mix Augmentation. Furthermore, we trained and evaluated various encoder models to assess their performance in the English and French text domains. Our best-performing model ranked first in the English Text subtask and second in the French Text subtask, highlighting the effectiveness of our approach in advancing NLP capabilities for ESG issue identification.

2 SharedTask ML-ESG

The SharedTask ML-ESG focuses on identifying ESG issues in news articles written in multiple languages. It builds upon the FinSim4-ESG shared task(Kang and El Maarouf, 2022) from FinNLP-2022. Our participation was specifically in the English subtask and the French task. The goal is to classify news articles into 35 ESG key issues based on MSCI ESG rating guidelines. The dataset includes separate training and testing sets in English and French, with 1,119 English articles and 1,200 French articles in the training set, and 300 articles

Proceedings of the Joint Workshop of the 5th Financial Technology and Natural Language Processing (FinNLP) and 2nd Multimodal AI For Financial Forecasting (Muffin), Macao, August 20, 2023.

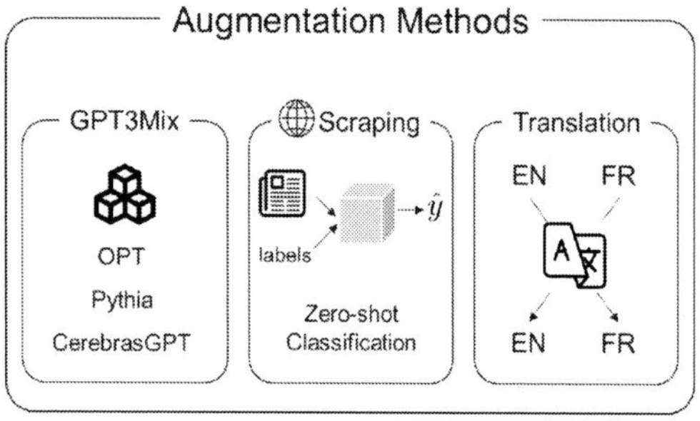

Figure 1: Overview of our approaches

in each language in the testing set.

3 Approaches

The primary objective of our work is to distill the capabilities of various well-known generative large language models to create a lightweight yet powerful encoder model. ESG Issue classification allows for generative model and sequence-to-sequence model approaches, but due to limitations in our computing resources and time constraints, we devised an approach focused primarily on the encoder models. Given the ML-ESG task's limited sample size (around 1200) and imbalanced label distribution, training on the available data alone is insufficient to fully train on 35 labels. To overcome these challenges, we employed three renowned open-source generative models: Pythia(Biderman et al., 2023), CerebrasGPT(Dey et al., 2023), and OPT(Zhang et al., 2022). Due to limitations in computational resources, we utilized a 12B model for Pythia, while CerebrasGPT and OPT utilized 13B models.

3.1 GPT3Mix

To augment the available data, we employed the GPT3Mix(Yoo et al., 2021) technique, which leverages large-scale language models to generate synthetic text samples. By blending real samples and leveraging soft-labels derived from the language models, GPT3Mix captures the intricacies of human language effectively. We integrated the MSCI guideline's label descriptions into the GPT3Mix template, enhancing the generation process and ensuring augmented data aligns with the desired label semantics.

3.2 Zero-Shot Classification

The ML-ESG task includes English and French subtasks, each with 35 classification criteria based on the MSCI guideline. However, the complexity of each criterion's decision boundaries poses challenges when relying solely on the available training data. To address this, we performed zero-shot classification(Xian et al., 2020) using ESG-related news collected through web scraping. To prevent prior exposure to the model, we excluded news articles from the training set originating from the same sources as the train set. We ensured label consistency by utilizing additional data only when Pythia, CerebrasGPT, and OPT provided identical labeling.

3.3 Translation

To train both multilingual and monolingual models, we leveraged translated versions of the English and French training sets as additional data. For translation, we utilized the widely recognized translation service, Deepl [1].

By employing these approaches, we aimed to optimize the use of generative models, apply data augmentation through GPT3Mix, perform zero-shot classification, and incorporate translated data to enhance the capabilities of our encoder models for the ML-ESG task.

4 Experiments and Results

Our experiments were conducted in two phases. In the first phase, our aim was to identify effective encoder models and approaches by combining various techniques. In the second phase, we aimed to build an optimal model based on the findings from the first phase.

All experiments were conducted using the same hyperparameters: learning rate of 3e-4, epoch of 20, and optimizer of AdamW(Loshchilov and Hutter, 2019). The experiments were run on a single A100 GPU.

4.1 First Experiment

In the first experiment, we aimed to validate the performance of various encoder models for the ML-ESG task. We utilized well-known encoder models, including DeBERTa(He et al., 2021), RoBERTa(Liu et al., 2019), and FinBERT(Araci, 2019) which is specifically designed for financial text. To ensure applicability across both English and French subtasks, we also incorporated multilingual encoder models, namely mDeBERTa(He et al., 2023) and mRoBERTa(Goyal et al., 2021).

[1] `https://www.deepl.com/translator`

Model	Subtask	Valid F1	Test F1
RoBERTa-base	English	0.66	0.67
DeBERTa-large	English	0.65	0.69
FinBERT	English	0.53	0.56
mRoBERTa-xl	English	0.61	0.69
DeBERTa-base	English	0.51	0.58
mDeBERTa	English	0.44	0.52
mRoBERTa-xl	French	0.76	0.75
mDeBERTa	French	0.49	0.47

Table 1: Overview of baseline experiment results

To evaluate the capabilities of these models, we employed stratified sampling to extract a validation set comprising approximately 5% of the training set. Due to the unbalanced label distribution, we utilized the weighted F1 score as the primary evaluation metric. Baseline scores were obtained for each model, and any model with a validation F1 score below 0.45 was excluded from further experimentation. The summarized performance results of the baseline models are presented in the table 1, serving as the baseline for further experiments.

Method	EN	FR
Original	1199	1200
GPTMix-OPT (opt)	2866	2867
GPTMix-Pythia (pyt)	2900	2901
GPTMix-CerebrasGPT (cpt)	2906	2907
GPTMix-Mixed Models (mix)	7473	7474
Crawled (da)	4816	-
Translation (ts)	2279	2279

Table 2: Size of dataset for each approaches, The content within parentheses represents the abbreviation of the respective datasets.

In addition to the initial experimentation, we employed data augmentation techniques to further enhance the performance of our models. We leveraged large-scale language models, including Pythia, CerebrasGPT, and OPT, for augmentation. For each news article, we generated additional samples and removed poorly generated ones to form a training dataset for each GPT3Mix augmentation technique.

Furthermore, we crawled ESG-related news articles in both languages, assigning labels to the collected data using Zero-shot Classification. Duplicate labels were removed, resulting in a cleaner dataset. Additionally, we added a translated version of the original training dataset to train monolingual models for English and French. We also constructed the 'GPTMix-Mixed Models (mix)' dataset by aggregating all GPT3Mix Augmentation datasets for further experimentation. Finally, we merged the augmented data for English and French to train a multilingual model.

Experiment Name	Subtask	Valid F1	Test F1
RoBERTa-base-mix	English	0.749	0.597
DeBERTa-large-ts	English	0.737	0.705
RoBERTa-base-pyt	English	0.735	0.629
RoBERTa-base-opt	English	0.730	0.603
RoBERTa-base-cpt	English	0.709	0.628
DeBERTa-base-da	English	0.694	0.615
mDeBERTa-mix	French	0.760	0.731
mRoBERTa-xl-cpt	French	0.702	0.714
mDeBERTa-pyt	French	0.671	0.663
mDeBERTa-opt	French	0.657	0.656
mRoBERTa-xl-ts	French	0.625	0.695

Table 3: Best performing models for each methodology

Among the English models, "roberta-base-mix" trained on data augmented by large language models OPT, Pythia, and CerebrasGPT and subsequently merged, achieved the highest validation F1 score of 0.7489. Furthermore, models trained on data augmented through translation and crawling obtained higher validation F1 scores than those trained on the original dataset. These results demonstrate the significant effectiveness of our proposed augmentation methodologies.

Similarly, for the French subtask, "mdeberta-mix" trained on data augmented using large language models, achieved a high validation F1 score of 0.7602, indicating that most of models trained on augmented data outperformed the baselines.

These experimental results highlight the efficacy of our approach and the positive impact of data augmentation on the performance of the encoder models in the ML-ESG task.

4.2 Second Experiment

Experiment 1 aimed to analyze the performance of various encoder models in multifarious ways. In contrast, experiment 2 focused on conducting experiments on several datasets using both base and large models from a specific subset of models, providing a more targeted investigation.

4.2.1 Effect of Model Size

The size of language models is a significant factor that impacts their performance. In this experiment, we compared the classification performance of two

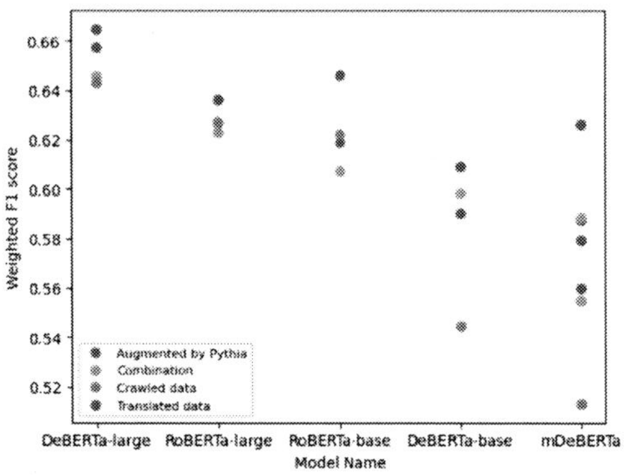

Figure 2: Experiment Results for experiment 2 on test set

well-performing language models from Experiment 1, DeBERTa and RoBERTa, at their base and large versions to analyze the effect of model size.

Figure 2 illustrates that the large models of RoBERTa and DeBERTa consistently achieved higher F1 scores compared to their base models. Notably, the F1 scores of the large models were concentrated within a narrower range, indicating a more reliable and accurate performance. This suggests that the base models do not offer superior performance and are more susceptible to bias in classification results, struggling to accurately distinguish certain labels.

4.2.2 Model Robustness

Despite our efforts to construct a training dataset with a balanced label distribution in Experiment 1, our language models faced challenges in handling out-of-distribution issues. The complexity arose from the large number of MSCI ESG standard labels (35 in total), which strained the models' predictive abilities. Certain labels, such as controversial sourcing, revealed noticeable weaknesses in our models' predictions.

To address these shortcomings and enhance the robustness of the language models, we modified our training and validation datasets in the second experiment. We allocated a greater number of samples to labels from web-crawled dataset that had proven challenging for the models to predict accurately.

4.2.3 Integration of data and ensembling

Our research aimed to enhance ESG issue classification in a multilingual context by adopting a diverse and multi-faceted approach. We utilized four types of datasets(ts,pyt,da,combined) and experimented with eight different models, exploring data mixing and ensemble methods to optimize model performance.

Although the combined datasets showed promising performance, they did not outperform models trained exclusively on translated data in second experiment. This indicates that incorporating data from diverse sources may introduce additional noise and potentially decrease performance. In such circumstances, ensembling the results from various models proved beneficial(Ruta and Gabrys, 2005). For the English task, we employed a hard-voting ensemble of the top-scoring models, trained on different datasets using various encoder models. This ensemble approach achieved the highest performance, with an F1 score of 0.69 on the test set and 0.81 on the validation set, demonstrating the effectiveness of combining diverse models and datasets. Similarly, for the French task, we applied an ensemble technique by combining predictions from three models trained on different datasets and diverse encoder models, resulting in an impressive F1 score of 0.78 on the test set (0.8 on the validation set), further highlighting the effectiveness of combining models in a multilingual context for ESG issue classification.

5 Conclusion

In this paper, we presented our approach for the FinNLP-2023 shared task on multi-lingual ESG issue identification. By leveraging advanced encoder models and techniques like GPT3Mix Augmentation, zero-shot classification, and translation, we achieved promising results. Our models ranked first in the English text subtask and second in the French text subtask, highlighting the effectiveness of our methodology across different languages. Our research contributes to exploring ESG topics and showcases the potential of advanced language models in identifying ESG issues. Future work would focus on exploring decoder and sequence-to-sequence architectures, expanding to other languages, and employing alternative models to improve the accuracy and generalizability of ESG issue identification systems.

Availability

The code is available at `https://github.com/finMU/ML-ESG_codes`.

References

Dogu Araci. 2019. Finbert: Financial sentiment analysis with pre-trained language models.

Stella Biderman, Hailey Schoelkopf, Quentin Anthony, Herbie Bradley, Kyle O'Brien, Eric Hallahan, Mohammad Aflah Khan, Shivanshu Purohit, USVSN Sai Prashanth, Edward Raff, Aviya Skowron, Lintang Sutawika, and Oskar van der Wal. 2023. Pythia: A suite for analyzing large language models across training and scaling.

Chung-Chi Chen, Yu-Min Tseng, Juyeon Kang, Anaïs Lhuissier, Min-Yuh Day, Teng-Tsai Tu, and Hsin-Hsi Chen. 2023. Multi-lingual esg issue identification. In *Proceedings of the Fifth Workshop on Financial Technology and Natural Language Processing (FinNLP) and the Second Multimodal AI For Financial Forecasting (Muffin)*.

Nolan Dey, Gurpreet Gosal, Zhiming, Chen, Hemant Khachane, William Marshall, Ribhu Pathria, Marvin Tom, and Joel Hestness. 2023. Cerebras-gpt: Open compute-optimal language models trained on the cerebras wafer-scale cluster.

Robert G. Eccles, Linda-Eling Lee, and Judith C. Stroehle. 2019. The social origins of esg?: An analysis of innovest and kld. *SSRN Electronic Journal*, 40:1–40. Last revised: September 14, 2019.

Naman Goyal, Jingfei Du, Myle Ott, Giri Anantharaman, and Alexis Conneau. 2021. Larger-scale transformers for multilingual masked language modeling.

Friede Gunnar, Timo Buschand, and Alexander Bassen. 2015. Esg and financial performance: aggregated evidence from more than 2000 empirical studies. *Journal of sustainable finance & investment*, pages 210–233.

Pengcheng He, Jianfeng Gao, and Weizhu Chen. 2023. Debertav3: Improving deberta using electra-style pretraining with gradient-disentangled embedding sharing.

Pengcheng He, Xiaodong Liu, Jianfeng Gao, and Weizhu Chen. 2021. Deberta: Decoding-enhanced bert with disentangled attention.

Juyeon Kang and Ismail El Maarouf. 2022. FinSim4-ESG shared task: Learning semantic similarities for the financial domain. extended edition to ESG insights. In *Proceedings of the Fourth Workshop on Financial Technology and Natural Language Processing (FinNLP)*, pages 211–217, Abu Dhabi, United Arab Emirates (Hybrid). Association for Computational Linguistics.

Yinhan Liu, Myle Ott, Naman Goyal, Jingfei Du, Mandar Joshi, Danqi Chen, Omer Levy, Mike Lewis, Luke Zettlemoyer, and Veselin Stoyanov. 2019. Roberta: A robustly optimized bert pretraining approach.

Ilya Loshchilov and Frank Hutter. 2019. Decoupled weight decay regularization.

Dymitr Ruta and Bogdan Gabrys. 2005. Classifier selection for majority voting. *Information Fusion*, 6(1):63–81. Diversity in Multiple Classifier Systems.

Yongqin Xian, Christoph H. Lampert, Bernt Schiele, and Zeynep Akata. 2020. Zero-shot learning – a comprehensive evaluation of the good, the bad and the ugly.

Kang Min Yoo, Dongju Park, Jaewook Kang, Sang-Woo Lee, and Woomyoung Park. 2021. GPT3Mix: Leveraging large-scale language models for text augmentation. In *Findings of the Association for Computational Linguistics: EMNLP 2021*, pages 2225–2239, Punta Cana, Dominican Republic. Association for Computational Linguistics.

Susan Zhang, Stephen Roller, Naman Goyal, Mikel Artetxe, Moya Chen, Shuohui Chen, Christopher Dewan, Mona Diab, Xian Li, Xi Victoria Lin, Todor Mihaylov, Myle Ott, Sam Shleifer, Kurt Shuster, Daniel Simig, Punit Singh Koura, Anjali Sridhar, Tianlu Wang, and Luke Zettlemoyer. 2022. Opt: Open pre-trained transformer language models.

A Appendix

A.1 GPT3Mix Prompt Details

Based on the GPT3Mix paper, we developed a Task Specification Template for the MLESG Shared Task and randomly extracted examples. However, considering the high probability of introducing imbalanced data when extracting augmented data with imbalanced labels, we equalized the extraction probability for each label to mitigate the imbalance issue. In this process, including descriptions for all 35 labels in the prompt could lead to excessive context, so we only utilized label descriptions for the labels present in the samples. Below is an example showcasing a partial portion of the prompt we employed.

A.1.1 Example of Task Description

```
Each item in the following list should contain
#ESG News headline, #ESG news and the related
#ESG key issues. #ESG key issues are based on
MSCI ESG rating guidelines.
```

A.1.2 Example of Label Description

```
Access to Finance: This label is about their
efforts to expand financial services to
historically underserved markets, including
small-business lending and the development of
innovative distribution channels.
```

A.2 Data distributions

In our study, we utilized GPT3Mix to augment the dataset, resulting in a well-balanced distribution of labels. Each of the 35 labels accounted for approximately 2.85% (plus or minus 0.7%) of the dataset. However, when performing zero-shot classification on the data obtained through web crawling, we encountered limitations. This was due to either the scarcity of relevant data available on the web or the presence of insufficient labels caused by model bias. To provide further insights, we present a detailed table 4 showcasing the label distribution exclusively based on the crawled data.

Label	Percentage (%)
Board	8.80
Carbon Emissions	6.94
Responsible Investment	5.64
Accounting	5.53
Pay	5.36
Packaging Material & Waste	4.57
Business Ethics	4.35
Water Stress	4.23
Financing Environmental Impact	4.01
Opportunities in Renewable Energy	3.89
Human Capital Development	3.84
Community Relations	3.78
Consumer Financial Protection	3.78
Product Carbon Footprint	3.67
Opportunities in Clean Tech	3.50
Biodiversity & Land Use	2.99
Electronic Waste	2.82
Chemical Safety	2.60
Raw Material Sourcing	2.54
Opportunities in Green Building	2.48
Ownership & Control	2.37
Climate Change Vulnerability	1.81
Toxic Emissions & Waste	1.58
Health & Demographic Risk	1.24
Access to Finance	1.24
Opportunities in Nutrition & Health	1.24
Access to Health Care	1.19
Privacy & Data Security	0.96
Access to Communications	0.73
Product Safety & Quality	0.68
Supply Chain Labor Standards	0.62
Labor Management	0.51
Controversial Sourcing	0.51

Table 4: Label Distribution of Crawled Data

Jetsons at the FinNLP-2023: Using Synthetic Data and Transfer Learning for Multilingual ESG Issue Classification

Parker Glenn*, **Alolika Gon***, **Nikhil Kohli***, **Sihan Zha***, **Parag Pravin Dakle**, **Preethi Raghavan**
Fidelity Investments, AI Center of Excellence
{parker.glenn, alolika.gon, nikhil.kohli, sihan.zha, paragpravin.dakle, preethi.raghavan}@fmr.com

Abstract

In this paper, we describe the various approaches by the *Jetsons* team for the Multilingual ESG Issue Identification Task (ML-ESG) to classify articles into ESG (environmental, social, and corporate governance) issues they are related to. For English and French articles, we finetune multilingual BERT with synthetic data in a single-label classification setting. For the Chinese articles, we employ transfer learning to leverage the full breadth of the multilingual training data. Our methods achieve 1st place on the leaderboard for French, and 5th place for both English and Chinese.

1 Introduction

ESG (environmental, social, and governance) investing introduces a set of standards to judge investments by values corresponding to specific issues. Examples of these issues include "Chemical Safety", "Controversial Sourcing", and "Carbon Emissions". The International Joint Conferences on Artificial Intelligence (IJCAI) shared task (Chen et al., 2023) presents a fine-grained multilingual classification task based on a taxonomy of these ESG issues.

We approach this task using several strategies, including 1) transfer learning to the multi-label Chinese data using mBERT (Devlin et al., 2018), 2) augmentation with synthetic data generated with LLMs in zero-shot and few-shot settings, and 3) T5 variants (Xue et al., 2021, 2022) for multiclass text classification.

2 Related work

Language models have been used for various financial tasks like named-entity recognition, sentiment analysis, or document classification. Previous works have performed domain-specific pre-training of language models for different financial tasks (Araci, 2019; Huang et al., 2022; Shah et al., 2022; Lu et al., 2023; Wu et al., 2023). However, until recently, only a few works have explored using language models for ESG-related tasks. Raman et al. 2020 evaluate the impact of using embeddings generated by language models on the classification of sentences concerning their relevance to the ESG domain. Mehra et al. 2022 pre-train a BERT model on ESG-related text to show improvement on classification tasks. Nugent et al. fine-tune an English BERT-style model on an ESG document classification dataset and evaluate using data generation as an augmentation strategy.

Kær Jørgensen et al. 2021 extend the idea of pre-training on financial text to multilingual text and evaluate different sentence classification tasks in seven languages. Jørgensen et al. 2023 evaluate various language models on a multilingual financial topic classification dataset to highlight areas of improvement for low-resource languages.

The work of Nugent et al. 2021 is closest to work presented in the paper. The authors use the back-translation task to generate additional input data. This work, however, performs ESG document classification in a mono- and multilingual setting. Additionally, we use a large language model to generate additional data using just the ESG topic compared to performing back-translation.

3 Data

We use the dataset described in Chen et al. (2023) for this task. The training dataset consists of articles in three languages: English (en), French (fr), and Chinese (zh). Alongside the articles are the corresponding ESG issues these articles are related to. The English and French dataset each contains about 1200 articles. These datasets are single-labeled with one out of 35 ESG classes, as designated by the MSCI[1]. The Chinese training set

*These authors contributed equally to this work

[1] https://www.msci.com/our-solutions/esg-investing/esg-industry-materiality-map

Proceedings of the Joint Workshop of the 5th Financial Technology and Natural Language Processing (FinNLP) and 2nd Multimodal AI For Financial Forecasting (Muffin), Macao, August 20, 2023.

contains 996 articles. The Chinese labels merge the MSCI classes with those designated by the SASB[2] for a total of 46 total labels. These Chinese data points are multilabel, and each article is classified with a minimum of one and a maximum of 13 labels. Figure 1 shows the distribution of training and validation instances on the 24 most popular classes.

3.1 Synthetic Data Generation with large language models

We leverage the power of open-source large language models (gpt-3.5-turbo[3]) in generating text for augmenting the dataset to improve the class imbalance. For all three languages (English, French, and Chinese), given an ESG label, we generate 'News Title' and 'News Summary' for each instance. We generate a total of 413 data points for 11 different labels. We choose these labels based on the class-wise performance metrics and class distribution.

We categorize the ESG labels into two categories - ambiguous and non-ambiguous. Here we define ambiguity as a label being open to more than one interpretation and requiring some domain expertise to resolve the ambiguity. We employ two different strategies for generating samples for these two categories. For non-ambiguous topics, we use zero-shot generation. For ambiguous topics, we use few-shot generation to ensure that the generated samples are related to the ESG domain. Below is an example of a zero-shot prompt.

```
Give 10 examples of news related
to ESG (Environmental, Social, Governance)
topic 'Electronic Waste'. Each example
should have a news title, news summary and
tags related to the article. Generate
these examples in french language.
```

4 Models

4.1 Chinese

Given the disjoint task setup of the Chinese data with the English and French data (multilabel vs. multiclass, respectively), it is difficult to train a single multilingual clasifier for all three languages. To utilize the value of English and French data, we adopt a transfer learning technique to train a model

[2]https://www.sasb.org/standards/materiality-finder/?lang=en-us

[3]https://platform.openai.com/docs/models/gpt-3-5

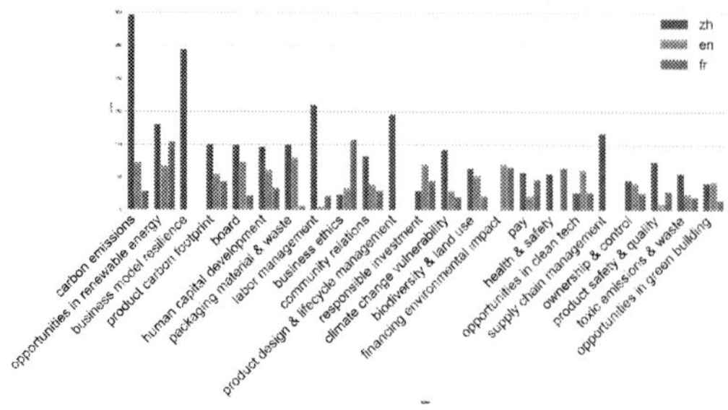

Figure 1: Frequency of the most popular 24 labels in the Train and Validation splits across the 3 languages.

to classify Chinese texts. We use the bert-base-multilingual-cased[4], which is based on the BERT model (Devlin et al., 2018), as our base model to reconcile different languages. We first fine-tune the base model using the English and French data to do single-class classification. Subsequently, we further fine-tune the model from the previous steps using Chinese data, changing the output layer to enable multi-class classification.

After observing the mean, median, and standard deviation of the number of labels in the training data, we adjust our label selection criteria to mimic that distribution of labels. For this multi-label classification problem, we apply the sigmoid function on the raw output and use the resulting probabilities to select labels. We found that selecting up to 10 labels with a probability larger than 0.2 yields a similar distribution of labels to that in the training data so that the mean, median, and standard deviation are roughly comparable between the training data and our model outputs. For all Chinese models, we discard those articles with empty ESG label fields[5].

4.2 English and French

Given the small size of the individual English and French datasets, we finetune bert-base-multilingual-cased on the combined datasets for single-label classification. We concatenate the article title and content separated by "||" and use it as input for the model. 80% of the combined dataset with 2,399 French and English articles is used for training, and the rest is used for validation. We perform 5-fold cross-validation and use a majority vote from the five predictions to choose the final

[4]https://huggingface.co/bert-base-multilingual-cased

[5]As there was no specific [not ESG-related] label provided and some non-labeled articles appeared related to ESG issues, we believed these datapoints represented noise.

ESG label. The learning rate is set at $2.5e-5$ and the model is trained for 10 or 20 epochs.

We also finetune multilingual BERT for single-label classification by augmenting the training data using synthetic data described in subsection 3.1 and/or using the given Chinese dataset. We validate these models using the given English and French articles. We train different models using three levels of augmentation - (1) use synthetic data in English and French, (2) use the given Chinese dataset for augmentation, and (3) use synthetic articles in all three languages along with the given Chinese dataset. At inference time, we generate our predictions on the test set using a majority voting ensemble from the models trained on each fold.

T5-based Filtration In converting the ESG labels to indices on a probability vector, we ignore features embedded in the labels' text. For example, the semantic distance between "Toxic Emissions & Waste" and "Packaging Material & Waste" is arguably smaller than between "Board" and "Pay". In the traditional multiclass classification paradigm, these relationships are ignored.

To remedy this, we experiment with using variants of T5 for multiclass classification. Specifically, we take those labels from the French and English data with the top-k highest softmax probabilities as judged by the classifier described in Section 4.2 and encode them with T5 alongside the article content and title. The T5 decoder selects one of the top-k labels as a final prediction. Setting k too high results in too large of a search space, sometimes resulting in context overflow. Setting k too low can cause the fatal mistake of the gold label being absent in the input to T5, dooming the filtration model to an incorrect prediction. We experiment with two multilingual T5 variants: ByT5 (Xue et al., 2022) and MT5 (Xue et al., 2021).

5 Results

5.1 Chinese

Due to the reasons stated in Section 4.1, we exclude those non-labeled data points. Thus, the reported model results do not consider those articles. Our Chinese model achieves the following results on the Chinese validation dataset obtained from the training data provided: **F1 score: 36.81, precision: 29.10, and recall: 52.62**. The three versions of our submissions to the official test set are the results from the single model with the above performance

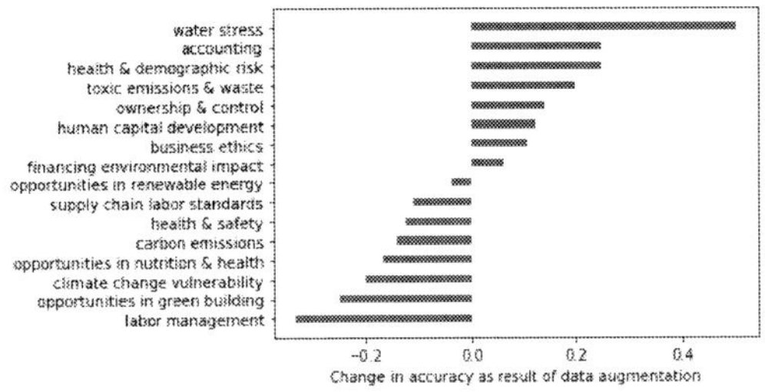

Figure 2: Classes with change in accuracy in the French test set due to augmentation using synthetic English and French data on training for 20 epochs.

using different label selection criteria.

5.2 English and French

Table 1 shows the precision (P), recall (R), and F1 score for English and French articles in the test set. Figure 2 shows the change in class-wise performance when using the synthetic counterparts.

Best French Result Finetuning multilingual BERT for 20 epochs on the original English and French training dataset augmented with synthetic articles in English and French achieves the F1 score of 79.96 for the French articles in the test split. Using data augmentation increases the F1 score by 1.39 when trained for 10 epochs. When trained for 20 epochs, using data augmentation increases the F1 score by up to 0.63.

Best English Result Finetuning multilingual BERT for 20 epochs on the original English and French training dataset augmented with the original Chinese dataset achieves the best F1 score of 66.33 for the English test split. As shown in Table 1, the augmentation increases the F1 score by a maximum of 0.66.

5.3 Classification with T5

As shown in Table 2, the multilingual variants of T5 were not successful in filtering the top-k predictions of the original BERT-based classifier. In the best setting, an mt5-large[6] model was able to boost the English F1 score by +0.77 when provided with the ranked top-5 predictions of the BERT classifier.

Analyzing the outputs of the mt5-large model, it suffered from a strong tendency to hyper-fixate on the positional signal provided by the ranked inputs. Specifically, the mt5-large model only predicted a label different from what the original classifier

[6] https://huggingface.co/google/mt5-large

Training Data	Epochs	$\mathbf{P}_{en}$	$\mathbf{R}_{en}$	$\mathbf{F1}_{en}$	$\mathbf{P}_{fr}$	$\mathbf{R}_{fr}$	$\mathbf{F1}_{fr}$
en + fr (**Jetsons_3**)	10	65.36	66.00	64.88	78.39	78.33	77.38
en + fr	20	66.77	66.67	66.01	80.00	80.00	79.33
en + fr + Syn (**Jetsons_2**)	10	64.11	65.00	63.75	80.34	79.00	78.77
en + fr + Syn	20	64.31	64.67	63.90	**81.32**	**80.33**	**79.96**
en + fr + zh	20	**66.96**	**67.33**	**66.33**	81.05	79.67	79.68
en + fr + zh + Syn_{all}	20	66.63	66.33	65.45	80.34	79.67	79.25

Table 1: Results of finetuning multilingual BERT on the English(en) and French(fr) articles in the test set with and without data augmentation. Official submissions on the test set are designated in bold. Syn - Synthetically generated en and fr articles, Syn_{all} - Synthetically generated en, fr, and zh articles.

	Model	K	EN F1	EN F1 Change	FR F1	FR F1 Change
Labels Shuffled	byt5-base	5	28.08	-28.39	32.08	-42.10
	mt5-base	10	25.58	-30.89	30.37	-43.91
	mt5-large	5	33.89	-22.58	39.1	-35.10
Labels Ranked by Logits	byt5-base	10	56.63	+0.16	74.18	+0.0
	mt5-large	5	**57.24**	**+0.77**	73.74	-0.44

Table 2: Results of the various T5-based models for filtering the top-k predictions made by the initial BERT-based classifier. We use the predictions from the 1st fold of **Jetsons_2** in these experiments.

predicted in 6 out of 600 instances, resulting in a 0.77 improvement in English samples. The model appears to get stuck in a local minimum in that merely predicting the label that appears first gives decent performance (whatever the original BERT-based classifier achieved). In an attempt to solve this hyper-fixation on positional signals, we run experiments with shuffled label inputs as well. This further highlighted the inability of the T5 variants to perform well in this task.

6 Analysis

6.1 Synthetic Data vs. Original

Surprisingly, the synthetic data generated using the methods described in Section 3.1 did not always improve performance on the final test set. To explore this further, we plot the embedding representation of the synthetic and original training data in Figure 3. Embeddings were generated using the paraphrase-MiniLM-L6-v2 model (Reimers and Gurevych, 2019), and cast to a 2-dimensional space using TSNE (Van der Maaten and Hinton, 2008). Qualitatively, we see that the synthetic data seems to have a lower variance in this embedding space than the original data.

Many of the synthetic data points appear to be simpler to classify than the original data points. Notably within the EN + FR data, 185 synthetic

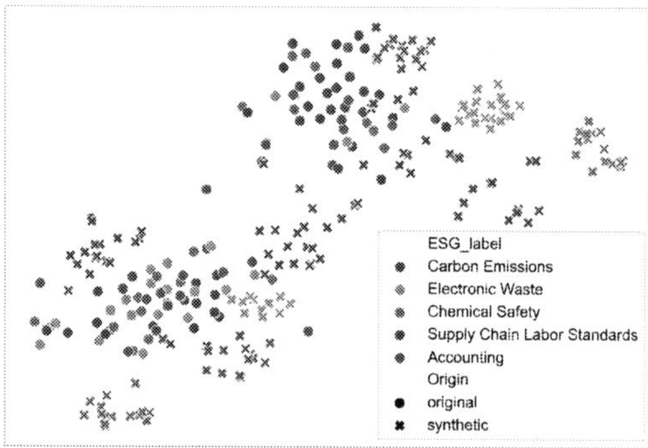

Figure 3: Plotting the embedding space of the original EN+FR articles against the synthetic articles generated with the LLM described in Section 3.1. The synthetic data points appear to be more tightly grouped together than the original training data.

article titles contained at least one token appearing in the gold label, whereas only 6 of the original data points contained this token overlap[7]. This represents a token overlap rate of 62.29% for the synthetic data and only 2.79% for the original data.

7 Conclusion

Excelling at the task of ESG issue identification moves the field of financial NLP to a more well-rounded state, where the primary focus of monetary factors is balanced with other qualitative, social factors. We carry out experiments on the FinNLP shared task of fine-grained ESG issue identification, and find that a BERT-based classifier augmented with synthetic data performs best on French and English data. Additionally, we see that utilizing transfer learning boosts performance on Chinese data.

[7]For example, the synthetic article with the title "BP announces net-zero emissions target by 2050" contains a token overlap ("emissions") with the gold label "Carbon Emissions".

References

Dogu Araci. 2019. Finbert: Financial sentiment analysis with pre-trained language models. *arXiv preprint arXiv:1908.10063*.

Chung-Chi Chen, Yu-Min Tseng, Juyeon Kang, Anaïs Lhuissier, Min-Yuh Day, Teng-Tsai Tu, and Hsin-Hsi Chen. 2023. Multi-lingual esg issue identification. In *Proceedings of the Fifth Workshop on Financial Technology and Natural Language Processing (FinNLP) and the Second Multimodal AI For Financial Forecasting (Muffin)*.

Jacob Devlin, Ming-Wei Chang, Kenton Lee, and Kristina Toutanova. 2018. BERT: pre-training of deep bidirectional transformers for language understanding. *CoRR*, abs/1810.04805.

Allen H Huang, Hui Wang, and Yi Yang. 2022. Finbert: A large language model for extracting information from financial text. *Contemporary Accounting Research*.

Rasmus Jørgensen, Oliver Brandt, Mareike Hartmann, Xiang Dai, Christian Igel, and Desmond Elliott. 2023. MultiFin: A dataset for multilingual financial NLP. In *Findings of the Association for Computational Linguistics: EACL 2023*, pages 894–909, Dubrovnik, Croatia. Association for Computational Linguistics.

Rasmus Kær Jørgensen, Mareike Hartmann, Xiang Dai, and Desmond Elliott. 2021. mDAPT: Multilingual domain adaptive pretraining in a single model. In *Findings of the Association for Computational Linguistics: EMNLP 2021*, pages 3404–3418, Punta Cana, Dominican Republic. Association for Computational Linguistics.

Dakuan Lu, Jiaqing Liang, Yipei Xu, Qianyu He, Yipeng Geng, Mengkun Han, Yingsi Xin, Hengkui Wu, and Yanghua Xiao. 2023. Bbt-fin: Comprehensive construction of chinese financial domain pre-trained language model, corpus and benchmark. *arXiv preprint arXiv:2302.09432*.

Srishti Mehra, Robert Louka, and Yixun Zhang. 2022. Esgbert: Language model to help with classification tasks related to companies environmental, social, and governance practices. *arXiv preprint arXiv:2203.16788*.

Tim Nugent, Nicole Stelea, and Jochen L. Leidner. 2021. Detecting environmental, social andnbsp;governance (esg) topics using domain-specific language models andnbsp;data augmentation. In *Flexible Query Answering Systems: 14th International Conference, FQAS 2021, Bratislava, Slovakia, September 19–24, 2021, Proceedings*, page 157–169, Berlin, Heidelberg. Springer-Verlag.

Natraj Raman, Grace Bang, and Armineh Nourbakhsh. 2020. Mapping esg trends by distant supervision of neural language models. *Machine Learning and Knowledge Extraction*, 2(4):453–468.

Nils Reimers and Iryna Gurevych. 2019. Sentence-bert: Sentence embeddings using siamese bert-networks. In *Proceedings of the 2019 Conference on Empirical Methods in Natural Language Processing*. Association for Computational Linguistics.

Raj Sanjay Shah, Kunal Chawla, Dheeraj Eidnani, Agam Shah, Wendi Du, Sudheer Chava, Natraj Raman, Charese Smiley, Jiaao Chen, and Diyi Yang. 2022. When flue meets flang: Benchmarks and large pretrained language model for financial domain. In *Proceedings of the 2022 Conference on Empirical Methods in Natural Language Processing (EMNLP)*. Association for Computational Linguistics.

Noam Shazeer and Mitchell Stern. 2018. Adafactor: Adaptive learning rates with sublinear memory cost. In *International Conference on Machine Learning*, pages 4596–4604. PMLR.

Laurens Van der Maaten and Geoffrey Hinton. 2008. Visualizing data using t-sne. *Journal of machine learning research*, 9(11).

Shijie Wu, Ozan Irsoy, Steven Lu, Vadim Dabravolski, Mark Dredze, Sebastian Gehrmann, Prabhanjan Kambadur, David Rosenberg, and Gideon Mann. 2023. Bloomberggpt: A large language model for finance. *arXiv preprint arXiv:2303.17564*.

Linting Xue, Aditya Barua, Noah Constant, Rami Al-Rfou, Sharan Narang, Mihir Kale, Adam Roberts, and Colin Raffel. 2022. ByT5: Towards a token-free future with pre-trained byte-to-byte models. *Transactions of the Association for Computational Linguistics*, 10:291–306.

Linting Xue, Noah Constant, Adam Roberts, Mihir Kale, Rami Al-Rfou, Aditya Siddhant, Aditya Barua, and Colin Raffel. 2021. mT5: A massively multilingual pre-trained text-to-text transformer. In *Proceedings of the 2021 Conference of the North American Chapter of the Association for Computational Linguistics: Human Language Technologies*, pages 483–498, Online. Association for Computational Linguistics.

A Appendix

A.1 Few-Shot Prompt for Data Generation

```
ESG label: Accounting

Type: few-shot prompt for english language

Prompt: Give 10 examples of news related
to ESG (Environmental, Social, Governance)
topic 'Accounting'. Each example should have
a news title, news summary, Tags related
to the article. Generate these examples in
english language. An example news for
'Accounting' topic - News Title:
```

```
"Institutional Investors: Fossil Fuel
Companies Must Align Numbers with Paris
Agreement", News Summary: "The group of
investors engaged bp in its campaign in
November, and sent parallel letters to
other energy majors, including Royal
Dutch Shell and Total. While Shell
and Total have also lowered their oil
and gas price assumptions, the statement
notes that most other companies have yet
to bring their assumptions in line with
the Paris Agreement, and calls on them
to do so: Other fossil fuel dependent
companies need to sit up and take note.
Based on our analysis of major European
fossil fuel companies 2019 financial
statements... it is clear that almost
none have aligned their critical accounting
assumptions with the Paris Agreement.
The level of BP's impairments demonstrates
the potential materiality of this risk
hidden in companies balance sheets."
```

Sample Generated Content:

French language -

Titre de l'article: Les entreprises doivent inclure la diversité dans leur comptabilité, selon une étude

Résumé de l'article: Selon une étude du cabinet de conseil PwC, les entreprises doivent inclure la diversité dans leur comptabilité. Cette étude a examiné les pratiques de comptabilité de 100 grandes entreprises aux États-Unis. Les résultats ont montré que seulement 10 informations sur la diversité dans leurs rapports financiers. Les experts affirment que l'inclusion de la diversité dans la comptabilité peut aider les entreprises à mieux comprendre leur personnel et à améliorer la prise de décision.

Tags : Accounting, Diversity, États-Unis.

English language -

News Title: The Impact of Diversity and Inclusion on Financial Performance

News Summary: Diversity and inclusion are increasingly seen as key drivers of financial performance, with studies showing that diverse companies outperform their peers. This article discusses the accounting implications of diversity and inclusion and the need for better diversity reporting standards.

Tags: ESG, diversity and inclusion, financial performance, accounting implications, reporting standards.

A.2 T5 Modeling

Hyperparameter settings All models are fine-tuned with Adafactor (Shazeer and Stern, 2018) and a learning rate of 1e-3, and a batch size of 32. A linear warm-up for the first 10% of training steps is employed, followed by cosine decay.

Inputs We display an example input to the T5 model described in Section 2 below, with the placeholder `{article_content}`.

```
Lenovo, Kuehne+Nagel Partner
on Solution to Offset
Shipping Emissions
with SAF Purchases
| {article_content}
|| LABELS:
opportunities in renewable energy,
carbon emissions,
financing environmental impact,
opportunities in clean tech,
opportunities in green building
```

In the example above, the BERT-based classifier predicted "Opportunities in Renewable Energy". However, the gold label is "Carbon Emissions". By passing in the ranked predictions from the BERT-based classifier, the T5 model is tasked with remedying the mistaken prediction and instead choosing the 2nd highest ranked ESG label.

Effect of k Figure 4 plots the relationship between k and the percentage of ranked data points which would contain the gold label.

A.3 Effects of Data Augmentation

Figures 6, 7, 5, 8 and 9 show change in class-wise accuracy in French and English test set as a result of different settings of data augmentation. For the French articles, performance for classes like Raw Material Sourcing, Labor Management, Opportunities in Green Building, Consumer Financial Protection, Community Relations, and Supply Chain Labor Standards improve on training for 10 epochs using augmented data.

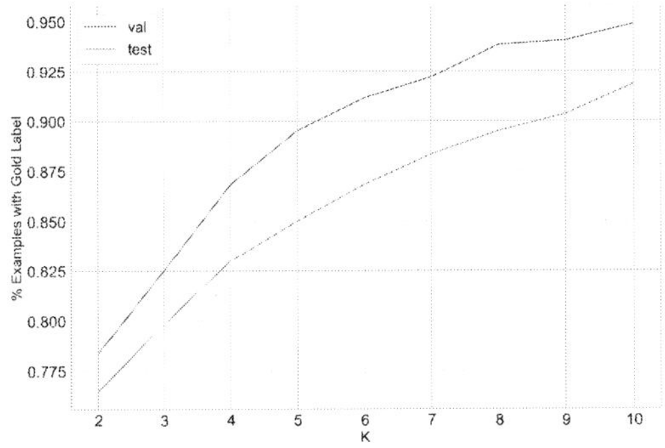

Figure 4: Plotting the relationship between k and the hypothetical upper-bound performance of the T5 model. By setting $k = 5$, 85% of the predictions we pass to T5 includes the gold label on the test split. This represents an upper performance bound of 87% for French and 83% for English.

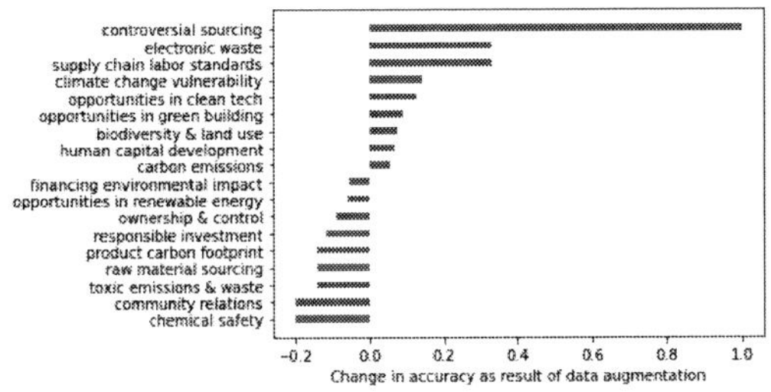

Figure 5: Change in the accuracy of English test instances on training for 10 epochs after augmentation using synthetic English and French data.

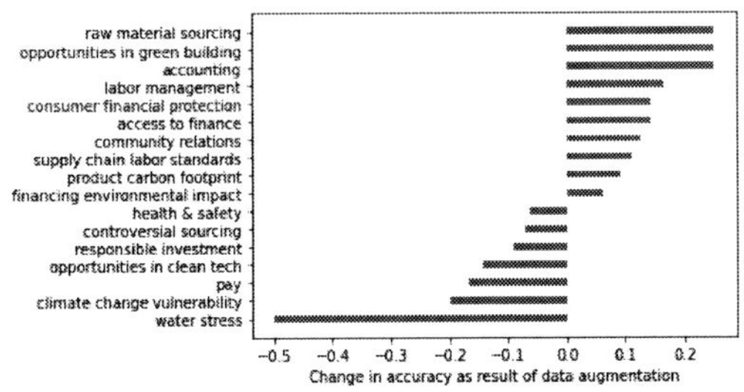

Figure 6: Change in accuracy of French test instances on training for 10 epochs after augmentation using synthetic English and French data.

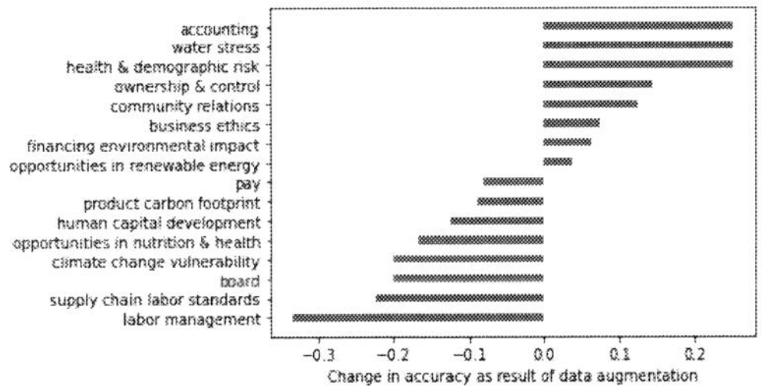

Figure 7: Change in accuracy of French test instances on training for 20 epochs after augmentation using original Chinese dataset.

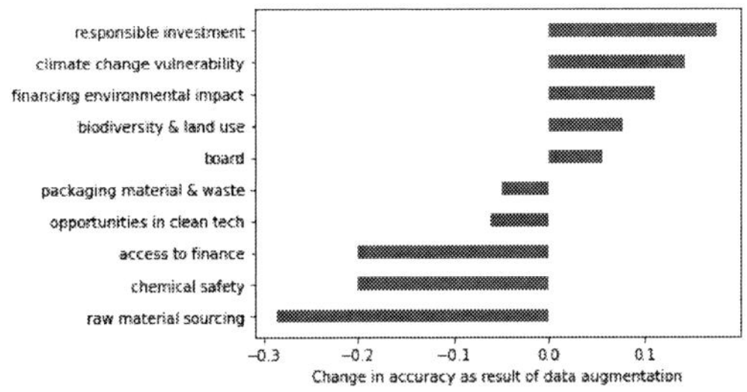

Figure 8: Classes with change in accuracy of English test cases due to augmentation using original Chinese dataset on training for 20 epochs.

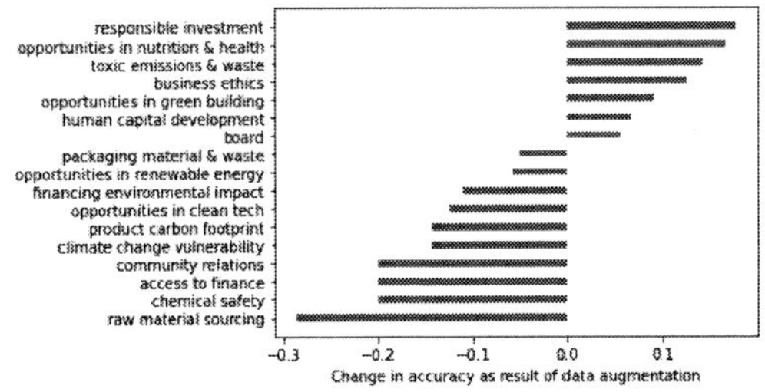

Figure 9: Change in accuracy of French test instances on training for 20 epochs after augmentation synthetic English and French data.

HKESG at the ML-ESG Task: Exploring Transformer Representations for Multilingual ESG Issue Identification

Ivan Mashkin
City University of Hong Kong
ivan.mashkin2018@gmail.com

Emmanuele Chersoni
The Hong Kong Polytechnic University
emmanuelechersoni@gmail.com

Abstract

Environmental, Social and Governance reports have to be periodically released by financial companies, as they represent an essential guide for the potential, socially-responsible new investors. Therefore, automatizing the analysis of reports and extracting the main ESG issues mentioned in the text is a goal of primary importance for financial Natural Language Processing (NLP) systems.

In this paper, we report our experiments for the FinSim4-ESG Shared Task, dedicated to the problem of multilingual ESG issue identification in English and French. Our results show that even simple classifiers trained on multilingual data and using crosslingual Transformer representations can achieve a strong performance in the task.

1 Introduction

Sustainable, Responsible and Impact investing (SRI) has gained a lot of prominence in the last decades (Serafeim and Yoon, 2022; Mehra et al., 2022). As a discipline, one of its primary goals is to specify environmental, social and governance criteria to generate long-term financial returns and produce a positive impact on the society (Mukherjee, 2020). For corporations, adherence to Environmental, Social and Governance (ESG) practices has become a requirement: for example, SEC filings in the US have to follow standard for Climate Change and Human Governance, and the European Commission stipulated, at the end of 2022, that all the companies providing investment products will have to disclose how their economic activity align with the taxonomy of the European Union and with the ESG regulations for sustainability (Kang et al., 2022). It is thus not a surprise that the demand for language technologies to automatize the analysis of ESG reports is correspondingly increasing.

With the rising popularity of machine learning and NLP technologies for Natural Language Processing (Loughran and McDonald, 2016), there is also a number of academic initiatives dedicated to research on development of systems for extracting relevant issues from ESG reports. The present paper aims at reporting our findings on the multilingual datasets of the FinSim4-ESG Shared Task (Chen et al., 2023). We participated in the English and in the French track and our best model, a simple SVM classifier relying on the crosslingual representations of the Distilled Universal Sentence Encoder (Reimers and Gurevych, 2019), achieves a F1-score of 0.62 and 0.71 on the English and the French test data, respectively.

2 Related Work

2.1 ESG and NLP

The field of corporate sustainability is interested in the set of self-regulatory acts that international business perform to mitigate the negative impacts on the society (Van Marrewijk, 2003; Sheehy, 2015; Feng and Ngai, 2020). Such practices are regulated by international standards and policies (Sheehy and Farneti, 2021). The issues ESG reports have to deal with are organized in taxonomies, and their automatic identification recently attracted attention in the NLP research community, in the form of the organization of a dedicated workshop at the LREC conference (Wan and Huang, 2022) and a shared task co-located with the IJCAI conference (Kang et al., 2022).

In the former, the topics of the contributions showed a varied interest in analyzing the language data in ESG reports, including machine learning models to fight stereotypes and improve inclusivity (Lu et al., 2022), corpus-based analyses of the metaphors in the legitimation strategies for the business of oil companies in China and in the United

Proceedings of the Joint Workshop of the 5th Financial Technology and Natural Language Processing (FinNLP) and 2nd Multimodal AI For Financial Forecasting (Muffin), Macao, August 20, 2023.

Category	Labels
Environment	Carbon Emissions, Climate Change Vulnerability, Product Carbon Footprint Biodiversity & Land Use, Water Stress, Electronic Waste, Packaging Material & Waste Toxic Emissions & Waste, Opportunities in Renewable Energy, Opportunities in Clean Tech, Opportunities in Green Building, Opportunities in Renewable Energy
Social	Health & Demographic Risk, Human Capital Development, Labor Management, Supply Chain Labor Standards, Chemical Safety, Consumer Financial Protection, Privacy & Data Security, Product Safety & Quality, Community Relations, Raw Material Sourcing, Access to Health Care, Opportunities in Nutrition & Health, Health & Safety
Governance	Ownership & Control, Accounting, Board, Tax Transparency, Business Ethics, Pay, Responsible Investment

Table 1: Map of the dataset labels, divided into the three main categories of Environment, Social and Governance.

States (Chen et al., 2022), and diachronic distributional methods to identify changes in the usage of ESG terms over time (Purver et al., 2022).

The shared task organized by Kang et al. (2022) was challenging the teams on two different subtasks: a taxonomy enrichment task, in the form of unsupervised discovery of hypernyms (Camacho-Collados et al., 2018) in sentences from ESG reports; and a binary classification task of the sustainability (sustainable / not sustainable) of excepts from the same type of reports.

2.2 Language Models for Financial Natural Language Understanding

Language models based on the Transformer architecture have been taking NLP by storm in recent years (Vaswani et al., 2017; Devlin et al., 2019), and a consequence of the success of Transformers, researchers working on NLP for specialized domains turned to domain adaptation techniques to exploit the full potential of such architectures (Guo and Yu, 2022). The financial domain makes no exception: the recently-developed models include adaptations of BERT (e.g. FinBERT, Araci (2019); Yang et al. (2020); Liu et al. (2020)), ELECTRA (FLANG-ELECTRA, Shah et al. (2022)) and even large language models such as BloombergGPT (Wu et al., 2023).

Transformers for financial NLP have been evaluated on a variety of tasks, either supervised (e.g. sentiment analysis, named entity recognition, numeral understanding; Peng et al. (2021); Shah et al. (2022); Wu et al. (2023)) or unsupervised ones (e.g. hypernym detection; Chersoni and Huang (2021); Peng et al. (2022)), showing important gains over the performance of general domain models.

Interestingly, models specialized for dealing with ESG issue identification have also been developed and made publicly available (Yang et al., 2020; Mukherjee, 2020; Mehra et al., 2022). Such models benefit from additional training on corpora of annual sustainability reports.

2.3 Multilingual Language Models

Transformers also led to impressive improvements in multilingual NLP, thanks to the introduction of large architectures that have been pretrained with language modeling objectives on multiple languages at the same time (e.g Multilingual BERT (Devlin et al., 2019), XLM-R (Conneau et al., 2020); BLOOM (Scao et al., 2022)). Such models are initialized with a large shared vocabulary, and utilize sophisticated sampling methods to balance the representation of high-resource and low-resource languages in the same semantic space.

In parallel with the development of Sentence Transformers (Reimers and Gurevych, 2019, 2020), which are able to generate vector representations of entire sentences and paragraphs, NLP researchers also introduced *multilingual sentence embeddings*. Those are based on the idea of having first a monolingual model generating sentence embeddings for a source language, and then having multiple student models trained on the translated sentences in other languages to mimic the original model.

3 Experimental Settings

3.1 Dataset Description

The organizers of the shared task made available training datasets in French and English, containing respectively 1200 and 1199 labeled examples. The 35 labels were defined on the basis of the MSCI ESG standard rating guidelines [1], and were generally related to three macro categories: Environment, Social and Governance (see Table 1). Finally, they released test sets for the two languages, each one

[1] `https://www.msci.com/esg-and-climate-methodologies.`

including 300 examples without labels. The gold labels were later made available for further evaluation and analysis.

The raw materials of the dataset were multilingual news articles, which were labeled by experts in ESG annotation: the news were collected, respectively, from ESGToday for English [2] and from RSEDATANEWS[3] and Novethic[4] for French. The English and French datasets are annotated by experts (2 annotators and 1 reviewer) in Fortia's Data & Language Analyst teams. The dataset instances include both the title and the main body of the news and the labels are mutually exclusive (in the cases where multiple labels could apply to one article, the texts were split into multiple instances). Noticeably, two of the labels ("Health & Safety" and "Tax Transparency") are present in the French but not in the English dataset, and thus we just excluded the examples with those labels (16 instances, in total) in the experiments in which we use French training data to make predictions on the English test set.

3.2 Systems Description and Settings

As a preprocessing step, we concatenated the text of the title and the text of the body of the news. Next, we adopted two different approaches for representing the ESG news with Transformers.

3.2.1 Approach 1: ESG Transformers with Sentence Translation

In the first approach, we used Transformer models that are specialized for ESG data, in particular the **ESG-BERT** model by Mukherjee (2020) [5] and the **FinBERT** model by Yang et al. (2020) with a previous fine-tuning on a dataset of 2000 ESG reports and three output labels (Environment, Social and Governance). [6] We chose to use ESG Transformers as they were fine-tuned on a similar type of textual data. Since both models are available only for English, we translated the French dataset with the help of the Google Translator API. [7]

We initially fine-tuned the models via 5-fold stratified sampling, to be sure that each fold had similar class distribution. However, we realized that the models were underfitting, probably because of the small size of the dataset. [8] Therefore we decided to use the fine-tuned Transformer models to generate vector representations of the dataset instances and to utilize different types of classifiers on top of them.

In particular, we used Logistic Regression (LR), Random Forests (RF), Support Vector Machine (SVM), all of them in the standard implementation in the Scikit-learn library (Pedregosa et al., 2011). For the classifiers, the parameters were optimized via the Skopt library for Bayesian optimization [9] and using 5-fold stratified sampling, similarly to what we originally did for model fine-tuning.

3.2.2 Approach 2: Sentence Transformers and Multilingual Training

In the second approach, we adopted a multilingual training approach: we used the Distilled Universal Sentence Encoder (**DUSE**) from the Sentence Transformers library [10] to encode directly the English and the French sentences, and then we simply merged the two datasets for multilingual training. We chose this approach because it maps the French-English data onto a unified vector space, so it allows us to simply merge the two datasets for training. Given the previous results, this time we used directly the pretrained Transformers to generate the input vectors for the classifiers (LR, RF and SVM) and we did not try to fine-tune the models. For finding the best parameters for the classifiers, we used the same procedure described above, combining 5-fold stratified sampling and the Skopt library for Bayesian optimization.

4 Results

The metrics for all the systems can be seen in Table 2 for English and in Table 3 for French.

A first notable finding in our result is that the multilingual representation of the Universal En-

[2] https://www.esgtoday.com/category/esg-news/companies/

[3] https://www.rsedatanews.net/

[4] https://www.novethic.fr/actualite/environnement.html

[5] https://huggingface.co/nbroad/ESG-BERT.

[6] https://huggingface.co/yiyanghkust/finbert-esg.

[7] For both approach 1 and approach 2, when the test dataset was the English one we excluded from the training data the 16 French instances with either "Health & Safety" or the "Tax Transparency" gold standard labels.

[8] With fine-tuned models, the preliminary results on the validation data always showed Accuracy scores in the low 40s, while the classifiers on top of the Transformer vectors performed more closely to the reported scores on the test set.

[9] https://scikit-optimize.github.io/stable/modules/generated/skopt.BayesSearchCV.html

[10] https://huggingface.co/sentence-transformers/distiluse-base-multilingual-cased-v1.

System	Accuracy	Precision	Recall	F1-score (Macro)
LR-ESG-BERT	0.59	0.55	0.59	0.56
RF-ESG-BERT	0.58	0.52	0.57	0.52
SVM-ESG-BERT	0.60	0.61	0.62	0.60
LR-FinBERT	0.59	0.54	0.56	0.53
RF-FinBERT	**0.62**	0.53	0.53	0.53
SVM-FinBERT	**0.62**	0.59	0.59	0.58
LR-DUSE	0.58	0.56	0.57	0.55
RF-DUSE	0.58	0.57	0.60	0.56
SVM-DUSE	0.58	**0.63**	**0.63**	**0.62**

Table 2: Results for all the systems on the English test dataset (300 examples, best scores per metric are in **bold**).

System	Accuracy	Precision	Recall	F1-score (Macro)
LR-ESG-BERT	0.67	0.66	0.67	0.66
RF-ESG-BERT	0.59	0.56	0.59	0.56
SVM-ESG-BERT	0.64	0.65	0.62	0.62
LR-FinBERT	0.70	0.69	0.70	0.68
RF-FinBERT	0.67	0.63	0.64	0.62
SVM-FinBERT	0.69	0.69	0.68	0.67
LR-DUSE	0.62	0.56	0.58	0.56
RF-DUSE	0.64	0.57	0.61	0.58
SVM-DUSE	**0.71**	**0.72**	**0.72**	**0.71**

Table 3: Results for all the systems on the French test dataset (300 examples, best scores per metric are in **bold**).

coder generally perform better than the domain-adapted ones of FinBERT and ESG-BERT. The translation of the French sentences to English to fit in the English-language domain-adapted Transformers does not seem to affect the trend too much. Among the classifiers that we explored, SVM is consistently the best option in the English dataset; it performs closely to LR on the French data with the two ESG Transformers, but it outperforms the other classifiers by a large margin with DUSE.

It is noticeable that when we compare Accuracy and F1-Score Macro, which is computed by using the mean of the F1-score of the single classes, most systems tend to have a higher value of Accuracy. We interpret this as an effect of imbalanced classes. However, SVM-DUSE is the only system for which F1-Score is the same, or even higher than Accuracy.

In the French dataset, the more frequent classes are generally predicted better: the accuracy is at least above 0.6 for all the classes with at least 10 examples in the test data. This does not hold for English, where we noticed that, for several classes with relatively high support, the accuracy is below chance level, e.g. **Electronic Waste, Health & Demographic Risk, Financing Environmental Impact, Privacy & Data Security**, which are all in the top-10 of the most frequent classes. We hypothesized that this might be due to diverging label distributions between the English test set and the joint training set. A Pearson correlation test revealed that, indeed, the class frequency correlation between the joint training and the English test data is lower than for the French data ($r = 0.62$ vs. $r = 0.74$), so this could be a partial explanation of the different performance across languages.

For the shared task, we submitted our systems with the following names: SVM-ESG-BERT as HKESG1, SVM-FinBERT as HKESG2 and SVM-DUSE as HKESG3. Our best ranks, both obtained by SVM-DUSE, are the 9th place out of 23 systems in the English track and the 10th place out of 21 systems of in the French track.

5 Conclusions

In this paper, we presented the systems that we used to compete in the ML-ESG shared task on Multilingual ESG Issue Identification. We took part in both the English and the French track, and our best system was -perhaps surprisingly- a simple linear SVM model relying on the sentence vector representation generated by the Distilled Universal Sentence Encoder (Reimers and Gurevych, 2019).

The dataset size was too small for the fine-tuning of Transformers. However, multilingual training was sufficient to obtain robust results on both dataset (0.62 of F1-score for English and 0.71 for French). The scores for the English dataset are generally higher, probably due to a more diverging distribution between training and test sets.

Acknowledgements

This work has supported by the Faculty of Humanities of the Hong Kong Polytechnic University (project "Analyzing the semantics of Transformers representations for financial natural language processing", code 1-ZVYU). We would like to thank the anonymous reviewers for their constructive feedback.

References

Dogu Araci. 2019. FinBERT: Financial Sentiment Analysis with Pre-trained Language Models. *arXiv preprint arXiv:1908.10063*.

Jose Camacho-Collados, Claudio Delli Bovi, Luis Espinosa Anke, Sergio Oramas, Tommaso Pasini, Enrico Santus, Vered Shwartz, Roberto Navigli, and Horacio Saggion. 2018. SemEval-2018 Task 9: Hypernym Discovery. In *Proceedings of SemEval*.

Chung-Chi Chen, Yu-Min Tseng, Juyeon Kang, Anaïs Lhuissier, Min-Yuh Day, Teng-Tsai Tu, and Hsin-Hsi Chen. 2023. Multi-Lingual ESG Issue Identification. In *Proceedings of the IJCAI Workshop on Financial Technology and Natural Language Processing (FinNLP) and the Second Multimodal AI For Financial Forecasting (Muffin)*.

Jieyu Chen, Kathleen Ahrens, and Chu-Ren Huang. 2022. Framing Legitimacy in CSR: A Corpus of Chinese and American Petroleum Company CSR Reports and Preliminary Analysis. In *Proceedings of the LREC Workshop on Computing Social Responsibility*.

Emmanuele Chersoni and Chu-Ren Huang. 2021. PolyU-CBS at the FinSim-2 Task: Combining Distributional, String-Based and Transformers-Based Features for Hypernymy Detection in the Financial Domain. In *Companion Proceedings of the Web Conference*.

Alexis Conneau, Kartikay Khandelwal, Naman Goyal, Vishrav Chaudhary, Guillaume Wenzek, Francisco Guzmán, Edouard Grave, Myle Ott, Luke Zettlemoyer, and Veselin Stoyanov. 2020. Unsupervised Cross-lingual Representation Learning at Scale. In *Proceedings of ACL*.

Jacob Devlin, Ming-Wei Chang, Kenton Lee, and Kristina Toutanova. 2019. BERT: Pre-training of Deep Bidirectional Transformers for Language Understanding. In *Proceedings of NAACL*.

Penglan Feng and Cindy Sing-bik Ngai. 2020. Doing More on the Corporate Sustainability Front: A Longitudinal Analysis of CSR Reporting of Global Fashion Companies. *Sustainability*, 12(6):2477.

Xu Guo and Han Yu. 2022. On the Domain Adaptation and Generalization of Pretrained Language Models: A Survey. *arXiv preprint arXiv:2211.03154*.

Juyeon Kang, Mehdi Kchouk, Sandra Bellato, Mei Gan, and Ismail El Maarouf. 2022. FinSim4-ESG Shared Task: Learning Semantic Similarities for the Financial Domain. Extended Edition to ESG insights. In *Proceedings of the IJCAI Workshop on Financial Technology and Natural Language Processing*.

Zhuang Liu, Degen Huang, Kaiyu Huang, Zhuang Li, and Jun Zhao. 2020. FinBERT: A Pre-trained Financial Language Representation Model for Financial Text Mining. In *Proceedings of IJCAI*.

Tim Loughran and Bill McDonald. 2016. Textual Analysis in Accounting and Finance: A Survey. *Journal of Accounting Research*, 54(4):1187–1230.

Lu Lu, Jinghang Gu, and Chu-Ren Huang. 2022. Inclusion in CSR Reports: The Lens from a Data-driven Machine Learning Model. In *Proceedings of the LREC Workshop on Computing Social Responsibility*.

Srishti Mehra, Robert Louka, and Yixun Zhang. 2022. ESGBERT: Language Model to Help with Classification Tasks Related to Companies Environmental, Social, and Governance Practices. *arXiv preprint arXiv:2203.16788*.

Mukut Mukherjee. 2020. ESG-BERT: NLP Meets Sustainable Investing. *Towards Data Science Blog*.

Fabian Pedregosa, Gaël Varoquaux, Alexandre Gramfort, Vincent Michel, Bertrand Thirion, Olivier Grisel, Mathieu Blondel, Peter Prettenhofer, Ron Weiss, and Vincent Dubourg. 2011. Scikit-learn: Machine Learning in Python. *Journal of Machine Learning Research*, 12:2825–2830.

Bo Peng, Emmanuele Chersoni, Yu-Yin Hsu, and Chu-Ren Huang. 2021. Is Domain Adaptation Worth Your Investment? Comparing BERT and FinBERT on Financial Tasks. In *Proceedings of the EMNLP Workshop on Economics and Natural Language Processing*.

Bo Peng, Emmanuele Chersoni, Yu-Yin Hsu, and Chu-Ren Huang. 2022. Discovering Financial Hypernyms by Prompting Masked Language Models. In *Proceedings of the LREC Workshop on Financial Narrative Processing*.

Matthew Purver, Matej Martinc, Riste Ichev, Igor Lončarski, Katarina Sitar Šuštar, Aljoša Valentinčič, and Senja Pollak. 2022. Tracking Changes in ESG Representation: Initial Investigations in UK Annual Reports. In *Proceedings of the LREC Workshop on Computing Social Responsibility*.

Nils Reimers and Iryna Gurevych. 2019. Sentence-BERT: Sentence Embeddings Using Siamese BERT-networks. In *Proceedings of EMNLP*.

Nils Reimers and Iryna Gurevych. 2020. Making Monolingual Sentence Embeddings Multilingual Using Knowledge Distillation. In *Proceedings of EMNLP*.

Teven Le Scao, Angela Fan, Christopher Akiki, Ellie Pavlick, Suzana Ilić, Daniel Hesslow, Roman Castagné, Alexandra Sasha Luccioni, François Yvon, Matthias Gallé, et al. 2022. BLOOM: A 176b-parameter Open-access Multilingual Language Model. *arXiv preprint arXiv:2211.05100*.

George Serafeim and Aaron Yoon. 2022. Stock Price Reactions to ESG News: The Role of ESG Ratings and Disagreement. *Review of Accounting Studies*, pages 1–31.

Raj Sanjay Shah, Kunal Chawla, Dheeraj Eidnani, Agam Shah, Wendi Du, Sudheer Chava, Natraj Raman, Charese Smiley, Jiaao Chen, and Diyi Yang. 2022. When FLUE Meets FLANG: Benchmarks and Large Pre-trained Language Model for Financial Domain. In *Proceedings of EMNLP*.

Benedict Sheehy. 2015. Defining CSR: Problems and Solutions. *Journal of Business Ethics*, 131:625–648.

Benedict Sheehy and Federica Farneti. 2021. Corporate Social Responsibility, Sustainability, Sustainable Development and Corporate Sustainability: What Is the Difference, and Does It Matter? *Sustainability*, 13(11):5965.

Marcel Van Marrewijk. 2003. Concepts and Definitions of CSR and Corporate Sustainability: Between Agency and Communion. *Journal of Business Ethics*, 44(2-3):95–105.

Ashish Vaswani, Noam Shazeer, Niki Parmar, Jakob Uszkoreit, Llion Jones, Aidan N Gomez, Łukasz Kaiser, and Illia Polosukhin. 2017. Attention Is All You Need. In *Advances in Neural Information Processing Systems*.

Mingyu Wan and Chu-Ren Huang. 2022. Proceedings of the First Computing Social Responsibility Workshop within the 13th Language Resources and Evaluation Conference. In *Proceedings of the LREC Workshop on Computing Social Responsibility*.

Shijie Wu, Ozan Irsoy, Steven Lu, Vadim Dabravolski, Mark Dredze, Sebastian Gehrmann, Prabhanjan Kambadur, David Rosenberg, and Gideon Mann. 2023. BloombergGPT: A Large Language Model for Finance. *arXiv preprint arXiv:2303.17564*.

Yi Yang, Mark Christopher Siy Uy, and Allen Huang. 2020. FinBERT: A Pretrained Language Model for Financial Communications. *arXiv preprint arXiv:2006.08097*.

Team HHU at the FinNLP-2023 ML-ESG Task: A Multi-Model Approach to ESG-Key-Issue Classification

Fabian Billert and **Stefan Conrad**
Heinrich-Heine University of Düsseldorf
{fabian.billert, stefan.conrad}@hhu.de

Abstract

In this paper, we discuss our submission to the Multi-Lingual ESG Issue Identification (ML-ESG) 2023, where we classify news articles into different ESG key-issues defined by MSCI. We use an adapter-based approach and evaluate different approaches and configurations, finally showing that it is advantageous to use multiple models in order to first classify articles into E/S/G classes before determining the final sub-issues.

1 Introduction

The surge in Environmental, Social, and Governance (ESG) research over the past few years is a testament to the growing importance of these issues in the corporate world (Zumente and Bistrova, 2021). Companies are increasingly recognizing that ESG-related matters can pose significant risks if not addressed properly (Aue et al., 2022). Beyond risk management, ESG topics are also crucial for a company's reputation, as they often reflect the company's values and commitment to sustainable practices (Schramm-Klein et al., 2016), (Islam et al., 2021).

Investors, too, are becoming more attentive to the ESG behaviors of companies. One common method of evaluating a company's ESG practices is through the human-curated scores provided by major rating agencies like MSCI[1] or Sustainalytics[2]. These agencies assess whether a company adheres to good ESG practices and assign a numerical value to represent the company's ESG performance. MSCI does this by considering 35 key-issues which they combine in different ways depending on the specific industry a company operates in (Nagy et al.). The final weight of a key-issues in the ESG score calculation is determined by quantitatively assessing each industry and consulting with investment practitioners.

Upon closer scrutiny of the evaluation metrics employed by the different ESG rating agencies, it becomes evident that these metrics do not completely incorporate sustainability principles into their process of assessing corporate sustainability (Escrig-Olmedo et al., 2019). In addition, (Crona, 2021) raises several concerns with the traditional rating agencies. One point of critique mentioned by them is that companies might self report data on positive environmental initiatives that are not connected to their negative environmental impact, but are similarly considered by the rating agencies. On the other hand, scoring mechanisms like the one used by MSCI are problematic in the sense that the weighting mechanism might not consider key ESG issues, depending on how the weights were created. These uncertainties in the evaluation process underscore the need for more comprehensive and nuanced methods of assessing ESG practices.

In order to create independent analyses, machine learning techniques, particularly those in Natural Language Processing (NLP), can be used. Over the past few years, NLP research has seen a significant uptick, with advancements in this field offering promising solutions for more in-depth ESG analysis (Min et al., 2021), (Chen et al., 2022), (Fischbach et al., 2022). By leveraging NLP, investors can conduct their own research to determine the sustainability of potential investment companies.

The Machine Learning for ESG (ML-ESG) task (Chen et al.) aims to motivate research in this direction and has annotated news articles in English, French, and Chinese based on the 35 key-issues used by MSCI. The task challenges participants to develop a system capable of classifying

[1] `https://www.sustainalytics.com/esg-data`

[2] `https://www.msci.com/our-solutions/esg-investing/esg-ratings`

Proceedings of the Joint Workshop of the 5th Financial Technology and Natural Language Processing (FinNLP) and 2nd Multimodal AI For Financial Forecasting (Muffin), Macao, August 20, 2023.

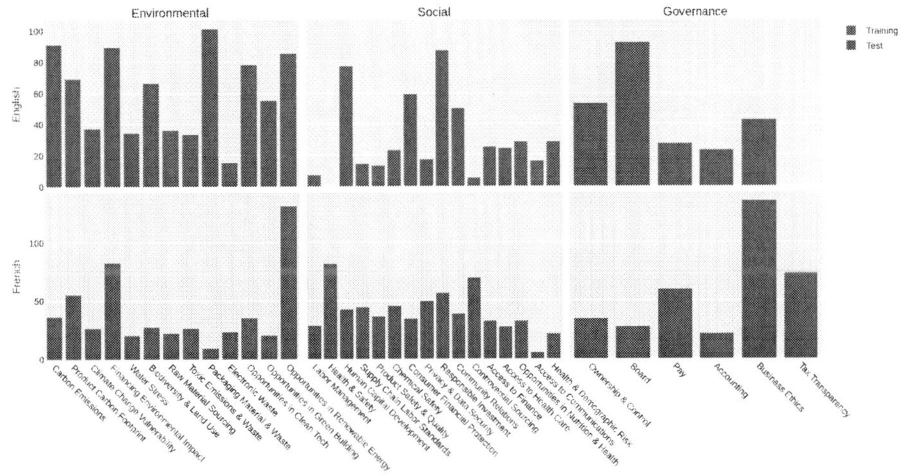

Figure 1: Occurrences of the different labels in the training- and test-data of the task. The top row represents the English data, the bottom row the French data. Each column represents one out of E/S/G as written above the figure. Training data is shown in red, test data in blue. **Note:** The test data was released after the task deadline and was not used during training unless mentioned.

articles in these languages into the appropriate ESG issues. This represents a significant stride towards more nuanced and comprehensive ESG analysis, ultimately enabling more informed and sustainable investment decisions.

In this paper, we present our solution for the ML-ESG task for the English and French datasets. We train a set of adapters for each language and try out different approaches to classify the news articles, ultimately showing that it is preferable to first classify a news article into one of the three main classes (Environmental, Social or Governance), before further classifying into the key-issues belonging to each category. Our approach achieves third place for the French language and nineteenth for the English language.

2 Task Description and Dataset

The dataset contains 1200 French and 1199 English news articles. Each article has the following properties: "URL", "news_title", "news_content", "ESG_label" (Chen et al.). The "ESG_label" is one of the 35 key-issues described in the ESG Industry Materiality Map of MSCI[3]. Each key-issue is attributed to one of the three top ESG components, "environmental", "social" and "governance". In Figure 1, different histograms for each ESG component show the occurrence of all the key-issues per language. Most news articles are classified as one of the environmental key-issues while the least articles belong to governance key-issues.

[3]https://www.msci.com/our-solutions/esg-investing/esg-industry-materiality-map

3 Experimental Approach

3.1 Adapters

Adapters are an efficient and flexible method for fine-tuning a foundational model for unique tasks (Houlsby et al., 2019) or transferring task-specific knowledge across different languages (Pfeiffer et al., 2020b). These tools are particularly useful when dealing with a dataset composed of multiple languages.

Adapter modules, which are incorporated into the layers of pre-existing models, are designed to master a particular task without altering the weights of the original model (Pfeiffer et al., 2020a). They are more parameter efficient than fine-tuning the full model while achieving nearly the same performance (Houlsby et al., 2019). Much like adapters that are trained for specific tasks, we can also train language-specific adapters. This is achieved by adding an adapter to a multilingual base model and then training it using Masked Language Modeling (MLM) (Pfeiffer et al., 2020b). If a task adapter is being trained with a multilingual base model, it is beneficial to also utilize a fixed language adapter because it captures and applies language-specific

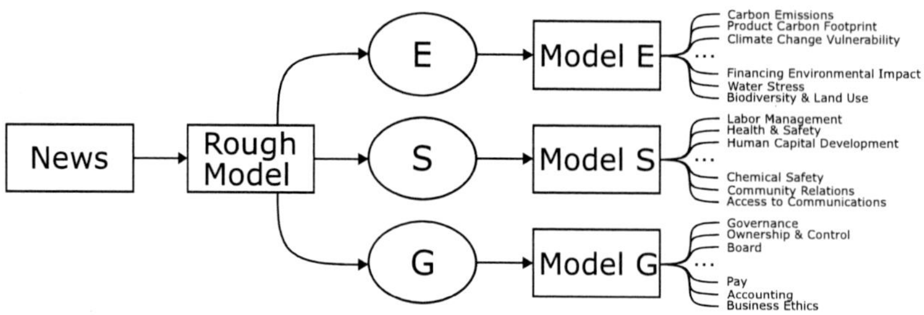

Figure 2: Schematic description of method 3. We first train a model to determine if a news article describes environmental, social or governance thematics. A second model then classifies the article with regards to the different key-issues belonging to that component. Each model in this case is constituted by a base-model, a language-adapter and a task-adapter as explained in subsection 3.1.

knowledge, which can enhance the final performance (Pfeiffer et al., 2020b).

3.2 Title or Content?

Classific. Target	Title	Content
Key-issues	0.63	0.41
Components	0.88	0.80

Table 1: Comparison of the F_1-macro scores when using the title vs using the content of the news articles for the French dataset. The first row shows results when directly classifying for the 35 key-issues while the second row classifies only for the rough E/S/G components.

We performed several experiments in order to determine if it is better to use the title or the content in order to classify the news articles. In Table 1, we show the F_1-macro scores when classifying the 35 key-issues directly in the first row, and the results for classifying the rough compontents (E/S/G) in the second row for the French dataset. In both cases, we achieve the best result when simply using the title to train the adapter. Since we observed a similar result for the English dataset, we decided to continue working without the "news_content" element.

3.3 Data Augmentation

Classific. Target	EN	FR
No Augmentation	0.58	0.69
Augmentation	0.68	0.67

Table 2: Comparison of the F_1-macro scores when augmenting the data by translating from the dataset in the other language and training on classifying the 35 key-issues directly. The top row shows the results without augmentation, the bottom row with augmentation.

Since we have data in two languages, we tried augmenting the data of each language by translating the data of the other language. For this, we use the OPUS-MT models published by (Tiedemann and Thottingal, 2020) from the huggingface-hub[4]. In Table 2, we show results on the key-issue classification for French and English. The results are conflicting, as we can see an improvement for the English dataset, while the French dataset performs slightly worse with the augmentation.

3.4 Configurations

We designed three different configurations:

- Method 1: Train an adapter on the 35 key-issues directly.
- Method 2: Augment the data by translating from the other language, then train on the 35 key-issues.
- Method 3: First train an adapter to classify an article into the ESG component, then train a set of three adapters, one for each ESG component, in order to classify the key-issues.

A rough schema for the third approach is shown in Figure 2. Since we achieved a better performance when translating for the English dataset (see Table 2), we decided to augment the data for the third approach for this language.

For all configurations, we evaluate the approach on 10% of the original training dataset. This is without augmentation, meaning the size of the eval dataset is only 5% the size of the total dataset for method 2.

As a base model, we use mBERT (Devlin et al.,

[4]https://huggingface.co/Helsinki-NLP

	Pre-Deadline			Post-Deadline	
Language	Method 1	Method 2	Method 3	Method 1	Method 3
EN	0.56	0.35	**0.57**	**0.61**	0.61
FR	0.75	0.73	**0.77**	0.78	**0.80**

Table 3: Weighted F_1-scores of the trained adapters for the test-set. On the left side, the official results. On the right side, the post-deadline results in which we evaluate on the test set during training.

2018). We then stack a pre-trained language adapter with fixed weights (from the AdapterHub [5], (Pfeiffer et al., 2020a)) on top of it followed by a task adapter (this setup is explained with more detail in (Pfeiffer et al., 2020b)). For training, we used a learning rate of $5 \cdot 10^{-5}$ and a simple cross-entropy loss-function.

4 Results

The submitted results of the three approaches are displayed on the left side of Table 3. Note that we display the weighted F_1-score here as opposed to F_1-macro we used in the previous section. For both languages method 3 shows the best performance, followed by method 1. However, while we placed third for French, the final placement for English was much worse. Our first guess at a reason for this was the imbalance of the training dataset, which we did not consider during the training. However, as we can see in Figure 1 in blue, the test data (which was released after the task-deadline) is similarly distributed as the training data.

4.1 Augmenting Key-Issues

Classific. Target	EN	FR
No Augmentation	**0.60**	0.77
Aug. Key-issue Model	0.58	**0.78**
Aug. Rough Model	0.59	0.77
Augmentation Both	0.57	0.77

Table 4: Comparison of weighted F_1-scores of the test-set when augmenting different parts of the data for method 3 (Figure 2). The first row shows the results without augmentation, the second row when augmenting only during training of the models classifying into the key-issues, the third row when augmenting only the first (rough) model and the fourth row when augmenting for all models.

In Table 3 we can see that the approach augmenting the data with the dataset of the other language (method 2) performs the worst for both languages. But since we augmented the English data for the method 3 and still measure good results (compared to method 1), we are unsure of the impact of the augmentation here. For that reason, we performed several tests where we train a model using augmented data at different stages. The results are shown in Table 4. We can see that the results are very similar among each language, especially for the French dataset where the configuration which augments the second models (classifying the key-issues) performs slightly better than the rest of the configurations. For the English dataset, the configuration without augmentation shows the best performance, while augmenting both models performs worst.

4.2 Evaluation on Test-Set

In order to determine the best performance possible with our setup, we train adapters on the whole training set, using the labelled test set to evaluate. The results are displayed in the right part of Table 3. Because method 2 performed the worst before, we do not include it here anymore. In addition, we do not augment the English approach for method 3 since we saw a better performance not augmenting in Table 4. We observe that the results improve slightly, but don't account for the difference in F_1-scores between the two languages.

5 Conclusion

We successfully trained several configurations capable of classifying news articles into the 35 key-issues defined by MSCI, showing that using the title instead of the content of the news article is more performant. We also tried to augment the datasets by translating from the other language but saw that this has little impact, even decreasing the performance in some cases. Out of the three different approaches, we observe that it is generally best to first classify the news articles into their rough ESG components (environmental, social & governance) before using a second model in order to determine the final key-issue.

[5] https://adapterhub.ml/

References

Tanja Aue, Adam Jatowt, and Michael Färber. 2022. Predicting Companies' ESG Ratings from News Articles Using Multivariate Timeseries Analysis. *arXiv*.

Chung-Chi Chen, Hen-Hsen Huang, Hiroya Takamura, and Hsin-Hsi Chen. 2022. An Overview of Financial Technology Innovation. *Companion Proceedings of the Web Conference 2022*, pages 572–575.

Chung-Chi Chen, Yu-Min Tseng, Juyeon Kang, Anaïs Lhuissier, Min-Yuh Day, Teng-Tsai Tu, and Hsin-Hsi Chen. Multi-Lingual ESG Issue Identification. In *Proceedings of the Fifth Workshop on Financial Technology and Natural Language Processing (FinNLP) and the Second Multimodal AI For Financial Forecasting (Muffin)*.

Beatrice Crona. 2021. Sweet Spots or Dark Corners? An environmental sustainability examination of Big Data and AI in ESG. *SSRN Electronic Journal*.

Jacob Devlin, Ming-Wei Chang, Kenton Lee, and Kristina Toutanova. 2018. BERT: Pre-training of Deep Bidirectional Transformers for Language Understanding. *arXiv*.

Elena Escrig-Olmedo, María Ángeles Fernández-Izquierdo, Idoya Ferrero-Ferrero, Juana María Rivera-Lirio, and María Jesús Muñoz-Torres. 2019. Rating the Raters: Evaluating how ESG Rating Agencies Integrate Sustainability Principles. *Sustainability*, 11(3):915.

Jannik Fischbach, Max Adam, Victor Dzhagatspanyan, Daniel Mendez, Julian Frattini, Oleksandr Kosenkov, and Parisa Elahidoost. 2022. Automatic ESG Assessment of Companies by Mining and Evaluating Media Coverage Data: NLP Approach and Tool. *arXiv*.

Neil Houlsby, Andrei Giurgiu, Stanislaw Jastrzebski, Bruna Morrone, Quentin de Laroussilhe, Andrea Gesmundo, Mona Attariyan, and Sylvain Gelly. 2019. Parameter-Efficient Transfer Learning for NLP. *arXiv*.

Tahir Islam, Rauf Islam, Abdul Hameed Pitafi, Liang Xiaobei, Mahmood Rehmani, Muhammad Irfan, and Muhammad Shujaat Mubarak. 2021. The impact of corporate social responsibility on customer loyalty: The mediating role of corporate reputation, customer satisfaction, and trust. *Sustainable Production and Consumption*, 25:123–135.

Bonan Min, Hayley Ross, Elior Sulem, Amir Pouran Ben Veyseh, Thien Huu Nguyen, Oscar Sainz, Eneko Agirre, Ilana Heinz, and Dan Roth. 2021. Recent Advances in Natural Language Processing via Large Pre-Trained Language Models: A Survey. *arXiv*.

Zoltan Nagy, Linda-Eling Lee, and Guido Giese. ESG Ratings: How the Weighting Scheme Affected Performance.

Jonas Pfeiffer, Andreas Rücklé, Clifton Poth, Aishwarya Kamath, Ivan Vulić, Sebastian Ruder, Kyunghyun Cho, and Iryna Gurevych. 2020a. AdapterHub: A Framework for Adapting Transformers. *arXiv*.

Jonas Pfeiffer, Ivan Vulić, Iryna Gurevych, and Sebastian Ruder. 2020b. MAD-X: An Adapter-Based Framework for Multi-Task Cross-Lingual Transfer. *arXiv*.

Hanna Schramm-Klein, Joachim Zentes, Sascha Steinmann, Bernhard Swoboda, and Dirk Morschett. 2016. Retailer Corporate Social Responsibility Is Relevant to Consumer Behavior. *Business & Society*, 55(4):550–575.

Jörg Tiedemann and Santhosh Thottingal. 2020. OPUS-MT – Building open translation services for the World. *Proceedings of the 22nd Annual Conference of the European Association for Machine Translation*.

Ilze Zumente and Jūlija Bistrova. 2021. ESG Importance for Long-Term Shareholder Value Creation: Literature vs. Practice. *Journal of Open Innovation: Technology, Market, and Complexity*, 7(2):127.